DOVER · THRIFT · EDITIONS

Aeneid

VERGIL

(Publius Vergilius Maro)

DOVER PUBLICATIONS, INC.
New York

DOVER THRIFT EDITIONS

GENERAL EDITOR: STANLEY APPELBAUM

Copyright

Copyright © 1995 by Dover Publications, Inc.

Bibliographical Note

This Dover edition, first published in 1995, is a republication of Charles J. Billson's English translation, *The Aeneid of Virgil*, originally published in two volumes (with facing Latin text) by Edward Arnold, London, in 1906.

Library of Congress Cataloging-in-Publication Data

Virgil.
    [Aeneis. English & Latin]
    The Aeneid / Vergil (Publius Vergilius Maro).
       p.   cm. — (Dover thrift editions)
    "Republication of Charles J. Billson's English translation, The Aeneid of Virgil . . . by Edward Arnold. London, in 1906"—T.p. verso.
    ISBN 0-486-28749-1 (pbk.)
    1. Epic poetry, Latin—Translations into English. 2. Aeneas (Legendary character) 3. Legends—Rome—Poetry. I. Billson, Charles J. (Charles James) II. Title. III. Series.
PA6807.A5B5   1995
873'01—dc20   95-40287
                                                 CIP

Manufactured in the United States of America
Dover Publications, Inc., 31 East 2nd Street, Mineola, N.Y. 11501

Note

PUBLIUS VERGILIUS MARO (70–19 B.C.) is universally acknowledged as the greatest Roman poet and one of the most important figures in Western literature. Having first gained prominence for his idyllic Eclogues and bucolic Georgics, the poet undertook the composition of the Aeneid, intended as the national epic of the Roman people.

In 31 B.C. Octavian (later given the title Augustus) had triumphed over Mark Anthony at the Battle of Actium, putting an end to the ceaseless civil strife that had ravaged Italy since the conflict between Marius and Sulla. It was Augustus' task to fashion a workable government while maintaining the appearance of time-honored forms and customs, and it was to this end that he encouraged Vergil in his task. The purpose of the Aeneid was twofold: to legitimize the new regime by expressing the divine mission of Rome to rule and spread the blessings of her civilization; and to reassert the personal qualities of the model Roman of the old Republic—a profound sense of obligation, strict adherence to duty, deep religiosity and seriousness of purpose—that were essential to the success of the new regime. (Although the character of Aeneas is frequently faulted by modern readers as wooden and insensitive, taken in this context, he merits sympathy.)

These elements are certainly to be found in the Aeneid, but Vergil's genius makes it far more than a simple propaganda piece. With faultless command of Latin and the dactylic hexameter (the meter of the original), the poet is able to assimilate and refashion the entire Homeric cycle of legend to create a work of refined sensibility. The characters he creates are notable for their humanity, most notably the tragic Dido and doomed Turnus, and a sense of profound sadness that is almost totally alien to Homer pervades the epic.

Vergil had not completed his revisions of the Aeneid when he died. He expressed the wish that the manuscript of the unfinished epic be burned, but its destruction was prevented by Augustus, to whom the world owes thanks for the preservation of this remarkable work.

Contents

Book I

ARMS AND THE MAN I sing, who first from Troy,
A Doom-led exile, on Lavinian shores
Reached Italy; long tossed on sea and land
By Heaven's rude arm, through Juno's brooding ire,
And war-worn long ere building for his Gods
A Home in Latium: whence the Latin race,
The Lords of Alba, and high-towering Rome.

Tell, Muse, the cause; how pained, how foiled in Will,
The Queen of Gods drove one whom Virtue crowned
Such toils to approach, and compass all that woe.
Can Heavenly hearts so unrelenting prove?

An ancient town, by Tyrian settlers held,
Far off faced Italy and Tiber mouth,
Carthage, well-dowered, and schooled in roughest war.
Before all lands, men say, 'twas Juno's haunt,
Before e'en Samos. There her chariot stood;
There hung her arms; there, if no Fates forbade,
She planned e'en then and nursed a world-wide Throne.
But fame had reached her that a race was sprung
From Trojan blood, her Tyrian towers to strew;
From whom a sovran People, proud in arms,
Should come to Libya's bane; so rolled the Doom.
Fraught with such fear, and that remembered feud
Once for dear Argos she had waged at Troy; —
Though still the smart remained, still deep at heart
Saturnia nursed the Judgment Paris gave,
Her beauty's cruel slight, the race abhorred,
The honours paid to Heaven-rapt Ganymede; —
Thus more inflamed, from Latium far she kept,
Tossed o'er all waves, the Trojans left by Greeks,
Achilles' leavings, and for many a year
From sea to sea they wandered, pushed by Fate:
Such work was wrought to build the Roman Race!

Scarce beyond sight of Sicily, they spread
All sail, and merry cut the salt sea foam,

1

When Juno, nursing deep the undying wound,
Thus to herself: "Am I to own defeat?
Not turn from Italy this Prince of Troy?
The Fates forbid me! Could not Pallas burn
The Argives' fleet, and drown them in the deep,
For one man's guilt, the madness Ajax wrought?
She, from the clouds down-flinging Jove's own fire,
Shattered their ships, and blew the waters high,
Him caught in whirlwind, and his cloven breast
Fixed on the pointed rock, outbreathing flames.
Yet I, Jove's Wife and Sister, I who move
The Queen of Gods, so many years make war
On one poor race! Henceforth shall any bow
To Juno, or lay tribute on her shrines?"

So mused her burning spirit, while she sought
The Storm Land, where the raging South is born,
Aeolia. Here King Aeolus commands
In cavern vast the loud unruly gales,
Bridled with chains and bondage, and they roar
Indignant round their bars, till all the mount
Howls discord. Throned on high, with sceptered hand,
He soothes their spirit, and controls their rage, —
Else would those raiding coursers sweep away
Seas, earth, and heaven's profound; but, fearing this,
The Almighty Father hid them in dark caves,
And piled above them high the mountains' mass,
And gave a King, whose chartered rule might know
To draw the reins, or loose them, at His word;
Whom Juno then, imploring, thus addressed:

"Aeolus, to thee Heaven's Sire and all men's King,
To smooth the waves gave charge, the storm to raise.
A race I love not sail the Tyrrhene Sea,
Bearing to Italy Troy's vanquished Gods.
Wing all thy Winds with rage! Submerge their ships!
Or widely scattering strew with dead the main!
Twice seven young Nymphs are mine, of faultless form,
Whose fairest, Deiopea, I will join
In wedding bands, and make her all thine own,
To live thy life with thee, and make thee sire
Of beauteous offspring, for such service done."

Then Aeolus: "Thine is the task, O Queen,
To choose thy wish, my duty to obey!
My realm thou gain'st me, and the grace of Jove;
Thou grantest me with the high Gods to feast,
To bear dominion over cloud and storm."

This said, he smote the hollow mountain's side
With spear reverse, and where a door is given
The embattled winds rush out, and scour the land.
Down-swooping on the sea, East Wind and South,
With Afric's squally blast, the deep abyss
Together rend, and roll vast waves to shore.
The seamen shout; the cordage screams aloft.
A sudden cloud has snatched from Trojan eyes
Daylight and sky. Black Night invests the sea.
The thunder rolls; the incessant lightnings flash;
And Death stares instant from all sides on all.
Aeneas' limbs relax with sudden chill.
Lifting his palms to Heaven and moaning sore,
Aloud he cries: "Thrice, four times happy, they
Whom under Troy's high wall their fathers saw
Die happy deaths! O bravest of the Greeks,
Tydides! might I but have fallen, my life
Yielding to thy right hand, on Ilium's plain,
Where Hector by Achilles' spear, where tall
Sarpedon fell, where Simois rolls deep
Such shields and helms and bodies of the brave!"

While yet he cries, the shrieking Northern storm
Strikes back the sail, and heavenward lifts the surge.
Oars snap: the prow swings off, and gives the sea
The ship's broad side; down breaks a mount of brine.
Some hang on the wave's crest; some see the floor
'Twixt gaping seas; the surges seethe with sand.
Three ships the South Wind hurls on ambushed rocks,
Rocks named by Latins "Altars," in mid main
Bristling immense; three more on shoals and banks
The East drives landward, piteous to be seen!
And strikes ashore, and heaps them round with sand.
One, leal Orontes' and the Lycians' bark,
Before Aeneas' eyes, a huge sea smites
Down on her stern. The helmsman, wrenched away
Rolls headlong: but the eddy round and round

Thrice spins the ship, and gulfs her in the flood.
Rare show some swimming in the vasty race.
Arms, planks, and Trojan treasures strew the waves.
Ilioneus' and bold Achates' ships,
Those which bore Abas and Aletes old,
Yield to the storm; their loosened joints admit
The ruinous deluge through each gaping chink.

Meanwhile the discord of the boiling sea,
The Storm let loose, the watery deeps up-cast,
Neptune perceived, and, gravely moved, looked forth,
Lifting above the wave his tranquil brow.
Strewn o'er the sea he saw Aeneas' fleet,
He saw the Trojans spent with wind and wave,
Nor did he not perceive his sister's guile.
East Wind and West he summons and bespeaks:

"What pride of ancestry hath swoll'n you thus,
That heaven and earth you now confound, and raise
Turmoil so wild, ye Winds, without my will?
Whom I — but first to smooth the troubled waves.
Not thus again shall you atone your deeds!
Speed instant back! and tell your King, not his
The Sea's dominion and the Trident stern,
But mine by lot. The craggy halls are his,
Eurus, where ye are lodged: there let him vaunt,
There let him reign, with all his Winds immured!"

More swift than speech, he calms the swollen flood,
Chases the gathered clouds, brings back the sun.
Cymothoe and Triton, from the rock
Thrust off the ships, by his own trident raised;
He channels the great Sands, the water smoothes,
And skims with printless wheels the level sea.
As when in some great concourse often springs
A tumult, and the rabble herd grow fierce,
Till stones and torches fly, the arms of rage, —
If then a man revered for worth and work
Face them, they listen, hush'd, with straining ears;
He governs them with words, and cools their heat.
So fell all Ocean's uproar, since the Sire
Looked o'er his waves, and gave his team the rein,
Speeding in cloudless blue his easy car.

The o'erlaboured Trojans, straining now to gain
What coast lies nearest, turn to Libya's shore.
There lies a haven in a creek retired,
Made by an island's arms, on which the sea
Breaks, and deep inlets hold the parted wave.
On either hand two peaks of towering rock
Menace the sky, and underneath wide-spread
Sleeps the safe pool, o'er which a scene impends
Of shimmering woodland, crowned by forest gloom.
Under the fronting bluff, a rock-hung cave,
With seats of living stone, and waters sweet,
A Sea-Nymphs' home; where the wave-weary bark
Needs not the cable, nor the anchor's tooth.
Here, with seven ships, the relics of his fleet,
Aeneas steers, and Trojans, sick for land,
Leap out at last, and gain the dreamed-of shore,
And on the sand their briny limbs repose.
And first from flint Achates struck a spark,
And caught in leaves, and with dry timber nursed
The flame, and fanned the fuel to a blaze.
Then Ceres' sea-sad grain, and Ceres' arms
They bring, world-wearied, and bestir themselves
To bake and bray with stones their rescued meal.

Meanwhile Aeneas climbs a rock, and scans
All the wide sea, to spy, if spy he may,
Antheus storm-toss'd, or Capys, or the arms
High on Caicus' stern, or Phrygian sloops.
No ships in sight, but roaming on the land
Three stags he saw; behind them all the deer,
In one long file, go browsing down the dales.
He paused; he seized the bow and flying shafts
Which leal Achates bore, and first laid low
The leaders of the herd, who proud bore up
Their branching heads, then aimed the crowd entire,
And drove into the glens their broken ranks;
Nor stayed, till seven huge bodies on the ground, —
To match his tale of ships, — the Victor stretched.
Who sought the haven, and divided all,
And shared the wine, which on Trinacria's beach
Acestes gave, a hero's parting boon,
Then thus with words their languish'd hearts consoled:

"Co-mates, — for troubles we have known before, —
O worse beset! these too some God will end!
Ye braved wild Scylla, and the rocks that roar
Through all their fissures, and the Cyclops' den
Ye entered. Cheer your hearts! Abandon fear!
To recollect even this may yet be sweet.
Through many a danger, many a chance and change,
We tend to Latium, where the Gods assure
Peace, and the realm of Troy again shall rise.
Endure! and keep yourselves for happy days!"

Such words he spake; and, pained with anxious thought
Masked under hopeful looks his heart-felt care.
They, hungry for the feast, prepare their prey,
Strip hide from ribs, and bare the inward meat.
Part carve and broach with spits the quivering flesh;
Part fix the brazen pans, and ply the flame.
Then, stretched on grass, recalling strength with food,
Of venison and of wine they take their fill;
Till, hunger stayed, they move the boards, and long
In anxious converse mourn their comrades lost,
'Twixt hope and fear surmising if they live,
Or lie at rest, and hear no voice that calls.
But good Aeneas mourns at heart the most
For Amycus, Orontes, and sad-starred
Lycus, brave Gyas and Cloanthus brave.

Now came the close, when Jupiter looked down
Over the sail-flecked sea, the lands outspread,
The shores, the peoples wide, and on Heaven's crest
Paused, and his downward gaze on Libya fixed.
Him then, thus pondering many an anxious thought,
Sadly, with tear-drops in her shining eyes,
Venus bespake: "Dread King of Gods and men,
Regent of rule eterne, the Thunder's Lord!
What wrong can my Aeneas or Troy's sons
Have done thee, that to them, so scourged by Death,
For Italy's sole sake, all lands are barred?
Firm was thy promise, Sire, that circling years
From Troy's replenished blood at last should raise
Romans, commanders, ruling sea and land
With sway imperial. What hath changed thy plan?
That pledge consoled me, weighing Doom with Doom,

For Troy's sad ruin; yet a woe not less
Still dogs the suffering heroes: O Supreme!
Where wilt thou place the limit of their pain?
Antenor, scaping through the Achaean hosts,
Might thread Illyrian bays, and make unharmed
Remote Liburnia and Timavus' fount,
Where through nine mouths, out of the roaring rock,
Spouts the loud sea, and drowns the furrowed field.
Yet there he built Patavium, gave a home,
A name to Trojans, hung up arms of Troy,
And now in happy quiet slumbers well.
But we, thy seed, to whom high Heaven thou giv'st,
Our ships all lost, for one heart's spite betrayed,
Far from Italian shores are sundered still.
Is this faith's meed? Is this our crown restored?"

On her the Sire of Men and Gods looked down,
Smiling as when he calms the fretful sky;
He gently kissed his daughter's lips, and said:
"Fear not, sweet Venus! Know, thy people's doom
Stands changeless: thou shalt see thy promised town,
Lavinium's walls, and bear to Heaven sublime
Great-souled Aeneas. Nought hath changed my plan.
Know, — since this trouble gnaws thee, I will speak
More fully, and unroll the leaves of Fate, —
Long shall he fight in Italy, subdue
Fierce tribes, and in wall'd cities school his men,
Till summers three have seen him Latium's King,
And three long winters crushed the Rutuli.
Ascanius then, Iulus now sur-named, —
Ilus he was, while Ilium's Kingdom stood, —
With thirty rolling years shall bound his reign,
Then from Lavinium move the royal seat,
And strongly fortify Long Alba's walls.
There thrice an hundred years the crown shall stay
In Hector's race, until a Vestal Queen,
Ilia, shall bear twin babes, the seed of Mars.
Then Romulus, proud in the tawny skin
Of his wolf-nurse, shall follow. He shall build
The Martial City, and stamp his name on Rome.
To her no bounds I give of Space or Time,
But Empire without end. Juno herself,

Who now with fear wears earth and sea and sky,
Will better her designs, and love with me
Romans, the Lords of Earth, the toga'd race.
So is my Will. A day shall come at last,
When Troy's great House beneath their yoke shall bring
Argos, and Phthia, and Mycenae's pride.
A Caesar from their glorious loins shall spring, —
Ocean his realm will bound, his fame the stars, —
Julius, a name from great Iulus drawn.
Him, rich with Orient spoils, shalt thou unvexed
Admit to Heaven, and vows he too shall hear.
Then wars shall cease, and the rude age grow mild.
Quirinus and his Brother, white-stoled Faith,
And Vesta shall give laws, War's iron Gates
Stand closed. Within, upon her savage arms,
Inhuman Rage will sit, by thousand links
Of brass chained back, and snarl with bloody fangs."

He spake; and Maia's Son from Heaven down sent,
That Carthage and her rising towers might give
Harbour to Trojans, lest, unware of Fate,
Dido should spurn them. Through the air he oars
His rapid vans, and lights on Libyan soil.
His task is done: the savage hearts are lulled
By God's own Will: but most o'er Dido's soul
Steal gentle thoughts, and ruth for Teucer's sons.

Now good Aeneas, tossed all night with care,
When the boon light was given, resolved to try
Those unknown shores, to what strange coast the blasts
Had blown them, and who held it, man or beast, —
Desert it seemed, — and bear true tidings back.
Beneath an arching rock, o'er-hung with trees,
He hid his vessels, wrapt in woodland shade,
And with Achates started, in his hand
Shaking two steel-bound spears.
                              Him in mid-wood
His Mother came to meet, a maid in looks,
Bearing the arms and habit of a maid,
Spartan, or like Harpalyce, whose feet
Outstrip the horse, outrun the Hebrus stream.
For huntress-wise o'er shoulders she had slung
The bow to hand, and given the winds her hair,

Bare-kneed, her folds up-gathered in a knot.

She first began: "Sirs, have you haply seen
One of my sisters wandering this wood,
With quiver girt, and spotted lynx's skin,
Or pressing clamorous on the foaming boar?"

Thus Venus, and thus answered Venus' son:
"None of thy sisters have I heard or seen,
O—how to call thee, Maid? No mortal face,
No human voice is thine,—O Goddess, sure!
Art thou Apollo's sister, or some Nymph?
Whoe'er thou art, be gracious, ease our pain;
And teach us on what shores, beneath what sky,
Outcast we wander, ignorant of place
And people, hither driven by storm and sea.
Oft at thine altars shall our victims fall."

Then Venus: "Nay, such rites are not for me.
To bear the quiver Tyrian maidens use,
And the red buskin on the leg bind high.
Carthage this realm, Agenor's Tyrian town,
But Libyans bound it, tribes intractable.
Here reigns, from Tyre and from her brother fled,
Queen Dido. Long her sorrows, long and dark;
But I will tread the surface of the tale.

"Sychaeus was her spouse, of Tyrian lords
The richest, and loved dearly to her woe.
To him her father yoked her still intact,
With virgin rites; but on Tyre's throne her brother,
Pygmalion, sat, in guilt out-shaming all.
Wrath came between those twain. He, blind with greed
And careless of his sister's love, struck down
Impious before the shrine with furtive steel
Unwarned Sychaeus, and long hid the deed,
Cheating with empty tales sick Dido's heart.
But in her dreams her lord's unburied shade
Came with a strange wan face, revealing all,
The guilty shrine, the dagger's bosom-thrust,
And all the sightless horror of the House.
He bad her haste to leave her native shores,
Disclosing ancient treasures underground,
Silver and gold unsummed, her journey's aid.

She, thus distract, sought friends to share her flight,
And all who loathed the tyrant King, or feared,
Muster, and seize what galleys lie to hand,
And load with gold. Pygmalion's hoarded wealth
Flies overseas: a woman rules the hour.
Where now thou see'st New Carthage lifting high
Yon towers they landed, and there bought them ground,
So much, — and thence the name of Byrsa sprang, —
As they could compass with one ox's hide. —
But who are ye, sirs? From what country come?
Or whither go ye?"
                              To her, asking thus,
With sighs he answered, drawing deep his breath:

"O Goddess! Ere from their prime source I traced
The annals of our woe, an thou could'st list,
Vesper would close heaven-gate, and lull the day.
From ancient Troy, — if haply to thine ears
Troy's name hath come, — we sailed contrary seas,
Till cast on Libya by the wayward storm.
I, good Aeneas, famed above the stars,
Bear in my ships our House-Gods saved from Greeks.
Jove's kin I seek, and Italy, my Home.
With twenty Phrygian barks I climbed the sea,
Led by my Goddess-mother, following Doom;
Scarce seven survive the ruining wave and wind.
I, poor, unfriended, roam these Libyan wastes,
From Europe thrust and Asia — " But no more
Brooking his moan, she interrupts his grief —

"Whoe'er thou art, not unbeloved of Heaven
Thou drawest breath, methinks, who hast arrived
This Tyrian city! Hence! On to the Queen's Court!
For news I bear, thy comrades are restored,
And altered winds have blown thy ships to port, —
Unless my parents taught me omens ill.
See yon twelve swans, in gallant trim array,
Whom dropping from the sky the Bird of Jove
Chased far and wide: they now, in column long,
Alight, or soaring scorn the earth they trod.
As they restored with clanging wings the sky
Circle in sport, and utter songs of joy,
Not otherwise thy ships and crews now hold

Gladly the port, or cross the bar full-sail.
Go, and step onward where thy path shall lead."

She said, and turned; all rosy flashed her neck;
The ambrosial locks a heavenly fragrance breathed,
Her vesture flowed to earth, and by her gait
The Goddess stood confest.
                              He, when he knew
His mother, thus pursued her as she fled:
"Thou too unkind! Why dost thou with false shapes
Mock me so oft? Why may we not clasp hands
Together, and with unfeigned lips converse?"
Thus he upbraiding paces to the town.
But round them, as they walked, the Goddess shed
A screen of mist and cloudy veil obscure,
That none might see or touch them, or delay,
Inquiring why they came. To Paphos she
Flies soaring, and delightedly regains
Her home, her fane, her hundred shrines that glow
With Orient gums and with fresh garlands breathe.

Meanwhile they hasten where the pathway points;
And climb at last the hill which hangs far-stretched
Above the city and on her towers looks down.

At that great town, once hovels, the thronged gates,
The clattering streets, Aeneas much admires.
Hotly the Tyrians work: some trace the walls,
The castle build, and roll up stones by hand.
Some trench a site for building. They ordain
Laws, magistrates, and senators august.
Here they are digging harbours; laying here
The Theatre's deep base, and hew from rocks
Tall columns, to adorn the future stage.
As bees in Springtime, through the flowering fields,
Work 'neath the sun; and train the nation's youth,
Or press the flowing honey and distend
Their cells with fragrant nectar, or their loads
From the new-comers take, or, ranged in line,
Drive from their fold the drones, a sluggard flock:
Work glows, and sweet with thyme the honey smells.

"O happy men, whose Home is rising now!"
Aeneas cries, and scans the towers above:

Then enters, screened in mist, most strange to tell!
And mingles with the crowd, himself unseen.

Amidst the town a grove spread lavish shade;
Where first the Poeni, tossed by sea and storm,
Dug up the Sign Queen Juno had foreshown,
A Horse's Head, — so should they be renowned
In war, and through the ages live in ease.
Sidonian Dido here to Juno a fane
Designed, magnific and divinely blest.
Steps rose to a bronze threshold, and bronze-bound
The lintels, and the grating doors were bronze.
A wondrous sight first lightened in this grove
Aeneas' fear: here first he dared to hope,
And in his fretted fortunes more confide.
For while he looks o'er all the mighty fane,
Waiting the Queen; while at the prospering town
And jealous labours of the craftsmen's hands
He marvels, lo! he sees the Trojan Wars,
Now blown about the world, sees Atreus' sons,
And Priam, and Achilles, foe to both.
He paused, and "O! What place," he sobbed, "what land,
Achates, is not filled with our distress?
See Priam! Even here Worth finds its meed;
Tears fall, and hearts are touched by mortal things!
Fear not; this fame will surely bear thee safe."

Thus on the pictured show he feeds his heart,
Sighing, and streaming tears bedew his cheek.
For there he saw how, fighting round the walls,
Pressed by Troy's chivalry, the Greeks took flight,
Or Phrygians, where Achilles urged his car.
Nor distant Rhesus' snowy tents he knew,
Which, in first sleep betrayed, Tydides heaped
With bloody slaughter, and his burning steeds
Turned back to camp, or ever they should taste
Fodder of Troy, or drink of Xanthus' stream.
Elsewhere flies Troilus, his weapons lost, —
Ill-doomed, ill-matched to meet Achilles' spear! —
Dragged by his steeds, fallen from the empty car,
But grasping still the reins; his neck, his locks
Are drawn in dust, where scrawls the inverted spear.
And Ilian wives were wending, supplicant,
To cruel Pallas' fane, with streaming hair,

And bare the Peplus, sad, and beat the breast:
Fixed on the ground the Goddess kept her eyes.
Thrice had Achilles round the walls of Troy
Dragged Hector, and would sell his corse for gold.
Ah! deeply then Aeneas sighed to view
His comrade's spoils, his car, his very corse,
And Priam stretching out his helpless hands.
Himself too, charging through Achaean chiefs,
The Eastern troops he knew, and Memnon's arms.
And, burning mid the fray, her Amazons
With moony shields Penthesilea led,
Who, girt with gold beneath her naked breast,
Dared clash with men, a warrior and a maid.

While all these wonders met the Dardan's eyes,
While lost he stood, in one long gaze entranced,
Queen Dido to the temple paced, a train
Of courtiers pressing round, supremely fair.
As on Eurotas' banks, or Cynthus' hill,
Diana leads the dance; behind her throng
A thousand Oreads: she the quiver bears,
And treads the earth, divine above them all.
Latona's heart with silent pleasure thrills.
Even such was Dido: so she passed in joy
Amidst them, busied in her city's growth;
Then in the sacred doors, beneath the dome,
High on a throne she sat, with weapons fenced,
Gave law and judgment, and the appointed task
Justly to each assigned, or fixed by lot:
When lo! Aeneas in the crowd discerns
Antheus, Sergestus, and Cloanthus brave,
With many a Trojan, whom the blinding gale
Had swept apart, and borne to distant shores.

Struck dumb together, both by fear and joy,
He and Achates fain would grasp their hands,
Yearning, but ignorance disturbs their minds,
And, veiled in hollow mist, they wait to see
What fate was theirs, and where they left the ships,
And why they came; for, chosen from all the fleet,
Clamorous they near the temple, praying grace.

When they had entered, and due audience gained,
Ilioneus, their eldest, with calm front

Began:
              "O Queen! by Heaven ordained to found
This city, and curb the unruly tribes with law!
Thee we poor Trojans, blown o'er every sea,
Implore. O save our ships from shameless fire!
Spare honest men; more nearly look on us!
We are not come with steel to overthrow
The Libyan's home, or harry prey to shore, —
Not ours, not conquered men's, such insolence!
A Land there is, by Greeks Hesperia named,
An old land, strong in arms and the glebe's fruit,
Where dwelt Oenotrians; now the younger men,
After their Chief have called it Italy.
Thither we took our course,
When stormy Orion rose with sudden swell,
And dashed us on blind shoals, and with bluff winds
O'er desperate seas and rocks unvoyageable
Dispersed us wide, and few have reached your shores.
What race of men is here? What land so rude
Permits this use? The welcome of the sand
Refused, they force us from their country's edge.
If men and mortal weapons ye despise,
Look yet for Gods remembering right and wrong!
Aeneas was our King, and none more just
Or righteous, or in battle more renowned.
Whom if Fate still preserves, if still he drinks
The air of heaven, nor lies in bitter gloom,
We fear not; nor shalt thou, if first to help,
Repent. Sicilian arms and towns remain,
Acestes too boasts the pure blood of Troy.
Grant us to beach our tempest-shaken ships,
To shape in woods new beams, and trim new oars,
And, if we may, with King and fellows found,
Joyous to Italy our course pursue.
If all is lost, if thou, great Prince, the seas
Hold, and Iulus' promise is no more,
Then seek we straits Sicilian, whence we came,
A Home now ready, Acestes for our King."

    So spake Ilioneus; the Dardans all
Acclaiming roared.
Then, casting down her looks, Dido in brief:

"Put off your anxious fears. To use these means,
And guard my frontiers well, my hard estate
Compels me, and the newness of my realm.
Who knows not Troy, and good Aeneas' race?
Their feats, their men, and that great flame of War?
Our hearts are not so dull; from Tyrian town
The Sun his horses yokes not so remote.
Whether Hesperia, Saturn's land, ye choose,
Or Eryx' country and Acestes King,
Safe I will send you, and with stores assist.
Or will you stay, this realm with me to share?
'Tis yours, this city I build. Here beach your ships.
Trojans and Tyrians, — I shall deem them one.
Ah! that your King were here himself, compell'd
By that same gale, Aeneas! Up the coast
Sure spies will I dispatch to Libya's ends,
Lest outcast he in town or forest stray."

   Roused by these words, long since Achates bold,
And Prince Aeneas were on fire to break
The shrouding mist. And first Achates urged:
"O Goddess-born! What purpose stirs thee now?
Thou see'st all safe, our ships, our friends restored,
Save one, whom in mid sea ourselves beheld
Drowned, to thy mother's words all else responds."
He scarce had spoken, when the veiling cloud
Parts suddenly, and melts into the air.
Aeneas stood revealed in radiant day;
In face and shoulders God-like, for on him
His mother shed the rosy light of Youth,
Fair tresses, and the charm of happy eyes,
As when man's hand adds grace to ivory,
Or Parian marbles are encinct with gold.
Then he, thus sudden, unforeseen of all,
Addressed the Queen:
                    "I whom ye seek am here,
Trojan Aeneas, saved from Libyan seas.
O thou sole pitier of Troy's untold woe!
Thou who with us, the leavings of the Greek,
By land and sea outworn, in want of all,
Would'st share thy city and home! To render thanks
Fitly, I cannot, Dido, nor could aught

Of Dardan blood o'er the wide world dispersed.
May Heaven, if any Spirits guard the Good,
If Justice aught avail, or conscious Worth,
Reward thee fitly! O what glad ages bore,
What mighty parents got thee so benign!
While brooks run seaward, while the shadows move
Round mountain vales, and star-flocks graze in heaven,
Thy fame, thy name, thy praise shall still endure,
Whatever shores call me."
                                        And both his hands
Sought dear Serestus and Ilioneus;
Then all, brave Gyas and Cloanthus brave.

Astonished by his looks, then by his plight
And sore distress, Sidonian Dido spake:

"What Doom pursues thee, Goddess-born? what spite
Casts thee so peril-tost on barbarous strands?
Art that Aeneas whom sweet Venus bore
Dardan Anchises by the Simois stream?
I mind how Teucer, from his land expelled,
To Sidon came, and sought to win new realms
By Belus' aid. My father Belus then
Laid Cyprus waste, and swayed the captive isle.
And from that day I knew the fall of Troy,
I knew thy name, and the Pelasgian Kings.
Thy very foe would give the Trojans praise,
And boast himself of Teucer's ancient stock.
O come, then, Sirs, pass underneath our roof.
Me too like fortune through a world of woe
Hath tossed, and in this land late rest hath given.
To grief not strange, I learn to aid distress."

She ended, and Aeneas led within
The regal halls, ordaining sacrifice.
And to his comrades on the beach meantime
Sends twenty bulls, an hundred bristled swine,
An hundred fatling lambs, their dams beside,
And joy the Wine God brings.

But in the centre of the Palace hall
A princely feast was set, where broidered cloths
Of royal purple on the boards were spread,
And massive silver; and brave deeds of yore

Shone, graved in gold, the legendary tale
Of all its heroes since the race began.

    Aeneas, since a father's love admits
No respite, to the ships Achates sends,
Ascanius to inform and thither guide,
Ascanius, the centre of all his care.
Gifts too he bids him bring, from Ilium's sack
Rescued, a mantle stiff with gold inwrought,
A veil with crocus-hued acanthus flowers
Bordered, which Argive Helen erst had brought
Out from Mycenae, when she came to Troy
And unpermitted love, her mother's gift;
The sceptre also which Ilione,
Eldest of Priam's daughters, bore of old,
Necklet of pearl, and jewell'd golden tiar.
Hasting for these Achates seeks the ships.

    But Venus in her heart new purposes,
New schemes designs, that Love shall be transformed
To sweet Ascanius' shape, and by his gifts
Stir into flame the Queen's impassioned heart.
The doubtful House she fears, the twi-tongued race;
Fierce Juno galls, and care with Night returns:
So in these words she speaks to winged Love:

    "Dear Son, my strength, my sole effectual might,
Son, who dost scorn the Father's thunder-stones
Which slew Typhoeus, to thy knees I fly,
And pray thy godhead. How through Juno's spite
Aeneas, thine own brother, roves the world,
Thou knowest, often hast thou shared my pain.
Him now Phoenician Dido with soft words
Keeps, and I fear how Juno's guest may fare.
On such a hinge of fate she will not sleep.
I plan to circumvent her, and the Queen
Invest with flame no deity may quench.
Love for Aeneas then shall bind her mine.
How thou canst compass this, our purpose hear.
E'en now the princely Boy, my chiefest care,
By his dear Sire's command, the city seeks,
With gifts that sea and Trojan flames have spared.
Him, sunk in sleep, I on my holy seat,

Cythera, or the Idalian hills, will hide,
Lest he should know the plot, and come between.
Thou, for one night alone shalt personate
His shape, thy boyish looks transform to his;
So, when the feast runs high, and wine-cups flow,
And radiant Dido takes thee in her lap,
And fondles thee, and gives thee kisses sweet,
A poisonous secret fire thou may'st instill."

Love, at his mother's word, puts off his wings,
And walks rejoicing with Iulus' gait.
But o'er Ascanius' limbs the Goddess sheds
Sweet rest, and bears him to Idalian glens,
Lull'd in her lap; there soft amaracus
Folds him in flowers and fragrance-breathing shade.

Now Love, obedient, by Achates led,
To Carthage gaily brought the regal gifts;
And coming found the Queen on golden seat
Throned in mid place, and proudly canopied.
There Prince Aeneas and the Lords of Troy
Reclined on purple strewings, and the slaves
Poured water on their hands, and served the bread,
And brought the fine-spun napkins; while within
Were fifty maids, whose care it was to keep
The feast replenished, and the fire aflame:
Another hundred, and as many boys,
All of one age, the tables spread with food
And wine-cups.
                    Surging through the festal doors,
The Tyrians bidden to the couches throng,
Admire the presents, and admire the Boy,
His face divinely flushed, his borrowed speech,
The mantle and veil with gay acanthus wrought.

But most the hapless Queen, to ruin doomed,
Her soul can never fill, and gazing burns.
The Boy, the gifts, both take her heart alike.
He, having hung upon Aeneas' neck,
And satisfied his feigned father's love,
Goes then to Dido. She with eyes and heart
Hugs him and fondles in her lap, nor knows
How great a God there lies. But, minding well

His Acidalian Mother, he prepares
To dim Sychaeus' image, and forestall
That heart long idle with a living love.

    Soon as the feast is lull'd, they move the boards,
And place great bowls, and wreathe the wine with flowers.
Din fills the house, and through the spacious halls
Roll voices. Burning lamps from the gilt roof
Depend, and torches overcome the night.
Then, calling for a jewell'd golden cup,
Pure wine the Queen pours in, after the use
Of Belus and his House, and silence falls.

    "Jove, since to thee the guest-rites are assigned,
For Tyrians and for Trojans make this day
Glorious, a day our children shall recall!
Come, Bacchus, Joy-giver, and Juno kind,
And ye, O Tyrians, give this gathering grace!"

    Ending, wine-tribute on the board she shed;
And first the cup touched lightly with her lips,
Then passed to Bitias, clinking it. Full slow
He quaffed the bowl, deep diving in the gold:
Then drank the other Chiefs.
                     Iopas too
Made sound his golden harp, whom Atlas taught.
He sang the wandering Moon, and the Sun's toils,
The source of Man and Beast, Lightning and Storm,
Arcturus and the rainy Hyades,
And the two Bears; why winter Suns so soon
Dip in the sea, what stays the laggard nights.
The Tyrians, then the Trojans, shower applause.

    Nor less with divers talk the hapless Queen
Protracts the night, drinking long draughts of love;
Of Priam and of Hector asking much,
Then of the armour of Aurora's son,
The steeds of Diomede, Achilles' might.

    "Nay, tell us all, O Guest! from first to last,
The Danaans' craft," quoth she, "the Trojans' fall,
Thy travels; for the seventh summer this
That bears thee wandering over lands and seas."

Book II

HUSH'D WAS EACH voice, and every face intent,
When from his lofty couch the Prince began:

"Unutterable, O Queen, the pain thy words
Bid me revive; how Troy's unhappy realm
Fell to the Greek; what piteous scenes I saw
And was great part of. Who, in such a tale,
From hard Ulysses' ranks, what Myrmidon
Would keep from tears? And dewy Night e'en now
Is riding down the sky, the sinking stars
Persuade to sleep. Yet, if so strong thy wish
To learn in brief our woes and Troy's last hour,
Although my memory shudders and recoils,
I will assay.

                "War-shattered, foiled by Fate,
As the long years roll on, the Danaan chiefs,
By Pallas' sacred art, build mountain-high,
Ribbed with sawn fir, a Horse; a votive gift
For safe return, they feign; so rumour spreads.
Men chosen by lot in its blind flanks are hid
In secret, and with armed soldiery
The monstrous cavern of its belly filled.

"In sight lies Tenedos, an isle renowned
Widely, and rich while Priam's kingdom stood,
Now but a bay and faithless anchorage.
They, sailing thither, on the desert coast
Lie hid; but we suppose them on the wind
For Argos bound. All Troy shakes off her grief;
The Gates are open thrown, the Doric Camp,
The shores forsaken, gaily visited.
Here the Dolopians pitched, Achilles here;
Here lay the ships, here was the battle-field.
Some at that fatal gift to Pallas gape,
Amazed at the vast Horse. And loudest cried
Thymoetes, 'Draw it inward, to the Keep!'
Traitorous, or so Troy's Doom already swayed:

But Capys, and the men of wiser wit,
Charged them to fling in sea that Danaan snare,
Suspicious gift, and burn it over flames,
Or bore and probe the hollow haunts within:
Contrary wishes rend the uncertain crowd.

"But foremost there, with a large concourse round,
Down from the Keep Laocoon runs hot,
Calling, 'O Burghers! What sad frenzy is this?
Think ye our foes are fled, or that one gift
Of Greeks is guileless? Is it thus ye know
Ulysses? In this frame lie Argives hid,
Or else this engine for our walls is built,
To spy our homes, and storm us from above.
Some fraud is there! O never trust the Horse!
Though Greeks bear offerings, I fear them still!'

"So saying, with great force his mighty spear
Against the flanks and belly of the beast
He hurled: it stood and quivered: at the impact
The cavern groaned; and had not Heaven's decree,
Had not our hearts been froward, on his charge
We had wrecked that Argive den, and thou, O Troy!
O Towers of Priam! ye were standing now!

"But lo! the while with uproar to their King
Some Dardan hinds were dragging one fast bound
With hands behind him, who, unknown to them,
Himself had given to work this very deed,
And open Troy to Greeks, one stout of heart,
Doubly prepared, to trick us or to die.
The Trojan crowd flow round from every side.
Eager to see, and vie in mocking him.
Hear now the Danaans' craft, and from one crime
Learn all the breed.

"For, standing in our midst, confused, unarmed,
And looking round the Phrygian ranks, he spoke:

" 'Alas! What land, what sea can now receive
Me miserable? What last resort is left?
No place for me with Greeks, and Dardans too
To satisfy their hate demand my blood!'

"His anguish turned our hearts, and all assault
Fell checked. We bid him tell us of his birth,

His news, the hope on which a prisoner leant.
He, when his fear is banished, thus returns:

" 'All I will tell thee true, O King! whate'er
Befall me, nor mine Argive birth deny.
That first: if Fortune moulded Sinon's life
Joyless, the jade shall never shape him false!
If haply to thine ears hath come the name
Of Palamedes and his high renown;
Whom, since he blamed the war, Greeks falsely charged,
On witness base doomed innocent to die,
And life-lorn now lament, — his friend was I,
A kinsman of his House, when at my prime
My needy father sent me to the wars.
While he stood firm in place, and wielded power
In the Kings' councils, we bore something too
Of name and fame; but when Ulysses' grudge, —
No news I tell, — had thrust him from the light,
In grief obscure I languished, sore at heart
Resenting my friend's fall; nor held my peace,
Infatuate! but I vowed, if Fate were kind,
If I regained my Greece a conqueror,
To avenge him. Thus I stirred relentless hate.
Hence first my ruin sprang. Ulysses hence
Kept threatening slanders, and among the mean
Sowed rumours dark, and sought conspiring arms:
Nor rested, till by Calchas' aid — But why
Recount the graceless tale? Why hold you back,
If Greeks rank all as one, and 'tis enough
That name to hear? Take vengeance now, and sate
Ulysses' hope, the Atridae's dearest wish!'

    "At that we, strangers to Pelasgian guile
And guilt so heinous, burn to ask his tale,
And trembling he proceeds with treacherous soul:

" 'Fain were the Danaans oft to make retreat
From Ilium, wearied of the endless war,
O would they had gone! As oft the storm-lashed sea
Bound them on shore, and the rude South deterred.
And loudest when this Horse stood ready framed
With maple beams, all heaven with tempest roared.
And when in doubt to Phoebus' shrine we sent

Eurypylus, this sad response he brought:
"With blood of maiden slain you calmed the gale,
When first, O Greeks, you came to Ilium's shore.
Seek now return with blood, and sacrifice
An Argive life!"
    The message went abroad,
And dazed our wits, and through our marrow shot
Cold shudders, who should be the victim doomed.
Ulysses then with clamour to our midst
Calchas, the Seer, drew, and charged to unfold
God's Will. — And many of that bad plot before
Warned me, and silently foresaw the end. —
Ten days within his tent Calchas is dumb,
Denouncing none, condemning none to death;
At last to loud Ulysses by concert
Scarce breaks a word, and me to the altar dooms.
All gave assent, and on one victim's head
Let fall the ruin each had feared his own.

 " 'The dreadful day had come; my rites were set;
The salted meal, the bands about my brow:
I broke away from death, I burst my bonds,
I do confess it! and all night lay deep
In darkling sedge, till haply they might sail.
And now no hope is mine to see my land,
Mine own sweet boys, my father dear-desired,
Who even for my escape may pay the cost,
And with their piteous blood my guilt atone!
But O! by Heaven I pray thee! by the Powers
That reverence Truth! by Faith, if any Faith
Stays in the world unspotted, to such woe
Give pity, and to sufferings undeserved!'

 "Life to his tears we grant, and pity too.
And Priam first his manacles and bonds
Himself bids loose, and thus benignly speaks:
'Whoso thou art, henceforth forget the Greeks!
Ours thou shalt be! Now make me answer true.
This monster Horse, why built they? Who conceived?
For what? what holy vow? what craft of war?'
He said; the other, in Pelasgian guile
Well-versed, to Heaven uplifts his unbound hands.

" 'Ye everlasting fires inviolable,
Be witness!' he exclaimed, 'O Shrines, O Knives
From which I fled! O victim bands I wore!
'Tis right to break the oaths I sware to Greeks,
Right to abhor those men, and spread abroad
Whate'er they hide: nor do my country's laws
Bind me. But thou, keep faith, thy saviour save,
If speaking truth, O Troy! I well repay.

" 'All hope, all heart the Greeks had in their war
Stood still on Pallas' aid; but since unjust
Tydides and Ulysses, rich in crimes,
From Pallas' holy fane her fateful Sign
Adventuring to tear, the sentries slew,
Seized the pure image, and with bloody palms
Dared touch her maiden chaplets, — since that day
The hopes of Greece ebbed refluent, her strength
Broke, and the Goddess turned her heart away.
No doubtful portents showed Tritonia wroth.
The Statue scarce in camp, a blaze of fire
Flashed from her lifted eyes, and o'er her limbs
Ran a salt sweat, and thrice, O wondrous tale!
With shield and shivering spear from earth she leapt!
"Fly!" Calchas cried, "Fly back across the main!
Troy cannot fall, unless again you seek
In Greece new omens, and bring back the grace
Which once was seated on your seaward keels!"
So now they run toward Argos on the wind
For arms and Gods; and soon remeasuring sea,
Will front you unawares. So taught the Seer:
And on his charge this image they have built
For outraged Pallas, to atone their sin.
This mass immeasurable he bade them rear
With oaken beams, and build it up to heaven,
So that it might not pass within your gates,
And under old religion succour Troy.
For if your hand profaned the Goddess' gift,
Ruin and death, he said, — God sooner turn
The curse on him! — would fall on Priam's realm;
But if your hands should draw it up to Troy,
Asia herself should bring a world of war
On Pelops' town, and Doom await our sons.'

"Such lying tales, by Sinon's glozing art,
Gained credence, and a traitor's tears entrapped
Whom not Tydides, not Achilles' self,
Not ten years mastered, nor a thousand ships.

"Now fell on us accurst a greater woe,
More dreadful far, confusing our blind wit.
Laocoon, Neptune's allotted Priest,
Stood by his shrine, to sacrifice a bull:
When lo! from Tenedos, o'er tranquil sea, —
I shudder to recall! — with endless coils
Two Serpents pressed together toward the shore.
Their bosoms rose above the wave, their crests
Blood-red o'er-topped the surge; their hinder parts
Trailed on the flood in mighty sinuous folds,
And lashed the roaring brine. They reach our fields,
Their blazing eyes suffused with blood and fire,
And with lithe tongues beslaver mouths that hiss.
Pale at the sight we flee. Unswerving still,
They near Laocoon; and first enfold,
In snaky coiled embrace, the tiny limbs
Of his two sons, and gnaw their piteous flesh.
Him then with weapons running to their aid
They seize, and swathe him in huge spires, and twice
Fold in their scales his waist, and twice his throat,
And lift above him head and towering necks.
He strains his hands the while to burst those knots,
His chaplets sprent with gore and venom black,
And with such roars of anguish fills the sky
As when a wounded bull shakes from his neck
The uncertain axe, and from the altar flees.
But those twain snakes to the high fanes glide off
On stern Tritonia's mount, and shelter there
Beneath the Goddess' feet and orbed shield.

"Fresh terror then through every shuddering heart
Creeps, and men say Laocoon hath paid
Due forfeit for his crime, who impious hurled
Against that sacred oak his guilty spear.

" 'Draw the dread Image home!' so all out-cry,
'Sue we the Goddess' grace!'
We cleave the walls, we lay the fortress bare.

All speed the work; and lay the rolling wheels
Beneath its feet, and ropes around its neck
Draw tight. The doomful engine, big with arms,
Surmounts our wall. Boys and unwedded girls
Chant hymns around, and touch the rope with glee.
It comes; it glides into the city's heart!
O Fatherland! O Ilium, home of Gods!
O war-famed walls of Troy! Four times it stopped
Even at the gate, four times the arms within
Clashed, yet we urge it, blind, ill-memoried men!
And store the monster in our hallowed Keep.
Cassandra e'en then her boding lips unclosed, —
Those lips which Heaven forbade us to believe.
We miserable men on our last day
Went wreathing all our fanes with festal green.

"The sky wheels round, and from the sea springs Night,
In her great umbrage wrapping earth and sky
And Argive fraud. We through the town lay stretched
Silent, while slumber folded the worn flesh.
And now from Tenedos the Greek array
Came sailing through the moonlight's friendly hush,
And neared the well-known strand, when the King's ship
Uplifted flames. Then, by Fate's malice saved,
Sinon by stealth undoes the wooden door,
And frees the captive Greeks. Them the opened Horse
Restores. Thessander first and Sthenelus,
With dire Ulysses, from the hollow oak
Slide down a rope: then Thoas, Acamas,
Machaon, Menelaus, Peleus' seed,
And he who forged the snare, Epeus' self.
They seize the city, plunged in sleep and wine,
And slay the watch; through open gates admit
All their allies, and join colleaguing bands.

"It was the hour when first o'er suffering men
Slumber, the boon of Heaven, most sweetly steals;
When lo! in dreams before mine eyes appeared
Hector in anguish, shedding floods of tears;
Torn by the car, as once, with dust and blood
Blackened, his swollen feet pierced through by thongs.
O in what guise he was! O how unlike
Hector returning in Achilles' spoils,

Or on Greek ships from launching Phrygian fire!
A squalid beard he wore, blood-boltered hair,
And all the wounds which round his native walls
So thickly scarred him. Weeping too methought
I first addressed him, drawing thus my moan:

" 'O Light of Dardans! Surest Hope of Troy!
What kept thee hence so long? Whence art thou come,
Dear-hoped-for Hector? O for us outworn
After thy people's deaths and all our pain,
To see thee now! What shamelessness hath marred
Thy happy visage? O what scars are these?'

"He nought replies, nor heeds my idle speech,
But, sighing deeply from the inmost heart,
'Fly, Goddess-born!' he says, 'Escape these flames!
Foes hold the wall. Down falls the pride of Troy!
Enough for King and Country! If man's arm
Had power to save, they had been saved by mine!
Troy gives to thee in charge her sacred Gods;
These take to share thy doom; for these at last
Build great thy walls across the o'erwandered main!'
He ceased, and from the holy place brought out
Vesta, her chaplets and undying fire.

"Meanwhile confusion through the city spreads:
Loud and more loud, though far-withdrawn the house
My sire Anchises owned and deep in trees,
The clamour rose, and shuddering strife drew near.
I start from sleep; I climb the topmost roof,
And stand with straining ears. As when a fire
Falls on a cornfield from the raging South;
Or when a mountain torrent drowns the land,
Drowns happy crops, and all the oxen's toil,
And headlong sweeps the trees; amazed and dumb,
From some tall rock, a shepherd hears the roar.
Then truth shone clear; bare lay the guile of Greeks!
O'ertopped by flames, Deiphobus' great house
Falls, and beside it burns Ucalegon.
The broad Sigean frith reflects the blaze.
Up rise the shouts of men, the trumpets' blare.
Madly I seize my arms, in arms not less
Unpurposed, hot at heart to muster friends,

And seize the Keep. Wild anger thrusts me on,
And bright before me gleams a soldier's death.

"But Panthus lo! escaped from Argive spears,
Priest of the Keep and Phoebus, Othrys' son,
Clasping his little grandson and his dear
Defeated Gods, flew to my door distraught.

" 'Panthus, how goes the day? What fort is held?'
Scarce had I asked when groaning he replied:

" ' 'Tis the last day, the inevitable hour!
Trojans we are not, Troy is past, and all
That glory gone. To Argos cruel Jove
Takes all. O'er the fired city Danaans rule;
High in our midst the Horse stands pouring out
Armed men; victorious Sinon, hurling fire,
Insults us. Some are at the wide-flung Gates,
As many thousands as from Greece e'er came, —
Some stand to arms across the narrow ways
To bar them: edge and glittering point of steel
Stand drawn, for slaughter ripe: scarce at the Gates
Our Guards give battle, and in blind strife resist!'

"Such words of Panthus, and the Will of Heaven
Mid flames and weapons drive me, where the roar
The rising shouts and the grim Fury call.
Then through the moonlight, prowest Epytus,
Rhipeus and Hypanis with Dymas came,
Who rallied to our side, — with Mygdon's son,
Coroebus, who at such a time to Troy
Coming, with wild love for Cassandra fired,
Brought a son's aid to Priam and his town, —
Unhappy that the bodings of his bride
He would not hear!

"Them when I saw for battle ranked and bold,
Thus I began: 'O Sirs! O hearts in vain
Most valiant! If your will be strong to join
A desperate venture, how things are ye see;
The Gods, through whom we stood, from fane and shrine
Departed all; a burning town to save;
To death! and charge with me on serried arms!
One chance the conquered have, to hope for none!'

"Thereat their rage waxed fiercer, and like wolves,
Raiding in darkness, whom the belly's lust
Drives blindly forwards, and their whelps at home
Wait with dry jaws; so we through foes, through steel,
Make for sure death, and to the city's midst
Press on. Around us hover night and gloom.

"Of that night's work who could the tale unfold,
Or weep a tear for every murder done?
An ancient city falls, that long held sway.
In streets, in houses, at the Gods' own doors,
Lie unresisting bodies everywhere
Thick-strewn. Not Trojans only pay their blood;
Oft to the conquered too manhood returns,
And the Greek conquerors fall. On every side
Panic and woe, and Death's wide-looming shade.

"There first of Greeks, among a goodly troop,
Androgeus met us, and our ranks unknown
Misdeeming friendly, thus bespoke us fair:
'Haste, men: what sloth hath kept you back so long?
The rest have fired and pillage Troy, but you
From the tall ships come hither only now!'

"He spoke, and instant, — for our answer won
No credence, — knew him fallen amidst his foes.
Amazed he started, checking voice and foot.
As when one toiling through a copse of briers,
Treads on a snake unseen, and shuddering shrinks
From the blue neck puffed out, and rising hate;
So, scared at us, Androgeus turned to flee.
We charge; we gird them with a hedge of steel,
And strew them broadcast, strangers to the ground,
And panic-struck. Fate speeds our first assay.
Then, flushed by victory, bold Coroebus cries:
'Come, follow, friends, where Fortune early points
The way to safety, where she shows us grace!
Shields let us change, and gird Greek harness on.
Courage or craft, who ask which foemen use?
They, they shall arm us!'
                              Saying thus, he dons
Androgeus' plumy helm, and blazoned targe,
And fastens to his side an Argive brand.

Rhipeus and Dymas, all the troop, with glee
Do likewise, arming from our spoils new-won.

"Mingling with Greeks, by favour not our own,
Through the blind night we press, in many a fray
Closing, and many a Greek to Orcus send.
Some to the ships escape, and running seek
The trusty shore: some in base panic climb
The Horse, and hide in that familiar vault.

"Against God's Will, alas! all faith is vain!
Lo! Priam's daughter with dishevelled hair,
Cassandra, dragged from Pallas' sacred shrines,
Vainly to heaven uplifts her burning eyes, —
Her eyes, for bonds her tender hands restrain.
That sight Coroebus bore not, mad with rage,
But flung himself amid the deep array,
Death-doomed. We follow, close our ranks, and charge.
But Trojan missiles from the temple's roof
O'erwhelm us now: a wretched carnage springs
From our arms' fashion, our mistaken plumes.
With yells and anger for the rescued maid,
Greeks from all sides attack us, Ajax keen,
Atreus' two sons, all the Dolopian host.
As, when a whirlwind breaks, South Wind and West,
And Eurus, with his orient coursers proud,
Conflicting shock: the forest roars; the sea
Neptune with savage trident stirs to foam.
They too, if any in the dark of night
Our craft surprised, and routed through the town,
Show themselves now; our shields and cozening arms
At once they know, and mark our uncouth tongue.
Numbers o'erwhelm us, and Coroebus first
Before the War-Maid's altar, by the hand
Of Peneleus falls dead; and Rhipeus falls,
Our purest, and of honour most compact, —
The Gods gainsaid! — Dymas and Hypanis
Die, pierced by friends, nor all thy piety
Could save thee, Panthus, nor Apollo's crown!

"O Ilian ashes! Death-flames of my kin!
Be witness, that I shunned not at your fall
Greek spear or perilous warfare; that my hand

Earned death, had death been doomed! But sundered thence
With Pelias and with Iphitus I pass,—
One Age retards, and one Ulysses' wound,—
Where calls the clamour, straight to Priam's house.

"Here found we battle fierce, as though no fray
Elsewhere, no other carnage filled the town;
War to the death, our very roofs assailed,
And to beleaguered doors the Tortoise driven.
Their ladders hug the walls; they storm the Gate;
And with their left hand to our shafts oppose
Shields, while they grasp the coping with their right.
From tower and roof the Dardans pluck defence;
And, since Death meets their gaze, prepare to wield
In that last hour such missiles; gilded beams,
The stately splendours of their ancient sires,
Roll downward. Some behind the doors below
Stand with drawn blades, and guard them, closely ranked.
Our spirit rose to save this House of Kings,
To help such men oppressed, and swell their force!

"A door there was, a way through Priam's house
To every room, a blind deserted gate
Rearward, whereby, while Ilium's kingdom stood,
Oft unattended to her husband's kin
Came sad Andromache, and brought his boy.
Hence to the roof I pass, from whose high top
Despairing Trojans cast their bootless spears.

"High toward the stars up-built on the sheer brink
A turret stood, from whence they used to scan
Troy, and the Achaean camp, and Danaan ships.
This we assailed with iron, where loose it joined
The roof's high floor, and wrenched it from the base,
And forced it forth. With sudden fall it bore
A crushing ruin down, which smote the Greeks
Wide-spread: yet more come up, nor stones the while,
Nor any missiles cease.

"Lo! Pyrrhus at the Gate, who proudly flashed
Before the porch in arms of brazen sheen;
Most like an adder, crammed with evil herbs,
In wintry earth long hidden, puff'd and cold,
Who throws his weeds, and, sleek with youth, involves

His slippery length to day, and rears his breast
Tall to the sun, and darts his triple tongue.
With him huge Periphas, Automedon,
Who drove Achilles' steeds, and Scyrian hosts
All made the roof at once, up-hurling fire.

"But Pyrrhus 'mongst the first with two-edged axe
The portals rent, and from their hinges tore
The brass-bound doors, hewed out a plank, and made,
Breaching the solid oak, a yawning gap.
The house lies open, the long halls revealed,
Priam's own chambers, chambers of dead Kings
Revealed, and warriors in the doorway massed.

"But in the house lament and woeful din
Confusedly rise: the vaulted mansions wail
With women's sobs, and clamour mounts the sky.
Through the vast house mothers run to and fro,
And hug the doors, and kiss them, wild with fear.
Fierce as his father, Pyrrhus presses on;
Nor bolts nor men may hold him. Doors give way
Beneath his frequent ram, and fall unhinged.
Force finds a road. The Danaans swarming in,
Slay those in front, and fill the house with troops.
Not so enraged a river bursts in foam
O'er dyke and dam, and plunges on the fields,
And sweeps o'er champaign wide both flocks and folds.
I saw the ravening Pyrrhus there; I saw
The Atridae in the Gate, and Hecuba
Beside her hundred daughters, and the King,
Staining with blood the flames himself had blest.
The fifty bowers that promised fruit so fair,
Doors proud with plunder and barbaric gold,
In ruin fell. Greeks take what fire hath left.

"Thou askest me perchance of Priam's fate.
He, when he saw the captured city's fall,
His doors wrenched off, the foe within his home,
Old as he was, his long disused arms
Threw on his feeble back, his useless sword
Girt on, and went to die among his foes.

"Amidst the house, beneath the naked sky,
Stood a great altar, and a time-worn bay

Leant over, and the House-gods wrapped in shade.
Here, round the barren shrine, sat Hecuba
And all her daughters, huddled up like doves
In the black tempest, clinging to their Gods.
But when she saw her lord in arms of youth,
'Unhappy spouse! what madness makes thee take
Those arms,' she cried, 'or whither would'st thou go?
Not such the aid, nor such defence the times
Require, not were my Hector here himself.
Draw here at last: this shrine will save us all,
Or thou shalt die with us.' And by her side
She placed the age-worn King in holy seat.

   "But lo! Polites, one of Priam's sons,
Flying from Pyrrhus' sword, through foes, through spears,
Down the long corridors and vacant halls
Runs wounded. Pyrrhus, burning on the stroke,
Chases, and grasps, and threats him with the spear;
Till, just emerging in his parents' sight,
He fell, and shed his life in streaming blood.
Then Priam, though with death now compassed round,
Withheld not, nor his voice or anger spared.

   " 'For such a crime,' he cries, 'for such a feat,
May Heaven, if Pity dwell in Heaven to mark
Such deeds, requite thee well, and give the meed
Thou earnest, who before mine eyes hast slain
My son, and marred his father's sight with death.
Not thus Achilles, whom thou feign'st thy sire,
Dealt with his foeman Priam; he revered
The suppliant's plea, and to the tomb restored
Hector's cold corse, and sent me home to Troy.'
He spake; and hurled his weak unwarlike spear,
Which, straight recoiling from the raucous bronze,
Hung idly from the buckler's central boss.

   "Then Pyrrhus: 'Thou shalt go then with the news
To Peleus' son, my sire! Tell him, be sure,
The wicked deeds of his degenerate son!
Now die!' So saying, to the very shrine
He dragged him trembling, slipping in the blood
Of his own son, and held his hair, and flashed
The blade, and hid it in his side hilt-deep.

"So ended Priam's day: such doom he met,
Seeing his Troy in flames, and all her towers
Down-cast; once Lord of lands and peoples wide,
Regent of Asia. Now a mighty trunk
Lies headless on the shore, a corpse unnamed.

"Then first wild fear embraced me, and I stood
Awe-struck. The form of my dear father rose
Before me, as I watched that King like-aged
Pant out his life. I saw Creusa left,
My house destroyed, the peril of my boy.
With backward glance I sum the force around.
All wearied out have flagged, and on the ground
Tumbled, or aching dropt into the flames.

"Now I alone was left; when, by the shrine
Of Vesta crouched, silent and close, I saw
Tyndareus' daughter, for the fires shone bright
As to and fro I passed, surveying all.
She, Trojans' hatred for their towers o'erthrown,
The Greeks' revenge, her long-left husband's wrath
Fore-dreading, — common Fury of Greece and Troy! —
Had hidden, and by the altar lurked unseen.

"My heart burned hot: wrath spurred me to avenge
My falling land, and take the price of sin.
Was she to look on Sparta and her land
Unscathed, and in her triumph walk a Queen,
With Trojan maids in train, and Phrygian boys,
And see her wedded home, her sons, her kin?
Had Priam died for this, and Troy been burned,
And Dardan blood so often poured like sweat?
Not so. For though no memorable name
Springs from a woman's death, no victor's palm,
Yet to quench evil, and repay desert
Shall bring me praise. O sweet to glut my soul
With vengeful fire, and sate my slaughtered kin!

"So raving, I advanced with furious heart;
When in my sight, not seen before so clear,
And in pure radiance gleaming through the dark,
A very Goddess, in such mien, such state
As Gods behold, my gracious mother came.
She caught my hand, her rosy lips unclosed:

'Son, what great anguish stirs thy lawless wrath?
Whence is this rage? Where lurks thy love for me?
Wilt thou not rather see where, worn with age,
Thou hast left Anchises? if Creusa lives,
And young Iulus? All the Grecian hosts
About them range; and, did my care not shield,
Flames and the hostile blade had swept them off.
Not Helen's hateful beauty thou must blame,
Nor Paris: 'tis the Gods, the severe Gods,
Who wreck this wealth, and raze the pride of Troy.
Look! for the cloud which dims thy mortal sight
With mist and darkness, I will take away; —
Whate'er thy mother bids thee, have no fear,
Nor disobey her counsels. Where thou see'st
Yon mighty blocks uptorn, stone rent from stone,
And eddying up together smoke and dust,
Neptune is shaking with his trident huge
The walls' foundations, and uprooting all
The City. Here most awful Juno holds,
Steel-girt, the Scaean Gate, and her allies
Calls from their ships with rage.
And lo! Tritonia on the topmost towers
Stands with her lurid cloud and Gorgon dread!
Courage and strength to Greeks the Sire himself
Gives; He himself stirs Heaven to cope with Troy.
Flee hence, my son, and give thy travail pause.
Ne'er absent, I will guide thee safely home.'
She spoke; and hid herself in darkest night.
Dread Shapes appear, and, warring against Troy,
The mighty Hosts of Heaven.

"Then all the city seemed to sink in flame,
And Neptune's Troy, uprooted from its base,
Fell, like some world-old ash-tree on the hills
Smitten with steel, which woodmen try to fell
With frequent hatchets: still it threatens long,
And nods the tresses on its trembling head,
Till, overcome with wounds, with one last groan
Torn from its ridge, it drags a ruin low.

"Down, Goddess-led, I haste, through foes, through fire.
The spears give passage, and the flames recede.

"But when my home was reached, our ancient house,
My father, whom I first desired to bear
High up the hills, and whom I first approached,
Refused, since Troy was shattered, to prolong
His days in exile. 'Ye, O ye whose blood
Runs fresh,' he cried, 'in your own vigour strong,
Turn ye to flight!
If the high Gods had willed that I should live,
They would have spared my home. Enough and more
One sack to see, one conquered town survive!
Here, here my corpse is laid; bid that farewell!
Death mine own hand will find. The pitying foe
Will spoil me soon; a tomb is little loss.
A weary while I linger, banned by Heaven,
Useless, since me Heaven's Sire, and all men's King
Swept with his thunder's blast, and smote with fire!'

"So he kept prating, and unshaken stayed.
With tears we plead, my wife, my little son,
And all our house, that he involve not all
In ruin, nor press on the insistent doom.
Still he says nay, not changing mind nor place.

"Back to the fight I rush, and choose to die,
Most wretched! for what plan, what chance remained?
I to escape, O Father! and to leave
Thee! Fell such slander from a parent's tongue?
If the Gods will that nought be left of Troy,
And thou art firm, and wilt to wreck so large
Add thee and thine, Death's door will gape anon,
When Pyrrhus comes, who sheds the father's blood
Before the shrine, the son's before his sire.
Was it for this, sweet Mother, me through shafts,
Through flames thou barest, in the heart of home
To see my foes, to see my son, my sire,
My wife, all butchered in each other's blood?
Arms, men, bring arms! Death calls the conquered on!
Give me again to Greeks! Let me renew
Battle! Not all shall perish unavenged!

"I gird the steel again, and my left arm
Strap to the targe, and step beyond my house:
But on the theshold lo! my wife embraced

My feet, and to his father held my boy.
'If death thou seekest, bear us with thee too!
But if, well-tried, thou hast some hope in arms,
Shield first this house! To whom shall we be left,
Thy son, thy sire, and I, once called thy wife?'

    "Loudly she cried, and filled the house with moans:
When suddenly a wondrous Sign uprose.
For lo! between his parents' arms and lips
Above Iulus' head there seemed to glow
A thin peaked light, a harmless flame, that played
About his wavy locks, and licked his brow.
With fear we trembled, and the burning hair
Shook, and with water quenched the holy flames:
But old Anchises to the stars upturns
Joyful his eyes, to Heaven lifts hand and voice.
'Almighty! If any prayers bend thy Will,
Look on us, only look! If worth deserve,
O give us help! Confirm this augury!'

    "Scarce had the old man said, when on the left
Thunder outcrashed, and, sliding from its sphere,
A Star shot through the darkness, trailing light.
Above our palace roof we saw it glide,
And bury its splendour in dark Ida's woods,
Marking a path: the long-drawn furrow glows,
And widely spreads around a sulphury fume.
Then vanquished quite my father rose erect,
Worshipped the holy Star, and prayed to Heaven.

    " 'No more delay. I follow where you lead.
Save, Guardian Gods! my house; my grandson save!
Yours is this omen; in your hand is Troy!
I yield; to go with thee I not refuse!'
He ceased; and now more loud the fire is heard,
More near the conflagration rolls its heat.

    " 'Then come, dear Father! rest upon my neck;
My shoulders shall sustain thine easy load.
Whate'er befall, one peril there shall be,
One safety for us twain. With me my son
Shall walk; my wife shall follow far behind.
Ye servants, heed my words. A mound there is
Beyond the city Gate, an ancient fane

Of lonely Ceres, and a cypress nigh,
Saved through long years by reverential awe.
To this one spot from divers let us come.
Thou, Father, take our holy Gods of Home.
For me, fresh come from battle and from blood,
'Tis sin to touch them, till in living streams
I wash me clean.'

"Then over my broad shoulders and bent neck
A cloak I spread, a tawny lion's hide,
And lift my load. Iulus clasps my hand,
And follows with small steps his father's stride.
My wife comes after. Dusky ways we tread;
And I, whom late not any shafts dismayed,
Not any Greeks in adverse battle ranged,
Now fear each breeze, and start at every sound,
Trembling for both, my burden and my boy.

"Now, drawing near the Gates, I deemed my way
All traversed, when a sound of many feet
Springs on our ears, and, peering through the gloom,
My father cries, 'Fly, fly! my son, they come!
The gleam of brass I see, and glowing shields.'

"Then in my fear some deity unkind
Stole my distracted wit; for while I tread
By-ways, and leave the street's familiar round,
Alas! my wife Creusa, rapt by Fate,
Or stopped, or lost the way, or sank foredone,
Uncertain which, ne'er to my sight restored.
Nor looks for her thus lost nor thoughts I bent,
Ere to the mound we came and hallowed seat
Of ancient Ceres. Here, when all were met,
She only lacked, and failed both son and spouse.
What man, what God did not my fury accuse?
What sight more cruel was in all Troy's sack?
My son, my sire, my Trojan Gods of Home,
Hid in a winding glen, I trust to friends,
The town regain, and don my shining arms;
Firm to renew each risk, and through all Troy
Returning, thrust my head on peril again.

"The walls and dusky portals whence I passed
First I regain, and follow through the night

My foot-prints back, and with close eye peruse.
Dread fills my heart; the very silence daunts.
Thence home I turn, if haply there she tread,
If there! The Greek invader fills the house.
The hungry fire is rolling up the roof
Wind-swept; the flames leap up and roar to heaven.

"Again I pass to Priam's towered seat.
In the void cloisters, Juno's sanctuary,
Phoenix and dire Ulysses, chosen guards,
Watch o'er the spoil. There Trojan treasures, torn
From blazing shrines, and tables of the Gods,
Bowls of pure gold, and captive vestments lie
Promiscuous heaped. Around, in long array,
Stand boys and trembling mothers.

"Nay more: I dared to pierce the night with cries,
Filling the streets with noise; and vainly again,
Again redoubling, called Creusa's name.
Thus storming as I ranged, in ceaseless quest,
A Phantom sad, mine own Creusa's Shade,
Rose to my sight, greater than her I knew.
Spell-bound, my hair uprose, my tongue was tied.
She spake, and with these words dispelled my care:

" 'Why wilt thou yield thee to such frenzied woe,
Sweet Husband? Not without the Will of Gods
It happens thus. To bear me hence with thee
Fate not permits thee, nor Olympus' Lord.
Long exile shall be thine, vast seas to plough,
And thou shalt reach Hesperia, where by tilth
And wealth of men smooth-sliding Tiber flows.
There joy and kingship and a royal wife
Are thine. For dear Creusa weep no more.
I shall not see the Myrmidons' proud seats,
Nor go to dwell a slave for Grecian wives,
I of the Dardans, wife of Venus' son!
Nay; me the mighty Mother of the Gods
Here keeps. Farewell! Love still thy son and mine!'

"Thus when she had said, into thin air diffused,
She left me weeping, fain to tell her much.
Thrice round her neck I tried to throw my arms:
Thrice fled the Vision from my empty grasp,

As light as wind, and like a flying dream.

"So night was spent, and I rejoined my friends;
And wondering there a mighty host I find
Of comrades streaming fresh, mothers and men
For exile thronged, a piteous group, who met
From every quarter, ready to embark
Their hearts and fortunes for what lands I chose.

"And now the Day Star rose o'er Ida's crest,
Leading the morn; and still the Danaans held
The leaguered gates: no hope of help was given.
I turned; I raised my sire, and sought the hills."

Book III

"WHEN ASIA'S WEAL and Priam's guiltless race
The Immortals doomed to ruin, and proud Troy
Falls, and all Neptune's city smokes in dust,
To banishment remote and lands forlorn
Gods' voices call us; and in Ida's shade,
Beneath Antandros' wall, we build a fleet;
Uncertain to what bourne our fates will lead,
And muster men. When summer scarce had sprung,
And oft my sire bade spread our sails to Fate,
I left my land with tears, I left the plain
That once was Troy, to sail the homeless seas,
With friends and son, with Troy's great Gods and mine.

"Far off, in Mavors' land, the Thracians plough
Their vasty plains, where erst Lycurgus reigned;
To Troy once friendly, and our Gods allied,
Ere Fortune fled. There landing, on the bay,
With fates unkind, my earliest town I trace,
And name it from my name *Aeneadae*.

"Oblations to my mother and the Gods,
To bless our works, I paid; and to Heaven's King
A shining bull would slay. A mound was nigh,

Whereon grew dogwood bushes, and dense spears
Of prickly myrtle. Drawing near, I strove
To crop the leafy wood, and wreathe with green
Our altars, when behold! an awful sign,
Wondrous to tell! for from the uprooted stem
Which first I tore from earth, black drops of blood
Gushed forth, and stained the soil. Cold horror shook
My limbs; fear froze my blood. Yet once again
Out of another tree, I sought to tear
A stubborn shoot, and probe the hidden cause.
Black from that other bark forth issued blood.

   "Deep pondering, I prayed the Woodland Nymphs,
I prayed Gradivus, Lord of Getic fields,
To bless that portent, and all harm remove.
But when with greater effort, 'gainst the sand
Pressing my knees, a third green spear I seize —
O shall I speak, or hold my peace? — a moan
Deep in the mound is heard, a tearful moan,
And a voice meets my ears: 'Why dost thou rend
A wretched man, Aeneas? Spare my grave;
Spare to pollute pure hands. Not strange to thee
Troy bore me; no strange blood is oozing here;
Fly, fly this cruel land, this greedy shore!
For I am Polydorus. Here the steel,
Sown in my flesh, hath sprouted into spears.'

   "Then doubt and dread oppressed me, and I stood
Spell-bound; my hair uprose, my tongue was tied.
This Polydorus with a weight of gold
Once sad-starred Priam sent in secret charge
To Thracia's Prince, mistrusting Dardan arms,
Seeing his walls girt close. When Troy was crushed,
And Fortune ebbed, to Agamemnon's arms
Turning in victory's wake, the Prince breaks through
All law, slays Polydorus, and the gold
Grasps. To what acts thou drivest mortal men,
Thou impious greed of gold! When fear had fled,
To all our chiefest lords, my sire the first,
These portents I disclose, and ask their will.
One mind have all, to quit that guilty land,
Leave treason's home, and give our barks the breeze.
So funeral rites we pay, earth high the mound,

And altars raise to Polydorus' shade,
Mourning with dusky cypress; and all round
Stand Ilian wives with streaming tresses free;
Cups with warm milk afoam, and bowls we bear
Of sacred blood, and lay his soul to rest,
And cry aloud for him the last long cry.

"From thence, when waves are trusted, and the breeze
Spreads calm, and South winds whisper to the sea,
Launching our ships, my comrades fill the strand.
We clear the haven; lands and towns recede.

"Amid the sea there lies a sacred isle,
To Neptune and the Sea-Nymphs' Mother dear,
Which, as it roamed the main, the Archer God
To Myconos and Gyaros fast bound,
And bade it lie unmoved, and scorn the gale.
I thither sail; the unruffled port receives
Our weary crew; we hail Apollo's town.
King Anius there, men's King and Phoebus' Priest,
Crowned with the laurel, met us, and recalled
The friend Anchises whom he loved of yore.
Kind hands we join, and pass beneath his roof.

"Then to the Temple's hoary stones I bend:
'Grant us a home, Thymbraean! Grant us walls,
A biding city and race! O keep and save
This second Troy, these leavings of the Greek!
Whom follow we? and whither? where to fix
Our Home? Give omens, Lord, our souls inspire!'

"I scarce had said; a sudden tremor stirred
The doors, the holy laurel, all the hill
Shook, the shrine opened, and the tripod moaned.
Prostrate to earth we fell, and heard a voice:

" 'Enduring Dardans! That same land which bore
Your parent stock, again shall take you home
To her rich breast. Your ancient Mother seek!
There shall Aeneas' House all nations sway,
And sons of sons, till generations fail!'

"Thus Phoebus; and a joyous uproar rose,
And all demanded, to what Home the God
Called us, and bade the wanderers return.

"My father then revolves the lore of old.
'Listen, O lords!' he cries, 'and learn your hopes.
Crete lies amid the sea, Jove's island home,
Mount Ida, and the cradle of our race,
An hundred cities fair, luxuriant fields.
Thence our first father Teucer, — if the tale
I well recall, — first sailed to Phrygian shores,
And chose his realm. Not then had Ilium raised
Her towers to heaven; in sunken dales they dwelt.
Hence Cybele's Queen, the Corybantic brass,
The Idaean grove, the silence-guarded rites,
And lions yoked beneath their mistress' car.
Up, then, and follow where God's bidding leads;
Appease the winds, and make for Gnossus' realm!
Not far the vessels' course; if Jove be near,
Three days shall bear them to the coasts of Crete.'
A bull to Neptune duly then he slew;
A bull to thee, fair Phoebus! and two lambs,
One black to Storm, one to boon Zephyrs white.

"A rumour flies, Idomeneus hath left
His realm an outcast, and deserted homes
In Crete await us, of all foemen void.
We leave Ortygia's port, and skim the main,
By Naxos' Bacchic ridge, Donusa green,
White Paros, Olearos, o'er straits that foam
Round many a shore of sea-strewn Cyclades.
Loud cry the straining mariners, 'To Crete!'
Cheerly they urge, 'On to our fathers' home!'
A wind that follows wafts us on our way,
And to those ancient shores we glide at last.

"My long-craved walls I trace, and call the town
Pergamea, praying Trojans, who rejoice
In that great name, to love the towers they raise.
And now our vessels on the beach were drawn,
And all on marriage bent, and tillage new;
Laws, homes I gave; when from the tainted sky
On human limbs a sudden sickness fell,
A blight on trees and crops, a year of death.
Sweet life they left, or dragged enfeebled frames,
While Sirius seared the fields, the herbage died,
Sick crops refused their yield. My father then

Bade us remeasure sea, and reach once more
Ortygia, and implore of Phoebus' grace
When pain should end, and whence he bade us try
Our weariness to heal, and whither steer.

" 'Twas night, and sleep held all the living world.
The Holy Shapes, the Phrygian Gods of Home,
Whom with me I had borne from Troy and flames,
Seemed in my sleep to stand before mine eyes,
Revealed in streaming light, where the full moon
Poured through the deep-set windows: who thus spake,
Dispelling care. 'What Phoebus hath to say,
When thou hast reached Ortygia, here he sounds.
He sends us to thy door. When Troy was burned,
We followed thee and thine, measured in ships
The tumbling waves with thee; we too will raise
Thy children to the stars, and give thy town
Empire. Thy walls build greatly for the great.
Nor shun long pain and exile. Thou must rest
Elsewhere: not hither did the Delian prompt,
Apollo called thee to no shores of Crete.
A place there is, by Greeks Hesperia named,
An old land, strong in arms and the glebe's fruit,
Where dwelt Oenotrians; now the younger men
After their Chief have called it Italy.
This is our proper seat: hence Dardanus
Sprang, and Iasius, founder of our line.
Up! and thine ancient father tell with joy
No doubtful tidings; Corythus to seek,
Ausonian lands. Jove doth not give thee Crete.'

"Awed by such vision and the voice of Gods, —
Nor was that sleep, but openly I saw
Their very features and their cinctured hair,
And chilly sweat bedewed my every limb, —
Up from the bed I leap, and raise aloft
Heavenward both hands and voice, and offer gifts
Pure on the hearth. And when my vows were paid
All to Anchises I unfold with joy.
He owned the ambiguous line, the rival sires,
His strange confusion of familiar lands.
'O Son!' he said, 'long tried by Ilium's doom!
Cassandra only warned me of this fate.

Now, I recall, thus she foretold our lot,
And named Hesperia oft and Italy.
But who could dream that Trojans should approach
Hesperian shores? Whom could Cassandra move?
Now, better counselled, let us own the God.'
He said; we all obeyed his words with joy.
We quit our second home, where few were left,
And spread our sails, and skim great plains of sea.

"Far on the deep, when no more land we saw, —
Sky everywhere, and everywhere the sea, —
Then overhead a blue-black cloud of rain
Bore night and storm; the shuddering water gloomed.
Blasts rolled the sea; the mountain billows rose,
And scattered wide our ships: the rainy clouds
Shrouded the day, and hid the darkened sky,
While fire flashed frequent from the riven rack.
Swept from our course, we drift on blinding surge.
E'en Palinurus in the sky confounds
Noontide with night, nor recollects his course.
Three days we drift in doubt and blinding gloom,
As many starless nights, till land at last
Rose the fourth morn, disclosing distant hills
And curling smoke. Down drop the sails; on oars
Rising, our mariners with no delay
Lustily toss the foam, and sweep the blue.

"Saved from the deep, isles of the Ionian main
Receive me first, by Greeks named Strophades,
Where weird Celaeno and the Harpies dwell,
From Phineus' house debarred, who fled in fear
Their ancient board. No monster boding worse,
Not any deadlier plague and wrath of Heaven,
Rose from the Stygian flood. Winged things, they wear
Girls' faces; foul the droppings of their vent;
Claws are their hands; their features evermore
With famine pale.

"Borne thither, and the haven made, behold!
Rich droves of cattle scattered o'er the leas,
And flocks of goats untended we descry.
We flesh our blades, and Jove himself invite
To share with Gods our spoil, then by the bay,

Pile grassy seats, and feast on goodly cheer.
But sudden from the cliffs, with awful swoop,
Those Harpies fall, and flap their clangorous wings,
Snatching the feast, and with polluting touch
Spoil all; their shrieks are mixed with odours foul.
Once more, far-drawn within a caverned cliff,
In shady trees embowered, we spread the board,
And on our altars lay the fire afresh;
Once more from hidden lairs the screaming rout
Fly round the prey, with beaks and crooked claws
Tainting our meal. My comrades then I charged
To take their arms, and fight the grisly tribe;
And they obeying lay their swords apart,
Buried in grass, and hide their ambushed shields.
Then when they drop, and scream along the shore,
Misenus, from his watch, on hollow brass
Signals; and in strange battle we engage,
Slashing with steel those Ocean Birds obscene.
But not one stroke their plumes, their bodies take
No wound; and swift in flight upsoaring high,
Half-eaten meat they leave, and traces foul.

"Only Celaeno, evil-boding Seer,
Lights on a lofty crag, and thus breaks forth:
'War would ye wage for kine and oxen slain?
Sons of Laomedon! with war to drive
Innocent Harpies from their fathers' realm!
Learn then, and fix in heart these words of mine,
Which Jove foretold to Phoebus, he to me,
And I, the Furies' Queen, to you reveal.
To Italy you sail: the summoned winds
Unharmed shall bear you to Italian ports.
But, ere you ring with walls your promised Home,
Fierce famine and this outrage of our blood,
Shall make you champ and gnaw your very boards.'

"She ceased, and to the forest winged her flight.
Then cold with sudden awe my comrades' blood
Froze, and their spirit fell. No more with arms,
With vows and prayers they bid me strive for peace,
Whether divine they be or fowls obscene.
My father on the beach, with palms outspread,
Invokes the Gods, ordaining sacrifice.

'O curb her threats, great Heaven! avert the curse!
With mercy guard the good!' The cable then
He bids us pull from shore, and loose the sheets;
The South winds fill the sails; through foaming waves
We skim the track where breeze and pilot call.

   "Wooded Zacynthus, and Dulichium
Rise from the sea, and Neritos' tall crags,
And Same, and we skirt Laertes' land,
Steep Ithaca, and curse Ulysses' home.
Soon too the cloudy peaks of Leucas show,
And that Apollo whom the seamen dread.
Wearied we steer to make the little town,
Cast anchor from the prow, and beach the stern.

   "Thus gaining land unhoped, our lustral dues
To Jove we pay, and, kindling altar-fires,
With Trojan Games we throng the Actian shore.
There, stripped and sleek with oil, my comrades try
Their country falls; so many an Argive town
Rejoicing to have passed, and fled the foe.

   "The Sun rounds all the year, and Winter frore
Chafes with North winds the sea. Then on the gates
I fix a hollow brazen shield, the wear
Of mighty Abas, with this legend graved:
These arms Aeneas from victorious Greeks!
I bid the seamen weigh, and man the thwarts:
Stoutly they smite the waves, and sweep the sea.
And soon we lose Phaeacia's skiey tops,
Skirt by Epirus' shore, Chaonia's port
Enter, and climb to steep Buthrotum town.

   "Rumours beyond belief there filled our ears,
That Helenus, the son of Priam, reigned
O'er those Greek towns, his bride and sceptre won
From Pyrrhus, and Andromache once more
Had found no alien spouse. My heart amazed
Burned to salute him, and to learn his tale.
Forth from the port I wend, from ships and shore,
When haply in a grove beyond the town,
By some feigned Simois stream, Andromache
Was shedding her sad gifts, and called his ghost
To Hector's tomb, an empty mound of turf,

And altars twain she hallowed but for tears.
Me coming when she spied, and saw distraught
The arms of Troy, by such great wonders awed,
Even still in gaze she froze, heat left her bones;
She swooned, and scarce failed speech recovered late.

  " 'Art thou alive, with real face and voice,
O Goddess-born! or, if sweet light be fled,
Where is my Hector?' Weeping thus, with moans
She filled the grove. I hardly in brief replied
To her despair, gasping with broken words.

  " 'Alive I am, through all extremes I live.
Doubt not, the sight is real.
But O! what chance hath fallen thee, declined
From such a man? What worthy fate hath found
Hector's Andromache? Art Pyrrhus' wife?'

  "She bowed her head, and in low accents spake.
'O blest alone of all the maids of Troy,
Before the foeman's tomb, neath Ilium's wall,
Bidden to die! who bore no lottery's shame,
Nor captive pressed a conquering master's bed!
We, from our burning town borne oversea,
The pride and insults of Achilles' son
Endured, and the slave's child-bed. Wooing then
Leda's Hermione, the Spartan bride,
To Helenus he passed me, thrall to thrall.
But him Orestes, burning with great love
For his rapt bride, and by Crime's Furies driven,
Took unawares, and at his altars slew.
At Pyrrhus' death, part of his kingdom fell
To Helenus, who named the land entire
Chaonia, after Trojan Chaon's name,
And built this towered Ilian citadel.

  " 'But thee what wind, what fate hath driven? What God
Thrust thee unweeting on our coast? How fares
Ascanius? Drinks he yet the living air,
Whom once in Troy—
Doth the boy pine for his lost mother still?
Is he to ancient valour by his sire
Aeneas, by his uncle Hector roused?'

"She ended weeping, and long sobbed in vain;
When from the town the hero Helenus
Came, thronged with friends, and recognised his kin,
And gladly led us in, and at each word
Shed many a tear. I go, and round me see
A lesser Troy, dwarf towers like her great,
A dried-up stream named Xanthus, and embrace
A Scaean Gate. My Trojans too the while
Enjoy the friendly city; them the King
Welcomes in spacious cloisters, and they pour
In the Hall's centre votive cups of wine,
And feast on golden plate, and lift the bowl.

"A day hath passed, and twain; and now the South
Calls to the sails, the canvas swells with wind,
When thus imploring I address the Seer:

" 'Troy-born, Interpreter of God, inspired
By bay and tripod and Apollo's Will,
Stars and birds' tongues and auguries of flight!
Tell me, — for holy voices all my course
Named happy, and all the Heavenly Ones advised
To make for Italy and lands remote, —
The Harpy alone Celaeno boded strange
Prodigious things, and told of cruel wrath,
And famine foul, — what perils shun I first?
How guided, may I win that hard assay?'

"Then Helenus the grace of Heaven first sues
With oxen duly slain, and from his head
Undoes the holy bands, and leads me himself,
O Phoebus, to thy doors, thrilled with the God!
Then with prophetic lips the Priest declaims:

" 'O Goddess-born! High auspices indeed
Direct thy voyage: so the King of Heaven
Thy lot awards; so rolls thy ordered course.
Few things of many I will set in words,
That safer thou may'st sail the homeless seas,
And rest in Italy: more Fate conceals
From Helenus, and Juno locks his lips.

" 'First; that Ausonia which thou deemest near, —
Blind soul! prepared to make a neighbour port! —

Far hence lies sundered by a pathless road.
First in Trinacrian waves the oar must bend,
The Ausonian brine be passed, the Aeaean Isle
Of Circe, and the Infernal Lakes, or e'er
Thy City thou may'st found on harbouring shores.
Signs I will show thee: keep them close at heart.
When thou, perplexed, shalt find beneath the holms
That fringe a secret stream one monstrous Sow
Stretched on the ground, with thirty young new-born,
White, and the brood about her udders white,
There shalt thou build, there rest from pain secure.
Nor heed that future gnawing of thy boards, —
Fate shall find means, and Phoebus called be near.
But fly those lands, fly that Italian coast
Washed by our orient tides. In every town
Dwells the bad Greek. Locrians of Naryx there
Have built their walls. Idomeneus of Crete
Hath poured his warriors o'er Sallentine plains;
And there that Meliboean chieftain's town,
Little Petelia, clinging to her wall.

" 'Nay, when thy barks lie stayed across the main,
And vows thou payest, raising on the beach
Altars, thine hair with purple covert veil,
Lest in thy worship any hostile face
Crossing the hallowed fires thine omens spoil.
Keep thou and thine this mode of sacrifice:
Pure in this rite let thy descendants bide.
But when thou leavest, to Sicilian shores
Blown, and Pelorus' narrow straits unfold,
Make the left coast, and sail with compass wide
The Southern waters, but the Northern shun.
Those lands long since, by some vast force uptorn,
(So strong to change is the slow lapse of Time,)
Were cleft apart, men say, though once the twain
Were both one land. The sea broke in between,
Hesperia rent from Sicily, and pours
'Twixt fields and towns divorced a narrow tide.
Scylla the right, Charybdis guards the left
Insatiate, and thrice sucks the swirling flood
Sheer down her gulf, and thrice again upspouts
Alternate, lashing the high stars with spume.
But Scylla, crouched in her blind cavern's lair,

With jaws out-thrust, pulls vessels on the rocks;
A human face above; a maid's fair breast
Down to the waist; below a monstrous shark,
With dolphin's tail to wolfish belly joined.
Better to round Pachynus' goal, and fetch
A long and weary compass, than to sight
Scylla but once within her vasty cave,
And hear rocks echo to her sea-green hounds!

" 'Now if some prescience, some prophetic fame
Pertain to Helenus, if Phoebus fill
His soul with truth, this one thing, Goddess-born!
One above all I warn thee, o'er and o'er
Repeating, first to mighty Juno pray;
To Juno chant thy vows, and win with gifts
The potent Queen; so, leaving Sicily,
Victor at last, Hesperia thou shalt gain.

" 'And when thou drawest near to Cumae town,
The mystic pools, Avernus' murmuring grove,
There shalt thou see the Prophetess inspired,
Who sings the fates of men and writes on leaves.
Whate'er she writes on leaves she sorteth well,
And in her cave keeps close. There they remain
Unchanged, in sequence true. But when the hinge
Turns, and a light air stirring through the door
Blows the thin leaves about, no care hath she
To catch them as they flutter through the cave,
Nor set them right, nor make the verses meet. —
Men leave unhelped, and hate the Sibyl's den. —
Here count not thou delay too dearly bought,
Though comrades chide, though strongly calls the sea,
And thou may'st fill the happy-bosomed sail.
Go to the Prophetess, and beg her sing
Herself thine oracles with willing lips.
The tribes of Italy, and wars to come,
How to escape each pain, and how to bear,
She will unfold, and, worshipped, grant success.
So much my voice may warn thee. Forward, then,
And by thy deeds to Heaven uplift great Troy!'

"Thus when the Seer's befriending lips had said,
Gifts to our ships he sent, of heavy gold
And carven ivory, and stowed our hulls

With massive silver, and Dodona's ware,
A coat of mail thrice-wove with rings of gold,
A fair peaked helmet, and a plumy crest,
The arms of Pyrrhus. And my sire hath gifts.
Steeds too he gives, and guides;
And finds us oars, and lends my comrades arms.

"Meanwhile Anchises bade the fleet set sail,
Nor lose the blowing wind. Whom Phoebus' Priest
Thus reverently bespake: 'Anchises, dear
To Heaven, by Venus' glorious nuptials crowned!
Twice rapt from Trojan ruins! Lo, for thee
Ausonia waits. Sail hence to yonder shores!
Yet them thou needs must skirt by sea: far off
Lies that Ausonian land Phoebus reveals!
Go, happy in thy son! Why further add,
Or with my talk delay the rising gales?'

"Andromache, at this last parting sad,
Brings for Iulus too a Phrygian vest,
And robes of golden broidery, nor stints
Her favour, loading him with woven gifts.
'Take these,' she saith, 'memorials of my hands,
Long to attest the love of Hector's wife,
Andromache, the last gifts of thy kin.
O boy! sole image of my Astyanax
Now left! Such eyes he had, such hands, such face!
And now like-aged were growing up with thee!'

"Leaving, I spoke to them with rising tears;
'Live happy, ye whose blessedness is won,
Won now, while we are called from fate to fate!
Your rest is gained: no sea remains to plough,
Nor those Ausonian ever-fading fields
To chase. A feigned Xanthus you behold,
A Troy your hands have made; a Troy, I pray,
Of happier fate, beyond the range of Greeks.
If e'er I enter Tiber, and the fields
That Tiber laves, and see our promised Home,
Twin cities there, and peoples closely bound,
Epirus and Hesperia, with one fate,
From Dardanus each sprung, our hearts shall make
One second Troy. Such charge await our sons!'

"Thence onward sailing by Ceraunian cliffs,
Our briefest course towards Italy we steer,
Till the sun sets, and the grey hills grow dim.
In the dear lap of earth we fling ourselves,
Allotting oars, and on the dry sea-sand
Comfort our limbs: sleep bathes the weary flesh.

"Night, driven by the Hours, her arch's crown
Not yet had climbed, when Palinurus rose,
Alert, and tried the wind, and on his ear
Caught it, and scanned the stars in the still sky,
Arcturus and the rainy Hyades,
The Bears, and great Orion, armed with gold.
And when he sees all heaven's unclouded calm,
He sounds his signal clear; we move our camp,
Launch forth anew, and spread our vessels' wings.

"The stars had fled before the reddening morn,
When far dim hills we saw, and lying low
Italy. 'Italy!' first Achates cries;
And merrily the crews hail 'Italy!'
Then Sire Anchises crowns a mighty bowl,
And fills with wine, and calls upon the Gods,
High standing on the stern:
'O Gods, supreme o'er earth and sea and sky!
Waft us with aiding wind, and breathe benign!'

"The wished-for breezes freshen, and the port
Widens more near, and on Minerva's Hill
A Temple shines. We, furling sail, our prows
Turn shoreward. Hollowed by the Eastern tide,
The port lies hid, its jutting horns afoam
With the salt spray: twin walls of towered rock
Stretch down, and from the shore the fane recedes.
Four horses, our first omen, here we saw,
Cropping the grassy lea, as white as snow.
Whereat Anchises: 'War, strange Land, thou bearest,
For war the steed is armed; these threaten war.
Yet this same beast will learn the harness' use,
Drawing the car, and bearing concord's yoke;
Hope too for peace,' saith he. Invoking then
Armed Pallas' might, who first our hail received,
Before her sacred shrine we veil our heads;

And duly, upon the Prophet's prime command,
To Argive Juno pay the sacrifice.

    "On, without stay, when all our vows were made,
Turning our sail-yard horns, those Greekish homes,
Suspected fields, we leave; and soon descry
Tarentum's bay, once home, if fame not errs,
Of Hercules, Lacinia's answering fane,
And Caulon's cliffs, and Scylaceum's strand,
Wreck-strewn. Then Aetna rises from the wave;
And far away we hear the loud sea moan
On beaten crags, and the shore's broken voice.
The surf leaps high; the sands and surges mix.
Then spake Anchises: "Tis Charybdis, sure,
Those rocks, those awful crags the Seer foretold!
Make off, my friends, rise on the oars in time!'
They straight obey; and Palinurus first
Swings South the roaring prow, and all our host
With oar, with wind, strain South. Now up to heaven
The arched wave lifts us; now, the wave drawn in,
We sink to shades below. Thrice roar the rocks
Through caverns deep; thrice the showered spray we see,
And stars bedewed with brine. But now the wind
Sinks with the sun, and leaves us weary men,
Who float unknowing to the Cyclops' coast.

    "A haven wide there lies, by beating winds
Unstirred, but near it Aetna thundering vents
Terrific deluge. Now a cloud of smoke,
Whirlwinds of pitch, and embers glowing white,
To the frayed stars he flings, and globes of fire.
Now shattered stones and entrails of the mount
He belches forth, and volleys molten rocks,
Roaring, and boiling from his deep abyss.
Below that mass, Enceladus, 'tis famed,
Lies, scorched by lightning, while above his head
Through riven ducts great Aetna blows his flames.
And all Trinacria, when he turns his side,
Trembles and moans, and shrouds in smoke the sky.
That night those uncouth wonders we endure,
Hidden in woods, nor see what makes the din.
No planet sheds its fire; no starry sheen
Brightens the sky; the louring rack rolls up,

And sullen Night holds fast the clouded moon.

"Now morn uprising with her orient star
Chased the dun mist, when sudden from the woods
Stept a strange shape of man, piteous in guise,
With extreme famine spent, who to the beach
Stretched forth entreating hands. We turn and gaze.
Sad filth, and beard unkempt, a garment held
By thorns; yet else a Greek, and one of old
Sent armed to Troy. He, when the Dardan dress
The Trojan arms he saw, awhile stopped short,
Scared at the sight, but to the beach anon
Ran headlong, and with weeping us implored:
'Now by the Stars I adjure you, by the Gods,
And by this lucent heavenly air we breathe,
Uplift me Trojans! Take me to what lands
Ye seek soe'er. I know that I am Greek;
And own I warred against the Gods of Troy;
For which, if wrong so deep my guilt hath done,
Sink me in sea, and strew me o'er the flood!
Dying, by human hands I fain would die!'

"He ceased, and clasped our knees, and to our knees
Clung writhing. Who he is, we bid him tell,
Whence born, what fortune drives about his days.
With scanty pause Anchises gave the youth
His own right hand in pledge, and cheered his heart;
Who, when his fear was banished, thus returned:

" 'Ithaca bore me, Achemenides,
Ulysses' mate, whom Adamastus poor,
My father, sent to Troy, — woe worth the day! —
In the vast Cyclops' cave, those cruel doors
Fleeing in dread, my comrades left me here,
Forgetful. Blood and bloody feasts pollute
That great dark house. The Giant — O ye Gods,
Take such a pest from earth! — strikes heaven itself,
Unfit for sight, unfit for speech of man,
On wretches' entrails fed and purple blood.

" 'Myself I saw him seize, with monstrous hand,
Stretched in his cave supine, two of our crew,
And break them on a rock, and the splashed floor
Ran blood. I saw him champ their gory limbs,

And the warm trembling flesh between his teeth!
Yet not unvenged: Ulysses bore not that,
Nor in such straits forgot his native wit.
When, gorged with meat and buried deep in wine,
The Monster bowed his neck, and lay immense
Along the cave, and vomited in sleep
Gobbets with blood and wine, we, casting lots,
And praying the great Gods, together all
Surged round, and with a pointed weapon bored
The one huge eye, which like an Argive shield,
Or the Sun's orb, sank in his glooming brow;
And glad at last avenged our comrades' ghosts. —
But fly, poor wretches, fly; and from this strand
Your hawser tear!
Like Polyphemus, in his cave who pens
And milks the woolly flock, so gross and grim
An hundred other one-eyed monsters dwell
About these bays, and roam the mountain sides.
Three moons e'en now have filled their horns with light,
While I among the forest haunts and homes
Of the lone beasts live on, and on the Rock
Spy those great giants, and their voice and tread
Hear trembling. Branches give me sorry fare,
Berries and cornels crude; uprooted herbs
Feed me. Far gazing round, at last I saw
Your barks, to which I turned, whate'er might hap.
Enough for me to escape this cursed crew;
Ye rather take my life howe'er ye will!'

    "He scarce hath said, when from the hills we see
The shepherd Polyphemus with his flocks
Moving gigantic to the well-known shore;
A Monster grim, huge, shapeless, reft of light.
A fir his hand hath lopped supports his steps;
The woolly sheep attend him, sole delight,
Sole solace of his pain.
When the deep flood he touched and reached the sea,
There, gnashing loud his teeth, the oozing blood
From his gouged eye he laves, and through the main
Strides to the midst, nor wets his lofty sides.
Far thence in fear we fly, with him that prayed
And earned our grace, in silence cut the rope,

And bend with straining oars, and sweep the sea.
He hears, and turns his footsteps to the sound.
But when he fails to grasp us and to match
The Ionian waves in chase, a great uproar
He raised, whereat each billow of the sea
Shook, and the soil of Italy far down
Trembled, and Aetna's hollow caverns roared.
Then from the woods and mountain sides aroused,
The one-eyed clan down rush, and fill the beach.
Vainly, with angry looks, we see them stand,
Brothers of Aetna, with sky-towering heads,
An awful conclave! as high oaks uplift
Their airy tops, or coned cypresses,
Jove's lofty forest, or Diana's grove.

  "Fear urged us then to slacken sheets, and spread
Our canvas to the wind. Far other charge
The Prophet gave us, not to hold our way
'Twixt Scylla and Charybdis, on each hand
The edge of ruin: so our sails are backed;
And lo! the North wind from Pelorus' strait
Blows, and Pantagia's living stones I pass,
And Megara's gulf, and Thapsus' lowly strand.
Such shores the comrade of Ulysses' pain
Showed us, recoasting where he sailed of yore.

  "Off the Sicanian bay, an Island lies,
Against wave-washed Plemyrium, named of old
Ortygia. There Alpheus, Elis' stream,
Stole underseas, men say, by secret paths,
And through thy fount, O Arethusa! pours
Into Sicilian seas: to whom, forewarned,
We pay our vows; then, past the luscious meads
Of still Helorus, graze Pachynus' reefs:
Till Camarina, whom the Fates forbade
To move her marsh, shows far, and Gela's plain,
Gela that bears its churlish river's name.
Then Acragas the steep, the getter once
Of noble steeds, shows her great walls afar.
Thy palms, Selinus, on the granted gale
I leave, and thread the Lilybaean shoals,
And sunken reefs, till on the joyless strand
Of Drepanum I stay. There, tempest-tost

So long, ah me! my father, comforter
Of every ill, I lose. There me outworn,
Thou leavest, father, rescued all in vain!
Not Helenus, foretelling things of dread,
Told me this sorrow, nor Celaeno grim.
This was my latest woe, my long road's end.
Departed thence, God drove me to your shores."

    One before all intent, Aeneas thus
The doom of Heaven retold, and all his ways;
Then hushed, and rested, when the tale was done.

Book IV

BUT DIDO, SICK long since of painful love,
Feeds with her veins the wound, by fire unseen
Wasted. The hero's prowess haunts her much,
Much his great race. Fast in her heart are fixt
His looks, his words, and love denies her rest.

    The morrow morn with Phoebus' lamp the earth
Gan traverse, and the dewy shades dispersed,
When her twin-hearted sister thus distraught
She addressed:
                "What dreams, O Anna! scare my soul!
O what a guest is this to us new-come!
O what a mien, what front, what arms are his!
Not vain my faith that he is Heavenly born.
Fear stamps the baser soul. O how the Fates
Have vext him! How he told of battles waged!
Were not my mind irrevocably fixed
With none to mate in wedlock, since by death
Love, turning traitor, robbed me at the prime;
Were I not tired of bridal torch and bower,
To this one fault perchance I might succumb.
Anna, I own it, since Sychaeus fell,
And by a brother's blood our House was stained,
He only hath moved my heart, or made my will

Falter; I know the marks, the flame of old!
But O! may Earth yawn deep, may Heaven's high Sire
With all his thunders hurl me to the shades,
Pale shades of Erebus, and Night profound,
Ere, Honour, thee I soil, or break thy law!
He who first made me his took with him all
My heart; still let him keep it in his grave!"
She ceased, and rising tears her bosom filled.

   Then Anna: "Dearer far than light is dear,
O Sister! wilt thou wither all thy Spring
Lonely, with no sweet babes, no crown of Love?
Think'st thou the buried ghost heeds aught of that?
What though no lover moved thee in thy grief,
In Tyre, or Libya; not Iarbas scorned,
Nor any Prince of Afric's conquering clime,
Yet wilt thou wrestle with a welcome love?
Hast thou no thought in whose domains we dwell,
Tameless Gaetulians here, and all around
Unreined Numidians and the Syrtes waste;
There desert drought, and Barce's savage hordes?
What need to tell of wars that spring from Tyre,
Thy brother's menace?
Guided by Gods I hold and Juno's love
Troy's fleet was hither blown. O what a city,
Sister, wilt thou see here, what kingdoms rise
On such a wedding! To what heights, allied
With Trojan arms, will Punic glory ascend!
Nay; sue the grace of Heaven with holy vows,
Give entertainment room, and weave excuse
To stay him, while with storms Orion wet
Smites sea and ship, while heavens refuse a track."

   Thus speaking, she made flame her glowing heart,
Filled her racked mind with hope, loosed Honour's rein.
They seek the shrines; they pray for peace, and slay
Choice ewes to Ceres, Bearer of the Law,
To Phoebus and Lyaeus, but in chief
To Juno, Guardian of the marriage bond.
Dido herself, most fair, with bowl in hand,
Pours o'er a white cow's horns, before the Gods
Paces to their rich altars, and the day
Hallows with gifts, and in the victim's breast

Gazing takes counsel of the breathing heart.
O blind Diviners! How can vow or shrine
Help passion's slave? The flame is biting deep
E'en then, and dumb within the wound lives on.
Unhappy Dido, burning, through the town
Roams frenzied, like an arrow-stricken doe,
A heedless doe some swain in Cretan glens
Hath pierced from far, and left the flying steel
Unknowing. She o'er Dicte's forest lawns
Flies, bearing in her flank the reed of death.

Now through the streets she leads him, and displays
Her Tyrian wealth, her city built and made;
Begins to speak, and checks the half-spoken word:
Now to the banquet goes at ebbing day,
And asks again to hear the Tale of Troy,
Infatuate! and again hangs on his lips.
But when they part, and the dim moon in turn
Sets, and the sinking stars are urging sleep,
Sole in her halls she mourns, his empty couch
Clasps, and him absent hears far off and sees.
Or, by his father's looks entranced, she hugs
Iulus, to beguile her untold love.
No more the towers rise; no more the youth
Exercise arms, nor ports or bulwarks make
Defensive: interrupted hang the works,
The giant threatening walls and engines huge.

Her thus infected when the Wife of Jove
Saw, and to passion yielding up her fame,
To Venus thus she spake: "A noble prize,
An ample spoil ye win, a glorious name,
Thou and thy Boy! One woman by two Gods
Subtly subdued! Nor do I fail to see
Our town thou fearest, this high Punic House
Holding suspect. But what shall be the end?
What boots our rivalry? Nay, let us make
An ever-during peace, a bridal pact.
Thou hast thine heart's desire. Dido with love
Burns, and through every vein draws passion in.
Rule we this people then with equal sway
Jointly, and let her serve a Phrygian lord,
And hand to thee for dower her Tyrian men."

To whom thus Venus — for beneath that speech
She marked what craft to Libya would divert
The Italian crown: " 'Twere madness to prefer
A war with thee! If when thy plan were done
'Twould issue well! But I am swayed by Fate
Uncertain if the Will of Jove intend
One city for the men of Tyre and Troy,
Both peoples blent and federate; but thou,
Thou art his wife; thou may'st his mind essay.
Lead, and I follow."
                   Juno then replied:
"Mine be that task. How to achieve our aim,
Hear now, and briefly learn. To hunt the glade
Aeneas and the woe-doomed Queen will ride
Together, when the morrow's sun new-risen
Unveils the radiant world. While ranging scouts
Circle the wood with toils, a sleety storm
On them will I pour down, and shake the sky
With thunder. Then their train, dispersing wide,
Will vanish into gloom: the selfsame cave
Dido shall enter and the Trojan Prince.
There I shall be, and, if thy will be toward,
Joined in firm wedlock I will make her his.
There shall her bridal be!"
                   Assent was given,
And at her plot the Cytherean smiled.

And when the dawn rose shining from the sea,
Forth from the city flowed the chosen train,
Nets, snares, and steel-bound spears, Massylian horse,
And the shrewd scent of hounds. Before her door
The Tyrian princes wait their Queen, who still
Tarries in bower, while her horse, adorned
With purple and gold, stands chafing the flecked bit.
At last she issues with an ample train,
Wrapped in a Tyrian scarf; and all of gold
Her quiver gleams, with gold her hair is bound,
A golden brooch clasps up her purple cloak.
Phrygians and blithe Iulus pace beside;
And with them joined, above them all most fair,
Aeneas; like Apollo, when he quits
Xanthus and wintry Lycia, and seeks

His mother's Delos. There he leads the dance,
And round his altars Cretans, Dryopes,
And painted Agathyrsi meet with din.
He treads the Cynthian slopes, and with soft green
Enwreathes his flowing locks, and binds with gold.
Behind him ring the shafts. So lightly trod
Aeneas, and so shone his glorious brow.

They climb the mountains, and the pathless wilds;
And lo! the goats, from rocky heights dislodged,
Bound down from crag to crag; and startled deer
In dusty masses fleeing from the hills
Scour the broad moor. But down the dales the boy
Iulus glories in his mettled steed,
Out-galloping them all, and longs to see
Among that cattle tame some foaming boar,
Or yellow lion coming down the fells.

Meanwhile the sky, with muttered peals convulsed,
Breaks in a storm of sleet. The Tyrians flee:
The scattered Trojans, and the Dardan child
Of Venus' son, for shelter scour the fields
Fearful, while torrents from the mountains plunge.
One cave holds Dido and the Trojan Prince.
Primaeval Earth and spousal Juno give
The sign: fires glitter, and the conscious sky
Their bridal lights, and mountain Nymphs cry hail.

Death's earliest day, the primal source was that
Of all her woes. She heeds nor eye nor tongue,
Nor dreams of secret love, but calls it now
Marriage, and with that name would screen her fault.

Forthwith runs Rumour through the Libyan towns;
Rumour, the swiftest bane. She thrives on change,
And gathers strength by going. Small at first,
And timorous, but full soon, to heaven uplift,
She treads the earth and hides in clouds her head.
Her Earth, infuriate with the Gods, conceived,
To Coeus and Enceladus, fame saith,
Last sister born; swift-footed, swift of wing,
Grim, monstrous, huge: and every plume she bears
Hath under it a glaring eye, a tongue,
Wondrous! a speaking mouth, and ears erect.

By night she flies from earth and heaven midway,
Strident, nor droops her lids in pleasant sleep.
By day she sits on roof or lofty tower,
A sentinel who keeps great towns in fear,
Truth's herald, but as oft in falsehood bold.
She now rejoicing fills the people's ears
With wild discourse, and tells both false and true;
How one of Trojan blood, Aeneas, came,
Whom Dido deigns to wed; all winter long,
Delights they share, and both their realms forget,
Enthralled by shameful love. Such tales abroad
The loathly Goddess spreads on every tongue;
And, speeding straight to Prince Iarbas, him
With words she kindles, heaping high his wrath.

He, Ammon's seed by Garamantian nymph,
An hundred fanes in his wide realm to Jove,
An hundred altars built, and hallowed fire,
The Gods' unsleeping sentry, and enriched
The soil with victims' blood, and with gay blooms
Festooned the courts: who, by that bitter tale
Maddened, before his shrines, amidst his Gods,
Jove long in prayer besought with uplift hands.

"Almighty Jove! to whom on broidered couch
The feasting Moor now pours Lenaeus' gift,
Dost thou behold? or do we vainly shrink,
O Father, from thy bolts, and do thy fires
Blindly affright, thy thunders idly roll?
The woman, straying in our bounds, who built
A little purchased town, to whom we gave
Ploughland and rights of fief, our hand refused,
Now takes Aeneas for her lord, and he,
This Paris, with his eunuch train, his chin
And essenced hair by Phrygian bonnet bound,
Takes and enjoys! And yet to fanes of thine
We carry gifts, and nurse an idle faith!"

Him, praying thus and clinging to his shrines,
The Almighty heard, and on the royal town
Looked, and on those who loved forgetting fame,
Then thus to Mercury his mandate gave:
"Go, Son, the Zephyrs call, and slant thy flight

Down to the Dardan Prince, who dallies yet
In Carthage, and of cities given by Fate
Heeds nought. To him my words bear swiftly down.
Not such his mother promised him to us,
And not for this twice saved him from the Greek;
But o'er the Imperial Mother's warrior sons,
O'er Italy to reign, from Teucer's blood
Prolong the line, and bind the world by law.
If no such glory fires him, if no toil
For his own fame he takes, yet doth he grudge
His son Ascanius the high towers of Rome?
What makes he there with foes? why not regards
Ausonian seed, and fair Lavinium's land?
To Sea! This sums it. Thus our message bear."

He ceased; the other, his great Sire's command
Obeying, first the golden sandals tied,
That bear him over seas and lands sublime,
Winged with the flying gale; then took the wand,
With which he calls the pallid phantoms forth
From Orcus, or to Tartarus sends down,
Gives sleep and takes away, and the dead eyes
Unseals, and drives the hurricane, and swims
The cloudy rack. Then flying he descried
Worn Atlas' sides and sky-supporting top,
Atlas, whose piney head is ever wreathed
In cloud and darkness, beat by wind and rain.
Snow cloaks his shoulders; rivers o'er his chin
Plunge downward, and his beard is stiff with ice.

Here first Cyllenius, weighing his spread wings,
Paused, and with all his body headlong dived
Sea-ward, as when a bird about the shores
And fishy crags flies low, and skims the wave.
So flew Cyllene's son, his grandsire left,
Between the earth and sky, and cut the winds
To Libya's sandy shore.
                              And when he touched
With his winged feet the land where hovels lay,
He spied Aeneas planning towers and town.
His sword shone starry with the yellow sheen
Of jasper, and a cloak of Tyrian dye

Hung from his shoulders which the sumptuous Queen
Had worked for him, and shot the web with gold.
Prompt rings the challenge: "Is it thou, O Prince!
Uxurious! building now this towered town,
This Carthage, ah! forgetful of thy doom,
Thy Kingdom. Me the Regent of the Gods,
Whom heaven and earth obey, Himself hath sent,
To bear this mandate through the buxom air:
'What mak'st thou here, in ease on Libyan soil?
If no such glory fires thee, if no toil
For thine own fame thou takest, yet regard
Thy rising heir and young Ascanius' hopes,
To whom the crown of Italy is owed,
The Roman world.' " He said, and ended not,
Ere mortal eyes he left, and passed from sight
Into thin air away.
                              Aeneas stood
Perplexed to see, his hair in terror rose,
His tongue was tied, and by that warning dread
And Heavenly mandate awed, he burns to fly,
And leave that pleasant clime. Ah! what to do?
How dare he now approach the impassioned Queen
To tell her? What beginning can he choose?
On every side dividing the swift mind,
This way and that he casts it, scanning all,
Till in his doubt this counsel overruled.
Mnestheus, Sergestus and Cloanthus brave
He charged to equip the fleet, to call the crews
And furbish arms in secret, and the cause
Disguise, and he the while, since that fond Queen
Knows not, and dreams not of such love undone,
Will try to meet her in her softest hour,
And tell when chance is kind. Then all with joy
Speed to obey his bidding.
                                        But the Queen —
Who can deceive a lover? — she foreknew
His guile, and early caught the coming stir.
She fears when all is safe; and hears distraught
The same cold Rumour tell of launching ships.
Helpless she storms, and through the streets incensed
Raves like a Thyiad, stirred by holy din,

Whom the triennial orgies of the God
Madden, and all night through Cithaeron shouts.
At last Aeneas she assails with speech.

"And hast thou hoped, O false one! to disguise
Thy crime, and leave my land without a word?
Not thee our love, not thee thine hand once given
Restrains, nor Dido doomed to death and woe.
Nay, even under winter's star thou strivest
To launch thy ships and stem the northern gales.
O cruel! If thy goal were no unknown
No alien land, if ancient Troy remained,
Would Troy be sought across this blustering sea?
Me dost thou fly? O, by these tears, I pray,
By thine own hand — for I have left but these —
O by our loves and bridal days begun,
If I have won thy thanks, and gave thee once
Some joy, have pity! Spare our House! and O!
If room be left for prayers, undo thy will!
For thee the Libyans hate me, Nomad chiefs
Scorn, yea, my kin turn from me: for thee, too,
Honour is dead, and all my Heavenly hope,
My once good fame. To whom thy dying Queen
Leav'st thou, O Guest! — my Love's sole title now! —
Why wait I till my brother raze these walls,
Or Moor Iarbas lead me captive hence?
Ah! if I had but held, before thy flight,
A child of thine! if in my halls might play
A little Aeneas, to bring back thy looks,
I should not seem all captured and forlorn."

She ended. He by Jove's command his gaze
Kept fixed, and deep at heart suppressed his pain.
At last thus briefly: "I will not deny,
I owe thee all, O Queen, thy words could tell;
And to remember thee will still be sweet,
While memory lasts, while breath commands my frame.
Words need be few. I did not think to flee
In secret; feign not so. I never lit
The bridal torch, nor plighted troth with thee.
If Fate allowed me choice, to live my life
And heal my woes at will, I first would honour
Troy, and the dear-loved remnant of my race;

Priam's tall house would stand, and Ilium's towers
My hand had for the vanquished built anew.
But Phoebus now and Lycia's oracles
Italy bid me seek, great Italy.
There is my love, my home. If Punic towers,
And Libyan city enthrall thee, Tyrian Queen,
Why dost thou grudge that Teucer's kin should hold
Ausonian fields? Doom drives us too abroad.
Me, when the world is veiled in dewy night,
When stars rise bright, my father's troubled ghost
Warns oft in sleep, and awes: my little son
Haunts me, so dear a head, of destined fields
Wrongly defrauded and the Hesperian crown.
Now the Gods' Herald, sent by Jove himself,
(Be witness both!) through the fleet air hath borne
His mandate: yea, I saw him pass the gate,
A God, in light revealed, and drank his voice.
Cease with thy plaints to inflame thyself and me:
I seek not Italy by choice."

    While thus he speaks, she glares at him askance,
And with swift rolling eyes surveys him o'er,
Silent; and now, inflamed with anger, cries:
"No Goddess bore thee! Thine no Dardan stock!
Traitor! The flinty peaks of Caucasus
Got thee, Hyrcanian tigers gave thee suck!
Why should I mask myself? why wait for more?
When hath he sighed, or looked upon my tears?
When hath he wept, or pitied her who loved?
Where should my charge begin? Not Juno now,
Not Father Jove now looks with righteous eyes.
No faith is sure! Wrecked, starved, I bade him hail,
Madly with him I shared my realm; I found
His missing ships; I saved his friends from death.
Ah, Furies burn me! Now Apollo calls,
Now Lycia bids! now, sent by Jove himself,
Comes the Gods' Herald with his mandate harsh.
What work for Gods! What care to vex their calm!
I hold thee not; I answer not. Away!
Pursue thine Italy with wind and wave!
Yet on the rocks I hope, if Heaven can smite,
Drinking thy doom, on Dido thou wilt call.

There I shall reach thee, wrapt in sulphury flames;
And when cold death hath stript my living flesh
My ghost shall haunt thee! Well shalt thou requite,
And I shall hear the rumour in my grave!"

Therewith she breaks off speech, and from the air
Turns anguished, and from sight withdrawing leaves
Him faltering in his fear and fain to speak.
Her maids uplift her and her fainting limbs
Lay on a couch within her marble bower.

But good Aeneas, though to soothe her pain
Sore yearning, and with words to avert her woe,
Sighing and fainting with the stress of love,
God's mandate still obeys, and seeks the ships.

From all the beach the Trojans launch with toil
Their high-built barks: again the smooth keel swims,
And oars they fetch yet leafy from the woods,
Unshaped, in haste to go.
From all the city you can see them swarm.
As when the ants, remembering winter, spoil
A heap of corn, and store it in their home.
Across the grass they move, a black thin line,
Bearing their booty; and with shoulders some
Push heavy grains, while others drill the ranks,
And scourge delay: the pathway glows with toil.

Then, Dido, seeing that, what heart was thine?
How didst thou sigh, from thy tall tower to see
The wide shore glow with men, and all the deep
Torn by their shouts? O whither, tyrant Love,
Driv'st thou not human hearts! Again to tears
Forced, and again to entreaty, she submits
Her humbled pride to love, lest any means
Be left untried, and she should vainly die.

"Anna, thou see'st the hurry on all the beach:
They gather round; the canvas calls the breeze:
The merry sailors crown the stems with green.
If I had strength to look for such a woe,
I shall have strength to bear it too. But grant,
Sister, this only boon. With none but thee
Conversed that traitor, gave his secret thoughts
To thee; thou only know'st his softer hours.

Go, sue for pity my disdainful foe.
I never swore at Aulis to uproot
The Trojan race: I sent no ships to Troy:
I never tore Anchises from his grave.
Why to my utterance doth he seal his ears?
Where hastes he? Let him grant his wretched love
This one last boon, and wait till winds be fair.
No more I plead for bridal vows betrayed,
Nor ask him to give up his Latian crown:
For time I pray, rest for my heart and room,
Till Fortune school me to endure defeat.
For pity, O Sister! grant my latest prayer,
And well will I repay thee, when I die!"

    Thus she implores: such moans her sister takes,
And takes again: but him no moans affect.
Intractable he hears: Fate bars the way;
And God has sealed his unperturbed ears.
As when the Alpine winds together strive
Some many-wintered oak with veering blasts
To uproot. It creaks, and from the storm-lashed trunk
Leaves strew the ground; yet to the rock it clings,
And high as it uplifts to heaven its head,
So deep to Tartarus its roots extend.
Thus, buffeted by veering voices, stands
Aeneas; and his mighty heart is wrung.
Firm stands his will; and idly tears roll down.

    Then, awed by Doom, unhappy Dido prays
For death, and wearies of the vaulted sky.
And more befell to urge her from the light:
For while on incensed shrines she laid her gifts,
The holy lymph turned black before her eyes,
O horrible! the wine was changed to blood!
From all, from Anna's self that sight she hid.
And in the Palace stood a marble shrine,
Sacred to her dead lord, with snow-white wool
Lovingly wreathed, and crowned with festal green.
Thence, when the world was veiled in gloomy night,
Voices were heard, her husband seemed to call,
And on the roof, with wailing long drawn out,
A solitary owl would chant her dirge.
And many a word of many a prophet old

Scared her with boding fears. In fevered dreams
Aeneas goads her on; and still she seems
Forsaken, walking one long road alone,
And looking for her kin in lands forlorn.
So raving Pentheus sees the Furies' rout,
Two suns, and double Thebes: so o'er the scene,
Haunted Orestes, Agamemnon's son,
Flees from his mother armed with snakes and fire,
While vengeful Terrors on the threshold crouch.

And when, subdued by anguish, she conceived
Madness and death, alone she planned the hour,
The method, and sad Anna thus bespake,
Masking with hopeful countenance her design:

"O Sister, give me joy! The way is found
To bring him back to me, or set me free.
Near Ocean's end, beside the setting sun,
Lies the far Aethiops' land, where Atlas huge
Turns on his back the star-yspangled sky.
Thence a Massylian priestess I was shown,
The Hesperian temple's guardian, who preserved
The sacred boughs, and strewed with honey dews
And drowsing poppy-seed the dragon's food.
She with her charms can free what hearts she will,
Or flood with passion; stay the rivers' flow;
Turn back the stars, and wake the ghosts of Night.
Earth moans beneath her feet, and down the rocks
The rowans dance. By Heaven I swear, I swear
By thy sweet life, dear sister, I am loth
To don such magic! But in the inner court
Raise thou by stealth a pyre beneath the sky:
There let them lay the arms he impious left
Hung in my bower, his dress, the bridal bed
Where I was slain. All relics of his guilt
I fain would cancel, as the Priestess shows."

Thereat she paused, and pallor took her cheek.
Yet Anna guessed not those strange rites concealed
Her sister's death, nor dreamed of such despair;
No worse she fears than when Sychaeus died,
And carries out her charge.

But when the pyre rose high with oak and pine
Within the inmost court, Queen Dido wreathed

The spot with garlands, and with funeral boughs
Crowned it, and laid thereon the sword he left,
His dress, his image, mindful of the end.

　　Around rise altars, where the Priestess calls
Three hundred Gods, Chaos and Erebus,
The tri-form Hecat, Dian triple-faced;
And sprinkles water from Avernus feigned.
Herbs too are sought, which brazen sickles reaped
By moonlight, juicy with black poison's milk.
And from the forehead of a newborn foal
The mother's love is reft.

　　Then Dido, by the shrine, with one foot bare
And robe ungirdled, holds the sacred cake,
And dying prays the Gods, the Stars that know
Men's doom, the Powers, if any Powers there be,
Justly regarding hearts that love in vain.

　　'Twas Night, and all Earth's weary bodies culled
The peaceful sleep. The woods, the savage seas
Lay husht, and midway rolled the sliding stars.
Each field is still: each beast, each painted bird,
That haunts the liquid mere or tangled brake,
Beneath the silent night in slumber's lap
Heals all its cares, and all its pain forgets.

　　But not the woeful Queen. She never sinks
To sleep; she draws not into eyes or heart
The quiet night. Her sorrow grows; her love
Surges again, on seas of anger tossed;
And thus the thoughts are rolling through her soul:

　　"Ah! what to do? Shall I derided now
Try my old loves, and beg the marriage bond
From Nomads whom I spurned? Or shall I track
The Trojans' ships, and serve their utmost will?
As though they still had thanks, and held my aid
To memory dear! And who would grant my wish,
Or take to his proud fleet the hated Queen?
Know'st thou not yet Laomedon's false sons,
O broken heart? What? Shall I flee alone
With those exulting crews? or shall I sweep
With all my Tyrian guard, and drive again
O'ersea, with canvas to the breezes spread,

Whom scarce I tore from Sidon? Nay; with steel
Thy pain avert, and die, as thou hast earned.
Won by my tears, thou, sister, thou wert first
To heap these ills and give me to my foe.
O might I but have lived like free wild things,
That know no bridal curse, nor love like mine!
The faith I swore upon Sychaeus' grave
I have not kept!" Such sorrow wrings her heart.

But in his high-built ship Aeneas lay
Sleeping, resolved and ready to depart.
Whom, in his dreams, the God's returning shape
Seemed once again to warn, in voice, in hue,
Mercury's image, with his golden hair,
His youthful grace.
                              "And canst thou, Goddess-born,
Sleep even now, nor mark the perils dire
Close gathering round, O madman! listing not
The happy Zephyrs? She in heart explores
A treacherous evil crime, resolved to die,
On seas of anger tossed. Fly hence in haste,
While fly thou may'st! Soon thou shalt see the waves
Thronged with her keels, see the wild firebrands flash,
The beach aglow with flame, should morning find
Thee dallying here. Up, up! Break off thy sloth!
A light inconstant thing is womankind!"
He said, and mingled with the shades of night.

Scared by that sudden ghost, Aeneas leaps
From slumber, and upbraids his sleeping crew.
"Wake, men, and hasten! Man the thwarts! Unfurl
The sails with speed! A God from Heaven sent down
Spurs us again to cut our mooring-ropes
And flee apace. Blest God, whoe'er thou art,
Joyous we come, again to do thy will.
O aid us with thy grace, and in the sky
Set favouring stars!"
                              He spake, and drew his blade,
And with a lightning flash the hawser smote.
All catch the flame at once, and strive and stir;
The beach is bare: ships cover all the sea:
They churn the foam, and stoutly sweep the blue.

Now Morning from Tithonus' saffron bed
Rose, and o'er earth dispersed the virgin light,
When Dido from her tower beheld the gleam
Of whitening day, and saw the ships move out
With swelling canvas, and the harbour void.
Thrice and again she strikes her lovely breast,
And tears her golden hair.
                       "Dear God!" she cries,
"And shall he go, and flout my kingdom thus?
No arms leap out, not all my city chase
And drag the ships from dock? Go! Fetch me quick
Firebrands; bring arms! ply oars! — What words are these?
Where am I? O, what madness turns my wit?
Unhappy Dido, now thy guilt comes home
Too late, thy crown once shared. So loyal proved
This famous saviour of his country's gods!
This famous son who bore his ageworn sire!
O, might I not have torn him limb from limb,
To strew the sea, and slain his friends, aye, slain
His son, and served him for the father's meat?
Such strife had doubtful issue? Yea, but who
Could daunt me dying? Brands I should have borne,
And filled his decks with flame, burned son and sire,
With all their kin, and slain myself the last!

"Sun, who surveyest all the works of Earth!
Thou, Juno, conscious herald of my pain!
Hecat, whose name the midnight crossway howls!
Avenging Terrors, and ye Gods that guard
Dying Elissa, hear! O, turn your power
To punish evil! If that godless head
Must voyage safe to port; if so the doom
Of Jove demand, and there his goal is set,
Yet by a gallant nation from his land
Outcast with galling wars, torn from his son,
Help may he beg, and see his kinsmen die
Unworthy deaths, nor, to unequal peace
Submitting, may he enjoy the wished-for day,
But fall too soon unburied on the sand.
So be it! This last word with my blood I shed.
Thenceforth, O Tyrians, all his seed pursue
With hatred! To my ashes grant this boon!

No love, no league between you. From my bones,
Avenger, rise, and chase with fire and sword
The intruding Dardans, now, hereafter, yea,
Whenever power is thine! May shore to shore
Be adverse, sea to sea, and sword to sword,
For fathers and for children endless war!"

    She ceased; and in her thoughts explored each way
To slit the hateful life: and briefly thus
To Barce spake, Sychaeus' nurse, (for hers
Lay black in ashes in her native land):

    "Fetch me my sister, Nurse, and bid her haste
To wash in flowing water, and to bring
The victims and sin-offerings ordained.
Thus let her come. Thou too thy temples veil
With holy bands. The rites of Stygian Jove
Duly commenced fulfilling I will end
My pain, and fire the Dardan's funeral pile."
She said: the Nurse made haste her aged feet.

    But Dido, trembling, wild with purpose dread,
Rolling her blood-shot eyes, and on her cheeks
Bright burning spots, else white with coming death,
Burst through the inner door, and madly climbed
The lofty pyre, and drew the Dardan blade,
Not for such purpose given! Then, when she espied
The Trojan dress, and the familiar bed,
Awhile she paused in thought, and on the couch
Sank, full of tears, and spoke a last farewell.

    "O relics sweet, while God and Fate were kind!
Receive my spirit, and free me from this woe!
I have lived my life, and run my destined course;
Now underground my mighty shade will pass.
I built a famous city: I saw it rise;
Avenged my lord, my cruel brother punished:
Happy, too happy, ah! if Dardan keels
Had never touched our shore!"
                                        She spake; and kissed
The bed, and "Shall I die then unavenged?
Yet let me die," she adds. "Thus, thus I go
Gladly to darkness. Dardan! watch this flame!
And with thee take the curse of Dido's death!"

She ceased; but ere she ceased, her handmaids saw
Her fallen upon the steel, the sword with blood
Foaming, her hands besprent. A loud uproar
Fills the high halls, and Rumour through the town
Riots, and houses wail with many a moan
And women's shrieks. Heaven rings with loud lament,
As though all Carthage to the invading foe
Or ancient Tyre were falling, and o'er house
And holy temple rolled the raging fire.

Death-pale her sister heard; and through the crowd
Ran, mad with fear, and rent her cheeks with nails,
And beat her breast, and called the dying Queen.

"O Sister, was it this? Didst play me false?
Thy pyre, thine altars, O, was this their end?
What moan is mine, forsaken, scorned to be
Thy death-mate? To thy doom thou shouldst have called
Me too; and let one blow, one hour take both!
Have these hands built it, calling on our Gods,
That I, unkind, might fail thee lying thus?
Thou hast slain me too, thy people, and thy lords,
Thy Carthage. Give me water; let me wash
The wounds; and if one last breath stir, my lips
Shall catch it!"
                              Saying thus, she climbed the steps,
And to her heart her dying sister pressed,
Moaning, and with her vesture staunched the blood.

She tried to lift her heavy eyes, again
Fell back. The death-wound grated in her breast.
Thrice, leaning on her arm, she raised her head;
Thrice on the bed fell back, with wandering eyes
Sought heaven's light, and, when she found it, moaned.

Then mighty Juno pitied her long pain
And hard departure; and from Heaven sent down
Iris, to loose from flesh the struggling soul.
For since she died not fated nor condemned,
But hapless ere her day, by sudden rage,
Not yet had Proserpine the golden tress
Cut, nor to Stygian Orcus doomed her head.

So dewy Iris flew on saffron wings,
Trailing against the sun a thousand tints,

And stood above her.
                    "This thy lock I take,
Sacred to Dis, and thee from flesh release."

    She spake, and cut the tress. Then all the warmth
Fled, and all life went out upon the wind.

Book V

MEANWHILE AENEAS HIS unwavering way
Sailed on, and cut the billows dark with wind;
Yet shoreward gazed, where now the death-flames shone
Of woeful Dido. What such blaze hath lit,
They know not, but the pangs of blighted love,
What woman's rage can do, these draw their hearts
Through sad foreboding.
                        Now their vessels held
The open main, and no more land was seen—
Sea everywhere, and everywhere the sky—
When overhead a blue-black cloud of rain
Bore night and storm: the shuddering water gloomed.
The pilot Palinurus from the stern
Himself cried out: "What clouds invest the sky!
What wilt thou, Father Neptune?" Saying thus,
He bade them reef the sails, and bend the oars,
Sloped to the wind his canvas, and outspake:
"Great-souled Aeneas! Not if Jove himself
Gave warrant, could I make Italian shores
With such a sky. From the black West the winds
Rise roaring adverse; air is crushed to cloud:
No strength is ours to thwart and stem the gale.
Since Fate is mistress, let us turn our course,
And follow where she calls. Not far, methinks,
Sicilian ports, thy brother Eryx' coast,
If rightly I recall the stars I watched."

    Then good Aeneas: "Yea; long since I marked
The winds' exaction and thy vain revolt.

Shift the sails' tack! Were any shore more sweet?
Where would I sooner beach my sea-worn barks
Than on that land which keeps Acestes still,
And in its lap enfolds my father's bones?"
He ceased. They steer for harbour, while the sails
Boon Zephyrs fill; and scudding o'er the waves
Joyous at last they touch the well-known strand.

   Amazed, Acestes from a distant peak
Their coming saw; and, rough with hunting-spears
And Libyan bear-skin, met the friendly ships;
Whom to Crimisus stream his mother bore
A Trojan. Not forgetful of her race,
He bade them hail, his rustic treasure showed,
And with kind cheer consoled the wearied men.

   And when the next day brightening in the East
Had chased the stars, Aeneas on the shore
Summoned his crews, and from a mound held speech:

   "Dardans, O breed of high and holy blood!
The circling months have measured all the year
Since when my sacred father's bones we laid
In earth, and hallowed his funereal shrines.
Now is that day, that ever-bitter day,
Ever to be revered, God wills, by me!
Yea, were I outcast on Gaetulian Sands,
Caught in Mycenae or the Aegean main,
Even so with solemn pomps would I perform
The yearly vow, and strew his shrine with gifts.
Now, not without the will, not without care
Of Heaven, methinks, my buried father's bones
We visit, to this friendly haven borne.
Let all pay homage glad, and pray for winds,
That, when our Home is planted, I may bear
Each year such tribute to his sacred fanes.
Troy-born Acestes sends to every ship
Two head of oxen: to the feast invite
Your Guardian Gods, and those your host reveres.
And should the ninth glad morning lift the light
O'er mortals, and unveil the radiant world;
First will I frame a race for Teucrian ships;
And who is fleet of foot, or brave of thews,

Or vaunts his skill with spear and flying shafts,
Or with the untanned cestus trusts to fight,
Let all attend, and hope for victory's palm.
Seal every lip, and wreathe your brows with green."

He with his mother's myrtle crowns his head.
Ascanius too is crowned, and Helymus,
Age-worn Acestes, and the Lords of Troy.
Then from the council to the funeral mound
He passed, the centre of the thronging host,
And poured upon the earth two bowls of wine,
Two of new milk, and two of hallowed blood,
And, showering rosy blossoms, thus he spake:
"Hail, Father, hail once more! O sacred dust,
Rescued in vain! Hail spirit of my sire!
Not mine with thee the Ausonian fields of fate,
Nor Tiber's stream to seek, where'er it flow!"

He ceased; when from the grave a slippery snake
Drew seven great coils, and with seven spires embraced
The tomb in quiet, gliding by the shrine.
Blue-spotted was his back, and flecks of gold
Shot fire across his scales, as Heaven's great Bow
Throws in the sun a thousand various hues.
Awe-struck Aeneas gazed. With long slow trail
Winding among the bowls and burnished cups,
He licked the food, then harmless to the tomb
Passed back, and left the altars where he fed.
More gladly he renews his father's rites,
Doubting if there his sire's familiar went,
Or Genius of the place. Two sheep he slays,
As many swine, as many dark-backed steers;
And, pouring wine, Anchises' mighty soul
Calls, and his shade from Acheron set free.
Blithely his comrades of their plenty too
The altars load with gifts, and slay the steers,
Or set the braziers, or, on turf reclined,
Lay coals beneath the spits, and roast the flesh.

The wished-for-day had come. In cloudless light
Phaethon's horses brought the ninth glad morn.
Fame and Acestes' glorious name had stirred

The countryside; gay parties throng the beach,
To view the Trojans, or on contest bent.
Midmost are prizes placed in all men's sight,
Green coronals and palms, the victors' meed,
Arms, holy tripods, robes of purple stain,
Talents of gold and silver. Then the song
Of trumpet from the central mound proclaims
The Games begun.
                  Four ships, the choice of all,
Sweep their great oars, well-matched. With rowers keen
Mnestheus the Shark commands, soon Mnestheus he
Of Italy, from whom the Memmian clan;
Gyas the huge Chimaera's town-like mass,
Which Dardan rowers urge from triple banks,
And in three rows the level oars uprise.
Sergestus too, from whom the Sergian House,
Sails the great Centaur; and Cloanthus, sire
Of Rome's Cluentian line, the Scylla sails.

   Fronting the foamy beach, far out in sea,
Rises a rock, which oft, when stars are hid
By winter gales, the tumbling billows drown.
In calm it lifts above the unruffled sea
A peaceful mead, which sunning gulls love well.
Here Prince Aeneas plants a leafy goal
Of green-sprayed ilex, for the sailors' sign
Homeward from thence their weary course to bend.
They take the allotted places: on each stern
In gold and purple proud their captains shine,
While, crowned with poplar wreaths, the bare-backed crew
Gleam bright with oil. They man the thwarts, their arms
Strain to the oar, and straining they await
The signal. Every heart beats fast and faint
With throbbing fear and eager lust of fame.
Loud peals the trumpet; all with no delay
Spring from their posts; the sailors' shouts resound.
Under their swinging arms the water foams.
In time they cleave the furrows; all the sea
Gapes to the rending oar and trident prow.
Less swift the racing chariots seize the course,
And from the barriers plunge; less fiercely fly
The bounding horses when the charioteer

Bends o'er his lash, and shakes the streaming reins.
Then cries of men and tumults of applause
Fill all the grove: the embosomed shores roll back
Shouts, and the hills rebound, by clamour beat.

Gyas before the rest the throng and stir
Cleaves, shooting first: Cloanthus follows hard;
More skilled his oarsmen, but his weight of pine
Retards. Behind, at equal distance, Shark
And Centaur for the foremost lead contend.
Now the Shark holds it; now the Centaur huge
Wins past her; now together both abreast
Move, and the brine with long keels furrow through.
They near the rock; the goal is in their grasp;
When Gyas, victor in the midway surge,
Menoetes thus his helmsman stern upbraids:

"Why steer to starboard thus? Turn hitherward!
Hug close the shore, and graze the leftward rocks!
Let others hold the deep!" But, of blind reefs
Fearful, Menoetes turned his helm to sea.
"Whither away, Menoetes? Make the rocks!"
Again cried Gyas, and looked back, and lo!
Cloanthus pressed him hard, and nearer drew.
'Twixt Gyas' vessel and the sounding cliff
Gliding within to lee, he shot ahead,
And gained safe water as he passed the goal.

Then Gyas blazed with passion, and his cheeks
Lacked not for tears; and headlong to the waves,
Forgetting pride and safety, from high stern
He flung the slow Menoetes, and himself
Holding the tiller, and himself their guide,
Cheered on his crew, and shoreward turned the helm.
But old Menoetes, when the sea at last
Gave up its burden, in his dripping weeds
Climbed forth, and sat upon a rock's dry crest.
Loud laughed the Trojans as he fell and swam:
Now, as he spews the brine, they laugh again.

Sergestus then and Mnestheus, far behind,
Burned with gay hope to pass the slackening ship.
Sergestus wins the lead, and nears the rock,
Not first by all his boat, but first by half,

Half the Shark passes with her jealous prow.
But Mnestheus in mid-ship among his crew
Paced cheering on: "Now, now swing back the oar,
Co-mates of Hector, whom in Troy's last hour
I chose companions! Now put forth that strength,
That mettle, once you showed in Afric Sands,
Ionian seas, and Malea's chasing waves!
Not pride of place I crave, nor victor's palm,
But O!—though those may win whom Neptune crowns,—
Last to return were shame. O win but this,
O shun disgrace!"
                    They, straining every nerve,
Shake with their mighty strokes the brazen poop.
Back sweep the seas: their limbs and parching lips
Quiver and pant, and sweat flows streaming down.

Chance brings the prize they seek; for, wild at heart
Sergestus inward to the rocks his prow
Turning, and entering on a perilous way,
Strikes on a jutting reef. The splintered oars
Crash on the flint; embedded hangs the prow.
Up spring the hindered crew, and shouting use
Their iron-shod pikes and sharply pointed poles,
While from the swirling water they collect
Their broken oars. But Mnestheus in delight,
And by success enlivened, plying fast
His ordered oarage, with the winds at call,
Runs down the open shoreward-sloping sea.

As when a dove, that makes in crannied rock
Her home and pleasant nest, is startled forth,
And flies afield. She, from her dwelling scared,
Flaps loud her feathers, then in quiet air
Skims with unmoving wings her liquid way.
So Mnestheus, so the Shark her final path
Cuts, so her impulse bears her floating on.
He leaves Sergestus struggling in the crags
And shallow seas, who vainly cries for aid,
Still studying how to row with broken oars.
Then Gyas, and the huge Chimaera's mass,
He holds in chase, who, of her helmsman robbed,
Yields, and Cloanthus now alone is left.
On him he steers; on him he drives amain.

Loud ring the shouts; all eager urge the chase;
The heavens with cries resound. Ashamed were these
To lose the glory gained, and very life
For fame would barter; these success inspires;
And power is theirs, because they think it theirs.

Now, prow to prow, the prize they might have shared,
Had not Cloanthus to the sea his palms
Outstretching prayed, and called the Gods to aid:
"Gods of the Sea, whose Ocean realm I sail!
This vow shall bind me at your shrines on shore
To offer a white bull, and o'er the waves
His entrails cast, and pour the flowing wine!"
He said; and deep below all Phorcus' choir,
Maid Panopea and the Nymphs of Sea,
Heard him. Portunus with his own strong hand
Impelled him on: more swift than wind or shaft
Shoreward he sped, and vanished in the port.

When all were summoned, then Anchises' son
Proclaimed Cloanthus by the Herald's voice
Victor, and with green laurel crowned his brow.
A silver talent and three steers and wine
For every ship he gave; and for their chiefs
Added his choicest meeds; a golden scarf
The victor gained, around whose ample marge
Ran in twin waves the Meliboean dye,
And broidered there the princely boy with spear
Chased the fleet stags on leafy Ida's side,
Keen, as if panting, whom in crooked claws
Jove's armour-bearer carried thence sublime;
Vainly the aged servitors lift up
To heaven their palms, and fiercely bay the hounds.
And he whose valour held the second place,
A hauberk won, with gold and polished rings
Triply inwove, which under Troy's high wall
From Demoleus he stripped by Simois stream,
A glory and guard in war; and scarce the slaves,
Phegeus and Sagaris, on bended backs
Could bear the many links, though Demoleus
Wore it of old, and chased the flying foe.
Two brazen cauldrons, and two silver bowls

Were the third gifts bestowed.
       Thus all had now
Their prizes, and in wealthy pride went forth
Flouting the scarlet ribbands on their brows;
When, from the cruel rock scarce torn by skill,
With oars all lost, and one tier crippled, home
Sergestus sailed, inglorious, amid jeers.
Most like a serpent on the highway caught
Which some brass wheel hath crushed, or with a stone
Some wayfarer hath struck, and left half-dead.
Vainly to escape it twists its body's length;
One half is fierce with burning eyes, and lifts
A hissing neck: one half the maiming wound
Clogs, and its knots upon themselves recoil.
So, with her oarage maimed, the ship moved slow,
Yet spreading canvas crossed the bar full-sail.
Rejoicing then in ship and crew restored,
Aeneas to Sergestus gave his prize,
A Cretan slave, in weaving not unversed,
Pholoe, that bare two boys below her breast.

 This contest o'er, towards a lawny mead
Aeneas bent his steps, where, girt by woods
And winding hills, within a valley's lap,
A circus lay. There he, with thousands round,
Sits in their midst enthroned, and now invites
Whoe'er would run fleet races, by rewards
Courting their ardour, and displays the gifts.
There muster Trojans and Sicilians mixed,
Euryalus and Nisus first:
One famed for beauty and the bloom of youth,
Nisus for love of him; whom followed next
Diores, Prince of Priam's lofty line,
Salius and Patron, Acarnanian one,
But one of Tegea from Arcadian blood.
There too stood Helymus and Panopes,
Twain forest lads, of old Acestes' train;
With many more whom fame in shadow hides.
In midst of whom Aeneas spake and said:
"Hear now, and blithely to my words give heed!
None of your tale shall leave without reward.

Two Gnossian lances, bright with polished steel,
A silver-studded axe, to each I give,
To each and all. The foremost three shall take
Prizes, and with pale olive bind the brow.
The first shall have a charger richly trapped,
The next an Amazonian quiver fraught
With Thracian arrows, which a belt of gold
Encircles and a jewelled buckle clasps;
The third with this Greek helm must go content."

He ceased. They take their ground, and when they hear
The signal, seize the track, and from the line
Scud like a cloud, all eyes upon the goal.
But far before them all, more fleet than wind
Or wings of lightning, Nisus flashes first.
Next him, but next with ample room between,
Comes Salius, and a little space behind,
Euryalus is third.
Him Helymus pursues, and lo! on him
Diores flying presses heel to heel
Hard on his shoulder, and had space remained,
He had shot ahead, and passed the doubtful man.
Exhausted near the end, their final bourne
Almost they reach, when Nisus, evil-starred,
Slips in some blood as on the ground by chance
Shed from slain steers it soaked the herbage green.
He in the hour of triumph could not keep
His feet from stumbling, but amid the filth
And sacrificial blood to earth fell prone.
Not then, not once Euryalus his love
Forgetting, he uprose in Salius' path,
And tripped, and rolled him on the slippery field.
Victorious through his friend, Euryalus
Flies flashing first, mid tumults of applause.
Next him comes Helymus, Diores third.
The whole wide concourse and the fronting ranks
Of Elders then with clamour Salius fills,
Claiming the prize snatched from him by a trick.
But tears and favour for the other plead,
And worth, more pleasing in a pleasing form.
Loudly for him Diores too appeals;
Who the last prize hath reached, but reached in vain,

Should the first meed to Salius be returned.
Then spoke Aeneas: "Your rewards shall stay
Unchanged, and none their order shall disturb.
Be mine to pity my unlucky friend."

So said, to Salius a great lion's hide
Heavy with hair he gives and gilded claws.
"If such the guerdons for defeat," exclaims
Nisus, "and thou canst pity those who fell,
What prize may Nisus claim? The first were mine,
Had I not been, like Salius, Fortune's foe."
And with his words he showed his face and limbs
Foul with the slime. Then laughed the gentle Prince,
And bade them bring a targe, from Neptune's fane
Reft by the Greeks, of Didymaon's art,
And dowered the hero with this noble gift.

The races ended, and the gifts bestowed,
"Come hither, ye whose hearts are stout and true!
Bind on the gloves," he cried, "and raise the arm!"
Offering a double prize; for him who wins
An ox fair-garlanded and decked with gold;
A sword and helm, the vanquished to console.

Uprose at once, amid the hum of men,
Dares in brawny might, who once alone
With Paris dared to strive, and at the mound
Where mighty Hector lies, struck Butes down,
Seed of Bebrycian Amycus, who bore
His haughty bulk unquelled, till Dares' arm
Outstretched him dying on the yellow sand.
E'en such was Dares, who with head upraised
For early battle, showed his shoulders' breadth,
And flung alternate arms, and smote the air.
His match is sought; but none of all that crowd
Dare meet the man, or bind the gauntlets on.
Then, deeming all to him resigned the palm,
Before Aeneas' feet alert he stood,
And grasped the bullock's horns, and thus cried out:
"O Goddess-born! If none dare trust himself
To fight, how long should Dares stand and wait?
Bid me bear off the prize." The Dardans all
Applauding, claimed for him the promised meed.

Then old Acestes, on the grass reclined
Beside Entellus, thus upbraiding spake:
"Entellus, is thine old puissance vain?
And wilt thou tamely let such prize be won
Without a fight? Where is thy guardian god
Thy boasted Eryx? Where the spoils hung up
On all thy walls, thy wide Sicilian fame?"
Then he: "No fear hath beaten off the love
Of praise and glory; but my blood runs cold
With loitering age; my waning strength is numb.
Had I what once I had, what yonder knave
Exults in, had I now that youth of mine,
No need of prize or ox to lead me on,
I count not the reward." He spake, and threw
Two gauntlets in their midst, of monstrous weight,
Wherein fierce Eryx, binding on his arms
The toughened hide, oft entered on the fray.
Amazement reigns; such mighty bulls were those
Whose seven huge hides are stiff with lead and steel.
But Dares, most amazed, far back recoils.
And great Aeneas felt their weight, and turned
Over and over the large twisted thongs,
While thus the veteran: "What if any here
Had seen the gloves of Hercules himself,
And that grim battle on this very shore!
These arms thy brother Eryx bore of old,
Stained yet with blood, thou see'st, and scattered brain;
With these he fought Alcides; these I used
While fresher blood gave strength, ere niggard age
Sprinkled my brows with white. Yet if these arms
Dares declines, if so Aeneas wills,
And so Acestes sanctions, let us fight
An equal match; I waive thee Eryx' hides;
Take heart, and doff thy Trojan gauntlets too."

So saying, from his back he threw the cloak,
His mighty limbs, his mighty shoulder-blades
Bared, and amidst the ring gigantic stood.
Then gauntlets fairly matched the Prince brought forth,
And bound with equal gloves the hands of both.
Each sprang on tiptoe, and undaunted raised
His arms aloft, and from the blow far back

Withdrew his head, while hand with hand commixed
Provoked the fray. One on his youth relied,
More light of foot: the other's limbs and bulk
Rose stalwart, though his trembling knees were slack,
And painful gasping shook his giant frame.
Now each at each aims many a fruitless blow,
And many on hollow side or chest resound
Loud-ringing, and the hand round ear or brow
Plays oft; with heavy blows their jaw-bones creak.
Firm stands Entellus, in one posture fixed,
And with his body only and quick eyes
Eludes each stroke. Dares as one who storms
A city, or invests a mountain fort,
Tries each approach, and all the ground with skill
Surveying presses many a vain assault.
Entellus rising shows his hand on high
Uplifted; Dares swift the coming blow
Foresees, and slips with nimble limbs aside.
His strength is spent on air, and heavy falls
Entellus' ponderous bulk, as often falls
Some hollow pine uprooted on the side
Of Erymanthus or great Ida's mount.
Eagerly Trojans and Trinacrians rise,
Shouts rend the sky. And first Acestes runs,
And from the earth in pity lifts his friend;
Who, by his fall nor stayed nor daunted, springs
Fiercer to fight, and anger wakes his force.
Then, all ablaze with shame and conscious worth,
Dares he chases headlong o'er the field,
Redoubling blows with right hand and with left.
No stay; no rest: as hailstones on the roof
Incessant rattle, so with stroke on stroke
Ceaseless with either hand he smites his foe.

    Then Prince Aeneas would no further brook
The bitter madness of Entellus' rage;
But set an end to strife, and took away
Exhausted Dares, and with words consoled:
"Unhappy man! What madness seized thy soul?
Know'st thou not altered strength and Heaven estranged?
To the Gods yield!" He spake, and stayed the fight.
But Dares to the ships his faithful friends

Lead, dragging his weak knees, and to each side
Swaying his head, while from his mouth the blood
Pours mixed with teeth. They take the helm and sword,
But to Entellus leave the palm and bull.

    Proud of the bull, and high of heart, then spake
The victor: "Goddess-born, and Trojans! Learn
What might was in me in my prime of youth,
From what a death you take your Dares saved!"
He spake, and by the bull, the victor's prize,
Confronting stood, and with his right hand swung,
And, rising to the blow, his gauntlet drove
Between the horns, and shattered bone and brain.
Dead, quivering, prone to earth the great ox fell.
Then over it he spake: "This better life,
Eryx, to thee I yield, in Dares' stead.
My gloves, mine art, here, victor, I resign!"

    Who now were fain to match the flying shaft
Aeneas summons, and their meed proclaims;
And with his mighty hand Serestus' mast
Uprears, and from it hangs a fluttering dove,
By twining cords tied fast, the arrows' mark.
All muster; and a brazen helm receives
The lots cast in: and first leaps out ere all
Amidst applauding cries Hippocoon's name:
Whom follows Mnestheus, in the galleys' race
Triumphant, Mnestheus still with olive crowned;
Eurytion third, thy brother, Pandarus,
O famous! who, to break the truce erst bidden,
First hurled thy bolt upon the Achaean host!
Last in the helmet lay Acestes' name:
He too was bold to try the toils of youth.

    Then each with all his strength the bended bow
Strings, and the weapons from his quiver draws:
And first Hippocoon's arrow through the sky
Sped from the shrilling cord, and cut the air,
And struck and in the wooden mast stood fixed.
The mast was shaken, and the affrighted bird
Fluttered, and widely rang the loud applause.
Then Mnestheus keen stood forth and drew the bow,
High-aiming, and with eye and shaft at one.

The bird, alas! his arrow failed to reach,
Which sundered yet the knots and hempen bonds
That tied her foot, and held her from the mast.
She to the winds and stormy clouds took flight.
Then swift Eurytion, who had kept his shaft
Long on the string, and prayed his brother's help,
Saw in the void rejoicing, and transfixed
Beneath a sable cloud the winging dove.
She fell, and in her body fixed the shaft
Brought back, but left her spirit with the stars.
Acestes only without prize remained;
Who yet his arrow launched on heavenly air,
And showed his aged skill and sounding bow.
Then glared a sudden portent, boding much
For future days, as one great issue taught,
When dread diviners read the sign at last.
For, flying in the clouds, the reed caught fire,
And marked its path with flame, and, burning out,
Passed to thin air; as when loose flying stars
Shoot in the sky, and trail their streaming locks.
Spellbound in wonder to the Heavenly Gods
Trinacrians pray and Trojans; and the Prince
Scorns not that omen, but embracing loads
With gifts the happy veteran, and bespeaks:
"Take these, O Father! for Olympus' King
Wills by these signs that thou this added prize
Shouldst draw, this gift of old Anchises' self,
A bowl embossed with figures, which of yore
For guerdon rich Cisseus the Thracian gave
My sire, a pledge and memory of his love."
He spoke; and with green laurel wreathed his brow;
And named Acestes victor before all.
Nor did Eurytion grudge the prize preferred,
Though he alone had brought the bird to earth.
Next, he who brake the fetters wins reward;
Last, who with flying reed the mast transfixed.

    But Prince Aeneas, ere that match was o'er,
Called to his side Iulus' guardian friend,
Epytides, and told his trusted ear:
"Go, tell Ascanius, if his troop of boys
Be ready now, and all his horse drawn up,

To lead the squadron in his grandsire's praise,
And show his arms." Then all the invading throng
He bids withdraw, and the long course leave free.

    Forth come the lads, and ranked before their sires
Shine on curbed steeds; and, as they pass, the hosts
Of Troy and Sicily admiring shout.
Trim garlands bind their hair: two cornel spears,
Pointed with steel, they wield, or quivers bright
Across their shoulders; and the bended gold
Entwines the throat, and falls upon the breast.
Three troops of horse are there; and captains three
Ride to and fro, and twelve boys follow each,
Like masters ruling each bright several band.
The first triumphal line young Priam leads,
Bearing his grandsire's name, thy glorious seed,
Polites, who shall breed Italian men.
A Thracian horse rides he, with pasterns white,
Piebald, and tossing high a snowwhite front.
Then Atys, whence the Latin Atii sprang,
Young Atys, young Iulus' boyish love.
Last, fair above them all, Iulus rides
A Tyrian steed, which radiant Dido gave
To bear the pledge and memory of her love.
The rest on horses of Trinacria ride,
Acestes' chargers.

    Joyful the Dardans gaze, their tremors greet
With cheers, and recognise their fathers' looks.
When gaily they had ranged on horseback round
Before all eyes, Epytides from far
Gave the awaited sign, and cracked his whip.
They gallop off, and into equal files
Breaking each band, diverge; and then, recalled,
Wheel round, and bear their lances at the charge,
Now they advance, and now in full retreat
Contrary move, alternate orb in orb
Entangling, as they wage a phantom war;
Now bare their backs in flight, now turn the spear
Fronting the foe, now ride at peace together.
As once the storied Labyrinth in Crete
Screened in its sightless walls a baffling road,
A thousand paths, where every clue was lost

In undiscovered maze without return;
In such a track the sons of Troy their steps
Entangling weave their game of flight and fray;
Like dolphins, that in wet Carpathian seas
Or cutting Libyan waves disport and swim.

These sports, this mode of riding, when he built
Long Alba's walls, Ascanius first revived,
And taught the pristine Latins to observe,
As he had learned them and the youth of Troy.
The Albans taught their sons; thence mighty Rome
Received them, and the ancestral use preserved.
"*Troy*" now the boys are named, "*The Trojan troop*."

So sped the contests to that hallowed sire,
Till Fortune changed, and broke at last her faith.
While at his tomb they held those solemn Games,
Saturnian Juno to the Trojan ships
Sent Iris down, and breathed a speeding wind,
Much scheming, and her ancient pain unslaked.
She by the many-coloured Bow her way
Runs quickly down, a maiden seen of none,
Scans the vast crowd, and, as she tracks the coast,
Sees ports abandoned and forsaken ships.
But Ilian wives, far on the lone sea-bank,
Wept for Anchises; and all weeping viewed
The unfathomed main. "Ah! voyage-worn, what seas
Await us still!" — on every lip one cry.
Tired of the toiling waves, they crave a Home.
So in their midst, in mischief not unschooled,
Lighting, she doffed her Heavenly mien and dress,
Transformed to Beroe, the age-struck wife
Of Doryclus, who once had race and name
And sons; so came she to the Dardan dames.
"Oh hapless ye," she cries, "whom warring Greeks
Dragged not to death beneath your native walls!
Unhappy race! what bane hath Fate in store?
Now, since Troy fell, the seventh summer wanes,
Whilst we o'er seas and lands outwatch the stars
By crags unharboured, and through rolling waves
Chase those Italian shores which ever fly.
'Tis Eryx' land; Acestes is our host:
Who disallows us here to build our Home?

O Fatherland! O Housegods saved in vain!
Shall not a Troy be told of? Shall I see
Simois no more and Xanthus, Hector's streams?
Nay, up! and burn with me the accursed ships!
For, while I slept, Cassandra's boding shape
Gave me these brands. 'Here seek your Troy,' said she,
'Here is your Home!' The hour is come: delay
Such portents brook not. Lo, yon altars four
To Neptune! God himself lends heart and fire!"

So saying, she seized first the baleful flame,
And raised her hand, and swung it blazing round,
And threw. Amazement seized the women's hearts,
And one, their eldest, Pyrgo, royal Nurse
To Priam's many sons: "Not Beroe,
I tell you, dames," she said, "no Trojan wife
Of Doryclus is this. The Heavenly grace
Mark, and the beaming eye, her presence note,
Her looks, her tones, the movings of her feet!
Nay, I myself left Beroe but now
Sick, fretting that she only missed our rites,
Nor paid due worship to Anchises' shade."
Such words said she.
But first they glared upon the ships in doubt;
Halting between sore passion for the land
Already theirs, and Fate's imperial call.
But, when the Goddess rose on level wings,
And, flying Heavenward, clave the Bow's great arch,
Then, awed by portents, and by fury driven,
From inner hearths they seize the flame, or rob
The altars, clamorous, hurling leaf and bough
And torch. The Fire-God with unbridled rage
Leaps over thwarts and oars and painted stems.

News of the burning ships Eumelus bore
To tomb and circus; and they turned and saw
Black clouds of floating ash. And foremost still,
Ascanius, gaily as he led the horse,
Thus to the stirred encampment rode in haste,
Nor could the breathless masters hold him back.

"What frenzy is this?" he cries. "What make you now,
O wretched wives? No hated camp of Greeks,

But your own hopes ye burn! 'Tis I, your own,
Ascanius!" And he flung to earth the casque
In which he played his mimicry of war.
Up speed Aeneas and the troops of Troy.
But those affrighted women o'er the beach
Scatter, and hide themselves in woods and caves.
They hate their deed: they hate the day: they know
With altered eyes their own, and from their hearts
Juno is banished. Yet no less the fire
Rages untamed. Beneath the moistened oak
Lives the slow-smoking tow, and creeping fumes
Prey on the keels, infecting all the frame.
No might of man, no water streams avail.
Then good Aeneas rent his clothes, and prayed
To Heaven for succour, lifting up his palms.

"Almighty Jove! If yet thou dost not hate
Each son of Troy, if thine old pity look
On human sorrows, let my ships escape
This flame, and snatch our little world from death!
Or hurl to dust this remnant with thy bolt,
If so I merit, by thine hand o'erthrown!"

He scarce had cried, when black with volleying rain
A storm broke wildly, and the hills and plains
With thunder shook. A watery deluge fell,
With driving South winds dark, from all the sky,
And filled the ships, and soaked the half-burnt wood,
Till every flame was quenched, and all the ships,
Save four that perished, from the bane were saved.

But Prince Aeneas, by that sad mischance
Sore stricken, rolls the burden of his thoughts
This way and that. There should he make his Home,
Heedless of Fate, or grasp Italian shores?
Whereon old Nautes, he whom more than all
Pallas had taught, and given wondrous skill,
And how to answer what the Gods' stern wrath
Threatens, and what the course of Fate demands,
He thus consoling to Aeneas spake:
"Follow we, Goddess-born, Fate's ebb and flow.
Whate'er befall, we conquer when we bear.
Dardan Acestes is of Heavenly birth!

Him take a ready co-mate in thy plans;
To him give all whose ships are lost, and all
Who of thy mighty purpose faint and tire;
The aged men, the mothers worn with sea,
Whate'er is weak, whate'er is timorous
Search out, and here let those faint-hearted dwell.
Acesta they shall call their city's name."

So spake his ancient friend, and cheered his heart
Racked yet with care, while darkling o'er the sky
Night drove her steeds. Then sudden on his sight
Falling from heaven the semblance of his sire
Anchises came, and uttered thus his voice:
"Son, dearer far than life, while life was mine!
Son, tried by Ilium's doom! I hither come
By Jove's command, who from thy ships hath driven
These flames, and pitied thee from Heaven at last.
Obey the counsel aged Nautes gives
Most seemly. Bear thy chosen bravest hearts
To Italy. A people rude and rough
There wait thy quelling. But the infernal halls
Of Dis first enter, and, Avernus passed,
Meet me, my son! Me no sad shades enfold,
Nor Tartarus; but converse of the pure,
Elysian bliss is mine. There shall the Maid,
The Sibyl, lead thee with black victims' blood.
There shalt thou learn thy promised race and home.
Farewell! The night rolls midway; and I feel
The savage panting of the steeds of Morn!"

He ceased; and fled like smoke into thin air.
"O whither, whither now?" Aeneas cried,
"Whom dost thou fly? Who keeps thee from our arms?"
So saying, he aroused the sleeping fire,
And with blest meal and incense paid the vow
To Trojan Lares, and white Vesta's shrine.

Forthwith he calls his friends, Acestes first,
Jove's mandate teaches, and the precepts given
By his dear father, and his own firm will.
Nor halt his plans, nor doth the King refuse.
The mothers are enrolled, and those who will
Debarked, poor souls who nought of glory crave.

The rest their thwarts renew, replace the wood
Eaten by flames, fix oars and cordage fresh;
Few by the count, but hearts of living fire.

Meanwhile Aeneas with a plough marks out
The town, allotting homes: makes here a Troy,
An Ilium here. Acestes reigned content,
Stablished a court, and gave a Senate laws;
And near the stars upreared, on Eryx' crest,
A Fane for Venus, and to Anchises' tomb
A Priest assigned, and widely hallowed grove.

Nine days had all men feasted, and each shrine
Honoured, and quiet winds had calmed the main.
Again the South blew up and called to sea.
Then on the hollow shores lament was loud;
And fond embraces stayed the night and day.
The mothers and the men who lately shrank
From sight of sea, and shuddered at its name,
Now fain would go and bear their travail out;
Whom good Aeneas soothes with words benign,
And to their King and kinsman trusts with tears.
Three calves to Eryx, to the Storms a lamb
He bids them slay, and cast the cable loose;
Then, wreathed with leaves of olive, on the prow
Standing afar, he holds the cup, and sheds
Entrails upon the flood, and flowing wine.
A wind that follows wafts them, and they dip
Stoutly their rival oars, and sweep the sea.

But Venus in the meanwhile, racked with care,
Addressing Neptune, thus her trouble breathed:
"Juno's great wrath, O Neptune! Juno's heart
Insatiate, make me stoop to every prayer.
Nor time nor goodness cure her; not Jove's Will,
Nor Fate, have stilled her rage. 'Tis not enough
From Phrygia's heart with hate to have devoured
Troy town, and dragged her through all pain and woe.
Troy's remnant still, her very bones and ash,
She hunts; I pray she knows what makes her wrath!
Thyself art witness what a coil she stirred
On Libyan waters, mingling sea and sky,
In vain reliance on Aeolian storms.

This in thy realm she dared.
And lo! to crime the Trojan dames she hath driven,
Burning his vessels, and, his ships all lost,
Forced him to leave his friends on alien shores.
Let what remains, I pray, in safety sail
Thy waves: O! let them reach the Tiber's stream,
If Fate permit, if there she grant their Home!"

To whom the Lord of Ocean, Saturn's son:
"Venus, 'tis very right to trust my realm,
Whence thou art sprung. And I deserve it; oft
I quelled such ravings of the sky and sea.
Nor less on land, Xanthus and Simois know,
I cared for thine Aeneas. When Troy's ranks
Achilles on their ramparts breathless hurled,
And dealt a thousand deaths; when every stream
Roared choking, nor could Xanthus find his way,
And roll to sea, then from Pelides bold
When Gods nor strength were matched in hollow mist
I rapt Aeneas, though I longed to raze
Those walls of perjured Troy mine hands had wrought.
Now too that purpose holds; dispel thy fear.
Safe, as thou wilt, Avernus he shall gain:
One only shalt thou look for, lost in sea;
One life for many shall be paid."

He with such words the Goddess' heart made glad:
Then yoked his steeds with gold, the foamy bits
Fixed, and the reins let slacken in his grasp,
While in his sea-blue car he skimmed the main.
The waves sink down; beneath his thundering wheels
Rough seas are smoothed; aloft the storm-clouds fly.
Strange shapes are in his train; unwieldy whales,
Old Glaucon's choir, Palaemon, Ino's child,
Swift Tritons, Phorcus' host, and on his left,
Nesaee, Spio, Panopea fair,
Thalia and Thetis and Cymodoce.

With peace and joy Aeneas' anxious heart
Again is thrilled. He bids them raise the masts;
And spread the arms with sail. Together all
They set the sheet; together left and right
They slacken sails; together twist and turn

The soaring horns. Fair breezes blow the ship.
But Palinurus first the close array
Leads, and by him the rest obedient steer.

Now dewy Night to the mid goal of heaven
Was drawing near. On benches by their oars,
With limbs unbent, the laboured crews lay still;
When Slumber, lightly parting the dun air,
Slid from the starry sky, and came to thee,
O Palinurus! bringing thee sad dreams,
Guiltless! and on the high-built stern the God
In Phorbas' semblance sate, while thus he spake:

"Pilot! the sea itself bears on the ship.
Fair blows the wind: the hour to rest is given.
Lie down, and steal thy wearied eyes from toil.
I, in thy stead, will ply thy task awhile."
With eyes scarce raised, the pilot answered him.
"And am not I to know the sleek sea's face?
Am I to trust this monster, and shall I
Confide Aeneas to the fickle winds,
I, by the false fair heavens so often duped?"

So saying, to the helm he clung, nor lost
His hold, but kept his eyes upon the stars.
When lo! the God shook o'er his brows a branch
Sleepy with Stygian drench, and wet with dews
Of Lethe, and declined the lingering lids.
Scarce had the stealing peace unbent his limbs,
When Slumber stooped, and him to weltering seas
Flung headlong down, with helm and half the stern
Shattered, oft calling on his mates in vain.
Then to the viewless winds he winged his way.

Not less the ships speed safely, undismayed
In Neptune's promise o'er the watery track;
Until they neared the Sirens' cliffs, of yore
Perilous, and white with many a sailor's bones.
Still the hoarse sea was moaning round the rocks.
Then, when he saw his ship, with helmsman lost,
Drifting, Aeneas, in the midnight seas,
Steered her himself, and mourned his friend's mischance:
"Dupe of fair skies and sea, thy corpse shall lie
Bare, Palinurus, on an alien shore!"

Book VI

WEEPING HE SPAKE, and gave his fleet the rein;
And touched at last Euboean Cumae's shore.
Seaward they turn the prows; the anchor's tooth
Holds fast each galley; and the beach is fringed
With curving sterns. A band of hope-flushed men
Leap on Hesperia's soil; and part from flint
Strike hidden seeds of fire; part scour the woods,
The wild beasts' home, and point to streams new-found.

But towards the hill which high Apollo rules
Aeneas hastens, where the Sibyl's cave
Lies vast and lone, on whom the Delian breathes
An ampler soul, unfolding things to come.
The Trivian Grove they reach, the House of Gold.

'Tis famed that Daedalus, from Minos' realm,
Trusting the air with wings, to the cold North
Fled, swimming far his unaccustomed way:
Till, lightly dropping on Chalcidian cliffs,
To thee, O Phoebus! safe on land, he vowed
His oary pens, and built thy mighty fane.
Androgeus' death he graved upon the doors,
And Cecrops' sons atoning year by year
With seven young lives; the urn, the lots new-drawn
And opposite Crete standing out of sea;
Pasiphae's passion, to the cruel bull
Joined by deceit, the mingled birth that told
Of monstrous love, the twiform Minotaur,
The House of toil, the maze which none might flee,
Till Daedalus, in pity for the love
Of the King's daughter, broke the snare himself,
Guiding blind steps by thread. Thou too hadst shone
Icarus! in that great work, had grief allowed;
Twice he essayed to grave thy fate in gold;
Twice fell the father's hands.
                      And all the tale
Their eyes had read, but now Achates came,

Returning, with the Priestess of the Grove,
Deiphobe, who thus the Prince bespake:

  "This hour asks no such shows: 'twere better now
Out of a herd ne'er yoked to sacrifice
Seven oxen, and as many chosen ewes."
She ended; and, her sacred charge performed,
Within the high-built temple bade them pass.

  A hundred avenues, a hundred doors
Lead to the cavern, hewn in Cumae's cliff,
Whence, hundred-voiced, the Sibyl's answers ring.
The threshold reached, "Now," cried the Maid, "'tis time
To ask thy fate! The God! ah me! the God!"
And suddenly her face, her colour changed,
Her locks disordered fell, her bosom gasped,
Her wild heart swelled, her stature grew, her voice
Seemed more than human, as the God, drawn near,
Breathed influence:
               "And spar'st thou vow and prayer,
Aeneas, spar'st thou? These alone will breach
The mighty-portals of this spell-bound hall!"
She ended. Horror through the Trojans' bones
Ran cold, and from his heart Aeneas prayed:
"Phoebus, still pitiful to Troy's long woe!
Who to Achilles' heel didst guide the shaft
And hand of Paris; who hast led me on
To seas that wash great countries, to remote
Massylian tribes, beyond the Syrtes' sand!
Those fleeting shores of Italy at length
We grasp: no further may Troy's fate pursue!
Ye too, O Gods and Goddesses, whom Troy
And all her glory vexed, you now may spare
The Dardan race. And thou, most holy Seer,
Foreknowing things to come! — I ask no crown
Unpledged by Fate — O grant in Latium yet
Troy's sons may rest, and all her wayworn Gods!
To Phoebus then and Trivia will I build
A marble fane, and name his holy days.
Thee also in our realm great shrines await,
Where I will place thy mystic words of doom
Told to my race, O Holy! and ordain
Thy chosen Priests. But trust them not to leaves,

To fly disordered on the frolic winds,
Chant them thyself!" He ceased, and spake no more.

    But in her cave, impatient of the God,
The frenzied Seer would shake him from her breast.
So much the more he tires her rabid mouth,
Tames her fierce heart, and moulds her with his hand,
Till all the hundred doors with one accord
Fly open, and her answers thrill the air.

    "O scaped at last from perils of the sea!
Yet worse remain on shore! Lavinium's land
Dardans shall reach — put from thy soul this care —
But they shall rue the day. Wars, awful wars,
I see, and Tiber foaming streams of blood!
Xanthus nor Simois nor Doric camp
Shall fail thee. There another Goddess-born
Achilles waits: there Juno shall not leave
The Trojans' track, while in thy need what tribes,
What towns of Italy shalt thou not sue!
A foreign love once more Troy's bane shall be,
Once more an alien bride!
But yield not thou! Meet care with bolder step
Than Fate concedes! The path of Hope shall rise,
Where least thou dreamest, in a Grecian town!"

    Thus Cumae's Sibyl from her shrine declaims
Dread mysteries, and, moaning through the cave,
Wraps truth in darkness: so in her mad mouth
Apollo shakes the reins, and goads her breast.
When frenzy fell, and raving lips were still,
Aeneas spoke: "No face of grief, O Maid!
Springs strange on me or sudden: all I scanned,
And in my soul ere now have traversed all.
One boon I ask. Since here the Gates are famed
Of nether Dis, and Acheron's dull sluice,
O let me see the face of him I love,
My father! Teach the way! the gates unfold!
Him on these shoulders through the flames I bore
Through thousand bolts, and saved from swarming foes.
O'er all the seas he shared my path, and braved,
Though weak, each threat of Ocean and of Sky,

Beyond the strength and destiny of Age.
He too, entreating, bade me seek thy doors,
And sue thy grace. O pity son and sire!
All things thou canst, O Holy! Not in vain
O'er dark Avernus Hecat gave thee rule!
If Orpheus with his lyre's melodious strings
Might call his wife from Hell; if, to and fro
Passing so oft, Pollux, by death's exchange,
Redeems his brother — why of Theseus tell,
Or Hercules? — I too am Heavenly born!"

Such pleas he uttered, and the altar clasped.
When thus the Seer began: "O seed of Gods!
Easy, great Trojan! is the downward path.
All night and day Hell Gates stand open wide.
But to return, to reach the air of Heaven,
There is the task and toil! A few had power,
Whom Jove hath loved, or manly zeal upraised
Heavenward, the sons of God. Woods lie between,
And winding black Cocytus flows all round.
Yet if so strong thy passion and thy will
Twice over Styx to swim, twice to behold
Dark Tartarus, on such mad errand bent,
Hear what must first be done.
                              A bough there is,
Golden in leaf and stem, and consecrate
To Stygian Juno. On a shadowy tree
It lurks, deep-folded in the sunless dells.
But none may tread the secret ways of Earth,
Ere from that tree he tear the golden tress.
This for her tribute Proserpine ordains.
When one is plucked, another doth not lack,
Golden, and burgeoning with leaves of gold.
Search throughly then; and, when thine eyes have found,
Pull off the branch, for freely will it come
If Fate be calling thee; else all thy strength
Will fail to pluck it, or to shear with steel.
Moreover the dead body of thy friend
Lies — ah, thou know'st not! — tainting all the fleet,
While thou for counsel laggest at our door.
Him first entomb, and carry to his rest;

And lead black ewes, thy first peace-offerings;
So shalt thou visit Styx, and walk the road
None walk alive." She ceased, and locked her lips.

Aeneas then, with downcast visage sad,
Wends from the cavern, pondering in his heart
The hidden things of Fate. Nor troubled less
The leal Achates paces at his side.
And many a word they wove, surmising each
Of what dead friend she spake, what body lay
For burial, when on coming they beheld
Misenus on the beach, unduly slain,
Misenus, son of Aeolus, most skilled
To wake the war-flame with his sounding brass;
Great Hector's comrade, who by Hector's side
Won glory both with bugle and with spear.
Him when Achilles slew, no lesser lord
The dauntless hero followed, to the train
Of great Aeneas joined: who, blowing late,
Madman! across the seas his hollow shell,
Challenged the Gods with music, and was seized
By jealous Triton, if the tale be true,
And in the rocks and foaming waters drowned.
So all around him mourn with loud lament,
And most Aeneas. Then with tears they ply
The Sibyl's charge, and heavenward pile with trees
The altar of his Tomb. Primaeval woods,
The wild beasts' lairs, are entered; the pine falls;
The smitten ilex rings; the ashen beams
Are cleft with wedges and the splintered oak,
And lofty rowans from the hills are rolled.

Amid such work, Aeneas cheers them on,
Foremost, and wielding weapons like their own.
But with his own sad heart he communes thus,
Scanning the boundless wood, and prays aloud:
"O to discover here in this green world
That Golden Bough! for all was true, too true,
Misenus, which the Sibyl spake of thee!"
He scarce had said, when from the sky two doves
Before his very eyes came flying down,
And on the green turf lit. His mother's birds

The mighty hero knew, and prayed in joy:
"O be my guides, if any way there be,
Fly straight to dingles where that sumptuous bough
Imbrowns the lawn! O fail me not in need,
My Goddess Mother!" Thus he spake, and paused,
Noting what signs they bore, and whither sped.
They feed and fly as far as following eyes
Can keep them still in ken; but when they come
To foul Avernus' jaws, rise swiftly up,
Skim through the liquid air, and side by side
Alight upon a tree, that wished-for goal,
Through whose dun branches shoots a gleam of gold.
As, sown on some strange tree, in winter woods
The mistletoe with alien leafage blooms,
With yellow fruit enfolding the smooth stem:
So on that shadowy oak the leafy gold
Glimmered, and tinkled in the rustling air.
Forthwith Aeneas grasped the clinging bough,
And plucked, and bare it toward the Sibyl's cell.

Meanwhile the Trojans on the beach still wept
Misenus, honouring the thankless dead.
And first with firs and oaken logs they piled
His mighty pyre, and wove about its sides
Dark boughs, and set before it cypresses,
The trees of death, and on it shining arms.
And some heat water, leaping to the flame,
In braziers, and anoint the cold man's corpse,
Moaning, and lay him on the bed, and there
Spread his gay raiment, the familiar dress.
Some, with sad ministry, the heavy bier
Raised, with averted heads, as custom bade,
Holding the torch below. Then blazed the pile,
Incense, and meats, and bowls of flowing oil.
But when the fire slept, and the ashes fell,
With wine they soaked the thirsty embers left,
And Corynaeus in an urn of brass
Hid the gleaned bones, and sprinkled thrice around
Pure water with a prospering olive's bough,
And cleansed the men, and spake the last farewell.
But good Aeneas made a high-built tomb,

And laid thereon his trumpet and his oar,
Under a skyey hill which bears his name,
Misenus, and preserves it ever green.

  This done, he hastens on the Sibyl's charge.
A pebbled cave there was, with yawning mouth,
Safe screened by forests and a sombre mere,
O'er whose great chasm no flying thing unharmed
Might wing its way, such breath from those black jaws
Issued and streamed to heaven; and hence the Greeks
Avernus named it, or *The Birdless Place.*
Here first the Priestess four black bullocks set,
And on their brows poured wine, between their horns
Cropping the topmost bristles, which she laid,
The first burnt-offerings, on the sacred fire,
Invoking Hecat, Queen in Heaven and Hell.
Others draw knives beneath, and the warm blood
Receive in bowls. Aeneas with his sword
To Night, and Night's great Sister, a black lamb
Slays, and to Proserpine a barren cow,
Dark altars raises to the Stygian King,
And, laying on the flame great bulls entire,
Pours on their burning flesh rich streams of oil.
And lo! toward sunrise and the prime of light,
Earth underfoot fell moaning, and the woods
Were stirred, and dogs seemed howling through the dark,
As the Divine One came. "Far hence, Unclean!
O hence," the Priestess cries. "Leave all the grove!
And thou, march on, and draw the steel. Now needs,
Aeneas, all thy prowess, all thy strength!"
She spake, and passed in frenzy to the cave.
He not with timid steps beside her paced.

  O Gods that rule the Dead! O silent Shades!
Chaos and Phlegethon, dumb fields of Night!
Let what I heard be told; O grant me grace
Things deep in Earth to unbare and gulfed in gloom!

  Darkling they fared, in desolate dim night,
Through ghostly homes and shadowy realms of Dis;
Like men in forests, when the inconstant moon
Throws peevish rays, and God has darkened heaven,
And sombre Night despoiled the hues of Earth.

Before the Porchway, in Hell's very throat,
Lay Grief, and pale Diseases, and Remorse,
And sad old Age, and Want, that counsels ill,
Fear, and gaunt Famine — dreadful shapes to see! —
And Death, and Pain, and Death's twin-brother Sleep,
And sinful Lusts of Soul. And full in face
Right in the gateway lay the Slaughterer, War,
The Furies' iron cells, and Discord wild
With blood-stained fillets round her snaky hair.

And in their midst an immemorial Elm
Spreads shadowing arms, where idle Dreams are lodged,
That cling beneath each leaf. And many forms
Of monstrous Beasts are there: within the gate
There stable Centaurs, Scyllas double-shaped,
Briareus, the hundred-fold, and Lerna's Worm,
Dire-hissing, and Chimaera, armed with flame,
Gorgons, and Harpies, and the tri-form Ghost.

In sudden dread, Aeneas seized his blade,
And turned its naked edge to bar their way;
And had his Guide not warned him all were frail
And flitting Ghosts, the semblances of life,
His sword had leapt and cleft the shades in vain.

Hence leads a road to Acheron, whose wild
And whirling torrent spews its slimy sand
On slow Cocytus; and as ferryman
Guarding the stream in awful squalor grim
Stands Charon; on whose chin the hoarness lies
Untrimmed and thick; his eyes are staring flame.
Foul from the shoulder hangs his knotted garb.
Himself he poles the boat, and tends the sail,
And bears the bodies in his dusky barge,
Ageing, but hearty with a God's green age.
All crowding to those banks the Phantoms streamed;
Mothers and Men, and bodies done with life
Of great-souled Heroes; boys, and maids unwed,
And sons on biers before their parents' eyes:
As many as leaves at Autumn's earliest cold
Falling to earth, or birds that landward flock,
O'er ocean routed, when the frozen year
Sends them to sunny lands. They stand, and plead

First to be ferried o'er, with hands outspread,
Craving for that far bank; but in his boat
The surly mariner takes these or those,
And keeps the rest far driven from the shore.

Aeneas at that throng astonied stood.
"Tell me, O Maid!" he cried, "what means this press?
What seek the souls? and why may some sweep o'er
The livid stream, while some the banks must quit?"
To whom the Ancient Priestess brief replied:
"Anchises' son, true seed of Heaven! thou seest
Cocytus' stagnant deep, the pools of Styx,
By which Gods swear, and fear to break their vow.
All this poor crowd thou seest due burial lack:
Yon ferryman is Charon: those who cross
Were buried: none that bellowing awful stream
Pass, till their bones are laid in quiet rest.
A hundred years they flutter round this shore,
Till, chosen at last, the wished-for pools they gain."

Aeneas paused, and in his pensive soul
Pitied their cruel lot. Leucaspis there,
Robbed of death's dues, he saw, and him who led
The Lycian barks, Orontes, both in woe;
Whom o'er the windy waters bound from Troy,
One storm had wrecked, engulfing ships and men.

And lo! the pilot Palinurus there!
Who, while he watched the stars by Libya's coast,
Late from the stern fell prone, and sank in sea.
Him woeful scarce amid the dusk he knew,
Then thus accosted: "O, what God from us
Hath torn thee and sunk beneath the shoreless sea?
O tell me! for Apollo, ne'er before
Found false, herein hath prophesied amiss.
Saved from the deep, he said that thou shouldst reach
Ausonian shores. Keeps he that promise thus?"
But he: "Apollo's tripod rang not false,
Anchises' son! for me no God hath drowned.
While clinging to my helm I ruled our course,
By chance I fell, and strongly wrenched it off,
And with me dragged. By the rude sea I swear,
Not for myself such fear as for thy ship

Seized me, lest she, with helm and pilot lost,
Might fail and founder in the leaping seas.
Me the wild South o'er leagues of ocean tossed
Three winter nights: scarce, as the fourth day dawned,
From the waves' crest I sighted Italy.
Slowly to land I swam; and now were safe,
But, heavy with dank weeds, when as I clutched
The splintered cliff, some savage men with steel
Assailed me thus, a prize to their dull wit.
Now billows roll me, and winds cast ashore.
But O, by heaven's sweet air! O, by thy Sire,
And by Iulus' rising hope, I pray,
Save me, Unconquered! Throw, for throw thou canst,
Earth on my corpse, and Velia's port regain!
Or if some way thy Heavenly Mother show —
For not, methinks, these streams and Stygian pools
Without Gods' aid thou'lt swim — O give thy hand
To me unhappy! take me o'er the waves!
That I may rest at least when I am dead."

He ended; and the Priestess thus began:
"Whence, Palinurus, is that wild desire?
Shalt thou, unburied, see the Stygian flood,
The Furies' stream, or reach the bank unbid?
Hope not by prayer to bend the doom of God!
Yet heed my words, to heal thy sorry plight,
For cities near and far to lay thy ghost
Portents from Heaven shall urge, and they shall raise
A Tomb, and pay the Tomb a yearly vow.
There Palinurus' name shall last for aye."
Such words awhile drove sorrow from his heart,
And cheered him with the land that bears his name.

So, wending on their way, they near the stream.
Then from the Stygian wave the boatman saw
Them pacing thither through the silent wood,
And thus accosted: "Whosoe'er thou art,
Our stream in arms approaching, halt! and there
Say why thou comest to this land of Shades,
Of Sleep and slumbering Night. My Stygian boat
May not convey the living. 'Twas no joy,
In sooth, I won, Alcides o'er the lake,
Nor Theseus bearing and Pirithous,

Though born of Gods, and great victorious men!
He sought the Guard of Tartarus to bind,
And drew him trembling from the throne of Dis:
They from his bower our Mistress strove to steal!"

  Whom thus the Amphrysian Priestess answered brief:
"But no such guile is ours. Be calm: our arms
No onslaught bear. Let that great gaoler bark
For ever in his den, to scare the ghosts!
Let Proserpine keep, chaste, her Uncle's home!
Trojan Aeneas, great in worth and war,
His father seeks, descending to the Shades.
If thee no image of such love can move,
Yet know this Bough!" And, hidden in her robe,
She showed the Bough. Then all his anger fell,
Nor spake he more, but that dread gift admired,
The mystic Branch, for many a year unseen.
He turns his dusky barge, and nears the shore;
And, thrusting from the thwarts all other souls,
He makes the gangways clear, and takes aboard
Large-limbed Aeneas, with whose weight the boat
Groans leaking, and admits the streaming fen.
At last he lands them both, in sea-green weed
And hideous slime, unharmed, across the stream.

  Here, with his three-mouthed bark, great Cerberus
Roars, lying huge within his counter den.
To whom the Maid, when on his neck she saw
The bridling worms, a drowsing honey cake
Threw down. He, wild with hunger, opened large
His triple throat, and caught it; then to earth
Sank his vast back, and sprawled o'er all the den.
The ward asleep, Aeneas gained the approach,
And left in haste the irremeable stream.

  Then on their ears a sound of wailing rose,
Where babies' souls were crying in the gate,
Life's joyless outcasts, whom the dismal day
Plucked from the breast unripe, and gulfed in gloom.
Near these are they on false accusal slain; —
Here, too, the Lots are drawn, the Verdict given.
Minos presiding shakes the urn, and cites
The silent Court, and learns each lifetime's plea. —

And next are those sad souls who to themselves
Dealt death unguilty, and threw away their lives
Hating the light. Ah! now how fain were they
In open day to suffer want and toil!
But Fate withstands, and that unlovely pool,
And Styx enfolds them, flowing nine times round.

    And not far hence lie, spreading near and far,
The Fields of Mourning, for such name they bear,
Where in blind alleys lost and myrtle bowers
They shun the light, whom Love's unpitying wound
Wasted; in death itself their pain remains.
Phaedra is there, and Procris; there he sees,
Sad Eriphyle, with her mad son's scars;
Evadne, and Pasiphae; and with these
Laodamia, and who once was man,
Caeneus, to woman's form again restored.
And there was Dido, roaming a great wood,
Fresh from her wound; whom when the Trojan Prince
Knew standing near, dim-seen in dusk, as when
At the month's prime, one sees, or thinks he sees,
The rising misty moon, then, dropping tears,
With loving blandishment he thus began:

    "Unhappy Dido! Ah! 'twas truly told
That thou wert dead, and sought the end with steel!
Was I the cause? O, by the stars I swear,
By Heaven, and all the sanctities of Hell!
Unwillingly, O Queen, I left thy shores!
But God's own word, which through this shadowy place
Now drives me, and these festering fields of Night,
Imperious thrust me forth; nor could I deem
My going thence would bring thee so much woe.
Stay! Turn not from my gaze! O, who is this
Thou shunnest? 'Tis my last permitted word!"

    He with such speech and many a tear essayed
To soothe her fiery spirit, glowering wrath.
Fixed on the ground she kept her eyes averse.
No more her visage by his speech was moved
Than if she stood all flint or Parian stone.
At last in scorn she fled, and refuge found
In that green umbrage, where her former lord

Shared all her pain, and gave her love for love.
But still Aeneas, stricken by her woes,
Pursued her far with pity and with tears.

Thence toiling on their path, they gain at last
The outer fields, where mighty warriors dwell.
There met him Tydeus; there, renowned in arms,
Parthenopaeus, pale Adrastus' shade;
And Dardans slain in war, long wept above,
Stood in one long array. With sighs he marked
Glaucus, and Medon, and Thersilochus,
Antenor's sons, and Polyphoetes, vowed
To Ceres, and Idaeus, holding still
His car, his arms. Full close they hedge him round.
One look contents them not; they pace beside,
Lingering in joy, and learning why he came.
But Danaan lords, and Agamemnon's host,
When through the gloom they saw him flash in arms,
Trembled with terror; and some turned to fly,
As to the ships of old, some lifted up
Thin cries of war from throats that vainly gasped.

There Priam's son, with all his body shent,
Deiphobus he saw, his shattered face,
Face and both hands, and earless, mangled head,
And nostrils by a wound inglorious lopped.
Him, cowering to conceal those grisly scars,
He scarcely knew, then thus familiar spoke:

"O great in arms! of Teucer's lofty line!
Who took such fell revenge? Who wrought on thee
Such licence? Rumour told me thou hadst sunk,
Spent with much carnage, on that final night,
Upon a heap of dead; and I myself
On the Rhoetean shore an empty tomb
Raised, and thrice called upon thy ghost aloud.
Thy name and weapons keep the spot, but thee
I found not in thy native earth to lay!"

Then he: "O friend, in nothing didst thou fail!
To him, and his dead shade, thou gavest all.
Doom, and the Spartan Woman's heinous crime
Plunged me in woe; these memories she left!
For that last night we spent in false delight,

Thou mindest all too well. When o'er our walls
The fatal Horse leapt down, and in its womb
Bore fruit of mailclad men, she, in feigned dance,
With songs and orgies, led the Phrygian wives,
And from the Keep a mighty firebrand held,
And called the Greeks. I in my bower unblest
Lay, worn with care, and sunk in slumber deep;
Deep sleep and sweet, Death's very image, weighed
My body down, while from our house my wife,
O peerless wife! bore every weapon out,
Drew from beneath my head the trusty sword,
Called Menelaus, and the door flung wide,
With such a gift in store to win his love,
And quench the fame of her nefarious past!
Why linger? In they burst; and with them came
Crime's counsellor, Ulysses. Do as much,
Just Gods, to them, if pure these lips that pray!
But tell me in thy turn what brings thee here
Living. Dost come from roaming of the seas,
Or charged by God? What fortune drags thee thus
To lands perplext and sunless homes of woe?"

   But while they talked, the Dawn in rosy car
Beyond mid-pole had made her heavenly way;
And thus the allotted time had all been spent,
Did not the guiding Sibyl warn him brief:
"Night speeds, O Prince! in tears we waste the day.
Here lies the place where twofold paths diverge.
One leads to Pluto's halls, by which we gain
Elysium; but the left to evil souls
Works woe, and brings them to the wrath of Hell."
To whom Deiphobus: "Dread Maid, forbear!
I go to fill the tale, and sink in gloom.
Pass on, our Pride! and happier prove thy fate!"
He said, and speaking bent away his steps.

   Aeneas turned, and 'neath the leftward cliff
A fortress saw, girt wide by triple walls,
Round which fierce Phlegethon poured out a flood
Of torrent fire, and tumbled thundering stones.
A gate in front, huge doors of adamant,
No might of man, not all the embattled hosts
Of Heaven might shake; high soars its iron tower,

Where, wrapt in bloody pall, Tisiphone
The entrance guards, nor sleeps by night or day.
And wailing rose therefrom, and cruel sounds,
Thongs, and the clank of iron, and dragging chains.

He stopped, and o'er that noise in terror hung.
"What shapes of guilt, O Maid! what penal scourge,
What loud lament is this assailing heaven?"
Thus spake the Sibyl: "Glorious Prince of Troy!
None pure in heart may tread these courts of sin;
But Hecat, when she throned me Queen of Hell,
Taught me God's punishments, and showed me all.
Here Rhadamanthus reigns with iron sway,
And chastens fraud, and hears and makes confess
Their poor fond secrets who on earth put off
Till death's late hour their unrepented sin.
Then, leaping on them with avenging lash,
The scourging Fury in the left hand shakes
Her grisly worms, and calls her sisters grim.
At last, on hideous hinges grating harsh,
The Infernal Doors fly open. Mark who sits
To watch the gate! what Shape the threshold guards!
Yet more abhorred within the Hydra lurks,
With fifty gaping throats. Then Hell itself
Yawns sheer, and twice as far through darkness drops
As sight can travel to the Olympian height.
Here, in the nethermost Abyss, hurled down
By lightnings, roll the eldest born of Earth,
The Titans. Here the giant twins I saw,
Aloeus' sons, whose hands essayed to thrust
Jove from his throne, and rend the vast of Heaven.
Salmoneus too I saw in throes atone,
Who mimicked Jove's own thunders and his fire.
Drawn by four steeds through the Greek Elis town
Exultingly he rode, with brandished torch,
Claiming the honours of a God. O Fool!
Who thought with brass and trampling hoofs to match
The storm-cloud and the inimitable bolt!
But him the Almighty Father, through dense air
Launching his shaft, — no smoking torch of pine, —
Hurled headlong in the raging whirlwind's blast.
There Tityos, nursling of great Mother Earth,

Lay stretching nine full roods, and with her beak
A monstrous vulture pecks for evermore
His liver, and his anguish-breeding heart.
She banquets shrewdly, in his bosom lodged,
And gives no respite to the new-born flesh.
Why name Ixion and Pirithous
Or Lapithae? o'er whom the impending rock
Seems slipping, slipping still. Before them gleam
Gold genial couches, and the feast is spread
With regal pomp: fast by the Furies' Queen
Crouches and guards the tables from their touch,
Rising with torch uplift and thundering tones.
Here they who hated brothers, or in life
A parent struck, or wronged a client's trust,
Or brooded over wealth in solitude
And shared it not, — there is the largest crowd, —
Those for adultery slain, and those who drew
The sword of treason, or their lords betrayed,
All wait their doom immured. Seek not to know
What doom, what shape of suffering falls on them.
Some roll a ponderous stone, or hang outstretched
On whirling wheels. There sits, and aye shall sit,
Unhappy Theseus: Phlegyas, most in woe,
Gives warning wide, and testifies through gloom:
'Learn to be just! Be warned, and fear the Gods!'
One to a tyrant lord his country sold,
Made laws for gold, and for a bribe unmade;
One forced a daughter's unpermitted bed.
All dared great guilt, and reaped their daring's fruit.
Had I a hundred tongues, a hundred mouths,
A voice of iron, I could not compass all
Their crimes, nor tell their penalties by name."

So spake Apollo's Priestess, old and hoar.
"On, now," she adds, "perform the unfinished task!
On let us haste! Cyclopian walls I see;
And lo! in front yon archway, where 'tis charged
To lay our gift." She ceased, and side by side
Threading the darkness they o'erleap the gap,
And reach the gate. Aeneas, hastening in,
His body sprinkles with fresh lustral dews,
And on the fronting threshold lays the Bough.

When thus at last the Goddess' gift was paid,
They came within a region green and fair,
Fortunate fields and groves, the homes of bliss.
An ampler ether decks those meads with light:
Another sun is theirs, and other stars.
There on the sward some vie in sportive bouts,
Or wrestle on the sand. Others their feet
Beat in the dance with songs. And there, long-robed,
The blessed Thracian to the measure sounds
His seven sweet notes; and now his fingers strike
The music out, and now his ivory quill.
And there is Teucer's old and stately race,
Great-hearted heroes, born in happier years,
Ilus, Assaracus, and Dardanus,
Troy's Founder. At their arms and shadowy cars
He marvels; fast in earth their lances stand,
Their steeds are pasturing free: their living joy
In car and weapons, all the love that fed
Their glossy steeds, still follow them below.
Others to right and left on grassy turf
Feasting he saw, and quiring Paeans glad,
Mid odorous laurels, whence Eridanus
Rolls up to Earth, full-brimmed, his woodland wave.
And there are those who for their country bled,
Priests who were pure in earth, and gentle Bards
Whose words were worthy of Apollo's choir,
Inventors rare whose arts have polished life,
And who by serving made their memory dear:
All these are crowned with bands of snowy white.

Them thus reposed the Sibyl then bespeaks,
Musaeus first, for him they most regard
Towering amidst their throng with shoulders tall:
"Say, happy Souls! and thou, O Bard most blest!
Where dwells Anchises, for whose sake we came,
And crossed the infernal streams?" Whom thus in brief
The Hero answered: "Here no settled home
Hath any; but by river banks we dwell,
In meadows fresh with rills and shady groves.
But climb yon height, if thus your hearts incline,
And I will lead you by an easy path."

And, walking first, he shows them spread below
The glittering plains, and they descend the hill.

There lay Anchises, in a far green vale,
And musing scanned the imprisoned souls that soon
Would rise to daylight, and the cherished line
Of all his offspring numbered, and reviewed
Their fates, their lives, their prowess, and their worth.
But when advancing o'er the sward he saw
Aeneas, eagerly both hands he stretched,
And raining down his tears, the silence broke:

"Art thou then come? and hath the love I hoped
Subdued the hard way? O may I see thy face,
And hear thee, Son, and answer, as of old?
Yet in my thoughts I deemed that this would be,
Counting the days, nor was my longing vain.
What lands, what wastes of water, O my Son,
Hast thou not traversed! by what perils tossed!
Ah! how I feared lest Libya worked thee woe!"

Then he: "O Father, 'twas thy phantom sad
That came to me so oft and hither urged!
My vessels ride the Tyrrhene Sea. O give
Thine hand, O Father, go not from these arms!"
He spoke, while streaming tears bedewed his face.
Thrice round his neck he tried to throw his arms;
Thrice fled the vision from his empty grasp,
As light as wind, and like a flying dream.

Meanwhile within a far ravine he saw
A glen of rustling foliage, and the stream
Of Lethe flowing before homes of peace.
And round it tribes and peoples numberless
Were hovering, as bees in the bright summer
Light on the damasked flowers, and stream around
White lilies, and the murmurous meadow hums.

Thrilled by that sudden sight, Aeneas asks
In wonder, what that distant river is,
And what great host is crowding all its marge.
Anchises then: "The Soul to which Fate owes
Another flesh, from yonder Lethe drinks

A lulling draught and long forgetfulness.
These have I wished to show thee many a day,
And count my children's children, to increase
Thy joy with mine, when Italy is found."

"O Father! May we think that any Souls
Pass upwards, and return to irksome flesh?
What is this strange sad longing for the light?"
"Son, I will hold thee in suspense no more."
And thus his Sire unfolds the gradual tale.

"Know first that Heaven and Earth and flowing Sea,
The Moon's far-shining orb, and Titan's stars
An inner Soul sustains; a Spirit infused
Moves in the mass, and sways the mighty frame.
Thence men are born, and beasts, and flying fowl,
And shapes that swim the deep: their seeds of life
Have fiery vigour, and celestial source,
Save for the fleshly taint, the numbing weight
Of earthy limbs, and bodies made to die.
Hence spring their fears, their love, and pain, and joy;
And, pent in gloom, the light they never see
From that blind dungeon. Nay, when life's last ray
Departs, not yet all evil, not all taint
Of carnal disappears; so long ingrained
Needs must that inward growth be wondrous deep.
Therefore they suffer chastisement, and purge
Past sins by penance. Some are stretched and hung
In the void winds, or under monstrous seas
Their guilt is washed away, or burnt by fire.
Each his own Doom we bear, (ere sent to dwell,
A happy remnant, in Elysian meads,)
Till Time fulfils the cycle, and takes out
That inbred flaw, and unpolluted leaves
The etherial sense and Heaven's authentic fire.
Rolled through a thousand years, God summons all
Yon Souls to Lethe, that remembering nought
The vault of Heaven they may behold once more
Resuming wistfully the mortal flesh."

He ceased, and drew through all that humming throng
Aeneas and his Guide, and chose a mound,

Whence he might scan the vast confronting ranks,
And recognise their faces as they came.

   "Now will I tell what glories shall pursue
The long Italian line of Dardan blood,
Illustrious souls, in distant years to bear
Our name! and teach what Fate hath stored for Thee!

   "Look, yonder, leaning on his maiden spear,
Nearest the light, is he who first shall rise,
Blent with Italian blood, to living day,
Silvius, the Alban name, thy youngest son,
Whom in green woods Lavinia late shall bear
To thee grown old, a King and Sire of Kings.
Through him our House o'er Alba shall bear sway.
Procas is next, our pride, and Numitor,
Capys, and he who shall renew thy name,
Silvius Aeneas, great in worth, as great
In prowess, should he gain the Alban throne.
What men are they! O what puissant fronts!
Behold the civic oak that shades their brows!
Nomentum they shall found, Fidenae's town,
Gabii, Pometii, and Collatia's fort,
Bola, and Cora and the Inuan Camp.
These shall be names which now are nameless land!
And there, beside his grandsire, Ilia's son,
Sprung from Troy's royal blood, the seed of Mars,
Lo, Romulus! O see the double plume,
His father's badge that marks him for the skies!
Beneath his auspices great Rome shall fill
Earth with her power, and with her glory Heaven,
Blest in her hero brood, and seated sole
On seven walled hills, even as through Phrygian towns
The towered Berecynthian rides her car,
Clasping a hundred sons, all denizens
Of Heaven, all tenants of the lofty skies!
Bend hither now thy sight. Behold thy sons!
Thy race of Romans! Caesar lo! and all
Iulus' seed, heirs of the heavenly day.
This, this is he so long thou hear'st foretold
Divine Augustus Caesar, who once more
Shall build, where Saturn reigned in Latian fields,

The Golden Age! O'er Garamant and Ind
His sway shall spread, beyond the stars, beyond
The range of Year and Sun, where on his back
Great Atlas turns the star-yspangled sky.
Ere his approach e'en now at Heaven's decree
The Caspian shudders, and Maeotia shrinks,
And Nile's seven mouths with terror are perplexed.
Yea, so much earth Alcides never passed
To pierce the brass-hoofed stag, or quell with shafts
Lerna, or silence Erymanthian brakes;
Nor conquering Liber, when with vine-clad reins
He drives his tigers from high Nysa's top. —
And doubt we still to give our prowess room?
Or shrink we in fear from that Ausonian land? —

"But who is this, that, crowned with olive, bears
The sacrifice? I know the hoary beard,
The Roman King, who first shall bind the State
By laws, from little Cures' needy soil
Sent forth to Empire. After whom shall come,
Ignoble peace to rend, and wake to war
The flagging State, to triumphs long disused,
Tullus. And next the braggart Ancus comes,
Even now too doting on the People's breath.
Wilt see the Tarquins? the avenging pride
Of Brutus, and the lictors' rods resumed?
He first the Consul's awful axe shall take,
And, when his sons provoke impetuous strife,
Doom them to death in Freedom's glorious name.
O Man of Grief! Howe'er thy tale be told,
Large honour there shall glow and patriot love!
Decii and Drusi see! Torquatus' axe!
Camillus see, who bears the banners home!
But those who shine like-armed, souls now at peace
In Death's dark durance, when they reach the light,
What wars between them, O what fields of blood
Will they awake! Across the barrier Alps
One from Monoecus' stronghold shall descend
To front his son-in-law's embattled East!
My sons, O cleave not to a strife like this!
Save Rome's own bosom from the swords of Rome!
Thou first, O seed of Heaven, thou first forgive!

Blood of my veins, cast down thine arms! —
Lo! who from Corinth to the high Capitol
Shall drive in triumph, flown with Grecian blood,
And yonder who shall lay Mycenae low,
Achilles' very seed, and vengeance take
For Trojan sires, and Pallas' outraged fane.
Thee, Cossus, thee, great Cato, who could pass?
The Gracchi, or the Scipios, Afric's bale,
Twin thunderbolts of war, Fabricius, strong
In penury, or Serranus on his glebe?
Spare my spent breath, ye Fabii! Great indeed
Thou by whose sole delay the State is saved!

"Some with more grace may mould the breathing brass,
And draw from stone, I trow, the living form,
Plead causes better, map the heavenly paths,
And tell the rising stars. Roman! be thine
To sway the world with Empire! These shall be
Thine arts, to govern with the rule of Peace,
To spare the weak, and subjugate the proud!"

He ceased, and, while they marvelled, added more:
"See how Marcellus, bright with splendid spoils,
In march triumphal above all men towers!
Rome, shaken by the invader, he shall stay,
Ride down the Poeni and the rebel Gaul,
And to Quirinus the third spoils hang up!"

And here Aeneas, seeing by his side
A graceful form, in shining armour clad,
But sad his brow, and downcast were his eyes:
"O Father! who is he, beside him thus?
His son, or one of his illustrious stock?
How the crowd hums about! How great he stands!
Yet round his head Night hovers dark and sad!"

Anchises then with rising tears began:
"Son, ask not of thy people's mighty grief!
Him Fate shall show to Earth, but not permit
Longer to live. Too great your Roman brood
Had seemed, O Gods! had this gift been their own!
What moan of men shall fill the Field of Mars
By the great city! What a funeral train
Shall Tiber see, and wash the new-made grave!

No boy of Ilian birth so high shall raise
His fathers' hopes; no Roman earth shall boast
So dear a nursling. O for love and faith!
O for the hand invincible in war!
Him none confronting in the shock of arms
Had met unscathed, or if he charged afoot,
Or if he spurred the horse's foaming flanks.
Ah, boy, the pity! Could'st thou sunder Fate,
Thou wert Marcellus! Give me purple flowers,
Handfuls of lilies: let me strew at least
O'er his dear Shade these unavailing dues!"

Thus o'er those misty fields they wandered wide,
Surveying all: and through each several scene
Anchises led his son, and with the love
Of coming glory made his spirit burn:
Then told of wars thereafter to be waged,
Laurentum's peoples, and Latinus' town,
And how to shun the toil, and how to bear.

Two are the Gates of Sleep, one fabled horn,
Through which true visions pass; the other shines
Polished, of ivory white, but false the dreams
To heaven sent upward from the shades of Hell.
With such discourse, the Sibyl and his Son
Anchises through the ivory Gate dismissed.
He with all haste regaining ships and men,
Steers straight by coastline for Caieta's port,
Casts anchor from the prow, and grounds the stern.

Book VII

THOU TOO IN death undying fame hast given,
Aeneas' Nurse, Caieta: o'er our shores
Thy memory broods; in great Hesperia still
A name (if aught that glory) marks thy bones.
Her burial dues were paid; her tomb was raised;
And sailing onward when the high seas fell,

Aeneas left the port. Far into night
The breezes blow, and on their track the Moon
Beams white; the waves in trembling radiance shine.
And soon they glide by Circe's sea-bound home,
Where, singing evermore, the Sun's bright child
Thrills her untrodden glens, and all night through
Burns odorous cedar in her stately halls,
And through the warp her humming shuttle runs.

And roaring thence was heard, and wrath of lions
Chafing their chains and growling late at night:
And bristled swine and bears within their pens
Ravined, and shapes of monstrous wolves howled forth,
Whom savage Circe from men's form had clothed
Through potent herbs with brutish face and mien.
But lest good Trojans, to that haven borne,
Should bear the spell, or near that dismal shore,
Neptune with prospering breezes filled their sails,
And sped their flight, and bore them past the surf.

The ray-lit sea flushed red, and Morning shone
Pale in her rosy car; the breezes died,
And every flaw lulled suddenly; the oars
Laboured in marble calm. Aeneas looked
Across the waters, and discerned a wood
Far-spread, through which the pleasant Tiber stream
In swirling eddies thick with yellow sand
Breaks to the sea. And divers birds that haunt
The river banks and bed, around, above,
Charm the sweet air with singing as they fly.
He bids the sailors turn their prows to shore,
And up the shady river sails with joy.

O come, instruct me, Erato! to tell
What Kings, what times, then were in Latium old,
When that invading host first drove on shores
Ausonian. Thou, O Goddess, aid me thou,
To unfold the dawn of War! Of battles sad
Thy Bard shall sing, and the brave deaths of Kings,
The Tyrrhene troops, and all Hesperia armed.
Now springs a loftier cycle; now I wake
A loftier theme!
                    The King Latinus reigned

Ageing in peace long time o'er field and town;
Born of the Nymph Marica, annals tell,
And Faunus, he of Picus, who from thee,
Saturn, was sprung, and thou didst found the line.
From him the doom of God all manly seed
Had reft and ravished in their prime of youth.
One only daughter kept the royal house,
Now ripe of years for man; whom many wooed
From Latium, and from all the Ausonian tract;
But goodliest of all the high-born prince,
Most noble Turnus; and the Mother Queen
Prospered his suit, full fain of such a son.
Yet many an awful sign from Heaven withstood.

Deep in the Palace Court a laurel grew,
Sacred, and saved in reverence many a year;
Which King Latinus, ere he raised his towers,
Found, and himself to Phoebus sanctified,
And thence *Laurentine* named his colonists.
And lo! a wonder! To this laurel's crest
A host of bees flew buzzing through the blue,
And settled; and, with feet enlinking feet,
Hung from the leafy bough in sudden swarm.
Then cried a Seer: "One coming from abroad
I see! A host from this same tract will make
The selfsame goal, to lord it o'er our Keep!"

Moreover, as the maid Lavinia stood,
Lighting pure altars at her father's side,
They saw, O horrible! her long loose hair
Flaming, and all her bravery consumed
With hissing fire, her queenly locks, her crown
Splendid with gems; and, wrapt in lurid smoke,
She strewed with sparks the Palace. 'Twas a sign
Held strange and terrible; and Prophets sang,
Fame should be hers, and glorious fate should crown
Her, but hard war should be her people's doom.
Then, vext by prodigies, the King consults
His father's oracles, in forest depths
Of vast Albunea, where the holy Fount
Sings, and the darkness breathes sulphureous breath.
Italians there and all the Oenotrian land
In troubles ask response; and when the Priest

Hath brought the gifts, and in the dead of night
Lain down to sleep on skins of slaughtered rams,
Strange hovering shapes he sees, and divers tones
Hears, and enjoys the converse of the Gods,
And speaks with Acheron and Hell's Abyss.
Here too Latinus sought response, and slew
A hundred woolly ewes, and laid him down,
Couched on the fleecy bed, when suddenly
A voice came from the thicket: "O my Son!
Seek not with Latin bridals to ally
Thy child, nor trust her to the bed prepared!
Sons coming from abroad shall set our name
High in the stars! and where the circling Sun
Scans either main, their progeny will see
The world spin underfoot, and own their sway!"
Such warnings Faunus in the silent night
Uttered, nor did Latinus hold them close.
Through each Ausonian city flying wide
Rumour had noised them, ere the sons of Troy
Had moored their galleys by the grassy bank.

    Beneath a branching tree Aeneas lay,
With fair Iulus and the Trojan lords,
Who set the meal, and on the sward spread out
Their meats on barley cakes, — so Jove inspired, —
And with wild fruits they crowned the cereal board.
Now when all else was spent, and, scant of food,
They bit the slender cakes, and turned to rend
With hands and venturous jaws that fateful bread,
Not sparing the wide trenchers; "Ho!" exclaims
Iulus, "we are eating boards as well!"

    Jesting he spake; and sounded with that speech
Their travail's bourne. His father caught the word,
And saved the amazing sign. "O hail!" he cried,
"My destined Country! Hail, ye Household Gods,
Faithful to Troy! Here is our Land; here lies
Our Home! For, I recall, my father left
Such secrets of my fate. 'When thou art borne
To shores unknown, my son, and, failing food,
Hunger shall drive thee to devour thy boards,
There hope to house thy weariness, and there
Thy bulwarks raise, and build at last thine Home!'

This is that hunger! this our final goal!
Here shall our ruin end!
Come then and let us blithe at earliest day
Explore the land and people, and, the port
Leaving by divers ways, their city seek.
Now pour the bowl to Jove, and on my Sire
Anchises call, and lay the wine-cup down."
He spake, and wreathed his brows with green, and prayed
The Genius of the Soil, the Nymphs, and Earth,
Eldest of Gods, the Rivers yet unknown,
Night, and Night's rising Signs, Idaean Jove,
The Phrygian Mother, and his Parents twain
In Heaven and Hell, invoking each in turn.
Then clearly from on high the Almighty thrice
Thundered, and with his own right hand shook out
A cloud that burned with rays of golden fire.
And swiftly rumour through the Trojans ran,
The day was come their destined Home to build.
They, in that Sign exulting, spread the feast,
And set the bowls, and wreathe the wine with flowers.

And when the next Day took the torch of dawn,
Champaign and coast they roamed, and peopled town,
Where sprang Numicus' pools, and Tiber stream,
Where dwelt the Latins bold.
                    And from all ranks
Anchises' son a hundred envoys chose,
Whom, wreathed with fronds of Pallas' tree, he bade
The royal Palace to approach with gifts,
And sue for grace. They on their mission speed
With rapid march; while on the strand their Prince
His City traces with a shallow trench,
And breaks the ground, and like a camp enrings
With battlement and scarp his first abode.

And when their way was measured, they were ware
Of roofs and towers, and neared the Latins' town.
Before it boys, and men in flowering prime,
Were training steeds, or steered the dusty car,
Or bent the bow, or from the shoulder hurled
Javelins, and challenged or to box or run.
And when a horseman bore the old King news
Of tall men coming in a garb unknown,

He charged to bid them in, and took his seat
On his ancestral Throne.

                    The stately House
Rose on a hundred columns, vast and tall
Above the city, Picus' royal home,
Where old Religion dwelt in horrent shade.
Here Kings must take the sceptre, here the rods
Of Empire rise. This temple was their Court,
Their sacred Feast-hall: here the Elders sate
At one long table when the ram was slain.
And in the porch the old dead Fathers stood
Imaged in antique cedar; Italus,
And the Vine Planter with his pruning-hook,
Sabinus, aged Saturn, and the form
Of Janus double-faced, primaeval Kings,
And all who for their country fought and bled.
And on the holy doors hung many arms,
Curved axes, captured cars, and crested helms,
Great portal bars, and spears, and shields, and beaks
From warships torn. There with the augur's staff,
The augur's scanty gown, on his left arm
Bearing the Shield of Mars, sate Picus' self,
The horse-subduer, whom with her wand his bride,
Impassioned Circe, struck, and by her drugs
Changed to a bird, and dyed his speckled wings.
In such a temple, on his fathers' throne,
Latinus sate, and bade the Trojans in;
And when they entered, mildly thus began:

   "Speak, Dardans! for not strange to us your race
And city, and not unfamed you cross the sea.
What seek ye? To the Ausonian coast what cause,
What need hath borne you o'er the dark blue main?
If driven by storms, or straying from your course,
(As oft it fares with mariners at sea,)
These river banks you gained, and lie in port,
Fly not our welcome! Know the Latins spring
From Saturn, by no laws to justice bound,
But self-controlled we serve our ancient God.
Indeed I mind, — though years have dimmed the tale, —
Auruncan elders told how Dardanus,
Born in these fields, reached Phrygian Ida's towns,

And Thracian Samos, now called Samothrace.
Hence, from Tyrrhenian Corythus, he sailed,
Whom golden mansions of the starry sky
Hold now enthroned, and swell the shrines of Heaven."

He ended; and Ilioneus returned:
"O King, great seed of Faunus! No black storm
In wintry seas hath washed us on your coast.
Nor star nor strand misled us; but by choice,
By purpose firm, thy city we arrive,
Driven from the mightiest Empire that the Sun
Once from the utmost ends of heaven surveyed.
From Jove our race began: descent from Jove
The Dardan boasts. Our King, Jove's lofty seed,
Trojan Aeneas, sent us to thy gates.
How wild a storm from fierce Mycenae broke
O'er Ida's plain, what shocks of Fortune thrust
Europe on Asia, world on clashing world,
That man hath heard whom Earth's remotest shore
Sunders by Ocean's verge, or whom the tract
Of pitiless Sun exiles in the mid zone.
We from that deluge borne o'er wastes of sea,
Crave for our Gods a roof, some harmless shore,
Water and air, in commonalty spread.
We shall not shame you, nor shall your renown
Fade, or the memory of your deed grow dim.
Ausonia shall not rue the embrace of Troy.
Yea, by Aeneas' doom, and by his hand,
Mightful in friendship tried or tried in war,
Peoples and tribes I swear — (O scorn us not
That suppliant wreaths we bear and suppliant words!) —
Sought our alliance oft, but Heaven's high doom
Imperious pushed us on to this your land.
Here Dardanus was born: Apollo hither
Recalls us, and by strong commandment drives
To Tiber, and Numicus' holy pools.
See! these poor bounties of the happy past
He gives thee, relics saved from burning Troy.
Anchises from this gold libations shed.
This was the wear of Priam, when he judged
The cited tribes, his sceptre, and his tiar,
And robes, the toil of Ilian wives."

While thus he spake, Latinus held his face
Downcast in muse, and fastened to the floor,
Rolling his eyes intent. Not purple bredes,
Not Priam's sceptre, moved the King so much,
As on his daughter's bridal bed he dwelt,
And pondered on the doom his father told.
Here was the Voyager from alien shores
Foreshown his Son, and summoned by the Fates
To share his rule, whose progeny should hold
In might pre-eminent the world entire.

At last thus briefly: "May God speed our course
By God foretold! Trojan, we grant thy boon.
Thy gifts I spurn not. While Latinus reigns,
Troy's wealth ye shall not lack, nor fruitful glebe.
But let Aeneas, if so strong his will
To join alliance and be called our friend,
Himself approach, nor tremble at our love!
To clasp his hand shall be my pledge of peace.
Now bear ye back your prince this word of mine.
I have a daughter, whom to mate with one
Of our own race, my father's oracles,
And many a sign forbid. Sons from abroad,
Shall set our name — so sing my country's Seers —
High in the stars. 'Tis he whom Fate hath called!
I think, nay, hope it, if my heart bode well!"

He ceased; and bade them lead from out his stalls,
Where thrice a hundred chargers shining stood,
A chosen horse for each, swift-footed, trapped
With purple bredes. Gold collars o'er their chests
Hang drooping: each is housed with gold, and champs
Red gold between his teeth. But to their Prince
He sends a chariot, and a harnessed pair
Of Heavenly seed, with nostrils snorting fire,
The bastard birth which daedal Circe once
Bred for her father from a secret mare.
They with such gifts and greetings of the King
High on their steeds take back the word of Peace.

But lo! from Argos Jove's relentless wife
Was holding through the air her homeward way,
When from Pachynus and the distant sky

She looked where blithe Aeneas and his crews
Were building homes, and all, from shipboard gone,
Trusting the land. She stood, transfixed by pain,
And thus, with head thrown up, her utterance poured:

"Ah! hated race! Ah, destinies of Troy
At odds with mine! And on Sigean plains
Could they not fall? And are the captives free?
Could Troy not burn them? Through all swords and flames
They found their way! My power at last, it seems,
Grows faint, and glutted wrath hath lulled my wit!
Nay, I dared chase them outcast on the deep,
And thwart them with my hate, where'er they sailed!
On them were spent all powers of Sky and Sea!
Syrtes, or Scylla, or Charybdis wild,
What skilled they? Safe in Tiber's bed they lie,
And fear nor waves nor me. Mars could undo
The giant Lapithae. To Dian's wrath
The Sire of Heaven himself gave Calydon.
What guilt doomed Calydon or Lapithae?
Yet me, Jove's mighty Queen, whose tortured heart
Shrank from no daring, stopped at no device,
Aeneas conquers! If my power be weak,
I shall not halt to crave what help is left,
And if I bend not Heaven, resort to Hell!
What though I may not thwart his Latin crown,
Though destined still Lavinia stays his bride,
Delays I yet may add, and ruin deal
On both their hosts. Yea, let their peoples pay
To make them one! Virgin, thy dower shall be
Troy's and Rutulia's blood! Bellona waits
To be thy bridesmaid! Not Cisseis only
Travailed with fire; nay, Venus hath a birth
Like hers, another Paris, bridal flames,
New flames of death against uprisen Troy!"

She finished; and, to earth descending fierce,
Called from the Dread One's seat in nether dark
Baleful Allecto, who delights in wars,
Slanders, and stratagems, and murderous wrath;
The grisly Terror, whom her very sire
And Hellish sisters hate, so many a form
She takes, so grim, so black with swarming snakes.

Whom Juno thus incites: "Concede me this,
O Virgin born of Night! for me this task
Accomplish, lest my fame and honour fade,
And lest these Trojans by a bridal gain
Latinus, and beset the Italian land.
One-hearted brothers thou canst arm for strife,
Blind homes with hate, and hurl thereon thy whips
And brands of death. A thousand names are thine,
A thousand plagues. Unload thy fruitful breast!
Dissever plighted peace, sow seeds of war!
Together wake to arms heart, voice, and hand!"

Allecto then, in Gorgon poisons steeped,
First seeking Latium and the royal roof
Before Amata's silent door sits down;
Whose woman's heart, with pain and passion hot,
O'er Turnus and the Trojans' coming seethed.
On her a serpent from her blue-black locks
The Goddess threw, to wind within her heart,
That she in madness might embroil the house.
Between her vesture and her sleeky breasts
The serpent glides unfelt, and stealing breathes
Its crazing viperous breath, and binds her neck
With golden circlet, and bedecks her brows,
And wreathes her hair, and o'er her body slides.
And while the subtle poison's clammy bane
Her senses thrilled, and filled her veins with fire,
Ere yet the flame o'er all her bosom spread,
Mildly she spake and mother-like, and long
Wept o'er her child and Phrygian bridal day:

"O Father, wilt thou give these outcast men
Lavinia's hand? Pity thyself and her!
Her mother pity, by the first wind duped,
When seaward he shall reave his maiden prey!
Stole not the Phrygian hind to Sparta thus,
And bare off Helen? Where is thy plighted word?
Where thine old love of kin? thy hand so oft
Pledged to thy Turnus? If an alien son
Our Fates demand, and Faunus' mandate stern
Constrains thee, every land from ours disjunct
And free is alien, as I deem, and thus
The Gods intend. Nay, Turnus, if his House

Be followed to its prime, from Inachus
Springs and Acrisius, from Mycenae's heart."

But when, for all her words, Latinus stands
Adverse, and deep the serpent's crazing harm
Sinks in her vitals, and pervades her frame,
Then, stung with horror, through the world of streets
She raves in anguish wildly, as a top
Flies to the curling lash, which eager boys
Spin in a circle wide through empty halls:
Urged by the thong, it reels in sweeping rings,
While over it the silly gaping crew
Admire the whirling box, and every stroke
Gives life; not duller was the speed she made
Through towns and peoples fierce. Even to the woods
She fled, a feigned Bacchante, greater crime
Daring and greater madness, and her child
On leafy mountains hid, that she might rob
The Trojans' bed, and stay the bridal torch.
"Ho! Bacchus, ho!" she shrieks, "'tis thou alone
Deserv'st the maid! For thee she takes the thyrsus,
Dances for thee, and feeds the holy tress!"

The rumour flies; each mother's heart grows mad
For strange adventure. They desert their homes,
They give the winds their hair; while others fill
The sky with shivering wail, and, clad in skins,
Brandish the vine-wreathed spears. She, fiery-fierce,
Lifts burning pine among them, while she hymns
The bridal song of Turnus and her child,
Rolling her blood-shot eyes, and sudden shrills:
"Ho, Latin Mothers! hear, where'er ye be!
If any love of sad Amata rest
In loyal hearts, if mothers' right be dear,
Undo your wreaths, with me the orgies dance!"
So through wild woods and deserts of the beast
Allecto goads the Queen with Bacchic rage.

But when she saw those seeds of frenzy sprout,
And the King's will undone and all his House,
The sombre Goddess-sought on dusky wing

The bold Rutulian's town, which Danae erst,
Blown thither by the headlong South, had built
For her Acrisian men; once Ardea called,
Ardea, a name still great, though Fortune dwells
No longer there. Here, in his high-built house,
Bold Turnus lay, and culled the midnight sleep.
The Fury then her Hellish face and mien
Changed to a beldam's countenance, and ploughed deep
Her obscene brow with wrinkles, and put on
Grey tresses bound and wreathed with olive spray,
To Juno's Priestess, Calybe, transformed;
Who with these words confronts the hero's sight:

"Turnus, shall all thy toil be spilt in vain?
Shall Dardan outcasts reave thee of the crown?
Thy bride, thy blood-bought dower, the King denies,
Seeking an alien heir. Go now, poor dupe,
And drive on thankless perils! Up, and rout
The Tyrrhene battle! Fold the realm in peace!
From mighty Juno's self this word I bear
To tell thee lying in the peace of night.
Up! Arm the men! Make ready! Take the field!
Be blithe! and burn these Phrygian men, and burn
Their painted barks in yon fair river moored!
High Powers of Heaven command. And if the King
Grant not the bride he promised, let him smart
Himself, and feel at last thine armed hand!"

To whom thus Turnus, answering in scorn:
"Not, as thou deem'st, without report to me,
They ride on Tiber's water. Prithee cease
To weave such bugbears. Nor doth Heaven's high Queen
Forget us yet.
But Age, that moulders, barren of all truth,
Frets thee with vain alarms, and mocks thy soul
With phantom terrors of encountering Kings.
To tend God's shrine and image is thy charge,
But leave to men, the warriors, peace and war!"

Thereat she blazed with anger, and the Prince
Yet speaking shuddered, and his eyeballs froze,

So thick the hydras hiss, to shape so large
The Fury expands. Then, rolling eyes of flame,
She spurns him while he falters, seeking speech,
And on her head uplifts a pair of snakes,
And sounds her lash, and thus, resuming, raves:

"See now, who moulders, mocked by lying Age
With phantom terrors of encountering Kings!
Behold! From Hell's dark Sisterhood am I,
And War and Death are in my hand!"

She spoke, and hurled her torch, and in his heart
Fixed the swart fuming brand. An awful dread
Shattered his sleep, and sweat from every pore
Streamed o'er his limbs. For arms he shrieks, for arms
He searches house and bed. The lust of steel,
The wild blood-fury wakes, and rage supreme.
As when the flame about a cauldron's ribs
Roars, and the water leaps; the flood within
Seethes fiercely as it smokes and tosses high
The frothy bubbles, till the wave at last
O'erleaps itself, and steam flies dark to heaven.

On King Latinus then, defiling Peace,
He charged his prime with armed force to march,
Save Italy, and drive her foemen out.
Trojans and Latins, he can match them both.
He gave the word, and prayed; and all his men
Clamoured and cheered for war; for one his youth
And beauty moved, and one his royal blood,
One the bright deeds of his puissant hand.

While thus he fired their souls, the Stygian bane
To Teucer's sons, fresh scheming, winged her way;
And marked where fair Iulus by the coast
Hunted and trapped the deer. There all his hounds,
Feeding their nostrils with familiar scent,
Hell's Daughter struck with fury and drove in chase
Hot on the deer. So first the woe began:
So woke in rustic hearts the flame of War!

A fair, large-antlered stag, by Tyrrheus' sons
Stolen from his mother, they were rearing up,
They and their father, whom the royal herds

Obeyed, the trusted Ranger of the field.
Their sister Silvia governed him with love,
And decked his horns with green, and washed him oft
In the clear spring, and combed the wild rough hair.
Tame to the hand, he knew his master's board,
Strayed in the forest, and came home himself
Though deep in night to the familiar door.

   Him straying far Iulus' furious dogs
Startled, as idly down the stream he swam,
And on the green bank swaged the summer heat.
Then, burning with desire of chiefest fame,
Ascanius bent the bow and launched his shaft.
God let not swerve the hand, but driven home
Through flank and belly sped the hissing reed;
And the hurt creature to the well-known roof
Fled, and with moans crept in, and, dripping blood,
Cried through the house like one imploring aid.
Then sister Silvia, beating hand on arm,
Called the rude hinds for help. They ere she wist
Stood by her, — for within their silent woods
The Fiend lay hid: — one held a stake burnt hard,
One a thick knotty club: whate'er they snatch
Wrath makes a weapon. Tyrrheus, breathing rage,
Incites them, axe in hand, as late he drove
The wedges home, and four-wise cleft an oak.
Hell's Daughter, watching, lit on mischief's hour.
High on the roof she perched, and from the top
Blew forth the shepherds' signal, through a horn
Stretching her Stygian voice, that all the wood
Shook, and deep forests rang, and Trivia's lake
Heard it afar, and Nar's white sulphury stream
Heard, and Velinus' wells, and mothers pale
Trembled, and clasped their children to the breast.
Then swiftly indeed, to that dread clarion's voice,
From every side wild peasants catch up arms,
And run together, while the men of Troy
Stream to Ascanius' help from opened camp.
They stand embattled; now no field is fought
With rustic cudgels, or with stakes burnt hard.
Steel must decide; and far the harvest waves
Of bristling sword-blades drawn, while radiant brass

Casts back to heaven the challenge of the Sun.
So, when the wind blows up the whitening wave,
The Sea gets slowly up, then, swelling higher,
Surges at last to heaven from his low bed.

  Before the battle's edge a hissing shaft
Laid Almo low, Almo the eldest son
Of Tyrrheus; for the wound was in his throat,
Closed the soft path of air, and stayed the life.
And there, with many, old Galaesus fell,
Pleading for peace between them, who was once
Their best, and richest in Ausonian lands.
Five flocks of sheep, five herds of kine came home
All his; his soil a hundred ploughshares turned.

  While thus in dubious strife the field is fought,
Her pledge redeemed, the Goddess, having shed
Red battle dews, and waked the war with death,
Hesperia quits, and through the aerial tract
Turns, and to Juno thus triumphing boasts:

  "Lo! how thy discord blossoms into war!
Speak, that they band in friendship, plighting troth!
Since I have sprent Troy's sons with Latin gore,
Yet more achieving, if thy will be mine,
The neighbouring towns to battle I will bring,
With rumours kindling the mad lust of war,
Till all bring help; till Latium teem with arms!"

  Then Juno thus: "Enough of fear and fraud!
War's seed is sown: the embattled forces close.
Arms lent by chance are newly dyed in blood.
Be such the bridal, such the wedding feast
Latinus holds, and Venus' peerless son!
Thee further licence in the fields of air
The Lord of high Olympus not permits.
Give place. Howe'er the hap of battle turn,
My hand shall rule."
                              So Saturn's daughter spake.
On hissing snaky wings the other rose,
And, flying Hellward, left empyreal air.
Among the mountains of mid Italy
Lies a famed spot, renowned on many a coast,
Amsanctus' Dale; on either hand pent in

By black and shaggy woods, and in its midst
A broken stream runs swirling among rocks.
A horrid pit, a breathing-hole of Dis,
Lies here; and from the chasm's pestiferous jaws
Bursts Acheron: where now the Fury hid
Her hateful might, relieving Earth and Heaven.

No less meanwhile Saturnia on the war
Laid her last touch. The herdsmen from the field
All hasten townward, bearing home the slain,
Young Almo and Galaesus' mangled face,
And pray the Gods, and on Latinus call.
Then Turnus, in that bloodshed's blaze and blare,
Sounds new alarms: "Our realm is pledged to Troy!
See Phrygia's shoot engrafted, me dislodged!"
And they whose mothers beat the pathless woods
In Bacchic dance, — so weighed Amata's name, —
Together swarm, and tire the Battle God.
All, deaf to omens, deaf to Heaven's own voice,
Clamour for war perverse, and eager throng
Round King Latinus' palace. He resists,
Like some old rock of ocean unremoved,
Some rock of ocean, when great breakers crash,
Which stands, while round it many a billow howls,
Firm in its mass: in vain the foaming crags
Roar, and the seaweed from its side is washed.

But when no power is his their purpose blind
To o'ercome, and all things bend to Juno's will,
To Heaven he pleads, and prays the vacant air:
"O, wrecked by Doom we drift on stormy seas!
Your impious blood this punishment shall bear,
Unhappy men! Thee, Turnus, thee remain
Reprisals stern: too late thy prayers shall be!
My rest is won: my haven all in view;
I am but spoiled of happy death." No more;
But, home withdrawn, he dropped the reins of rule.

A Latian use there was, which Alban towns
Kept ever sacred, and imperial Rome
Keeps now; whene'er they summon Mars to strife,
Or if for Goth or Arab they prepare
Sad war, or traverse Ind, and to reclaim

Their standards from the Parthian, chase the Dawn; —
Twain Gates of War there are, so named, from dread
Of awful Mars revered and holy fear,
Barred by a hundred bolts' eternal iron;
And Janus there the threshold constant guards.
Here, when the Fathers' sentence is for war,
The Consul, in Quirinus' gown, and cinct
In Gabine wise, unbars the door himself,
Himself calls battles forth, then all the rest
Call, and the trumpets blow with harsh assent.
And by this mode 'twas charged Latinus then
War to proclaim, and those sad doors unbar:
But, shrinking from their touch, the King forsook
That deed of shame, and in blind darkness hid.
Then from the sky Saturnia, Queen of Heaven,
Glided, and thrust the doors, and turned the hinge,
And threw herself War's iron portals wide.
Unroused before, Ausonia's fury blazed.
Some start afoot: some high on horseback stir
Fiercely the dust; and all for weapons seek.
Some with rich fat their targes and their spears
Rub bright, or whet their axes on the stone.
Gaily the banners rise, the trumpets sound!
Full five fair cities forge the sword anew,
Ardea, Crustumeri, Atina strong,
Proud Tibur, and Antemnae's towered hold.
They hollow helms, and for their bucklers plait
Osiers, or beat the brazen breastplate out,
Or silver shining greaves. So ends the pride
Of sickle and share, and all the ploughman's joy!
They smelt anew their fathers' swords. Loud rings
The battle horn: the sign of war goes round.
One grasps a helm; one yokes his neighing steeds,
His buckler dons, his coat of mail with gold
Thrice folded, and girds on his trusty sword.

　　Now open Helicon, O Muses! wake
The Song of warring Kings, and all their hosts
That filled the field, what flower of men, what blaze
Of arms fair Italy put forth of yore!

For ye remember, ye can all rehearse;
Though scarce to us blown rumours faintly come!

Mezentius first in field from Tuscan shores,
Fierce scorner of the Gods, his battle ranged.
Lausus, his son, came near, than whom was none,
Turnus except, more fair, Lausus that knew
To tame the horse, and the wild beast o'erthrow.
He from Agylla leads a thousand men
In vain! Ah! worthy of a father's rule
More kind, with no Mezentius for his sire!

Next o'er the sward fair Aventinus showed
His palm-crowned chariot and triumphal steeds,
Hercules' son, and on his targe he bore
His sire's device, the Hydra's hundred snakes;
Whom in the Aventine wood, by stealthy birth,
Rhea, the Priestess, gave the coasts of light,
Mixt with a God, when, after Geryon slain,
The proud Tirynthian reached Laurentine lands,
And bathed Iberian bulls in Tuscan stream.
Darts and fierce pikes they bear, and with light swords
And Samnite javelins fight. Himself on foot,
Swathed in a lion's hide, shaggy and huge,
With white teeth horrent o'er his head, thus goes
Beneath the royal roof, in terror clad,
And on his back the robe of Hercules.

From Tibur next, that bears their brother's name,
Came the twin Argive brethren, Coras brave
And brave Catillus, who before the van
Sweep through the swarm of darts, like Centaurs twain,
Sons of the Cloud, who, plunging down the steep,
Leave Homole and Othrys' snowy slopes
With rapid course: great forests, as they go,
Yield, and the roaring branches give them way.

Nor absent he who built Praeneste's town,
Deemed ever Vulcan's son, the Prince who dwelt
With country flocks, the foundling on the hearth,
Caeculus, followed by a rustic troop
From steep Praeneste, and the Gabian fields

Of Juno, and cold Anio, and the rocks
Of Hernicans rill-dewed, Anagnia rich,
And Amasenus stream. Not all had arms,
Nor shields, nor cars; the most sling leaden balls;
Part bear in hand two spears, and on their heads
Wear caps of yellow wolf-skin, and they plant
The left foot bare; a shoe of hide untanned
Covers the right.
            But lo! Messapus there!
The Sea-God's Son, the tamer of the horse,
Whom none might slay with fire, and none with steel!
Sudden to battle his flagging folk he calls
To wars not used, and wields the sword anew.
There are Fescennium's troops, Falerian men,
Men from Soracte, the Flavinian glebe,
Ciminus' lake and hill, Capena's glens.
Singing their King, they march with even step,
As through the filmy rack when snow-bright swans
Return from pasture, pouring through long necks
Melodious notes. The stream, the Asian fen,
Give back the sound.
No mail-clad squadron seemed that thronging host;
An airy cloud it seemed of screaming birds,
Pressing to landward from the boisterous sea.

   Lo! Clausus, born of Sabines' ancient blood,
A mighty host leads on, himself a host,
From whom the Claudian clan, since Rome was shared
With Sabines, spreads through Latium. With him march
Pristine Quirites, Amiternum's troop,
Eretum's force; who dwell Velinus' vale,
Nomentum town, Mutusca's olive-groves,
Severus' mount, the crags of Tetrica,
Casperia, Foruli, Himella's stream;
Who Tiber drink or Fabaris, whom cold
Nursia sent forth, and Horta, Latin tribes,
And whom the ill-omened Allia parts in twain.
Many as the waves that roll o'er Afric seas,
When fierce Orion sets in wintry storm;
Or thick as wheat-ears burned on Hermus' plain,
Or Lycia's whitening fields, by summer's sun.
They sound their shields; earth trembles at their tread.

There Agamemnon's kith, the Trojans' foe,
Halaesus, yoked his steeds, and sped to war
A thousand tribes, who hoe the Massic slopes,
Happy with vines, and whom Auruncan sires
Sent from the hills and Sidicinian meads;
And who leave Cales, and the shallow pools
Of slow Volturnus, rude Saticulans,
And Oscan bands. Their arms are rounded clubs
Bound to a pliant thong. A leathern targe
Fends their left side; and with the dirk they close.

Nor, Oebalus, shalt thou depart our song
Unnamed, whom Telon on Sebethus' nymph
Fathered, when old he swayed the Caprean realm:
But, ill-contented with his native fields,
E'en then his son in wide dominion held
Sarrastian folk, and Sarnus' water-meads,
Rufrae, and Batulum, Celemna's tract,
And perched Abella's apple-bearing slopes.
These throw the mace, like Teutons, and their heads
Helm in the cork-tree's bark; and brazen gleam
Their moony bucklers, brazen gleams the sword.

Thee too to war the hills of Nersae sent,
Ufens, renowned and prospering in arms;
Whose race most rugged of the hard Aequian glebe
Are used to hunt the forest, and the earth
Labour all-armed: and ever 'tis their joy
To harry spoil, and live on plundered gain.

And prowest Umbro, the Marruvians' Priest,
With leaves of happy olive round his brow,
Came, sent by King Archippus. Well he knew
On viper kind and noisome water-snakes
With charm and touch to shed the dew of sleep,
And lull their wrath by craft, and ease their bite.
But not to heal the stroke of Dardan spear
His power availed: no herb of Marsian hills,
No sleepy spells were medicine for his wound.
For thee Anguitia's glen, the Fucine mere,
The pure pool waters wept for thee!

Thee too, Hippolytus' great warrior son,
Virbius, thy mother, fair Aricia, sent,

Nursed in Egerian glens, where Dian's shrine
On the wet shore lies fair and peaceable.
Fame runs, Hippolytus, by frighted steeds
Torn through his step-dame's craft, to sate with blood
His father's vengeance, visited once more
Airs of the starry heaven, to life recalled
By herbs the Healer gave, and Dian's love.
The Almighty then, incensed that mortal man
From nether shades should rise to life and light,
Hurled down to Styx with thunder Phoebus' son,
Who such an art had found and healing skill.
But him for pity Trivia in the grove
Of Nymph Egeria hid, to spend his days
Among Italian forests, with his name
To Virbius changed, unfriended, unrenowned.
And horses thence from Trivia's fane and groves
Are kept away, since on the beach they flung
Chariot and man, scared by the wild sea-beasts.
Not less his son on the wide champaign trained
The fiery steed, and sped his wheels to war.

     And in the front, full-armed, supreme in grace,
Turnus advanced, a head above the rest.
His triple-crested helmet bore atop
Chimaera, breathing forth Aetnaean flames.
More wild she grew, more fierce her bale-fire glared,
As the long battle swelled in wrath and blood.
But on his burnished scutcheon bossed in gold
Horned Io shone, now bristled, now a cow, —
A great device, — and Inachus his stream
Poured from an urn, while Argus watched the maid.
A cloud of foot and troops of shielded men
Thickly behind him swarm; Aurunca's force,
Argives, and Rutuli, Sicanians old,
Sacranian troops, Labicum's painted shields,
Who till Numicus' coast, and Tiber's glades,
And labour with the plough Rutulian slopes,
Circaeus' ridge; whom Jove at Anxur guards,
And fair Feronia in her happy glens;
Where Satura's marsh lies black, and Ufens winds
Cold through deep valleys to the engulfing sea.

Last came Camilla of the Volscian race,
Leading her chivalry abloom with brass.
A warrior maid, her woman's fingers plied
Distaff nor crate, but she was strong to bear
Battles, and running to outstrip the winds.
She might have flown o'er standing blades of corn,
Nor hurt the tender ears, or skimmed the sea,
Poised on the swelling wave, and never dipped
Her feet in ocean. All men leave the house,
They leave the field admiring; and the crowd
Of mothers, gazing on her as she goes,
In wonder gape, how royal purple folds
Her shining shoulders, how the brooch clasps up
Her hair with gold, and how she bears herself
The Lycian bow and steel-shod shepherd's staff.

Book VIII

WHEN TURNUS ON Laurentum's tower raised high
The flag of War, and trumpets hoarsely brayed;
When Turnus spurred the horse, and shook the spear,
Confusion spread: Latium in hot revolt
Rose with infuriate manhood, all one will.
Ufens, Messapus and Mezentius,
Scorner of Gods, command, and from all sides
Enforcing aid rob ploughmen from the soil.
And Venulus to Diomede's great city
Posting for help, proclaims that Trojans lodge
In Latium, and Aeneas has disbarked
His conquered Gods, and claims a destined throne;
That many join him, and in Latian land
His name spreads wide: what plans he forges there,
What fruit of war he wishes, if success
Walk in his steps, he sees himself more clear
Than King Latinus or King Turnus see!

Thus then in Latium. But the Trojan Prince
Saw all, and tossed upon a sea of cares;
And here and there dividing the swift mind,
He casts it on all sides, revolving all.
As when the light of water, flashing back
In brazen bowls the sunshine or the moon,
Flies flickering to and fro, and leaps anon
Upward and strikes the fretted ceiling's dome.

'Twas night; and sleep o'er all the wearied world
Lay deep on bird and beast, when by the stream,
Beneath the cold sky's arch, Aeneas couched,
Heart-worn by piteous war, and late indulged
The stealing peace. Before whose vision rose
Among the poplar boughs the God himself
Of that fair river, Tiber, veiled in folds
Of thin grey lawn, and with his hoary locks
Enwrapped by shading reeds; who speaking thus
Dispelled his cares:
                              "O born of Heavenly blood!
Who bearest back to us, from foemen saved,
The eternal towers of Troy! expected long
In Latin fields and on Laurentine soil!
Here lies thine Home. O fail not! Here thy Gods
Rest safe. Nor fear the strife: all storm and wrath
Of Heaven is lulled.
And deem not these the forgeries of sleep;
For thou shalt find, beneath my fringing holms,
A Sow stretched out, with thirty young new-born,
White, and the brood about her udders white;
Here shalt thou build; here rest from toil secure!
Ascanius hence, when thrice ten years return,
Alba shall build, the city of spotless name.
Not vain my words. What plan the hour demands
Learn briefly. Not for hence Arcadian men,
A race from Pallas sprung, who followed King
Evander and his banners, on these hills
Choosing their ground, a city there have built,
Named Pallanteum from their grandsire's name.
These, who with Latins wage unresting war,
Take thou in plighted faith thy camp to join.
Myself will guide thee up these banks, to stem

The stream with oars. Arise, O Goddess-born!
And with the sinking stars to Juno take
Fit prayers, and win her from her threats and ire
By humble vows. Me, after victory won,
Worship. 'Tis I whose blue and brimming wave
Lapping the bank thou see'st through fertile fields,
Tiber, Heaven's dearest stream. Here my proud home
Rises to crown towered cities yet to be!"

　The River ceased, and in the water pools
Plunged deep. Aeneas Night and Sleep desert.
Rising, he scans the sunlit orient sky,
And from the stream in hollow palms uplifts
Water, and utters thus to Heaven his voice:

　"Laurentine Nymphs, from whom the streams are born!
And thou, O Tiber, with thy sacred flood,
Receive Aeneas! Shield him now from harm!
What pool soe'er, O pitier of our dole!
May hold thy fount, where'er thy beauty springs,
My gifts, my worship I will bring thee still,
O horned River, King of Western Waves!
O stay but near! Assure thy Heavenly Word!"

　He spake, and from the fleet two galleys chose,
Equipped with oarage and with full-armed men;
When lo! a sudden wonder! Mid the trees
A Sow all white, with young ones white as she,
Lay stretched before them on the margent green.
Whom good Aeneas with her brood to thee,
To thee, Queen Juno, sacrificed and slew.
Tiber, that livelong night, his swelling stream
Smoothing in silence, stayed the refluent wave
To spread his bosom like some mild still pool,
That nought should strain the oars. They onward speed
With happy cries. The pine-wood through the stream
Glides smooth, and wondering waves, unwonted woods,
Far-dazzling shields admire and painted hulls
That swim the river. They with oars wear out
A night and day, and through long windings pass
By various trees o'ershadowed, and cut through
Green-glooming woodlands in the placid stream.

　Half-way up heaven the fiery sun had climbed,
When roofs and towers far distant they descry

Rare-strewn, which now the might of Rome hath raised
To pierce the sky, then poor Evander's home.
They turn their prows with speed, and near the town.

It chanced that day the Arcadian King in woods
Beyond his walls, to great Amphitryon's son
And all the Gods paid worship. There his son,
Pallas, and all his Chiefs and Elders poor,
Gave incense, and the altars smoked with blood.
They through the greenwood shade saw high-built ships
Gliding, with all their silent oars at rest,
And shuddering saw, and rose and left the feast:
Whom boldly Pallas to break off the rites
Forbade, and flying with drawn sword himself
Cried from a mound aloof: "O Sirs, what cause
Drove you to paths unknown? What goal is yours?
What race, what home? and bring ye peace or war?"

Then Prince Aeneas from the high-built stern
Spake, holding forth a peaceful olive branch:
"Troy's sons thou see'st, the Latins' armed foes,
Whom they have banished in dispiteous war.
We seek Evander. Bear him word that Chiefs
Of Troy are come, who crave colleaguing arms."

So great a name struck Pallas with amaze.
"Whoe'er thou art, come forth; before my sire
Speak, and within our house find harbourage."
He grasped his hand in greeting, and they stepped
Beneath the greenwood trees, and left the stream.

Then spake Aeneas to the King thus mild:
"O best of Greeks! to whom, by Fortune's will,
Pleading I bear the fillet-braided bough!
I feared not that thou wert a Greekish chief,
Arcadian, and akin to Atreus' sons.
My prowess, and the oracles of Heaven,
Our fathers' kinship, and thy worldwide fame,
Have bound me thine, and led me on content.
For Dardanus, the original Sire of Troy,
Sailed to the Teucrian land, Greek legends tell,
Electra's son: her mighty Atlas bare,
Who on his shoulders holds the heavenly spheres.
Your sire was Mercury, white Maia's son,

Conceived by her on cold Cyllene's crest.
But, if fame err not, Maia sprang from him,
That Atlas who upholds the stars of heaven.
Thus from one blood our families diverge.
I sent no legates then, nor wooed thy grace
With artful preludes; mine own head myself
Humbly I offered, coming to thy gates.
One Daunian race with warfare harsh pursues
Thyself and us. If we be routed, nought
They ween shall stay them, till they hold subdued
Hesperia, and the Low and Upper Sea.
Take troth, and give it! Hearts in battle strong,
Proud hearts are ours, and manhood tried in deed."

   Aeneas ceased. The other long perused
The speaker's face, his eyes, and all his frame.
Then answered brief: "O bravest son of Troy!
How gladly I bid thee hail! How I recall
Thy father's voice, the great Anchises' face!
I mind how Priam, seeking Salamis,
His sister's realm, to visit, made his way
To cold Arcadia's bounds. The bloom of youth
Then clad my cheeks; and gazing I admired
The Trojan Lords, yea, Priam's very self
Admired; but taller than them all went forth
Anchises. Him my heart with boyish love
Flamed high to greet, and clasp his hand in mine.
Eager I led him up to Pheneus' walls.
And he, departing, gave me Lycian shafts,
A quiver brave, a scarf inwove with gold,
And two gold bridles which my Pallas keeps.
Therefore I take your proffered hand and troth;
And when the morrow dawns, my means shall aid
And speed you forth in joy. These rites the while,
Since here ye come as friends, (these yearly rites
'Twere sinful to defer,) perform with us,
And sit familiar at the board of friends!"

   This said, he bade replace the festal cups,
And gave them grassy seats, and chief in place
Aeneas welcomed with a maple chair,
And shaggy lion's skin. Then chosen men
Vie with the altar priest, roast flesh of bulls

Bearing, and heaping crates with Ceres' gift,
The laboured grain, and serving Liber's wine.
There feasts Aeneas, with the sons of Troy,
On oxen chine and sacrificial flesh.

When hunger fled and lust of food was stayed,
Evander spake: "This ritual, this feast,
This altar so divine, no shallow faith,
Ignoring ancient deities, on us
Imposed, O Trojan guest! but we repeat
This bounden service, as from peril saved.

"See first yon hanging cliff, the scattered rocks,
The mountain home made desolate, the crags
In mighty ruin rent. A cave was there,
Deep-vaulted, vast, the lair a monster kept,
Half-human Cacus, to the sunny beam
Impenetrable; and ever with fresh blood
Its floor was warm, and on the braggart gates
Hung sad with gore wan faces of dead men.
This monster Vulcan fathered. From his mouth
Swart flames he spewed, and strode a giant mass.
But Time at last to us too praying brought
Help, and a God's approach. The avenger came,
Proud with the spoils of triform Geryon slain,
Prowest Alcides. Here the Conqueror drave
Great bulls and oxen, filling vale and stream.
But Cacus, that his madding soul might leave
No crime undared, no treachery untouched,
Four noble bulls, as many glorious kine,
Reft from their fold, and lest the tracks should show
Advancing feet, he dragged them by the tail,
And haling to his den with prints reversed,
Would hide them, screened in stone; no mark should lead
A seeker to the cave. Now from their fold
Amphitryon's son gan move his pastured herd,
And as they went his lowing oxen filled
The woods with moaning, and the hills were left
With clamorous sound. Then from that savage cave
One heifer lowed, and giving back their cries
Baffled her gaoler's hope. Anger inflamed
Alcides' gall with frenzy: arms he seized
And heavy knotted club, and running sought

The skyey mountain's top. Then fear indeed
In Cacus first we saw, and in his eyes
Confusion. Swifter than the East he scuds, .
And seeks his cavern; terror wings his feet.
Shut fast within, he burst the chains, and dropped
A monstrous stone his father's craft had hung
With links of iron, and blocked the encumbered door:
And lo! the enraged Tirynthian coming scanned
All access, and his face turned here and there,
Gnashing his teeth. Thrice all the Aventine Mount
He traversed, hot with ire; thrice tried in vain
The doors of stone; thrice wearied sank to earth.

"Above the cave a flinty spire uprose,
Sheer-cut, a wondrous height, fit nesting-place
For fearsome fowls! which as it leaned aslant
Above the leftward river, from the right
With counter push he loosened, and unshook
From its deep roots, and sudden hurled it down.
Therewith the wide sky thunders, and the banks
Leap far apart; the frightened stream flows back.
But bare and roofless lies the Tyrant's hall;
The dark deep cave falls open; as if Earth,
At some great shock deep yawning, should unbar
The infernal gates, and the pale realms disclose,
Hated by Gods, and show the unfounded gulf,
And ghosts that shudder as the day flows in.
On Cacus, thus by sudden light surprised,
Immured in rock, and howling sounds uncouth,
Alcides fell, and summoned all his arms,
And smote him hard with boughs and massy stones.
But he (for other refuge none remains,)
Spews from his mouth a wondrous blinding smoke,
And wraps the house in darkness, and the eyes
Bereaves of sight, and through the cavern rolls
A midnight cloud of smoke with mingled fire.
Alcides bore not that, and plunging leapt
Right through the fire, where vapour o'er the cave
Poured thickest, and the smoky tide rose high;
And Cacus, spitting ineffectual flames,
He gripped, and wrenched, and throttled in his grasp
His strangled eyes, and gullet dried of blood.

"The doors are burst; the house of gloom laid bare.
Exposed to heaven are shown the stolen kine,
The theft forsworn, and by its feet the corpse
Drawn forth disfigured. None can gaze his fill
On face and dreadful eyes of that half-beast,
His bristly chest, his throat's extinguished fire.

"Thence came this worship; and a younger race
Have kept the day. Potitius taught it first,
And that Prinarian House who guard the rites
Of Hercules. This altar, built by him,
Greatest by name, our greatest aye shall be.
O come then, Sirs, such glories to extol,
Reach out the cup, and bind your hair with green,
Call on our common God, and pour the wine!"

He ceased. His hair the twi-hued poplar's shade,
Herculean umbrage, wreathed with hanging leaves.
He grasped the holy bowl. Then all with joy,
Invoking Heaven, their quick libations shed.

Nearer the welkin's rim sank Evening's star:
And now Potitius led the Priests in train,
Girt round with ritual skins, and bearing fire.
They bring fresh bounteous courses, and the feast
Renewing with full plates the altars heap.
Then round the burning shrines the Salii stand
Singing, their temples bound with poplar sprays;
One choir of young, and one of old, who chant
The Praise of Hercules; how first he seized
His step-dame's horrors, crushing the twain snakes;
And how in war he laid great cities flat,
Troy and Oechalia; how by Juno's spite,
A thousand labours in Eurystheus' halls
He bore. "Thou slay'st Hylaeus, Unsubdued!
And Pholus, cloud-begotten, double-shaped,
The Cretan Dread, and Nemea's monstrous Lion!
The Stygian pools, the bloody Guard of Hell,
Couched on his half-gnawed bones, trembled at thee.
No shape dismayed thee, not Typhoeus' self,
Towering all-armed; around thee not unmanned
The Snake of Lerna reared her swarm of heads.

Hail, Jove's own son! O Glory new to Heaven!
Us and thy rites attend with prospering feet!"

Such praise they hymn, and add the crowning lay
Of Cacus' cave, and Cacus breathing fire;
The woodlands ring with din, the hills rebound.

Such holy rites performed, all citywards
Returned. And as he walked the age-worn King
Beside him kept Aeneas and his son,
Cheering the way with talk. And all around
Aeneas turns his quick admiring eyes,
Charmed by the scenes, and gladly asks of each,
And hears old memories of bygone men.

Then spake the King who built the Roman Keep:
"Fauns of the soil and Nymphs these woodlands dwelt,
And men whose kind were born from trunks and trees.
Nor law nor arts had they: to yoke the bull
They knew not, nor to store or save their gains.
The branches fed them, and rough hunter's fare.
Then Saturn first from high Olympus came,
Fleeing Jove's arms, an exile from his realm;
Who fused the unruly mountain-scattered clan,
And gave them laws, and chose them for a name
Latium, since latent he lay safe with them.
Golden that Age was named, while he was King,
In such calm peace he ruled; till slowly dawned
A worse, a tarnished age, madness of war,
And greed of gain. Then came the Ausonian host,
Sicanian tribes, and Saturn's land full oft
Laid down her name. Kings then and Thybris reigned,
Thybris, the Giant, from whom in after time
We men of Italy called Tiber's stream,
And Albula then lost its true old name.
Forced from my land, I roamed the utmost sea;
Till sovran Fortune and avoidless Fate
Here placed me, by my mother's warnings urged
Carmentis, and by Phoebus' Heavenly voice."

So said, he pacing onward shows the Shrine,
And that Carmental Gate the Romans name,
Honouring the Nymph Carmentis, who long since

Forboded first Aeneas' lofty line,
And Pallanteum's pride prophetic sang.
The Grove he shows, where Romulus restored
Asylum wide, the cold Lupercal's vault,
Called from Arcadian Pan's Lycaean name.
Then Argiletum's Glen, the holy place,
Bears witness, while he tells of Argus' death.
Thence to Tarpeia's Capitolian seat,
Now all of gold, then bushed with shaggy thorn.
E'en then the trembling hinds in reverence held
That place of fear, and shrank from rock and tree.

   "This Grove," he said, "this leaf-crowned Hill, some God,
Some unknown God inhabits. Jove himself
The Arcadians deem they saw, when oft he shook
His glooming Aegis, and compelled the clouds.
And here two towns thou see'st and walls o'erthrown,
Relics and memories of the men of old,
This fortress Janus built, and Saturn that;
Saturnia and Janiculum their names."

   Thus interchanging talk, they neared the roof
Of that poor King, and heard the cattle low
Mid Rome's proud Forum and Carinae's pomp.
His dwelling reached: "These doors the Conqueror passed,
Alcides. Him this royal house received.
Thou too, O Guest! scorn riches, and put on
A God's great heart, not rough to poverty!"
He said, and under his low-vaulted roof
The tall Prince led, and left him to repose
On leaf-strewn bed and skins of Lybian bear.

   Night falls, and folds o'er earth her sable wings;
When Venus, with no idle mother's fear,
Moved by Laurentine threats and stern revolt,
To Vulcan turning in their golden bower,
Speaks, and her words inspire with Heavenly love:

   "While Argive Kings laid waste the fated towers
Of Troy, fore-doomed to fall by hostile fires,
No help for those in woe, no arms I begged
Of thy rich art, sweet husband, willing not
Thee or thy toil to exercise in vain;
Though much I owed to Priam's sons, and wept

Aeneas' hardships oft; who now is lodged
By Jove's commandment on Rutulian shores.
Yet craving arms, a mother for her son,
I pray my cherished God. Thee Nereus' child,
Thee with her tears Tithonus' wife could bend!
See the clans gather! See the gated towns
Sharpen the sword to murder me and mine!"

    She ceased; and softly in her snowy arms
Caressed him faltering: and anon he caught
The wonted flame: the dear familiar heat
Through bone and marrow shot, as when at whiles
The thunder flashes from a fiery rift,
And shoots in light across the storm-dark sky.
She in her arts rejoiced, and knew her charm.
Then spake the captive of immortal love:

    "Why are thy pleas far sought? Where lags thy faith
In me, my Goddess? Had such care been thine,
We might have armed thy Trojans even then.
Doom nor the Almighty had forbidden Troy
To stand, and Priam live ten further years.
Now if thine heart be set on war, whate'er
Mine art can compass, all that iron may found,
Or liquid ore's alloy, with utmost might
Of fire and wind— O ask no more! O cease
To doubt thy strength!"

                  He spoke, and granted her
The wished embrace, and on her bosom sank,
To steep his body in reposeful sleep.

    But on the waning middle of the night,
When rest had purged his sleep, while she who stays
A slender life by distaff and the loom
First wakes the sleeping ashes, to her toil
Adding the night, and sets her maids to spin
By firelight, so that she may keep unstained
Her husband's bed, and rear her little sons:
Even so, with not more sloth, the Lord of Fire
From his soft bed rose up to work the forge.

    An isle by Lipare's Aeolian rock
Lies off Sicania, steep with smoking crags,
Whereunder Aetna's vaulted smithy roars

With Cyclops' anvils, and the groaning forge
Rings with stout blows, and Chalybean ore
Hisses, and fire within the furnace pants.
Vulcan's that House; the land Vulcania named:
Whereto from Heaven came down the Lord of Fire.

    Cyclops in that vast cave were forging steel,
Bare-limbed Pyracmon, Brontes, Steropes;
Within whose hands a thunderbolt half-made
Lay, such as oft on earth from the wide heaven
The Father hurls; but half remained unwrought.
Three rays of frozen rain, of vapour three,
Three of red fire they made and winged wind.
Now awful flashes in their work they weave,
Thunder and Dread and Wrath's pursuing flame.
A chariot's flying wheels elsewhere they forge,
Wherewith the War-God wakens towns and men,
And the dread aegis, angry Pallas' arm,
With serpent scales and gold; and burnish bright
The twisted snakes and on her Heavenly breast
The Gorgon's severed Head with rolling eyes.

    "Away," he cries, "with all your toils begun!
Cyclops of Aetna, list! A Hero's arms
Must now be made. Use now your nimble hands,
Your strength, your master skill. Cast off delay!"
No more he spake; but they with speed fell to,
And fairly shared the task. In rivers flow
Brass and gold ore, and in the furnace vast
The deadly steel is molten. One huge shield,
To meet all Latin bolts, they forge, and weld
Sevenfold with orb in orb. Some take and give
Air in the windy bellows: others dip
The hissing brass in water. All the vault
Groans loud with beaten anvils. One by one
With mighty rhythmic strokes they lift their arms,
And with tenacious tongs turn round the mass.

    Thus in Aeolia sped the Lemnian Sire:
When the boon light, and birds in his low eaves
Singing their morning songs awoke the King.
The old man rose, and clad himself, and bound
His feet in Tyrrhene sandals, and to side

And shoulders girt his Tegeaean brand,
And o'er his left flung back a panther's hide.
Two dogs before him from the threshold walked,
Guarding their master's steps. He, minding well
Their converse and a hero's plighted word,
His guest's own lodging sought. Aeneas too
At dawn was stirring. Pallas went with one;
Achates with the other. They being met
Clasp hands, and, seated in the central court,
Unhindered intercourse at last enjoy.
Then first the King:

"O prowest Lord of Trojans! While thou livest,
Not vanquished will I own the State of Troy!
But though our name be great, our warlike strength
Is feeble. Here the Tuscan river hems:
Here the Rutulian clashes on our wall.
Yet mighty peoples I will join with thee,
Troops of a wealthy State, as saving chance
Reveals a way. For Fate hath called thee hither.

"There stands a town not far, the hoary stones
Of old Agylla, where on Tuscan hills
Lydians, a war-famed race, made once their home.
Long years they flourished, till a tyrant Lord,
Mezentius, crushed them with barbaric arms.
Why tell his heinous acts, his deeds of blood? —
God keep the like for him and all his tribe! —
Live bodies joined to corpses he would link
In torture, hand to hand, and face to face;
And thus embracing kill them with the drench
Of foul corruption in long throes of death.
At last the wearied people thronged in arms
Round raving King and Palace, slew his guards,
And stormed the roof with fire. He mid the broil
Escaped, and flying to Rutulian bounds
Found succour in the help of Turnus' arms.
Hence all Etruria in just ire hath risen,
With instant war demanding the doomed King.

"These hosts, O Prince, to thy command I add.
For all the beach was loud with thronging ships,
Advance was ordered; when a hoar old Seer,

Foreboding, checked them: 'O Maeonia's pride!
O flower of ancient valour! whom just wrath,
Against Mezentius blazing, bears to war!
By no Italian may such men be ruled:
Choose foreign leaders!' Then the Etruscan host
Pitched here, astounded by that voice from Heaven.

"Tarchon himself hath sent me embassies,
With crown and sceptre, proffering the Throne,
If I will come and take the Tyrrhene power.
But the slow frost of Age, my life outworn
And strength past prowess, grudges me such sway.
My son I would have urged, but half his blood
Flows Sabine from his mother. Thou, whom Fate
Blesses in years and race, Thou, Heaven's own choice,
Advance, brave Chief of Troy and Italy!
Yon Pallas, too, our comfort and our hope,
Shall join thee: let him learn, well-schooled by thee,
War's heavy pains to bear; to mark thy deeds,
And from his boyish years admire thee well.
Two hundred Horse, the flower of Arcady,
I give him: he will give the like to thee."

He scarce had said, and still with downcast eyes
Anchises' son and leal Achates stood,
And, sad at heart, on many a danger mused,
When Venus sent a sign in open sky.
A sudden flash with thunder from above
Shot wildly ruining downward, and the clang
Of Tyrrhene trumpets hurtled through the air.
Upward they gaze. Again, again the crash
Peals, and they see in cloudless air serene
Arms gleaming red through haze, and ringing loud.
The rest stood spell-bound; but the Trojan Prince,
Hearing that sound, his mother's promise heard.

"Ask not, O friend!" he said, "O ask not whither
These portents lead! 'Tis I whom Heaven demands!
This Sign my Goddess Mother vowed to send
If war beset, and bring me through the air
Vulcanian arms for aid!
Oh! Death and Sorrow round Laurentines close!
Turnus, revenge is mine! What shields, what helms

Shall Tiber roll, what bodies of the brave!
Now let them cry for War, and break their bond!"

He spoke, and rose; and first the sleeping fire
Woke on Herculean shrines, approaching glad
The small House-Gods he worshipped yestere'en;
And by Evander's side the men of Troy
Slay chosen ewes together. But from thence
To ships and men repairing, from their tale
He chooses out, to take the field with him,
Their bravest hearts. The others down the stream
Float idly onward with the flowing wave,
To tell Ascanius how his father fares.
Then to each Trojan bound for Tuscan land
A steed is given; and for their Prince led forth
One housed in lion's skin with fair gold claws.

Fast through the little town blown rumours fly
That Horse ride hot to join the Tyrrhene King:
And mothers pray and pray, and fear on peril
Treads close, and larger looms the shape of War.

Evander then his parting son embraced,
Held fast his hand, and, filled with tears, thus spake:
"O would God bring me back the years gone by!
As once I was, when by Praeneste's wall
I strewed the van, victorious burned their shields,
And with this hand King Erulus sent down
To Orcus, though Feronia at his birth
Gave him three lives, O horror! triple arms!
Thrice to be lain in death! whom yet this hand
Robbed of all lives, and all his arms stript off!
Then never from thy sweet embrace, O Son!
Would I be torn; ne'er had Mezentius dealt
Within my bounds so many a savage death,
Widowing the city of so many a man.
But Oh! ye Gods! O ruling Lord of Heaven!
Pity, great Jove, I pray, the Arcadian King,
And hear a father's prayers. If your decree
Keep Pallas safe for me, and if I live
To see, to meet him yet; for life I pray,
And any pain my patience can endure.
But if, O Fate! thou threatenest some great woe,

Now, let me now break off life's torturing hour,
While pain delays, while hope is trembling still,
While thou, dear boy, my last and lone delight,
Stay'st in mine arms, ere sorrow wound mine ear!"
Such parting words the father uttered forth,
While servants bore him swooning to his house.

And now the Horse had passed the open gates,
Aeneas and Achates in the van,
Then other Lords of Troy; and in mid troop
With blazoned arms and doublet Pallas shone:
As when the Day Star, washed in Ocean's wave,
Whom Venus loves above all other stars,
Lifts his pure head, and clears the gloomy sky.
Then fearful mothers, on the walls agaze,
Follow the dusty cloud and gleaming troops.
Right onward to their goal through briers they march,
With clang of arms, close-ranked. The crumbling plain
Reels with the thunder of their hurrying hoofs.

A grove there is by Caere's icy brook,
Hallowed by old religion, where all round
Fir-glooming hills embosom the green wood.
'Tis said, the old Pelasgians, who of yore
Peopled that tract, held sacred grove and day
To God Silvanus of the field and fold.
Not far from here Tyrrhenian Tarchon lay,
Safe-camped; and from the hill-top one might see
Wide spreading o'er the fields his legioned host.
And here Aeneas and his warrior band
Way-worn arrived, and rested steeds and men.

Now Venus through the clouds, divinely bright,
Brought down her Gift; and in a sunken dale
Descried her son by the cold stream apart:
To whom appearing sudden thus she spake:
"Behold the promised gifts my lord hath wrought!
Doubt not, my son, but soon defiance hurl
On proud Laurentines and on Turnus bold!"

She spake, and sought her son's embrace, and down
Before an oak-tree laid the radiant arms.
He, gazing on those gifts of Heavenly grace,
Eyes each insatiate, and admiring turns

In hands and arms the dreadful crested helm,
Vomiting flame, the doom-delivering sword,
The hauberk stiff with brass, blood-red, immense,
Like the broad splendour of some purple cloud
Burning with sun-fire, and the polished greaves
Of gold and wrought electrum, and the spear,
And all the Shield's inutterable frame.

　　There Roman triumphs, great Italian deeds
The Fire God made, a Prophet not unlearned
Nor blind to coming ages, all the line
Born from Ascanius, and the fields they fought.
There too he made, in Mavors' greenwood den,
The Mother Wolf, and round her udders hung
Twin boys, who played, and licked her without fear.
She bent her lissom neck, and each in turn
Caressing formed their bodies with her tongue.

　　Not far was Rome, and Sabine women rapt
From crowded seats amidst the Circus Games,
And War fast springing on that iron brood,
On Tatius, and the sons of Romulus.
Then, laying feuds aside, the two same Kings
Before Jove's altar stood, and held the bowl,
And with a sow's blood sealed their plighted peace.
Hard by was Mettus, by the parting teams
Sundered — (ah! Alban, hadst thou kept thy word!) —
And Tullus, harrying the false traitor's flesh
Through briers and bushes drenched with bloody dew.
Porsenna too bade take the outcast back,
Tarquin, and held the city sore in siege.
Aeneas' sons for freedom charged the steel;
While him you saw like one who fumes and threats,
As Cocles rent the bridge, and Cloelia brake
Her bonds, and swam the stream.
　　　　　　　　　　　　　　Before Jove's fane
Manlius stood guard, on steep Tarpeia's rock,
And held the Capitol, where recent straw
Thatched Romulus' rude hut. And here a goose,
Fluttering all silver through a gilded porch,
Proclaimed the coming Gauls. The Gauls were come
Through bushes, screened by darkness and the boon
Of obscure Night, to gain the Capitol,

Gold-haired, gold-vestured; and their kirtles branched
Shine brightly, and their milk-white necks are twined
With gold: in each right hand two Alpine spears
Flash, and long targes all their body fend.

And here he graved the dancing Salii,
And Pan's nude Priests, the fleecy crests, the shields
That fell from heaven, the Matrons' sacred pomp
In cushioned coaches.
                            And far off he adds
Tartarean seats, the lofty Gates of Dis,
The dooms of guilt; thee hanging, Catiline,
On dizzy steep, by Furies' forms appalled;
The pure aloof, in Cato's ruling care.

Round these the semblance of the billowy sea
Spread golden, but the dark waves foamed with white;
And silver bright the circling dolphins swept
The water with their tails, and cut the surge.

And in the centre showed the brazen fleets,
The Actian fight, where all Leucate seethed
With battle, and the waves were glinting gold.
Here on the stern Augustus Caesar stands
Leading to war, with Senate and with State,
And all his Gods; and round his happy brow
Flames shoot, and brightly dawns his fathers' star.

Elsewhere Agrippa, helped by winds and Gods,
On leads his line; and the proud battle-mark,
The beaked sea-crown, is shining on his front.
Here Antony, with strange barbaric arms
From Red Sea coast and nations of the Dawn
Brings Egypt, Bactra, and the utmost East,
Triumphing, and the Egyptian bride, his shame.
On, on they press together. All the brine
By oars and trident beaks is rent in foam.
On to deep sea, as though the Cyclad Isles
Were swimming loose, or mount were dashed on mount,
A mass so vast they drive of towered ships.
Now flying bolts are rained and fiery tow:
The fields of Neptune redden with strange blood.

Her troops the Queen with native timbrel calls;
Nor looks back yet on those twain snakes behind.
Howling Anubis, all her monstrous Gods,
On Neptune, Venus, and Minerva turn
Their weapons; in mid fray an iron Mars
Storms, and aloft the boding Terrors sit,
And Discord stalks in glee with vesture rent
Before Bellona and her bloody scourge.
Actian Apollo saw, and stretched his bow
From Heaven: awe-struck all Araby and Ind,
All Egypt, all Sabaea, turned and fled.

She seems to call the winds; she sets the sails:
Now, now she slacks the sheet! Amidst the slain
The Fire God made her, white with coming death,
Scudding on wave and wind; and opposite
Great Nile in sorrow, throwing wide his folds,
Calling the vanquished to his dark-blue lap
And streams of refuge.
                              But in Rome there rides
Caesar in threefold triumph, and performs
To Gods Italian his immortal vow,
Starring the city with three hundred shrines.
Joy, Games, and plaudits fill the roaring streets;
Altars in every fane, and matron choirs,
And steers before each altar sacrificed.

He, seated in bright Phoebus' snowy porch,
Reviews the nations' spoils, and hangs them up
On those proud doors. Long move the vanquished tribes,
In dress and arms diverse, diverse in speech.
Nomads, and ungirt Africans he graved,
Gelonian archers, Carians, Leleges,
Euphrates' sobered stream, the Morini,
Outmost of men, the Dahae unsubdued,
Araxes' unbridged wave, and hornèd Rhine.

He thus admires the Shield, his Mother's gift,
And, pleased with shadows of the hidden time,
Shoulders the destined glories of his sons.

Book IX

WHILE THUS IT fell in regions far remote,
Saturnia from the sky sent Iris down
To gallant Turnus. In Pilumnus' grove,
His father's hallowed vale, was Turnus found;
To whom rose-mouthed the child of Thaumas spake:

"Lo! what no God dare promise to thy wish,
Turnus, unsought the rolling day brings near!
Aeneas, from his town and vessels gone,
Evander seeks and Palatinum's crown.
Nay, to far towns of Corythus advanced,
He arms the Lydian hinds. Why falterest thou?
Now, now 'tis time to summon horse and car.
Break off delay, and seize the startled camp!"

She said, and, soaring high on level wings,
Fled o'er the clouds athwart her far-flung Bow.
Then Turnus knew her, and to heaven both palms
Uplifting, thus pursued her as she fled;

"Iris, O beauty of Heaven! Who brought thee down
Earthward to me? What sudden sheen of light
Breaks? for the skies are parted, and I see
Heaven's wandering stars! Such signs, whoe'er thou art
Calling to arms, I follow!" And he drew
Fresh water from the stream, and long in prayer,
Loaded the air with vows.

      Now all the host
Moved on the plains the pageant of their war,
Their shining steeds, and broidered gold array.
Messapus led the van, and Tyrrheus' sons
Rallied the rear; and in mid troop full-armed
Towering a head o'er all, great Turnus rode.
So moves broad Ganges with his seven calm streams
In silence rising, or the prospering flood
When refluent Nile sinks back within his bed.

A sudden cloud of dust the Trojans mark
Gather in gloom, and darken o'er the plain;

And from the counter mound Caicus cries;
"What misty globe rolls hither? Ho, to arms!
Bring swords, bring missiles! Burghers, climb the walls!
The foe is here!" And, with a load uproar,
They, plunging through each gate, the ramparts fill:
For so war-wise Aeneas, when he left,
Had taught them, if some chance should fall the while,
Not to array their line, nor trust the field,
But keep the safe-trenched rampart of the camp.
They then, though shame and wrath to battle point,
Yet close their gates, and, as he bade, remain
Armed in the hollow towers.
                              Now Turnus flew
Before his tardy files, and sudden came
With twenty chosen horsemen on the town,
Riding a dappled Thracian, and red plumes
Waved o'er his golden casque. "Ho, lads!" cries he,
"Who will be first with me upon the foe?
Look!" And he hurled a spear, preluding war,
And towering crossed the ground. They, with dire shouts
And clamour, pressed behind him, in amaze
At the dull hearts of Trojans, that they shrank
From the fair field, nor clashed in arms like men,
But hugged the camp. He, riding to and fro
Tempestuous, seeks approach where way is none.
As when a wolf at midnight prowling round
Some crowded sheep-fold in the wind and rain,
Yelps at the pens: beneath their mothers lambs
Bleat scathless; but the wild and angry beast
Rages at those unreached, to madness worn
By famine, and his jaws long dried of blood.
So burns the fierce Rutulian, as he eyes
Rampart and camp, and passion fires his frame;
How can he try approach? and how shake out
The fenced-in Trojans? On the ships he falls,
Which, hedged with earth-works and the flowing stream,
Lay hidden by the camp, and calls for fire
From his bold troops, and, flaming, fills his hand
With fiery pine. Then, by his presence urged,
All fall to work, and arm themselves with brands,
Spoiling the hearths: a pitchy glare is shed
From smoking torches, and the God of Fire

Flings to the stars on high the mingled sparks.

Say, Muse, what God such conflagration turned,
Who drove from Trojan ships that cruel fire?
Hoar the tale's faith, but ever fresh its fame.

What time Aeneas first on Ida's hills
Would shape his ships to sail the ocean wave,
The Gods' own Mother, Berecynthia, thus
Great Jove addressed; "Son, grant me what I ask,
Thy mother dear, who lulled the Olympian feud!
My forest pines long-loved, my grove that crowned
The mountain top, my grove of sacrifice,
Glooming with firs and maples, these I gave
The Dardan Prince, when he had need of ships,
Gladly; but now dread racks me and distress.
O free my fear, and let a mother's prayers
Keep them unshattered still by sea or gale!
Let it avail our mountains gave them birth!"
To whom her Son, who guides the circling stars:

"What fate, O Mother, dost thou crave for these?
Shall vessels wrought by mortal hands obtain
The immortal lot? Aeneas safely pass
Through straits unsafe? What God hath power so large?
Yet when their rest is gained, when once they hold
Ausonian ports, whichever scape the waves,
And to Laurentum bear the Dardan Chief,
Stripped from their mortal form, shall skim the main
Sea-Goddesses like Doto, Nereus' child,
Or Galatea breasting the white foam."
He said; and by his Stygian brother's stream
And black bituminous banks he sware the oath;
And, nodding, shook Olympus with his nod.

The promised day had come, and Fate had filled
The destined hour, when Turnus' insult warned
The Mother to defend her ships from fire.
Strange gleams shone forth; a splendour from the Dawn
Streamed o'er the sky, and Ida's choirs were seen.
Then, falling through the void, an awful Voice
Filled all the Trojan and Rutulian lines.

"Stir not to save my ships, O Men of Troy!
Arm not your hands. Turnus shall burn the sea
Before these holy pines. Go, Ocean Nymphs!
Go free; the Mother bids!" And straight each bark
Broke from her cable, and with plunging bows
Dipped like a dolphin in the water deeps.
Again they rise, O wonderful! O strange!
As many maiden forms that swim the sea,
As prows erewhile stood brazen by the shore.
Awe seized the Rutuli: Messapus' self
Quailed mid his startled steeds, and Tiber's stream
Paused, moaning hoarse, and from the sea drew back.

But gallant Turnus shrank not; nay, he fired
Their souls, rebuked their terror. "Lo! these signs
Are aimed at Trojans, whom high Jove himself
Robs of their wonted help! Our blades, our flames
They wait not! Now no path is theirs by sea;
No hope of flight, from half the world debarred,
While all the land is ours, such countless tribes
Bear arms in Italy. Me nothing daunt
These Phrygian boasts and oracles of Doom.
Enough for Fate and Venus that they touched
Ausonia's fields. Fate calls not less on me
That cursed race to uproot who stole my bride!
Not Atreus' sons alone such sorrows feel;
Not Argos only may upraise the sword!
One fall may serve? Nay, but one crime had served,
Had they abhorred thenceforth all womankind!
Who now from these poor hindrances of death,
This intervening wall, this trench's check,
Pluck heart. Yet saw they not the walls of Troy,
Which Neptune's hands had built, subside in flame?
But ye, my chosen! who will breach the wall,
And fall with me upon their quaking camp?
I need no Vulcan's arms, no thousand ships
To deal with Trojans! Let all Tuscany
Befriend them! 'Tis no dark and nerveless theft
Of Pallas' Sign, with castle sentries slain,
These need to fear: no Horse shall bury us!

Clear in broad day we will to fire their wall!
No Greeks, no raw Pelasgians, for ten years
Baffled by Hector, shall they deem my force!
Now, since day's best is o'er, for what remains,
Yourselves refresh; and, happy in success,
Hope, Heroes! hope for battle in procinct!"

Messapus now hath charge to fence the Gates
With pickets, and surround the camp with fires.
Twice seven Rutulian warriors hold the wall,
Their prime; each followed by an hundred men
Red-plumed, and bright with gold. These to and fro
Run, changing guard; or stretched along the grass,
Revel in wine, and tilt the brazen bowl.
The fires shine round. In games the sentries pass
The wakeful night.

Such view the Trojans from their rampart see,
Guarding the height. Alarmed, they try the Gates,
And join the towers with bridges, and bring up
Missiles, by Mnestheus and Serestus urged,
Whom Prince Aeneas charged, should peril call,
To rule the forces and command the day.
And all the legion, watching on the walls,
The danger share, and guard each post by turns.

Ward of the Gate was Nisus, bold in arms,
Hyrtacus' son, whom huntress Ida sent
To join Aeneas, quick with spear and bow;
And by his side Euryalus, than whom
No fairer Trojan donned the arms of Troy.
Youth bloomed unshorn upon his boyish cheek.

These, one in love, one in the battle-rush,
Together too were holding then the Gate,
When Nisus spake: "Does God thus fire the soul?
Or is his own wild craving each man's God?
For strife, for some high venture, long my spirit
Stirs in my breast, and chafes at stagnant calm.
Thou see'st how confident Rutulians keep!
Their lights gleams rare: unbent by sleep and wine,
They lie prostrated: all is still. Now learn
What doubt, what purpose, in my spirit soars!
All, high and low, demand Aeneas here,

And call for messengers to bear him word.
If what I ask they grant thee, — for to me
Fame is enough, — I think by yonder knoll
To find a path toward Pallanteum's wall."

　　Great love of glory dazed Euryalus,
While to his fiery friend he thus replied:
"Me dost thou ban from sharing deeds so high?
And shall I send thee to such straits alone?
Not thus my war-worn sire Opheltes taught,
Who in Troy's stress and terror of the Greek
Reared me; nor thus I bore myself with thee,
Following the great Aeneas and his doom.
A soul is here that scorns the light, and deems
Well-bought with life that glory thou dost aim!"

　　Then Nisus; "No such fear of thee was mine,
Nor could not be; so Jove, or whoso scans
These deeds with love, restore me conqueror!
But if, — as oft in such a strait thou seest, —
If me some chance, some God should overthrow,
May'st thou survive; thine age is worthier life.
May there be one in common earth to lay
My ransomed corpse; or, should Fate hinder that,
Pay my last dues, and raise an empty tomb.
Nor let me cause thy mother pain so deep,
She who alone of many mothers dared
Cleave to her son, and scorn Acesta's walls."

　　But he: "In vain thou weavest empty pleas:
My purpose fails not. Let us haste!" He cries,
And wakes the watch, who coming serve their turn;
While he and Nisus with him leave their post,
And hie to find the Prince.

　　　　　　　　　　　Now o'er the earth
All other living things in slumber loosed
The yoke of care, and all their pain forgot;
When the prime leaders and the flower of Troy
In council pondered on the public strait;
What course to find, what envoy to their Prince.
They, leaning on their lances, targe in hand,
Stand in mid camp. Euryalus and Nisus
Crave entrance both in haste, on matters high,

Well worth delay! Then first the impatient pair
Iulus welcomed, and bade Nisus speak.
Then he: "O fairly hear us, Men of Troy!
Nor let our offer by our years be judged!
Rutulia's sons, unbent by sleep and wine,
Lie silent. We ourselves have spied a way,
A passage by the gateway next the sea.
Their fires burn out: the leaden smoke goes up.
Grant us to use this chance, and let us seek
Aeneas and high Pallanteum's wall.
Soon will you see us here from heaps of dead
Return with spoil: nor can we miss our way,
In hunting oft down the dim dales we marked
The city's face, and learned the river's course."

Then many-yeared Aletes, ripe of soul:
"Gods of our Fathers, ever guarding Troy!
Our race not wholly you would ruin yet,
Such gallant youths you bring, and hearts so true!"
He spake, and clasped them both, by hand and neck,
Dewing his cheeks with tears. "What guerdon meet
For such deserts, O heroes! shall I deem
Fit recompense? Your first, your fairest meed
God and your hearts shall give; the rest anon
Aeneas shall repay; Iulus too
Shall not forget such service all his days."

"Yea!" cried Iulus, "I, whose sire's return
Is all my weal! by our great Guardian Gods,
Our Fathers' Spirit, and hoar Vesta's shrine!
Nisus, I pray you, on your knees I lay
My hopes, my fortune, O recall, give back
To sight my father, and all grief is gone!
Two beakers will I give thee, which my sire
Took when Arisbe fell, of silver, bossed,
Two tripods, two gold talents, and a bowl
Of ancient days, Sidonian Dido's gift.
If ours it be to conquer Italy,
To grasp the sceptre, and divide the spoil,—
Thou saw'st his horse, his arms, when Turnus passed
All gold,—that horse, his shield and crimson crest
Henceforth I keep, O Nisus! for thy meed.
Yea too, my sire will give twelve mothers fair,

Twelve captured men, with all their harness on,
And eke Latinus' sovran own domain.
Thee, whom mine age with nearer course pursues,
O princely boy! I take thee to my heart,
And greet thee as my friend in every chance.
No quest of glory shall be mine in peace,
In war, without thee: thou in deed, in word,
Shall have my chiefest trust!"

                                   To whom replied
Euryalus: "No day shall prove me false
To such high ventures, if my fate be kind,
Nor adverse fall. But thee, all gifts above,
One boon I pray. Of Priam's ancient race
My mother came, whom neither Troy, nor walls
Of King Acestes kept from following me.
Her blind to aught of danger now I leave
Without farewell (Night and thine hand avouch!)
Because I cannot brook a parent's tears.
O ease her need, and help her loneliness!
Thus let me hope in thee, and I shall go
Bolder to fate."

                          Heart-struck, the Dardans wept;
But more than all Iulus, as his soul
Mirrored that glimpse of the dear filial bond.
Then thus he spake;
"I promise all thy great assay deserves.
Thy mother shall be mine, and only lack
Creusa's name: great honour shall be hers
For such a birth. I swear, whate'er ensue,
By this mine head, by which my father sware,
All that I promise thee returned in joy
Shall wait unchanged thy mother and thy kin."

   With tears he spake; and from his shoulder took
The golden brand, Lycaon's Gnossian art
Had made, and fitted to the ivory sheath.
Mnestheus to Nisus gave a lion's fell;
And leal Aletes gave him casque for casque.
All armed they march; whom as they go each band
Of chieftains young and old, with farewell vows,
Speed to the gate. And fair Iulus sent,
With manly thought and soul above his years,

His father many a message; but the winds
Dispersed and gave them to the clouds untold.

They pass the fosse, and through Night's shadow seek
The perilous camp; yet first for many bear
Death. O'er the herbage strewn in sleep and wine
Bodies they see, and chariot poles upturned,
Men between reins and wheels, and by their side
Wine-cups and arms. Then Nisus spoke the first:

"Bold be the hand, O friend! Achievement calls!
Here lies our path. Thou, lest some arm be raised
Behind our backs, keep watch and ward afar.
Here I will waste, and make thee road enough!"

He spake, and hushed; and therewith turned his blade
On haughty Rhamnes, who on rugs heaped high
Lay, and from all his breast was breathing sleep;
A Prince, and eke Prince Turnus' dearest Mage, —
Though by no magic he might ward his bane!
Three slaves he slew, that heedless by their arms
Lay nigh, with Remus' charioteer and squire,
Beneath their steeds: their drooping necks he cut,
Severed their master's head, and left the trunk
Bubbling with warm black blood that soaked the ground,
And soaked the couch. Then Lamyrus and Lamus
Fell, with Serranus, who that night played late,
Fair boy! and lay subdued in every limb
By the strong God; ah, happy! had he spent
All night in play, and seen the morning light!
A famished lion thus, with hunger mad,
Storms through full sheep-folds, and with bloody teeth
Mangles the woolly flock all dumb with fear.

Nor less Euryalus, on fire with rage,
Slew many a nameless foe, and laid in death
Fadus, Herbesus, Abaris surprised,
And Rhoetus, who, awake, and seeing all,
Yet hid in fear behind a lofty jar,
And as he rose, the blade was buried deep
Straight in his breast, and full of death withdrawn.
He, vomiting the purple life, outpours
Wine mixt with blood. The raider fierce sped on:
He reached Messapus' troops; he saw the fire

Fade into ash; he saw the tethered steeds
Cropping the grass; when Nisus (for he marked
The o'erpowering lust of blood,) cried thus in brief:

"Here let us pause: unfriendly Dawn is near.
Revenge is glutted: we have pierced the foe!"
Behind they leave much armour silver wrought,
Fair bowls and carpets. But Euryalus
His golden-studded belt from Rhamnes strips;
A gift which once rich Caedicus bestowed
On Remulus, to pledge his absent friend,
Who dying to his heir the keepsake gave;
Then 'twas Rutulians' spoil on foughten field; —
He strips, and round him slings the bootless prize;
And dons Messapus' helm. They leave the camp,
And speed to safety.
                Now some Horse the while
Were riding forward from the Latin town,
While the main host lay marshalled on the plain,
With answers to King Turnus, shielded all,
Three hundred men, with Volscens in command.
Who, as they neared the rampart, saw the twain
Swerving to left; and in the glimmering night
His helmet, flashing back the moon, betrayed
Heedless Euryalus. No careless eye
Took note. "Stand, men!" cries Volscens from his troop
"Why go ye? Why in arms? and whither bound?"
They nought reply, but to the woods their flight
Quicken, and trust the night. The horsemen block
The well-known cross-ways on all sides, with guards
Crowning each outlet. Wide the forest spread,
Shaggy with thorn and ilex, and with briers
Each glen was choked, and through the hidden ways
Rare gleamed a path. The shadows of the boughs,
The loaded spoils, impede Euryalus:
Fear cheats him of the way. But through his foes
Nisus escapes unheeding to the tract
Named since from Alba's name the *Alban Meads*,
Then the deep pastures of the Latian King.
He stops, and for his friend looks back in vain.
"Where have I left thee? Ah, Euryalus!
Where may I trace thee back through all the maze

Of this deceitful wood?"
                                    So, threading back
His noted steps, he roams the stilly brake,
Hearing the horses, sounds and signs of chase.
Nor long the time, ere clamour meets his ears,
And he discerns Euryalus, whom now,
By wood and night betrayed, the squadron whole
With tumult seize, and all his strife in vain.
Ah, what to do! what force, what arms may dare
Rescue? Or shall he charge the serried swords,
Speeding a glorious death? With arm indrawn,
He poised his spear, and to the far-off Moon
Looked up, and prayed:
                                    "Thou, Goddess, aid me thou!
Assist our task, O Splendour of the Stars!
Ward of the woodland ways, Latona's child!
If to thy shrines my father Hyrtacus
Bare gifts for me, if I have added spoils,
Hung in thy dome, or from thy sacred roof,
Grant me to rout this throng! O guide my shaft!"

   He ceased, and, straining all his body, hurled
His lance. The spear flew speeding through the night,
Broke in the back of Sulmo as he turned,
And splintering pierced his heart. He from his breast
Pours the warm tide, and rolling cold in death
Heaves with long sobs. They peer on all sides round.
But he the fiercer lo! another bolt
Aims from his ear, and, while they doubt, the lance
Hisses through Tagus' brows, and piercing stops
Warm in his brain. Then fierce is Volscens' rage,
Who nowhere sees the sender of the spear,
Nor where to launch his wrath. "Yet thou meanwhile,
With thy warm blood," he cries, "for both shalt pay!"
And with drawn sword assails Euryalus.
Then wild, distraught with terror, Nisus called,
Nor could endure to hide, nor longer bear
Such pain:
                        "Me, me, 'tis I, who did the deed!
On me, Rutulians, turn your steel! the guilt

Is mine entire: he nothing dared nor could;
May heaven be witness and the conscious stars!
He only loved too well his luckless friend!"

While thus he speaks, the sword, thrust through the ribs,
Shatters the snowy breast. Euryalus
Is rolled in death: blood o'er his body streams,
And on his shoulder rests the drooping head;
As when some rose-red flower the plough hath shorn
Lies faint and dying, or as poppies bend,
Loaden with rain, and hang their weary heads.

But Nisus springs amid them; sole of all
Seeks Volscens out, at Volscens only stays:
Whom gathered round the foe from every side
Thrust back. Not less he presses, and his sword
Wheels flaming, till in Volscens' clamorous mouth
He buries it, and dying slays his foe.
Then, torn with wounds, he throws his body down
On his slain friend, and rests at last in death.

O happy pair! if aught my strains avail,
Time shall not steal your memory, while Troy's House
Shall stand on Capitol's eternal Rock,
And Rome's high Father own imperial sway!

Such booty gained, the conquering Rutuli
Bore back dead Volscens to their camp with tears.
Nor grieved they less to find pale Rhamnes there,
Serranus, Numa, and so many a lord
Slain at one bout. Around each corpse they crowd,
Around the dying men, the place still wet
With slaughter, and the streams of foaming blood.
All know the spoils, Messapus' glittering helm,
And all those blazons at such cost regained!

Now Morning from Tithonus' saffron bed
Rose, and o'er Earth dispersed the virgin light.
The Sun streamed down: the world lay bright and bare.
Turnus, himself all-armed, to arms awoke
His warriors, and each captain ranged for war
His brazen files by many a rumour fired.

Yea, and they bear in front on lifted spears,
A piteous sight, with clamorous din pursued,
Euryalus' and Nisus' heads.

But the stern Trojans on their leftward wall
Showed front; for round their right the river ran;
And held the fosse, and on the lofty towers
Stood mournful, saddened by those impaled heads,
Known all too well, and dropping the dark blood.

Now to the mother of Euryalus
Swift Rumour, winging through the startled town,
Slid with the tale. All warmth her body fled:
Her shuttle dropped; her web lay all unrolled;
And flying woeful with a woman's wail,
She rent her hair, and to the rampart's edge
Ran frantic, nor of men nor perilous bolts
Recked aught, but with lamenting filled the sky.

"Oh, do I see thee thus? O Son, my life's
Last comfort! Couldst thou leave me desolate,
O cruel! nor, when sent to perilous straits,
Speak to thy joyless mother one last word?
Woe! on strange earth, for Latin dogs and birds
Thou liest a prey! Not I, thy mother, closed
Thine eyes, nor washed thy wounds, nor laid thee out
Wrapt in that robe I hurried night and day
To weave for thee and soothed an old wife's care.
Where shall I follow thee? What country now
Holds thy dead mangled limbs? Is this, O Son!
All that returns? all that o'er lands and seas
I followed? O Rutulians! of your love,
Pierce me with all your weapons, slay me first!
Or with thy bolt, great Sire of Heaven! in pity
Smite down to Tartarus this hated head,
Since else I cannot slit the torturing life!"

Such sobs unmanned them, and a sigh of grief
Ran through all hearts, and numbed their strength for war.
Idaeus then and Actor bare her thence,
With sorrow burning, as Ilioneus
And sad Iulus bade them to her home.

But the dread trumpet's brazen song afar
Gives warning: shouts ensue; the heavens resound.

With tortoise even-driven the Volsci speed
To fill the trenches, and tear down the dyke.
Part, seeking entry, scale the walls where thin
The line of foemen, through whose sparser belt
Light gleams. The Trojans in defence shower back
Bolts of all kinds, and thrust them down with pikes; —
Long war had taught them how to guard their walls. —
Stones too they roll, their shielded line to break,
Of deadly weight; but they beneath their shell
Bear lightly all the storm: yet fail at last;
For where the throng looms large, the Trojans roll
A monstrous mass, and hurling strew their foes
Broadcast, and break the shelter of their shields.
No more the bold Rutulians care to strive
In warfare blind, but try with missile bolts
To clear the dyke.
Elsewhere with dread aspect Mezentius shook
The Etruscan pine, and hurled the smoking torch.
While horse-ruling Messapus, Neptune's son,
Tears down the dyke, and calls for scaling steps.

    Ye, O Calliope! inspire my song!
The tale of deaths, the blood that Turnus' sword
Shed, and each warrior down to Orcus sent.
Unroll with me the mighty page of war;
For well remembering ye can well record!

    There stood a tower of vantage, high upbuilt
With bridges tall, which all the Italian force
Were fain to storm, and with main might to o'erthrow.
With stones the Trojans hold it, and their bolts
Shower through its hollow windows. Turnus then
First cast a blazing torch, and to its side
Fixed fire, which, swelling in the wind, devoured
The planks, and clung consuming to the doors.
Confused within, they rush and flee from harm
Vainly; for as they throng, and backward fall
To where no ravage comes, with sudden weight
The tower falls prone, and thunder fills the sky.
To earth they drop, with that great mass behind,
By their own weapons pierced and splintered wood,
Half-dead. Scarce Lycus and Helenor only
Escape; Helenor in his youthful prime,

Whom to Maeonia's King a slave had borne
In secret, and with arms forbidden sent
To Troy, bare sword and blank unblazoned shield.
He, seeing Turnus' thousands closing round,
And Latins here, and Latins marshalled there,
As some wild creature in the hunters' pale
Foams at their shafts, and rushing on her death,
Well-knowing leaps and falls upon their spears;
Not otherwise amidst his foes he leapt,
Rushing on death, where thickest fell the darts.
But Lycus far more swift, through enemies,
Through weapons flies, and keeps the wall, and strives
To clasp its roof and reach his comrades' hands.
Whom Turnus chasing both with foot and spear,
Chides thus, triumphing; "Madman! dost thou hope
To scape our hands?" and grasps him where he clings,
And plucks him down, and with him half the wall;
As when Jove's Shield-bearer in horny claws
Lifts hare or snow-plumed swan; or as Mars' wolf
Reaves from its fold a lamb, which, bleating sore,
Its mother seeks in vain. From every side
Rose shouts. The assailers filled the trench with earth,
And others to the roof hurled flaming brands.
With one huge mountain crag Ilioneus
Laid low Lucetius, as he ran with fire:
Then Liger lanced Emathion: stealing far
Asilas' shaft struck Corynaeus dead.
Ortygius fell to Caeneus; he to Turnus;
To Turnus Itys, Clonius, Promolus,
Sagaris, and Idas standing on the tower.
Capys Privernus slew; Themilla's spear
Had grazed him, but he dropped his shield distraught,
And clasped the wound: the winging shaft his hand
Nailed fast to his left side, and, hid within,
Shattered with deadly hurt the cells of breath.
Fair-armed stood Arcens' son, in broidered vest
Brave with Iberian blue, of visage proud;
Sent by his father from his mother's grove
Beside Symaethus' streams, where stands the Shrine
Of old Palicus fair and peaceable.
Mezentius dropped his spears, and round his head
On tightened thong thrice drave the hissing sling,

And with the molten lead betwixt his brows
Smote him, and laid him stretched along the sand.

   Then first in war, 'tis said, Iulus aimed
His shaft, erst wont to scare the flying deer,
And bold Numanus by his hand struck down,
By surname Remulus, who late had wed
Prince Turnus' younger sister. He before
The van went forth, with shoutings fair and foul,
Flown with his new-won royalty, and thus
Clamoured aloud:

                 "Are ye not shamed once more,
O twice-caught Phrygians, to be held in siege?
To screen from death in walls? Lo! these are they
Who claim our brides! What God, what madness thrust
Your arms on Italy? No sons are here
Of Atreus, no Ulysses weaving words!
A sturdy breed, we plunge our new-born babes
To harden in the fierce and freezing streams.
Our lads ere dawn have tired the woods in chase.
They break the horse for sport, and bend the bow.
Patient of toil, to little used, they delve
And tame the soil, or shatter towns in war.
Iron is our life's sole wear. Our spears we turn
To goad the ox: no tardy Age our mind
Weakens, or saps our strength. Our last grey hairs
The helm constrains; and ever 'tis our joy
To harry prey, and live on plundered gain.
For you the crocus braids, the purple dyes!
Idlesse ye love, and in gay dances revel,
With tunics sleeved and ribboned bonnets fine,
O Phrygian wives, not men! Get hence, O hence
To Dindymus to list your wonted pipes!
The Idaean Mother's timbrels and the flutes
Call you! Leave arms to men, and sheathe the sword!"

   Him noising thus and chanting words of ill
Iulus brooked not, and the horse-hair drew,
Aiming a shaft; and as he stretched his arms,
Stayed, and to Jove sent first the suppliant vow.

   "Bless this bold deed, Almighty! and mine hand
Each year shall bring thee gifts, and to thy shrines

Lead a white steer gilt-fronted, with a head
Tall as his mother's, and his butting horn
Full-grown, who scatters with his hoofs the sand."

The Father heard, and thundered on the left
From cloudless sky. At once the fateful bow
Sang, and the hissing arrow left the string,
Flew through Numanus' head, and pierced the skull.
"Go! Mock at valour, insolent! 'Tis thus
The twice-caught Phrygians answer Rutuli!"
He adds not; and the Trojans roar applause,
And lift blithe hearts to heaven. And haply then
Long-haired Apollo, where he sat enskied,
Saw from a cloud Ausonia's ranks and camp
Far down, and thus bespake the conquering boy:

"Fair fall thy valour, lad! So stars are reached!
God-born and God-begetter! 'Neath thine House
All doomed wars shall sink again to peace:
Troy cannot hold thee!" Saying thus, he leaves
High heaven, and parts the blowing airs, and seeks
Ascanius, changed in visage to the form
Of Butes, who of old Anchises' arms
Bare, and was loyal henchman at his gates.
Him to Iulus then his sire had given.
Like him went Phoebus, like in voice and hue,
In hoary locks and savage-sounding arms,
And with these words addressed the ardent boy.

"Enough, Iulus, hurtless by thy shafts
Numanus to have slain. Such merit first
Phoebus allows, nor envies arms like his.
Yet now refrain from war!" So Phoebus spake,
Nor ended ere he left his mortal guise,
And into thin air vanished far from sight.
The God, those Heavenly shafts, the Dardan Chiefs
Knew, and in flight his sounding quiver heard.
So with his holy words they check the boy
Hungry for battle, but themselves the strife
Rejoin, and life on open hazards cast.

O'er all the walls' defence a clamour runs.
They draw the bow; they twist the sling; with bolts
The ground is scattered: shields and hollow helms

Ring to the blow, and fierce the battle swells.
As when at setting of the rainy Kids,
Rains lash the earth: as hailstones on the sea
Down pour, when God with blustering South stirs up
The watery rack, and rifts the hollow clouds.

Pandarus and Bitias, of Alcanor born,
Whom in Jove's grove Iaera of the woods
Bred tall as pines and mountains of their land,
Trusting their arms, the Gate they held in charge
Throw open wide, and bid the foe come in.
They right and left within before the towers
Stand sheathed in steel, flashing their lofty plumes;
As high in air, beside the flowing stream,
On Padus' banks, or pleasant Athesis,
Twain oak-trees rise, and lift their unshorn heads
With nodding crest sublime to the high heavens.

In rush their foemen, seeing entrance wide.
Quercens at once, bright-armed Aquicolus,
Tmarus' rash soul, and Haemon, with their troops,
Or turn their backs, or at the very gate
Lay down their lives. Then fiercer swells the wrath
In clashing hearts, and Trojans gathered round
Swarm to the spot, and dare with onset close
Make further sally.

                    Now as Turnus fought,
Dealing wild havoc on the field afar,
News reached him that the foe, with bloodshed hot,
Had opened wide their gates. He left his task,
And, stirred by monstrous anger, made all speed
To those proud brethren and the Dardan Gate.
And first Antiphates, (for first came he,)
Sarpedon's bastard by a Theban dame,
Hurling the shaft he slew; the Italian cornel
Cleft the thin air, and piercing deep the throat,
Entered his breast. The wound's black cavern foamed,
And in his lung the embedded spear grew warm.
Then Erymas, Aphidnus, Meropes,
Then flame-eyed Bitias' flaunting soul he sped;
No shaft it was, (no shaft that life had taken,)
But, hissing loud, a driven thunderbolt,

Came the slung pike, which not the two bulls' hides,
Nor trusty corslet's twofold scales of gold
Withstood: the vast limbs totter and fall down.
Earth groans; and on him thunders the great shield.
So falls at whiles on Baiae's shore a mass
Of mighty stones compact and cast in sea:
So prone it plunges ruining, and sinks,
And bedded deep lies still; the water seethes,
And darkly spreads the sand: then Prochyta
Shakes at the sound, and hard Inarime,
By Jove's commandment on Typhoeus laid.

Fresh prowess then the Lord of Arms instills
In Latin hearts, and goads them fiercely on,
Hounding on Trojans Panic and black Fear.
They gather, for the battle-feast is spread;
And every heart the War God spurs!

When Pandarus beheld his brother's fall,
How fate inclined, what fortune ruled the hour,
He with broad shoulders pushing swung the gate
Round on its hinge with force, and many a friend
Left from the walls shut out in desperate fray;
But others streaming onwards shut within.
Fool! not to see Rutulia's King break in
Amidst them, and himself to enclose him there,
Like some great tiger among helpless sheep!

Light from his eyes flashed strangely, and his arms
Rang terrible; his blood-red helmet plumes
Danced, and the lightnings dartled from his shield.
That hated giant form the Aeneadae
Know, suddenly dismayed. Then Pandarus
Springs, hot with anger at his brother's death,
And cries: "Not here Amata's dower hall!
Not here walled Ardea hugs her Turnus close!
Foemen thou see'st; hence is no power to flee!"

Smiling on him thus Turnus answered calm:
"Come, if thine heart be stout! close hand to hand!
Here too, tell Priam, was Achilles found!"
He ceased. The other with main might his spear
Threw, rugged still and knotty with the bark.

The breezes caught it: Juno turned aside
The wounding shaft, and fixed it in the gate.

"But not this blade my forceful hand impels
Shalt thou escape! This blow another deals!"
He said; and, rising on the lifted sword,
Clave him betwixt the brows, and sorely gashed
The young soft cheek. Din rose, and earth was shaken
By that great weight. He dying to the ground
Sank his faint limbs and weapons splashed with brain,
And the equal-severed head this way and that
Down from his shoulders hung. With terror shocked,
The Trojans turned and fled; and had the thought
Flashed on the victor's mind, to break the bar,
And let his comrades enter through the gate,
The war's, and Troy's last day that day had been!
But rage consumed him, and mad lust of blood
Drove him upon his foes.
First Phaleris he caught, and Gyges houghed,
Their lances seized, and in the flyers' backs
Hurled them: Saturnia steeled his hand and heart.
Halys to these he joins, and, with pierced targe,
Phegeus; then those who fought within unware,
Halius, Alcander, Prytanis, Noemon.
Lynceus withstood, and called his fellows on,
But from the mound the blade flashed on the right,
And caught him: helm and head at that one blow
Dropped severed far. Then fell the wild beasts' fear,
The shrewdest hunter to anoint his shafts,
And arm the steel with poison, Amycus;
Clytius, and Cretheus, whom the Muses loved,
Cretheus, the Muses' friend, whose heart was still
In songs and lyre and string-drawn melodies:
Steeds, wars, and warriors were his constant song.

Learning how Trojans fell, their Chiefs at last,
Mnestheus and bold Serestus, drawing nigh
Behold them routed, and their foe enclosed.
"Now whither, whither flee you?" Mnestheus cries;
"What other walls, what town is yours beyond?
One man, O Burghers, hedged by all your dykes!
Shall he thus unavenged throughout your town

Deal death, and send our very prime below?
Be shamed! and pity, cowards! your woe-worn land,
Your great Aeneas, all your Gods of old!"

   Thus fired they rally, and in dense array
Stand close. And Turnus, edging from the fight,
Makes for the stream, and where the river winds.
More fiercely then with shouts the Trojans press,
Swarming around: as when a band with arms
Fall on a savage lion, who, dismayed,
Glaring and grim, gives way: honour and rage
Forbid him turn his back; nor through armed men
However wistful may he make advance.
So Turnus doubtful his unhasting steps
Draws backward, and his spirit boils with rage.
Nay, twice e'en yet he charged amidst his foes;
Twice turned and drove their rout along the wall.
But all their force swarm quickly from the camp,
Nor does Saturnia give him strength to meet
Their coming; for Jove sent the Maid of Air,
Iris, to bear his sister bidding stern,
That Turnus leave the Trojans' lofty walls.
So he no more with targe, with hand no more
Hath power to stand, on every side o'erwhelmed
By showering darts. His casque with ceaseless clash
Rings round his brows: stones wear his solid brass.
His plumes are shent; his buckler cannot ward
The blows, as denser drive the Trojans' spears,
And Mnestheus' thunder. Sweat from all his frame
Flows in dun streams: he cannot breathe; sick gasps
His perished members shake. At last, full-armed,
He leapt into the stream, whose amber flood
Received him coming, and with gentle waves
Upholding him, washed off the stain of war,
And sent him joyous to his friends again.

Book X

WIDE OPEN NOW the Olympian Halls eterne;
And Heaven's great Regent to his starry seat
Convokes the Gods. The subject Earth from thence
The Dardan camp he views and Latian clans.
In the wide courts they sit. Himself begins:

"Empyreal Powers! Why is your purpose changed?
And why thus jealous are your hearts at strife?
Latins to war with Trojans I forbade.
What rebel feud is this? What terror urged
Or these or those to wake the clash of swords?
A time will come (provoke it not!) for war,
When savage Carthage through the sundered Alps
Ruin shall hurl one day on towered Rome!
Then hates may clash; then rapine may be loosed.
But now forbear, and own the appointed Peace!"

Thus briefly Jove; but not with answer brief
Spake golden Venus:
"Father! Eternal Might of Men and Things!
(For now what else is left us to implore?)
Look how Rutulians lord it! See how Turnus
Rides down the ranks, and on the heady tide
Sweeps to success! Walls succour Troy no more.
Nay, in her gates, and on her very dykes
The fight is joined, and trenches swim with blood.
Far thence the unwitting Prince! O wilt thou ne'er
Let sieges end? Walls of a new-born Troy
Again are threatened, and another host,
A new Tydides from Aetolia springs
On Teucer's sons. Pain waits me yet, I ween,
And I, thy child, abide the swords of men!
If Trojans in despite of thine high will
Sought Italy, their heads should bear the crime,
Nor give them aid: but if so many a word
From Heaven and Hell hath led them, why may aught
Change now thy mandate, or build fate anew?

Why tell of ships burnt up on Eryx' shore,
The King of Storms, the Aeolian blasts uproused
To fury, and Iris from the clouds sent down?
Now even the Shades, (a region yet untried,)
She moves; and suddenly on earth lets loose
Allecto raving through the Italian towns.
No dream of Empire moves me: all our hopes
Fell with our fortunes. Whom thou wilt may rule.
If thy hard wife give Teucrians no domain,
O by the smoking wreck of ruined Troy,
Grant, Father, that Ascanius may escape
The stroke of arms! Aeneas may pursue
O'er strange tumultuous seas his destined course,
But guard my grandson! Let my power avail
To shield and steal him from the perilous fray!
Cythera, Paphos, Amathus are mine,
The Idalian courts are mine: there let him live
Disarmed, inglorious. Then with mighty sway
Bid Carthage grasp Ausonia; he shall thwart
No Tyrian powers! What boots it to have fled
The plague of War, through Argive flames escaped,
And on wild shores and seas such perils drained
In quest of Latium and a Troy re-risen?
Best by their land's last ashes to have sat
On soil that once was Troy! O give them back
Xanthus and Simois! O let them pass
Once more through Ilium's doom!"
                              Then, full of wrath,
Queen Juno thus: "Why wilt thou make me break
My silence deep, and bare my hidden pain?
Hath man or God compelled the Dardan Prince
To take the field, and prove Latinus' foe?
Fate led him to Ausonia? Yes, the voice
Of mad Cassandra! Did one word of ours
Make him leave camp, commit his life to winds,
Trust to a boy his walls and all the war,
Or shake the Tuscans' loyalty and peace?
What God hath wrought this wrong? what spite of ours?
Was Juno there? or Iris sent from heaven?
It chafes thee that Italian flames should gird
A new-born Troy, and Turnus keep his land,
Pilumnus' seed, divine Venilia's son;

How then if Trojans hurl their fires on them,
And wear and waste the fields of other men,
And choose them brides, and sunder hearts betrothed,
And plead for Peace while arming ships for war?
Thou may'st remove Aeneas, with void air
Cheating the Greeks and substituted cloud;
Thou may'st transform his vessels into Nymphs,
And when we aid Rutulians we transgress!
'Far thence the unwitting Prince.' So let him stay!
Paphos is thine; the Idalian courts are thine;
Why tempt fierce hearts, and cities breeding war?
Who strove to lay thy reeling Phrygia flat?
We? or the man who brought the Greeks on Troy?
What woke all Europe and all Asia's power?
Whose theft dissolved their peace? Was mine the sword
That waved Troy's wanton on to Sparta's sack?
Did I lend arms, or kindle war with lust?
Then fears for thine were meet: now thou dost chide
Too late, not justly, throwing idle taunts!"

So pleaded Juno: and the Empyreal Powers
Murmured diversely; as when forests catch
The infant gale, and rolling hollow sounds
Murmur, and seamen learn the coming storm.

Then spake the Omnipotent, Supreme of All:
And while he spake the courts of Heaven were hushed;
Earth trembled; and the etherial vault was still;
The breezes fell, and silent lay the Sea.

"Hear now, and in your hearts my utterance fix!
Since your unending feud from peace debars
Troy and Ausonia; let each Trojan man,
Let each Rutulian carve his hopes this day
As Fortune wills: Myself will favour none.
Whate'er hath caused this siege, Ausonia's doom,
Or Troy's own wrong and counsels learnt amiss,
(Nor do I spare Rutulians,) each man's deeds
Shall ban or bless. Jove rules for all alike.
Fate will prevail!"
                              And by the Stygian streams
And black bituminous banks he sware the oath;
And, nodding, shook Olympus with his nod.

Then ended parle. He left his golden Throne,
And passed the doors, by Heavenly escort led.

Meantime round all the gates Rutulians press
To lay men dead, and gird the walls with flame.
But leaguered in their lines Aeneas' host
Lie without hope of flight. Helpless they stand,
And with a thin vain circle crown the towers.
Asius, Thymoetes, twain Assaraci,
Castor, and aged Thymbris head the line;
And hard by these Sarpedon's brethren stand,
Clarus and Themon from the Lycian steep.
Large as his father Clytius Acmon towers,
Menestheus' brother, with a monstrous crag,
Near half a mountain, in his straining grasp.
Some volley spears or stones; some handle fire,
Or fit the shaft to string. And in their midst
Venus' peculiar care, the Dardan boy,
Unbonnets his fair head, as when a gem,
Dividing the red gold on throat or neck,
Beams lustre, or as when, inlaid by art
In boxwood or Orician terebinth,
Ivory gleams; while o'er his milk-white neck,
Clasped by a golden band, his tresses flow.

Thee too, O Ismarus! proud peoples saw
Shoot anguish, and with poison arm thy reeds,
Lord of lush meadows, which Maeonian men
Farm, and Pactolus waters them with gold.
There too was Mnestheus, high uplift by fame
That erst he routed Turnus from the walls;
And Capys too, whence Capua takes her name.

These in stern hosting clashed. But through deep night
Aeneas clove the seas. For when he left
Evander, to the Etruscan King he hied,
And told his name, his race, and what he sought
What proffered, how Mezentius won allies,
How fiercely Turnus blazed, and how unsure
Man's brittle state. He pleaded while he warned:
And Tarchon tarried not, but joined his force,
And struck alliance. Then from fate released,
At Heaven's command the Lydian tribe embark,

Bound to an alien chief.
                                    Aeneas' prow
Rides foremost, with the Phrygian lions beneath,
O'erhung by Ida, dear to exiled Troy.
Here great Aeneas sits, and ponders deep
War's wavering turns; while Pallas by his side
Now asks him of the stars, the roads of Night,
Now how he travailed on the land and sea.

   Now open Helicon, O Muses! wake
The song of all who filled Aeneas' train,
Who launched from Tuscan shores and sailed the sea.

   First, Massicus the brazen Tiger sailed,
Leading a thousand men, who left the walls
Of Clusium and of Cosae, armed with shafts
And light slung quivers and the deadly bow.

   Next Abas grim, whose band in sunbright mail
Glowed, and astern a golden Phoebus shone.
Him Populonia gave her war-tried sons
Six hundred, and three hundred Ilva gave,
Ilva, boon isle of inexhaustive mines.

   Asilas third, the interpreter of Gods,
Whom hearts of beasts and stars of heaven obey,
The tongues of birds, the lightning's boding fire:
A thousand dense with bristling spears he ruled,
Whom Pisa gave, the Alphaean city throned
On Tuscan soil.
                        Then fairest Astyr came,
Astyr, made bold by horse and spangled arms.
Three hundred more (one spirit led them all),
Left Minio's meads and Pyrgi's ancient town,
And Caere and Graviscae's baneful air.

   Nor thee, Ligurian Chief, unmatched in war,
Cinyras, I pass; nor thy spare company,
Cupavo, from whose crest the swan-plumes rise,
Your father's badge, O badge of love and shame!
Cycnus, fame runs, amid the poplar boughs,
His sisters' shade, for Phaethon his love
Sang, and with music lulled his amorous woe.
Then, drawing on soft plumes of snowy age,

Left Earth, and winged melodious to the stars.
His son on ship-board mid his youthful peers
Oars the vast Centaur, which above the sea
Hangs lofty, threatening with a rock the waves,
And with long keel the deep brine furrows through.

And Ocnus left his home, of Tuscan stream
And boding Manto born, who gave her name
And walls to thee, O Mantua! Mantua dowered
With mighty fathers, but of strain diverse.
Three tribes are hers; four cities under each;
Herself their head, and Tuscan-born her strength.
Five hundred thence Mezentius made his foes,
Whom with grey sedges veiled Benacus' child,
Mincius, to battle led in floating fir.

Slow moves Aulestes, with his hundred trees
Beating the flood; the riven waters foam.
Him giant Triton bears, and with a conch
Shocks the blue deep: a hairy-breasted man
Ending in dragon's paunch, the great half-beast
Floats on the wave that hissing foams below.

So many chosen Chiefs in thrice ten ships
Went to Troy's aid, and cut the salt sea fields.

Now day had left the sky, and in mid-heaven
Mild Phoebe rode in her night-wandering car:
Aeneas, (for his care no respite gives,)
Governs himself the helm, and tends the sails.
When lo! before him in mid-course appear
His old companions, by Cybebe's grace
From ships transfigured into Nymphs of Sea,
Who cleave the billows swimming side by side,
As many as prows stood brazen on the shore.
They hail their King from far, and round him dance.
And sweetest-tongued Cymodocea grasped
The stern with her right hand, and rose breast-high,
And, oaring with her left the silent waves,
Bespake him ere he wist: "O Heavenly-born!
Wak'st thou, Aeneas? Wake, and loose the sheet!
Thy barks are we, tall Ida's holy pines,
Now Nymphs of Sea. When that Rutulian fierce
Scourged us with fire and steel, unwillingly

We broke thy bonds, and still we swim in quest
Of thee. This shape our Mother framed in love,
And with divine life dowered us under seas.
Thy son Iulus dykes and trenches still
In thorny battle keep mid Latin spears.
Already Tuscans, mixt with Arcad horse,
Their stations hold. 'Tis Turnus' firm resolve
With countering troops to bar them from their camp.
Rise! and betimes bid call thy troops to arm,
When morning comes, and take the unconquered Shield,
Rimmed round with gold, the very Fire-God's gift!
The morrow's light, unless my words sound vain,
Shall see Rutulian carnage heaped on high!"

She ceased; and, parting, with no uncouth hand
The tall ship pushed, which through the rolling sea
More swift than spear or wind-fleet arrow flew.
The rest behind her sped. Anchises' son,
Dazed, yet emboldened by that Heavenly Sign,
To the hollow sky looked up, and prayed in brief.

"Parent of Gods! whom Dindymus delights,
Towered cities, and the twi-yoked lions' team!
Guide me in war, boon Goddess! Prosper well
Thine augury, and give thy Phrygians peace!"

No more he spake: and when the darkness fled,
And light returning orbed to perfect day,
He taught obedience, bidding all prepare
For battle, and dispose their hearts for war,
Then, standing on the stern, now full in ken
The leaguered Trojans scanned. His flaming Shield
He lifted high. The Dardans, with new hope
Fanning their wrath, fling missiles, and to heaven
Upraise their cries; as when Strymonian cranes
Fly, shrilling signals, from the roaring South,
And trail harsh music through the storm-black sky.

But on Ausonia's captains and the Prince
Fell wonder; till they turned and saw the ships
Steered shoreward, and the whole sea sailing in.
The helmet blazed, and from its crest a flame
Streamed, and the golden targe was spouting fire;
As blood-red comets on the lucent night

Cast baleful gleams, or as the Syrian Star
Springs, when his angry glare brings thirst and pain
For woeful men, and saddens all the sky.

But Turnus' boldness shrank not from the task
To seize the shore, and force them from the land.
Nay, he incites his men, and chides their fear:
"Lo! what you prayed for! 'Tis the battle-grip!
The war is in your hands! Remember now
Your wives and homes! Recall the mighty acts,
Your fathers' glories! Meet them by the waves,
Confused with slippery footsteps as they land.
Fate aids the bold!"
He said; and pondered whom to lead in front,
And whom to trust with the beleaguered walls.

Meanwhile Aeneas from their ships debarks
His troops by gangways. Many wait the ebb
Of slackening sea, and leap into the shoals;
And some use oars. But Tarchon scans the beach
Where no shoal murmurs, and no breakers sound,
But the sea swells unhindered; there his prows
Turns sharply in, and thus his crew implores:

"Bend the stout blades, O chosen! Lift the ships!
On! On! Bite through with beaks this land of hate!
Let every keel her own deep furrow plough!
I grudge not shipwreck in a port like this,
If once we grasp the land!" So Tarchon spake;
And rising on their oars his seamen drive
Their foaming galleys toward the Latin land,
Till beaks grip shore, and all the keels lie fast
Unhurt, save thine, O Tarchon! for she dashed
On shallows, and upon a pitiless reef
Hung poised awhile in doubt, and wore the waves;
Then broke, and in deep water cast her crew,
Whom the wrecked oarage and the floating thwarts
Entangled, and the ebb drew back their feet.

No dull delay holds Turnus, but he hurls
All ranks on Trojans, fronting them on shore.
The trumpets peal. And first Aeneas routs
Their peasant bands, fair auspice of the fray!
And slays great Theron, striding up to fight

Hugest of men. Through brazen links, through coat
Scaly with gold, the sword-blade gashed his side.
Lichas he smote, from his dead mother ripped,
The babe who scaped the steel, and thence to thee,
Phoebus, was vowed. And not far off he felled
Cisseus and Gyas huge, who with their clubs
Laid low the lines: strength nor Herculean arms,
Nor could their sire Melampus aid them now,
Alcides' friend, while yet he toiled on Earth.
On Pharus, lo! who flung some empty word,
He whirled the lance, and stayed his noising tongue.
Thou, Cydon, too, pursuing thy new joy,
Clytius, whose cheek Youth dusted with its gold,
By Dardan hand o'erthrown, hadst lain in death,
Careless of all thy loves, but Phorcus' seed,
Thy seven close-banded brethren, interposed,
Showering their sevenfold spears, and some of these
Leapt ineffectual back from helm and targe,
And some fond Venus turned, that razed the skin.
Aeneas then to leal Achates cried:
"Hand me the shafts! My arm on Rutuli
Shall hurl in vain not one that in Greek flesh
Stood once at Troy!" A mighty spear he caught,
And cast; which flying through the brazen shield
Of Maeon broke, and rent both mail and breast.
Alcanor came, and with his hand upheld
His falling brother, but the spear flew on,
Keeping its path of blood, and pierced his arm.
Down by its sinews hung the dying hand.
Then Numitor the spear torn from his brother
Aimed at Aeneas, but he might not pierce
His mark, and grazed the tall Achates' thigh.
Clausus of Cures, in his prime of strength,
Came up, and Dryops with a far-flung spear
Smote neath the chin, and thrusting pierced the throat,
And quenched his voice therewith, and quenched his life.
His brow strikes earth, his mouth pours clotted blood.
Three Thracians too, of Boreas' ancient race,
Three sons of Idas from the Ismarian steep,
By divers deaths he slays. The Auruncan troops
Draw close, Halaesus, and the horseman proud,
Messapus, Neptune's seed. Now these, now those

Essay to expel them. Round Ausonia's gate
The battle swells: as when in the wide sky
Winds clash in equal conflict; and no wind,
No cloud, nor sea gives way: in doubtful poise
The battle hangs, and all things stand at strain.
Not otherwise Troy's files and Latin files
Clash, foot on foot and man pressed hard on man.

But where a spate had swept the uprooted briers,
And rolled the huddled rocks, when Pallas saw
His Arcad troops, unwont to charge afoot,
Turn on the foe their backs, (for the rough ground
Bade them dismiss their steeds,) in such a strait
Using the sole resource, he fired their hearts
With pleading first, and then with bitter words:

"Where flee you? O by all your valorous deeds,
By King Evander's name! by fields well fought!
By all mine hope to match my father's fame!
Trust not to feet! The steel must share our way!
Where clings most dense yon globe of hostile men,
Our glorious land calls you and Pallas home!
No Gods oppose us, but a mortal foe,
With mortal hands like ours, and lives as few!
See how the broad seas bind us! how on land
Flight fails us! Shall we turn to sea or Troy?"

So said, he broke amid the embattled foe;
When Lagus met him, led by no kind fate;
Whom, while he gathered a great stone, he lanced
Where the spine parts the ribs, and from the bone
Pulled back the embedded spear. Nor while he stooped
Might Hisbo catch him, though his heart was fain:
For while he plunged, distraught for his dead friend,
Him Pallas took unware, and hid the blade
Deep in his windy lungs. On Sthenelus
He charges then, and Rhoetus' daring seed,
Anchemolus, who shamed his step-dame's bed.
Ye too, O Thymber and Larides, twins
Of Daucus, died, whose parents each from each
Knew not, and oft in pleasing error fell.
Now Pallas made you cruelly distinct!
Thymber, thy head Evander's sword swept off;

And thy lopped hand, Larides, seeks its lord.
The half-dead fingers twitch, and clutch the steel.

Shame now and anger arm the Arcadians, fired
By Pallas' words, and seeing his great deeds:
Who next speared Rhoeteus, flying in his car.
Such space, such time gained Ilus; for his lance
Pallas had aimed at Ilus; which midway
Rhoeteus received, O Teuthras! fleeing thee,
Thee, and thy brother Tyres. He down-rolled
With dying feet beats that Rutulian soil.

And as in summer, when the wished-for breeze
Rises, some shepherd sows the woods with fire:
The thickets catch; and one long shuddering flame
Spreads o'er the lea: he sits in triumph throned
And eyes the exulting blaze; — so all in one
Closed thy brave hearts, O Pallas, thee to aid!
But bold Halaesus, gathered up in arms,
Fell on them. Ladon and Demodocus
He slew, and Pheres, and with flashing blade
Shared the hand lifted to Strymonius' throat,
Smote Thoas with a stone, and splashed his face
With battered brains and blood. His prophet sire
Had kept Halaesus in the woods concealed,
Till Death bedimmed his eyes; then Fate prevailed,
And doomed him victim to Evander's spear:
Whom Pallas aimed at, making first this vow:

"Grant, Father Tiber, to this steel I cast
Auspicious passage through Halaesus' heart!
His arms, his harness' spoil thine oak shall wear!"
The God gave ear: Halaesus to his lance,
Shielding Imaon, leaves his breast unarmed.

Not such a death Lausus, strong tower of war,
Lets scare his troops, but straightway meets and slays
Abas, war's knot and stay. Arcadia's sons
Fall, Tuscans fall, and you, O Men of Troy,
Whom Greeks undid not, fall! The battles close
In force and chiefs well matched. Their outer ranks
Press inward, and the throng permits nor spear
Nor hand to move. Here Pallas strains and strives,
Here Lausus fronts him, not far off in age, —

Two noble forms! but Fate denied them both
Home to return. Yet not between themselves
The Lord of high Olympus let them strive:
Soon waits their doom beneath a sterner foe.

His sister now bade Turnus bear the war
For Lausus; and his chariot clove the press.
He saw and hailed them: "Sheathe the sword! I fight
Alone with Pallas; he is mine alone!
I would his father were but here to view!"

They gave the space enjoined; and as they left,
Amazed at that proud mandate, Pallas stood
And stared at Turnus, o'er his giant frame
Rolling his eyes, and with stern gaze faced all.
The Prince's words he met with words like these:
"Praise for great trophies or for glorious death
Shall crown me now. Each fate my sire can bear.
Desist from threats!" And in their midst he strode.
Cold ran the blood to each Arcadian heart.
Turnus leapt down, to close with him on foot:
And as a lion from some distant height
Sees in the fields a bull heart-bent on war,
And springs: even so looked Turnus as he came.
Him when the other deemed in reach of spear,
Advancing boldly, that some chance might aid
Unequal strength, he called to the wide sky:
"O, by my father's home, where rest and cheer
Were thine, Alcides, bless my great assay!
May Turnus see me strip his blood-stained arms!
O, may the victor haunt his dying eyes!"

Alcides heard, and deep at heart suppressed
A heavy sigh, and shed the idle tear;
While thus his son the Sire addressed benign:
"Each hath his day. Irreparable and brief
Is mortal life: but to spread fame by deeds
That is man's work. Under Troy's lofty walls
Fell many a son of Gods; nay, mine own child
Sarpedon fell. And Turnus his own doom
Calls; yea, he nears his life's allotted goal."
He said; and from Rutulia turned his sight.

But Pallas with main might his javelin threw,
And from its scabbard tore the flashing blade.
The spear flew on, and where the harness rose
High o'er the shoulder struck, and thrust its way
Through the shield's rim, and razed great Turnus' skin.
Long Turnus poised his steel-tipped wooden lance,
Then launched it forth on Pallas, crying thus:
"See, if our spear hath not a sharper point!"
Then through the shield, through brazen plates and mail,
Through all the foldings of the great bull hide,
The quivering spear-thrust smote, and through the guard
Of sheathing hauberk pierced the mighty breast.
Warm from the wound he tore it out in vain;
Life passed one way with blood: down on the wound
Prostrate he fell; his armour rang above;
And on strange earth his dying lips were prest.
Above him Turnus stood:
"Arcadians, to Evander bear my words!
As he deserved, I send his Pallas home.
Such meed, such comfort as a tomb can give
I grant. Not little costs his Dardan guest!"
He spake; and on the dead man pressed his foot;
And tore away the heavy belt embossed
With crime, — the bridegrooms on one wedding night
All basely slain, the chambers dashed with blood, —
Which Clonus graved in gold, and Turnus now
Triumphing took, and gloried in the spoil.

Blind hearts of men! O blind to coming doom,
That, puffed by fortune, cannot keep in bounds!
A day will come when dearly he had bought
Dead Pallas back, when he shall hate those spoils,
That day! But on his shield a train of friends
Moaning, with many a tear, bear Pallas home.
O grief, O glory for thy parent's sight!
This thy first day of war, and this thy last,
While thick behind thee lie Rutulia's dead!

Of that sad ill no rumour but sure news
Flies to Aeneas; that his men have reached
Destruction's edge; 'tis time to save their rout.
His flaming falchion through the nearest files

To thee, O Turnus! flown with that fresh blood,
Mows broad approach. Pallas, Evander, all
Shine in his sight; the home where first he found
The hand of welcome. And four sons that sprang
From Sulmo's loins, as many Ufens bred,
Alive he takes, to offer his dead shade,
And wet with captive blood his burning pyre.

On Magus then his spiteful lance he threw,
Who deftly stooped; the spear flew quivering o'er;
And, clinging to his knees, he thus besought:
"By thy son's promise, by thy father's shade,
Spare me, I pray thee, to my son and sire!
A stately house is mine, where cellared deep
Chased silver lies. Weights of wrought gold are mine,
And gold unwrought. Troy's victory doth not hinge
On me: one life will never turn the scale!"
He ceased. To whom Aeneas thus returned:

"Spare for thy children all thy vaunted wealth
Of gold and silver! Such compacts of war
Turnus annulled e'en now by Pallas' death.
So thinks my son, so thinks my father's shade!"
Thus said, he grasped his helm, and, while he cringed
Deep drove the sword-blade in his backdrawn throat.

Not far stood Phoebus' and Diana's Priest,
Haemonides, his brows with fillets bound,
All radiant in his robe and sun-bright arms;
Whom far he chased, and felled, and standing o'er
Slew and in darkness wrapped. His arms for thee
A Trophy, O King of War! Serestus bare.

Then Caeculus, of Vulcan's seed, renewed
The fight with Umbro from the Marsian hills,
Meeting Aeneas' rage. His sword had shared
Anxur's left hand, and all his buckler's orb.
(Some vaunt he spake, and thought to match the word
With might, and haply in his soaring heart
Promised himself grey hairs and length of life!)
Then Tarquitus, whom Dryope the Nymph
Bare to a woodland Faun, his onset hot
Met shining-armed. He, drawing back his spear,
Transfixed the breastplate and the ponderous shield,

And vainly as he pleaded, full of prayers,
Smote off his head, and rolling the warm trunk,
With bitter heart cried o'er it: "Lie now there,
Long-dreaded! Thee no mother dear shall lay
In earth, or load thee with thy fathers' tomb.
Wild birds shall have thee, or the drowning seas
Toss thee, and foodless fishes lick thy sores!"

    Antaeus then and Lucas, Turnus' prime,
He routs, bold Numa, and great Volscens' son,
Red Camers, richest of Ausonian lords,
Who reigned in mute Amyclae. As of yore
Fame runs Aegaeon, with his hundred arms,
His hundred hands, his fifty mouths and breasts
Blazing with fire, against the bolts of Jove
Clashed all his fifty shields, and drew his swords,
So, once his blade grew hot, Aeneas stormed
Victorious o'er the field.
                   And lo! he turns
Full on Niphaeus' team. The four-yoked steeds
Espy him striding with a dreadsome cry,
And turn in terror and their lord o'erthrow
And shoreward whirl the car. With twain white steeds
Then Liger and his brother Lucagus
Amidst them plunged. One brother guides the team,
While Lucagus wheels fierce the naked sword.
Them raging thus Aeneas could not brook;
But charged, and faced them, large with levelled spear.
When Liger thus:
"No Phrygian plain is here, Achilles' car,
Nor steeds of Diomede! Now ends thy life!
Now ends the war!" So fly mad Liger's words.
Yet not with words the Trojan Chief rejoined,
But hurled his spear. As Lucagus bent down,
Urging his steeds, and hanging o'er the lash,
Even while he thrust his left foot out to fight,
The spear passed through the shining buckler's rim,
And pierced his groin. He, from his chariot flung,
Rolled on the field death-struck. Whom thus bespake
Aeneas harsh: "O Lucagus! no flight
Of craven horses hath betrayed thy car;
No empty shadows turned them from the foe;

Thyself leapt out and left them!" Thus he spake,
And seized the steeds. His brother from the car
Slid, and despairing stretched his helpless palms:
"By thine own self, by those who got thee brave,
O spare me, Trojan; pity him who prays!"
Aeneas, to more pleas: "Not thus erewhile
Thou spakest! Die! Let brother bide by brother!"
Then where life lay his falchion clove the breast.
Wide wasting thus the Dardan swept the field,
Like some black storm or torrent; till at length
Ascanius and his peers their passage force,
And leave the bootless leaguer of the camp.

Meanwhile Heaven's Lord to Juno thus began:
"Sweet Wife and Sister mine! thou canst not err!
'Tis surely Venus who upholds and aids
These Trojan men, and not their own fierce hearts
To danger schooled, or hands in battle strong!"

Then Juno meekly: "Why, fair husband mine,
Vex my sick heart that fears thy bitter words?
O were my charms as potent as they were
And should be, thou would'st not deny me this,
Almighty! to draw Turnus from the field,
And for his father Daunus keep him safe.
Now let him perish, and his righteous blood
Atone to Trojans; though from us his birth
Springs through his sire Pilumnus, and thy courts
His lavish hand hath heaped with many a gift!"

To whom the Olympian King thus answered brief:
"Soon must he fall; but if reprieve thou prayest
From present death, and know'st I thus ordain,
Take him away, and rob the instant fates.
So far my grace hath room. But if thy prayers
Hide larger boon; if all the war thou deemest
Reversed and changed, thy hopes are barren food!"

And she, with tears: "Yet if thine heart would give
What thy lips grudge, and he remain alive!
Sad death awaits him guiltless, or I stray
Vainly from truth; O grant my fears be false,
And thou, who canst, wilt turn some better way!"

She said; and straight from Heaven, involved in cloud,
Sped down to Trojans and Laurentum's camp,
Driving the storm. Then out of hollow mist
To bear Aeneas' form the Goddess wrought
A Phantom weird and frail. With Dardan arms
She arrayed it, and the semblance of his shield
And godlike crest. An empty voice she gave,
Gave soulless sound, and counterfeited stride;
Like shapes men tell of hovering after death,
Or visions that delude the slumbering sense.

Before the van that Image gaily danced,
With taunts and missiles calling on his foe;
When Turnus charged, and launched the hissing spear.
It turned and fled. Then Turnus deemed he saw
Aeneas yielding, and his stormy soul
Drank idle hopes. "Now whither dost thou flee,
Aeneas? O forsake not thy betrothed!
The land of thy sea quest this hand will give!"
So noising he pursues, and his drawn blade
Flashes, nor sees the breezes filch his joy.

Now haply moored beside a ledge of rock,
With steps and gangway spread, the galley lay
Which King Osinius sailed from Clusium's shore;
And there Aeneas' flying Image slips
In hiding close. Not slower Turnus speeds,
And leaping o'er the gangway thwarts delay.
He scarce had touched the prow, Saturnia rent
The cable, and drove the ship on ebbing sea;
And him far off Aeneas seeks to fight,
While slaughtering many a foe. No longer then
The flimsy Shadow seeks a hiding-place,
But soaring melts in mist, while Turnus drives
Storm-swept to sea. He, witless of the truth,
Ungrateful for his safety, looks behind,
And stretches to the stars both hands and voice:

"Almighty Father! Didst thou deem my guilt
So heavy and such a punishment decree?
Whence, whither go I? How or in what sort
Returning, shall I see Laurentum's camp?

What of the troops who followed me to war,
All left, O horror! to a shameless death!
I see them straggling, and their dying groans
I hear. What can I? How can earth for me
Yawn deep enough? Ye rather, Winds! be kind!
On cliffs, on crags, 'tis Turnus' hope and prayer,
My vessel drive, or dash on Syrtes' shoals,
Where no Rutulian and no shame may reach!"

    While thus he spake, he wavered to and fro,
If, crazed by such dishonour, he should fall
On his rude blade, and drive it through his ribs,
Or fling himself in sea, and reach the shore
Swimming, to rush on Trojan steel again.
Thrice either way he tried; thrice Juno's might
In pity held him back. He, gliding on,
Cleaves the deep seas; and, borne on prospering tides,
Floats to his father Daunus' ancient town.

    Meanwhile, by Jove's command, Mezentius fought
In Turnus' room, and charged the exulting foe.
The Tyrrhene troops press round, and all on one,
On one man press with hate and volleyed darts.
He, as a rock which juts into the deep,
Beaten by raging blasts, and swilled with sea,
Each onset fierce bears out of sky or wave
Moveless and fixed; — so he on earth laid low
The flying Palmus, Hebrus, Latagus,
Whom with a stone, a mountain fragment vast,
Full in the face he caught, and Palmus left
Helpless and houghed: on Lausus he bestowed
Their arms to bear, their plumes to deck his helm.
Evanthes too he smote; and Pallas' friend
And birth-mate Mimas, whom to Amycus
Theano bare, that night when Cisseus' child
Laboured with fire and Paris, who in Troy
Sleeps, but dead Mimas on Laurentine shores.

    As from the hills when biting hounds have driven
The boar on piney Vesulus nursed long,
Long fed in reed-beds of Laurentum's marsh;
Who, when the nets are reached, stands still and snarls,
Savage and bristling; and no man dare press

His anger nearer, but they send from far
Safe shouts and spears: so none whose righteous wrath
Mezentius woke, had valour to close in
With naked steel: aloof they stand, and taunt
With shouts and missiles. He to every side
Keeps facing, unafraid; and with his teeth
Gnashes, and from his back shakes off the spears.

Acron, the Greek, from time-old Corythus,
Leaving his bride half-wed, had come to war.
Whom when he marked, bright with the rose-hued plumes
Of his betrothed, wide wasting in the field,
As some starved lion, prowling round the folds,
Urged by mad famine, should he spy a goat
Or hart with springing horns, gapes savage-mouthed,
Exults, and lifts his mane, and on the flesh
Clings crouching, while his wicked mouth is washed
With loathly blood:
So fierce Mezentius plunged among his foes.
Down Acron rolled, and gasping spurned the soil,
And with his life-blood bathed the broken lance.

By cast of spear the Tuscan scorned to slay
Flying Orodes, with a wound unseen,
But met him man to man, and not by sleight
But by main strength prevailed, and o'er him stood,
Straining with foot and spear. "Here lies, O men!
Orodes proud, no sorry part of war!"
And all with shouts take up his triumph-song.
But dying he: "Not long, not unavenged,
Victor, whoe'er thou art, thy joy shall be!
Doom waits thee soon: this field shall hold us both."

To whom Mezentius, smiling in his wrath:
"Die now! My fate the Lord of Heaven and Earth
Shall see to!" And he drew the weapon out.
Peace fell upon his eyes, and iron sleep
Closed them in endless night. Alcathous falls
To Caedicus; Sacrator slays Hydaspes;
Rapo Parthenius and stout Orses' might;
Messapus Clonius and Lycaon's son,
One flung to earth by falling steed unreined,
One foot to foot. Forth Lycian Agis strode,

Whom Valerus felled, nor lacked his fathers' fire.
Salius smote Thronius; and Nealces, skilled
With the far-duping shaft, laid Salius low.

Now to each host grim Mars dealt pain and death
With equal hand. Alike they slay and fall,
Victors and vanquished; neither know retreat.
The Gods on high pitied their wasted rage,
And all those pains of sad mortality.
Here Venus watched, there Juno. Through the press
Tisiphone ran riot. Like a storm
Mezentius walked the earth with shaken spear,
Great as Orion, when he plants his feet
To cleave the pools of Nereus, o'er the waves
Lifting his shoulders high, or when he bears
A many-wintered oak from mountain heights,
And while he walks his head is veiled in clouds,
So huge in harness came Mezentius on.

Him in the long array Aeneas marked,
And went to meet. Unterrified he stood,
Waiting his great-souled foe, firm in his bulk,
And measured with his eye the range of spear:
"O Hand, my God! O weapon poised for flight!
Now aid me! Trophy for Aeneas' death
Thee, Lausus, thee I vow: the robber's spoils
Thy wear shall be!"
                        The hissing spear from far
He hurled, which flying from the shield glanced wide,
And pierced Antores' side, Hercules' friend,
Renowned Antores, who from Argos sent,
Clave to Evander and a Latin home.
Fallen by another's wound, he looks to heaven,
And dreams of pleasant Argos as he dies.

Aeneas cast his spear. Through hollow orb
Of threefold brass, through linen folds it passed,
Through work of three bull hides, and in the groin
Sank deep, but spent its force. He joyous saw
The Tuscan's blood, and from his thigh snatched up
His sword, and hotly pressed the quailing man.
Which Lausus saw, and for the sire he loved

Groaned deeply, and the tears rolled down his cheeks.
Thy grievous death, thy prowess, if the years
Shed credence on thy deed, I shall not pass
Unsung, nor thee, O thou to memory dear!

Back stept the Tuscan, dragging in his shield
The spiteful spear, a maimed and useless man.
Out springs his son; and, plunging in the fray,
Confronts the sword-blade which Aeneas' hand
Had raised to strike, and holds him thus in check:
And all cry out while shielded by his son
The sire draws off, and with far-volleyed darts
Harass the foe. Aeneas, full of wrath,
Keeps shielded close. And as, whene'er the clouds
Pour down a storm of hail, each ploughman runs,
Each peasant runs from field, each traveller stays
In shelter safe, beneath a river's bank
Or high-arched rock, while rain is on the land,
That they may toil their day when sun returns;
So, stormed by arrowy sleet, Aeneas bore
The cloud of war, while all the thunder roared,
And taunted Lausus, and on Lausus cried:
"Daring beyond thy strength! Why wilt thou rush
On death? Thy love beguiles thee of all care!"
Not less he springs, foolhardy. Higher swells
The Trojan's anger, and the Fates now spin
Lausus' last thread: for through his body sweeps
Aeneas' brand, and buries all its length.
It pierced his targe, light harness of the brave,
The vest his mother wove with threads of gold,
And blood filled all his breast, and from his flesh
Life to the Shades passed sadly on the wind.

But when Anchises' son his dying looks
Saw, and his visage growing wondrous pale,
He sighed for pity, and his hand outstretched,
His heart reflecting the dear filial bond.
"Unhappy boy! What shall Aeneas give?
What meed of valour for thy soul's desert?
Keep thou the arms thou lovedst. Thee I send
Home, if that move thee, to thy fathers' dust.
Yet in thy death be thine this solace sad,

'Tis great Aeneas' hand that lays thee low!"
He chides the tardy train, and lifts him up,
Whose well-sleeked locks are drabbled with his blood.

   Meanwhile his father lay by Tiber's stream,
Bathing his wounds, and leaned against a tree
To ease his limbs. His brazen helm aloof
Hangs from the boughs; his arms are on the field.
His chosen stand around: he rests his neck,
Gasping, and lets his beard flow o'er his breast;
Oft asks of Lausus, and to call him back
Oft sends with orders from his mourning sire.
But weeping friends are bearing on their shields
Dead Lausus home, a great man greatly slain.
With boding heart their distant wail he knew,
Soiled his white hair with dust, and both his palms
To heaven outstretched, and clung upon the corpse.

   "Son! did life bind me with so sweet a lust
That in my stead I let the foeman's hand
Strike him I fathered, saved by these thy wounds,
And living by thy death! Ah! now for me
Exile is pain; now deep the wound is driven!
I too, my son, have stained thy name with shame,
Hurled from our throne by hate. I owed my land
Her debt of vengeance: would a thousand deaths
Had paid the forfeit with mine own bad life!
And still I live, nor leave the light and men,
But leave I will!" And as he spoke he rose
On his hurt thigh, and, though the wound galled sore,
Unbeaten yet, called for his horse, his pride,
His comfort, who would bear him from all fields
Victor; and thus the grieving steed bespake:

   "Long, Rhaebus, if for mortals aught be long,
We two have lived. To-day shalt thou bring back
Aeneas' head, avenging Lausus' pain
With me; or, if power fail us, then with me
Die: for I think not, bravest! thou wilt bear
Another's rule, and brook a Teucrian lord!"

   And on his willing back the accustomed seat
He took, and loaded both his hands with shafts;
And, helmed with shining brass and nodding plumes,

He galloped thus afield. A mighty tide
Of shame and wild despair rose in his heart,
And love to madness wrought, and conscious worth.
He with a great voice called Aeneas thrice:
And, knowing him, Aeneas prayed in joy:
"Father of Heaven and great Apollo grant
Thou comest on to close!"
So said, he went to meet the assaulting spear.
But he: "Why threat me, now my son is gone?
Thou canst destroy me by that way alone!
We fear no death, and for no God refrain!
Cease; for I come to die, and bring thee first
These gifts." He said, and hurled at him a shaft,
And in wide circuit flying dart on dart
Aimed; but the golden boss withstood them all.
Thrice round Aeneas on the left he rode,
Throwing his darts: the Trojan thrice bore round
The monstrous thicket on his brazen targe;
Till tired of such delays and plucking out
So many a spike, pressed by the unequal fray,
He, fraught with wiles, at last leapt forth and launched
His javelin at the charger's hollow brow.
The steed reared up, and beat his hoofs in air,
His rider threw, and falling over him,
Lay with slipped shoulder in confusing heap.
Trojans and Latins burn the air with shouts.
Up ran Aeneas, and his sword unsheathed,
And o'er him thus: "Where now is that wild heart,
That Tuscan fierce?" Mezentius, looking up,
Drank the wide air, and spake, regaining sense:

"O bitter foe! Why taunt and threaten death?
Nought hinders it: not thus I came to fight.
Not such the bond my Lausus made with thee.
One thing I ask, if conquered foes may hope,
Hide me in earth. I know my people's hate
Enfolds me round; O ward their fury off,
And let me share a tomb beside my son!"

Then in his throat he took the awaited sword,
And o'er his harness poured the blood of life.

Book XI

MEANWHILE FROM OCEAN rose the dawning day:
And, though the burial of his friends engrossed
Aeneas' care, and death bedimmed his soul,
Yet first to Heaven he paid the conqueror's vow.

A mighty oak he planted on a mound,
Shorn of all boughs and decked with shining arms,
Mezentius' spoils, to thee, great Lord of War,
A Trophy! with his plumes bedewed with blood,
Snapt spears, and hauberk in twelve places slashed.
On his left arm he strapped the brazen targe,
And from his neck the ivory falchion hung;
And while his captains thronged him closely round,
To charge the exulting crowd he thus began:

"The greatest deed is done: fear not the rest.
Behold our first-fruits, a proud monarch's spoils!
My hands have made Mezentius what he is.
To Latin King and walls now lies our way.
Be bold, be ready, and forestall the fight,
That no delay surprise us, when the Gods
Grant us to raise our banners and our host
Lead forth from camp, nor sluggish fear retard.
Meanwhile the unburied bodies let us lay
In earth, sole honour that the dead may gain!
Go. Their last glory give to those great hearts
Who with their blood have made this land our own;
And to Evander's saddened city first
Be Pallas sent, whom no unmanly soul
Darkness assumed, and sank in timeless death."

Thus he with tears; then to the door withdrew,
Where an old man was watching Pallas' corse,
Acoetes, who was shield-bearer of yore
To King Evander, but with star less kind
Since followed that dear charge. Around him stand
The servitors, a throng of Trojan men,
And Ilian wives with mourning locks unbound;

Who, when Aeneas passed the high-built doors,
Beating their breasts, uplifted to the stars
Loud wailing, and the palace moaned with grief.
He saw the pillowed head, the snow-white face,
The open gash of the Ausonian spear
In that smooth breast, and spoke with rising tears:

"Unhappy boy! Hath Fortune come to bless,
Yet spared not thee to see a realm of ours,
And ride in triumph to thy fathers' home?
Not thus I promised when I left thy sire
Evander, who embracing sent me forth
To Empire, and who warned me in his fear
How bold my foes, how hard my strife should be!
Even now, perchance, by hollow hope enthralled,
He pays the vow, and loads his shrines with gifts;
While with vain rites in mourning train we go
By his dead boy, who owes the Gods no more.
Unhappy! Thou shalt see his woeful bier!
Is this our waited triumph and return?
This my firm pledge? Yet thou shalt see no scars
Of shame, Evander, nor shall thy son's life
Make death his father's prayer. O what a shield,
Iulus! Italy! ye both have lost!"

He ceased; and bade them lift the piteous dead;
And sent a thousand men, his army's prime,
To bear him escort on the final road,
And share his father's tears; for grief so great
Small comfort, yet the mourning father's due.
Others not slothful weave a lissom bier,
Wattled with arbutus and sprays of oak,
And heap a bed, with shady leafage screened.
Here, on his woodland litter, he is laid;
Like some soft violet or harebell faint
Plucked by a maiden's hand, which hath not lost
Its hue and fashion, but the Mother Earth
Feeds it no longer now, nor gives it life.
Then purple vestures twain Aeneas brings
Heavy with gold, that once in happy toil
Sidonian Dido's hands had worked for him
Threading the web with gold: and one of these,
A last sad tribute, on the dead he lays;

With one he shrouds the fire-devoted head.
Then many a prize of Latian field he heaps,
And bids them bring his spoils, a long array,
Steeds, arms from foemen reft; and binds the hands
Behind the backs of victims whom he doomed
For that dead shade, to wet the flame with blood.
Trees, clad with foemen's arms, he bids the Chiefs
Themselves to carry, scored with foemen's names:
And sad Acoetes, worn with years, is led,
Rending his breast and face, who falling prone
Casts all his length on earth. Then forth they lead
The chariot reeking with Rutulian blood;
And next his war-horse, with all trappings doffed,
Aethon, who with big tear-drops wets his face.
Some bear his lance and helm, (for Turnus keeps
All else). Arcadians then, with arms reversed,
Tuscans and Trojans follow, trooping sad.

When all the train had passed, Aeneas stopped,
And sighing spake: "Now hence to other tears
Calls this dread doom of War! Hail evermore,
Great Pallas, and for evermore farewell!"
He spake no more; and to the high-walled camp
Retraced his way.
                            Now from the Latins' town
Envoys were come, with fronds of olive dight,
Who prayed his mercy to restore their dead,
Whose bodies strewed the field, and let them lie
Ensepulchred in earth; for war was none
With crushed and life-lorn men: O let him spare
Whom once he called his friends, his bridal kin!

Their prayers the good Aeneas might not spurn,
But gave the boon, and added thus in words:

"What sorry Fortune in such coils of war
Hath wrapped you, Latins, that you shun our love?
Peace crave ye for the dead, the War-God's prey?
Fain would I grant it to the living too!
I had not come but Doom this lodging gave.
Not with your race I war. Your King forsook
Our bond, and trusted him to Turnus' arms.
'Twere fairer done, had Turnus faced this death!

If he would drive us forth and end the war
By battle, here he should have met my sword;
And one had lived, whom God or his right hand
With life had dowered. Go! Burn your hapless dead."

Aeneas ended. They, amazed and dumb,
Kept eyes and faces on each other turned.
Then Drances old, in heart and bitter tongue
Young Turnus' constant foeman, thus returned:
"O Trojan, great in fame, in arms more great!
How shall I praise thee to the skies? Shall first
Thy justice move me, or thy feats of war?
Home will we bear thy words with thankful hearts;
And, if Fate grant a way, to King Latinus
Yoke thee. Let Turnus look for friends himself!
Yea, gladly we will raise thy destined walls,
And on our shoulders bear the stones of Troy!"

He ceased; and all one voice assenting cried.
Twelve days at truce, in mutual bands of peace,
Trojans and Latins mixed the woodland slopes
Securely roam. The cloven ashtree rings.
Star-soaring pines they fell, nor cease to split
Wedged oak and scented cedar, and draw down
Great mountain-ashes on their groaning wains.

Now flying Rumour with her tale of grief
Evander fills, Evander's house and town,
Where late she told of Pallas' conquering arm.
Gateward the Arcadians rush, and with old wont
Snatch funeral torches. A long line of light
Gleams on the road, dividing the dim fields.
The coming band of Phrygians join their train
Wailing. The mothers see them reach the walls,
And make the mourning city burn with shrieks.
But nought can stay Evander: in their midst
He rushes; and, the bier set down, falls prone
On Pallas, clasping him with moans and tears.
And scarce at last pain leaves his voice a path:

"Not this thy promise to thy father, Pallas!
That thou wouldst trust thee to grim Mars with care!
I know how strong is the young battle glow,
How sweet the glory of the first affray!

O first-fruits reaped in pain! hard rudiments
Of looming War! O vows and prayers of mine
By no God heard! And thou, most blessed Wife,
Happy in death, nor spared for this sad day,
While I outlive my span, a father left
Surviving all! O that Rutulian spears
Had slain me in Trojan ranks, my life been shed,
And this sad pomp borne me not Pallas home!
Yet you I blame not, Trojans, nor our bond,
Our hands in friendship joined: this debt mine age
Owed. Yet if death untimely waited him,
'Twill cheer me that he first slew Volscian hosts,
And leading Trojans into Latium fell.
No other obsequies I deem thy due
Than good Aeneas and his Phrygians give,
The Tyrrhene captains, all the Tyrrhene force.
Great spoils they bring, — the men thine hand doth slay!
Thou too wert standing, a vast armoured trunk,
Turnus, had age been matched and strength of years!
But shall my grief stay Teucrians from the field?
Go! nor forget to bear your King these words:
'Thine hand it is that keeps me in life's pain
With Pallas dead. Both son and sire thou seest
Claim Turnus. For thy fortune, thy renown
But this is left. For life I ask no joy,
Nor may, but dead to gladden my dead son!"

Meanwhile the Dawn o'er woe-worn men had raised
Her kindly light, renewing task and toil.
And now Aenéas on the winding strand,
Now Tarchon built the pyres, and thither bore,
Each with ancestral rites, their comrades dead,
And lit black fires below them, shrouding all
The lofty heavens in gloom. Thrice round the pyres
In flashing arms they marched, on horses thrice
Wheeled round the funeral flames, lamenting loud.
Tears on the ground and on their armour shed
Fall frequent, and their cries go up to heaven,
With blare of trumpets. Spoils of Latin dead
Some cast into the fire, fair-fashioned swords,
Helms, bridles, glowing wheels; while others add
The men's familiar bucklers, and the arms

That brought no joy. And many an ox they slay
In sacrifice around, with bristled swine,
And cattle harried in from every lea
Kill o'er the flames; then on their burning dead
Gazing along the beach, they unremoved
Guard the burnt ash, till dewy Night wheels round
The shining heaven of stars.
                              Nor less elsewhere
The mourning Latins built unnumbered pyres;
Laid many a man in earth, or sent them home,
Or bare to neighbouring fields. The rest, a mound
Of indistinguishable slain, they burn,
Untold, unhonoured; and the long wide land,
Glowing with fire on fire, is all one light.
And when three suns had routed cold and gloom,
The bones and mingled ashes on each hearth
Mourning they heaped, and with warm earth o'erspread.

    But most in rich Latinus' city rose
The sound of long lament, where anguished brides,
And mothers, and dear sisters' aching hearts,
And boys left fatherless, all cursed the war,
And Turnus' bridal; bidding Turnus arm,
Himself to fight the issue, since he claimed
Himself the Italian crown and pride of place.
Fierce Drances goads them: Turnus, he attests,
Alone is called, and challenged to contend.
Yet many a various word for Turnus pleads.
The Queen's great name o'ershadows him, and fame
Lifts high the man who reaped such spoils of war.

    And lo! amidst their broil and hot debate,
The Envoys come from Diomede's great town
With sad response; that all the pains they spent
Were nothing worth; nought skilled or gifts or gold
Or forceful prayers. "Look now for other swords,
Or sue for peace," said they, "the Trojan Prince."

    E'en King Latinus by great grief is bowed.
God's anger warns him, and those new-made graves,
That Fate's clear purpose leads Aeneas on.
By sovereign call a council of his chief
He summons to his court; who streaming flock

Through crowded highways to the royal hall.
Full in their midst, with sorrow-laden brow,
Eldest and prime in power, Latinus sat,
And bade the envoys from the Aetolian town
Speak, and each answer tell in order due.
Then every tongue was hushed, and Venulus,
Obedient to his bidding, thus began:

"The Argive camp and Diomede we saw;
Measured the way, surmounted every hap,
And touched the hand which laid our Ilium low.
He near Garganus builds a conqueror's town,
Named from his Argive sires Argyripa.
When we had entered, and full audience gained,
We proffered gifts, and told our name and land,
Who showed us war, what drew us to his town.
He heard; and thus returned with aspect calm:

" 'O happy peoples! O Saturnian realm!
Ausonians old, how fate hath vexed your peace,
And lured you on to battle-shocks unknown!
We who with steel profaned the fields of Troy,
(Let pass the weary battling at her walls,
The dead whom Simois keeps!) we, for our guilt
Paid penalties world-wide. E'en Priam's self
Might pity us, as false Caphereus knows,
Euboea's crags, and Pallas' star of woe.
From that campaign on distant shores exiled
To Proteus' Pillars Menelaus roams,
And Aetna's Cyclops meet Ulysses' gaze.
Why tell of King Idomeneus' changed home,
Pyrrhus, or Locrians lodged on Libyan soil?
Mycenae's Lord himself, the Achaeans' Chief,
Even on his threshold by a vile wife's hand
Fell: an adulterer snared the conquered East!
Me too, O Gods! fair Calydon ye grudged,
My father's hearth to see, my dear-loved wife!
Yea, still weird visions haunt me. Friends I lost,
Ah, penance sad! now wing the air as birds,
Or roam the rivers, and with tearful cries
Fill the sea crags. Such fears I had to bear
Since when I thrust my blade in Heavenly flesh,
O madman! and profaned with impious hurt

The hand of Venus. Urge, O urge me not
To strife like that! Since Troy was overthrown
I wage no war with Trojans, nor delight
To think on evils past. Turn with your gifts
To Prince Aeneas. We have stood before
His ruthless steel, and fought him hand to hand.
Trust one who tried how large he looms above
His lifted shield, what tempest wings his spear!
Had Ida borne two more such men as he,
Dardans had fallen upon the Inachian Towns,
And Greece were mourning now her altered fate.
Howe'er we dallied by Troy's stubborn wall,
'Twas Hector and Aeneas stayed the Greek,
And till the tenth year held the conqueror's feet.
Both great in heart, both great in puissant arms,
But he most leal. Join hands with him you may;
But look ye that you clash not sword on sword!'
Great King, thou hearest what the King replies,
And how he counsels in this stress of war."

    Scarce thus the Envoys, when a various hum
Ran through the vexed Ausonians, as when rocks
Delay a river, and the pent-back stream
Cries, and the banks are loud with murmuring waves.
When hearts grew calm, and restless tongues were hushed,
Thus, after prayer, the high-throned King began:

    "Latins! I would, 'twere better, we had ruled
The nation's course ere now. No time is this
For council, when the foe is at our gates.
Ill war we make on men of Heavenly race,
Unworn, unconquered; men who in defeat
Can never drop the sword. Abandon hope
To win Aetolian arms: each in himself
Hath hope,—how frail ye see! How all beside
Lies sunk in ruin your own eyes behold,
Your hands can feel. I blame not any man:
No more could prowess do: with every limb
Our realm fought hard. Hear now what sentence holds
My doubting mind, which I will teach in few,
And heed my words.
              An old demesne is mine,
Nearest the Tuscan river, dipping long

Toward the far West, beyond Sicanian bounds.
Auruncans and Rutulians sow and plough
The stubborn slopes, and graze their rugged heights.
Let all this land and tract of fir-topped hill
Go to win Trojan hearts; and let us make
Fair pact, and bid them to our realm as friends.
There let them build their Home if so they crave;
But if on other lands and other men
Their mind is bent, and they can leave our soil,
Let us build ships of oak, twice ten, or more
If they can man them: by the water's edge
Wood lies at hand: and let them choose their size,
Their number; we will give them hands and gear.
And more: to bear our words, and seal the pact,
An hundred of our people's prime shall go
With proffered boughs of peace, and take as gifts
Talents of gold and ivory, our seat,
Our royal robes. Now for the common weal
Take counsel, and relieve our weary state!"

Then Drances, fraught with spleen, whom Turnus' fame
Still goaded with wry Envy's bitter stings;
Lavish of wealth and words, but cold in war;
No empty name in council, in cabals
A man of might; (his mother's proud descent
Gave rank to one of obscure father born,)
He then uprising high their anger piled.

"O King, thou mootest what is dark to none,
Nor asks my voice; since all confess they know
Our fortunes' bourne, but speak with bated breath.
Let him cease blustering and free speech allow,
By whose bad auspices and ways perverse
(Though death he threaten, yet will I speak out!)
Such stars of War have set, and all our city
Lies sunk in grief before us, while he storms
Troy's camp, secure in flight, and startles Heaven!
Add but one gift, O King! but one, to all
Thou bidst us take for Dardans! O let none
Compel thee by his fury not to give
Thy child well-wedded to a peerless son,
And by a lasting bond confirm this peace.
But if such panic hold us, let us call

On him, from him beg favour that he yield,
To King and Country giving back their own.
Why wilt thou fling so oft on peril's mouth
These sad-starred men, O source of Latium's pain?
War hath no salve. For Peace we pray thee, Turnus!
And that one pledge of Peace inviolable.
See! I whom thou would'st hate, (and if thou dost,
'Tis nought,) I sue thee first! For pity yield!
Go beaten hence! O we have seen enough
Of rout and death and the wide waste of War!
Or, if Fame stir thee, if such strength thy soul
Nurse, and such doting on thy palace dower,
Face now thy foe, indomitable heart!
And we, to win for thee a royal bride,
We, common men, must cover the wide plain,
Unwept, unburied! Nay, if thou art man,
If thou hast any of thy fathers' fire,
Face him who calls!"

But Turnus' fury kindled at his words:
He groaned, and thus broke forth in accents deep:

"Aye forward, Drances, is thy tongue, when War
Demands the Hand! No Senate House is here,
O ready Counsellor, to fill with words,
Though puffed and blown in safety while yon fosse
Swims not in blood, and ramparts check the foe.
Roll on thy wonted thunders, and charge me
With panic, Drances! thou whose hand hath piled
Such heaps of Trojan dead, and filled the land
With spoils so splendid! We can try what might
Lives in the brave! Not far we have to seek
Our enemies; they gird our walls about.
On! On! Why lagg'st thou? Will thy prowess dwell
In nought for ever but thy windy tongue,
Thy flying feet?
I beaten? Dog! Can any brand me thus,
Who sees the Tiber swell with Ilian blood,
Evander's House uprooted and laid flat,
Arcadians stript of arms? Not so I seemed
To Bitias and tall Pandarus; not so
To thousands whom I vanquished on a day,
And sent to Hell, though hedged in foemen's walls!

'War hath no salve!' Pour out such omens, Fool!
On Dardan heads and thine! Cease not to maze
The world with terrors! Magnify the men
Twice vanquished, and decry Latinus' arms!
Now quail the lordly Myrmidons; now quail
Tydides and Achilles! back recoils
From Adrian waters Aufidus in flight!
Or when he feigns to shrink before my threats,
Trickster! and whets his slander with his fear!
(Nay, such a life this hand shall never spill.
Stir not, but keep it in thy craven breast!)
Now, King, to thee I turn and thy great charge.
If in our arms thou hast no further hope,
If so forlorn are we, and by one rout
. So fallen that Fortune cannot turn again,
Peace let us plead for, stretching hands unarmed!
Yet, Oh! if any fire be in us still,
Great above all is he and blest in deed,
Who, shrinking from such sight, fell once for all,
And bit the dust! But, if we still have means
And manhood still intact, and for our aid
Italian tribes and cities still remain;
If fraught with blood the Trojans' glory came,
And they too have their dead, and over all
One storm hath swept, why on the grunsel edge
Faint we ere trumpet call in shameful fear?
Time and the changes of the toiling days
Have mended much; and oft to those she mocked
Fortune comes round, and firmly plants their feet.
Aetolian Arpi will not lend us aid,
But rich Tolumnius will, Messapus will,
And all the tribe-sent Chiefs; and no mean fame
Shall tend the Laurentine and Latium's prime.
Camilla too, of the great Volscian race,
Will lead her chivalry a-bloom with brass.
Or, if the Trojans challenge me alone,
And 'tis your will, and I thus thwart your weal,
Not with such hate doth Conquest shun my hand,
That I should shrink from aught with hope so large!
Bold will I face him, though Achilles' self,
And clad in Vulcan's arms! I, Turnus, I
Who yield in prowess to no man of old,

This life to you and King Latinus vow!
Me only Aeneas calls? So let him call;
Nor Drances rather by his death atone,
(Should Heaven be wroth), or bear the victor's palm!"

    While thus on doubtful issues they debate
Wrangling, Aeneas moves his camp a-field;
And, spreading tumult through the regal halls,
A rumour runs, which fills the town with fear,
That Troy's embattled host and Tyrrhene troops
Are marching on the plain from Tiber stream.
Then storm and ferment in the people's heart
Raged, and wrath pricked them with no gentle spur.
Hands clutch at arms: for arms the young men shout:
Sad fathers weep and mutter. On all sides
Clamour and wide confusion fill the air.
As in the tree-tops when a swarm of birds
Alight, or by Padusa's fishy stream
Swans make hoarse music o'er the voiceful pools.

    Then Turnus seized the time. "Yes, friends," he cried,
"Sit praising peace in council, while our foes
Clash on the realm!" And adding not, sprang up,
And left the hall in haste. "Volusus, ho!
Bid arm the Volscian maniples!" he cried,
"Lead forth the Rutuli! Thou and thy brother,
Coras, and thou, Messapus, spread the Horse!
Part fence the City gates, and man the towers!
The rest with me make onset when I charge!"

    The town runs to the walls. The King himself,
Stunned by misfortune, leaves the council, leaves
Postponed his purpose, and himself blames oft
That to the Dardan Prince he held not out
Greeting, and for his City gained a son.

    Some trench the gateways, or bring stones and stakes.
The clarion sounds the bloody note of War;
And boys and mothers, in a motley ring,
The ramparts crown: on each that struggle calls:
While, bearing gifts, to Pallas' towered fane,
Girt with a matron throng, the Queen ascends,
And by her side the maid Lavinia, cause
Of all that woe, with lovely eyes downcast.

They enter, censing the dim fane, and pour
From the high threshold voices of lament:

"Tritonian maid! O sovran Queen of War!
Break with thine hand the Phrygian robber's spear!
O cast him down! O dash him at our gates!"

And Turnus, arming furious for the fray,
Donned his red hauberk rough with brazen scales,
And sheathed his legs in gold, and to his side
Girded his sword, and with his brow still bare
Ran in a golden glitter from the Keep,
Bounding with hope, impatient of the foe.
As when a horse hath broken from his stall,
And roams the open meadow, free at last,
Where mares are grazing, or in his old stream
Splashes once more, and throws his head on high,
And neighs, and revels, while around his neck,
Around his shoulders, plays the flowing mane.

Him in the gateway with her Volscian files
Camilla met; and from her horse the Queen
Leapt down; at whose example all her troop
Slipped from their steeds to earth. Then thus she spake:

"Turnus! if in themselves the brave may trust,
I dare, I vow to meet Aeneas' turm,
And ride alone to face the Tyrrhene Horse.
Let me be first to try the perilous fray!
Hold thou the walls on foot, and guard the town."

And he, with eyes on the dread Maiden fixed:
"O Maid! O Rose of Italy! What thanks
Can I express or pay? But since thy soul
Soars high above all praise, share now my task!
Aeneas, as our spies bring sure report,
Hath sent on treacherously his light-armed Horse
To scour the plains, while he draws nigh the City
O'er the lone mountain ridge. I lay a snare
In his green winding path, to block with troops
The vale's twin throats. Do thou in battle meet
The Tyrrhene Horse; with thee Tiburtus' force,

Messapus bold and Latin bands shall be;
Take thou the Leader's charge."

                              And with like words
Messapus and the banded Chiefs he cheered
To take the field; then went to meet his foe.

There lies a vale far-folded, fit for fraud
And ambush, which the glooming forest clasps
On every side, and through each narrow throat
Leads a thin track, an avenue malign.
A plain lies on the beacon heights above,
Unknown, a safe retreat, whether from right
Or left you plan an onset, or would stand
High on the ridge and roll great stones below.
And hither Turnus by familiar paths
Went and took ground and held the faithless woods.

Meanwhile Latonia in the Heavenly seats
Thus to swift Opis of her holy band
And maiden sisterhood in sadness spake:

"To cruel war, O Maid! Camilla hies,
And all in vain hath girt our armour on,
Dear before all to me! 'Tis no new love,
No sudden rapture thrills Diana's heart!

"When Metabus, through insolence and hate
Thrust from his throne, from old Privernum fled,
To share his flight amid the press of war
He took his babe, who bore her mother's name
Casmilla, to Camilla lightly changed.
He bare her in his bosom while he sought
Lone mountain glens, though Volscian troops wide-spread
Hovered all round, and savage spears assailed.
Lo! Amasenus foamed athwart his flight,
Flooding his banks, such rain had rent the clouds.
Then, fain to swim, yet fearing for his child,
By that dear burden checked, he, weighing all,
Fixed suddenly upon this hard resolve.
In his strong hand a massy spear he bore,
Of knotted oak burnt hard, to which he bound
His daughter wrapt in bark and forest cork,

And lashed her featly round the middle shaft.
Then, in his great hand poising it, he cries:

" 'Boon Forest Maid, Latonia! This my child
To thee I vow! She holding first thy lance
Flies from our foes for aid! I pray thee, Goddess!
Take her for thine, whom now the wild winds bear!'

"He bent his arm, and threw the whirling shaft.
The waters roared. Camilla flew forlorn
On the shrill spear across the huddling spate.
But Metabus, pressed hard by thronging hosts,
Plunged in the flood; then victor from the grass
Plucked spear and child, his gift to Trivia vowed.

"No town, no roof received him, nor himself
From savageness had lapsed. He led the life
Of shepherds on the solitary hills,
And nursed his daughter in the thorny brakes
Of tangled forests from the wild mare's breast,
Milking the udders in her baby lips.
And when the child first set her feet and stood,
With pointed spear he armed her hands, and hung
Across her little shoulders shafts and bow.
Instead of gold-bound hair and flowing robe,
A tiger's skin fell hanging down her back.
Even then her tender hands threw childish darts,
Or, slinging round her head the twisted thong,
Strymonian crane brought down or white-plumed swan.
Her many Tyrrhene mothers for their sons
Desired in vain: with Dian sole content,
Her huntress heart she keeps and maiden mind
For ever pure. Would she had ne'er been swept
On such a feud, to charge the ranks of Troy!
Dear had she been and of my train this day.
Yet, Oh! since Fate on her untimely weighs,
Glide, Nymph, from Heaven, and hie to Latian fields,
Where that disastrous battle rolls in gloom.
Take these: the avenging shaft from quiver draw;
That whoso taint with harm, or friend or foe,
Her sacred limbs, may pay me with his blood.

Then veiled in mist her piteous corse unspoiled
In her own land I will ensepulchre."

She ended: but the other, wrapt in storm,
Sped down the buxom air her sounding way.

And now the Trojan and Etruscan Chiefs
Draw near the walls, with all their chivalry
Marshalled in equal troops. The prancing steed
Neighs o'er the field, and fighting the drawn rein
Swerves left and right. The iron field with spears
Bristles, and blazes with uplifted arms.

Opposed Messapus and the Latin scouts,
And Coras with his brother, take their stand,
And Maid Camilla's wing. They couch their spears,
Far drawing back the arm, and poise their darts.
Hot burned their coming and the noise of horse.
Now each in spear-throw of the other halt;
Then shouting charge, and spur the furious steed.
All round the showering missiles thick as snow
Darken the sky. And first with countering spears
Tyrrhenus and Aconteus charging meet,
And shock with mighty sound, and tear the breast
Of either charger dashed on broken breast.
Like thunder-bolt or heavy sling-shot ball
Aconteus falls far-flung, and on the air
Sheds forth his life. Confusion fills their files.
The Latins wheeling sling their shields behind,
And townward turn their steeds. The Trojans charge,
Led by Asilas, till they near the gate:
The Latins shout anew, and backward turn
Their horses' yielding necks. Their foes drop rein,
And fly, retreating far. As when the Sea
Sweeping to land with alternating flow
Now swills the rocks with foam, or softly spreads
A breast of water o'er the sandy marge;
Now, fast retreating, rolls the shingle down
Sucked back by ebbing waves, and leaves the shore.

Twice to their walls the Tuscans drive their foe;
Twice baffled look behind with shielded backs.

But when the third fight met, and all the lines
Grappled together, and man chose his man,
Then moaned the dying, then in blood lay deep
Bodies and arms, and wounded horses rolled
Mixed with slain men, and fierce the battle swelled.

 Afraid to close, Orsilochus threw lance
On Remulus' horse, and left it neath his ear.
With chest upthrown the maddened charger reared,
And pawed the air, impatient of his wound.
Down the flung rider rolled. Catillus smote
Iollas, and Herminius, great-threwed,
Great-hearted, with his yellow locks unbound,
And shoulders bare. No fear of wounds hath he,
So large he looms. The spear thrust in his back
Quivers transfixed, and doubles him with pain.
Blood flows on every side: each warrior sheds
Slaughter, and seeks in wounds a glorious death.

 Through that hot field, a quivered Amazon,
With one breast bare for fight, Camilla leaps:
Now showers the arrowy sleet; now takes in hand,
Tireless, the two-edged axe, while Dian's arms
Ring from her shoulder, and the golden bow.
And even if backward pressed she yields her ground,
Still with turned bow she aims the flying shafts.
Her chosen gird her round; Larina chaste,
Tulla, Tarpeia shaking the bronze axe;
Boon maids of Italy, in peace and war
Divine Camilla's help-mates and her pride.
So Amazons of Thrace to battle clash
In painted armour o'er Thermodon's flood,
Or round Hippolyte, or when her car
Penthesilea rides, and the loud rout
Of moony-shielded women leap with glee.

 Whom first, whom last, fierce Maiden did thy spear
Strike down, how many didst thou lay in death?
Euneus first, whose open breast she lanced
With the long pine-shaft's point, who falling poured
Rivers of blood, and biting the red ground

Writhed dying on his wound. Then Pagasus
And Liris, who, while gathering the reins,
From his stabbed horse rolled down; the other ran
Stretching his unarmed hand to help him rise,
When both together fell. To whom she adds
Amaster, and pursues with far-flung spear
Tereus, Harpalycus, Demophoon,
And Chromis. For each bolt the Maiden throws
A Phrygian man falls dead.
                                In harness strange
Rode Ornytus on Iapygian steed,
The hunter, with his shoulders clad for war
In bullock's hide, and on his beavered brow
A wolf's great mouth and grinning white-toothed jaws.
A wood-pike arms his hand. He through the press
Wheels to and fro, a head above the rest:
But him she caught (no toil among that rout),
And pierced, and o'er him thus relentless spake:

"Tuscan! didst dream of chasing forest deer?
The day is come when woman's arms shall show
How vain your boast! Yet to the dead thou'lt take
A name not mean, slain by Camilla's spear!"

Butes, Orsilochus, Troy's hugest men,
Follow: but Butes in the back she pierced
'Twixt helm and hauberk, where the rider's neck
Gleams, and the buckler from his left arm hangs.
Orsilochus she flees in circuit wide,
Then wheels within, and gives her chaser chase,
And rising high, through arms, through bone, her axe,
For all his begging, drives and drives again,
Till the hot battered brain wets all his face.

Then Aunus' son, who dwelt on Apennine,
(No least Ligurian in his hour of guile,)
Suddenly saw her, and stood still for fear.
And since no speed could now evade a fight,
Or shun the assaulting Queen, by wit and craft
Essaying to beguile, he thus began:
"Where is thy greatness, if a woman trust

In horse's strength? Prepare to fight on foot.
Dare in fair field to meet me, waiving flight,
And learn at once whom windy vaunts will dupe!"

But she, with indignation fired, her horse
Gives to her friend, and with drawn blade on foot
And maiden shield confronts him unafraid.
Then, deeming craft hath won, he, pausing not,
Turns rein, and rides in flight, with the iron spur
Chafing his horse.
                    "O false! O vainly puffed
With pride, Ligurian! Thou hast tried for nought
Thy fathers' wiles: no fraud shall bring thee back
Unscathed, O serpent, to false Aunus' home!"

She said; and, running swift as flame, his horse
Crossed, and the bridle caught, and front to front
Met, and took vengeance of his hated blood.
So lightly a bodeful hawk from some high crag
O'ertakes a soaring dove, and grips her fast,
And tears her heart out with his hooked claws,
While blood and scattered plumes fall from the sky.

But not blind-eyed the Sire of Men and Gods
High on Olympus sat, surveying all.
Tyrrhenian Tarchon to hot strife he roused,
His anger pricking with no gentle spur:
Who, through the slain and ranks of yielding men,
Galloped, and goaded them with shouts, on each
Calling by name, and gave the beaten strength:

"O dastard still! O dull to shame! What fear,
Tuscans! what sloth hath settled on your souls?
A woman turn and drive our ranks abroad!
What boots your steel, those idle arms we bear?
Not slow are you to frays of Love and Night;
Or, when the wry pipe wakes the Bacchic dance,
To look for feasts and tables crowned with cups,
(Your love, your life!) till the smooth Seer pronounce,
And the fat victim call you to the grove!"

So said, he spurred amidst them, daring death,
And charged on Venulus in turbid rage.
He tore him from his horse; he hugged his man,

And swept him off amain at saddle-bow.
A shout uprose; and every Latin eye
Turned on them. Tarchon, flying like a fire,
Bears his armed foe, from whose own lance's head
Rending the iron, he feels what part is bare
To take death's wound. The other from his throat
Holds off the hand, by strength repelling force.
As when a golden eagle high bears up,
Gripped in her feet, a snake, and claws him tight:
In waving folds the wounded serpent writhes,
Bristles his scales, and, hissing from his mouth,
Swells high: no less she digs her hooked beak
I' the struggling worm, and beats her wings on air.
So Tarchon from Tiburtine ranks his prey
Triumphant bore: whose fair example all
Pursued with onslaught. Arruns, doomed himself,
Round swift Camilla wheels, with shaft and skill
Preventing her, and waits the readiest chance.
Where'er the Maid rides hotly through the press,
He glides, in silence watching all her steps.
Where from her foes she comes victorious back,
Stealthy and swift, he turns the rein, and tries
Now this approach, now that, and wheels all round,
And shakes the unerring spear, with mischief fraught.

Now vowed to Cybele and once her Priest,
Chloreus, in Phrygian armour shining far,
Urged on his foaming horse caparisoned
With brazen feathery scales and cloth of gold.
He, in strange purples brave, from Lycian bow
Shot forth Gortynian shafts; a bow of gold
Rang on his back, and gold his Prophet's helm.
His saffron scarf, his folds of rustling gauze
The yellow gold bound up, and broidered fair
His outland breeches were and tunic gay.
Him, (to deck temples with his Trojan gear,
Or wear herself his captured gold,) him sole
From all that press of war the Huntress Maid
Chased blindly, and with woman's love of spoil
Burned reckless through the battle; till at last
Seizing his time, Arruns the hidden dart
Woke up, and thus to Heaven his prayer addressed:

"Supreme Apollo, whom we chief adore!
Soracte's Guard! for whom the well-fed pine
Blazes, and we thy votaries, through the fire
Tread the heaped embers, strong in faith; O grant,
Almighty! that our arms may purge this shame!
No prize I seek, nor trophies for a maid
Vanquished and spoiled; fame other feats will bring.
Let this dire bane but fall beneath my blow,
And without glory I will take me home!"

Apollo heard; and half his prayer allowed;
Half to the scudding winds he scattered wide.
To lay Camilla dark in sudden death
He gave: again to see his mountain home
He gave not; into air his words were blown.
So when the launched spear sounded through the sky
Swift minds and eyes all Volscians as one man
Turned on the Queen. But she nor wind nor sound
Heeded, nor spear descending from the blue,
Till under her bare breast the piercing shaft
Lodged, and deep driven drank her maiden blood.

Up run her maids, and lift their falling Queen
Awestruck. But fearful Arruns flies ere all,
In joy with terror blent. No more he dares
Trust to his spear, nor meet the maiden's arms.
As, when he slays a shepherd or an ox,
The wolf at once in mountain heights untracked
Buries himself, ere vengeance can pursue,
Knowing his boldness, and his cowering tail
Smooth to his belly draws, and seeks the woods:
So out of sight slunk Arruns in dismay,
And in thick battle plunged, content to fly.

She dying grasps the spear; but through her bones,
Deep in her wounded ribs, the steel stands fast.
Fainting she falls; her eyelids cold in death
Fall, and the rose-bloom from her cheek is gone.
To Acca then, her friend of equal years,
Sole friend of all who shared Camilla's heart,
Breathing her latest breath, she spake and said:

"So far my strength hath gone. Now my sore hurt
Speeds me, O Sister! All around grows dark.

Bear this last charge to Turnus, that he fight
Where I have fought, and beat the Trojans off.
And now farewell!"
                 She left the reins, and slipped
Unconscious to the ground; then, freezing slow,
Passed from the bonds of flesh, and hung her neck,
And dropped her arms, and bowed her head to Death,
And with one groan indignant life took flight.

Then rose a cry that struck the golden stars.
In fray more furious with Camilla slain,
Charged all the force of Troy, the Tuscan Chiefs,
And all Evander's wings of Arcady.

But Trivia's sentry on the mountain top,
Opis, unfeared had watched the battle long;
And when amid the madness and the noise
She saw Camilla done to piteous death,
Moaning, she uttered from her heart these words:

"Ah! too, too harshly, Maiden, hast thou paid,
Who challenged Trojans! It availed thee nought
To have served Diana in the thorny wilds,
Or on thy back to have borne our quivered shafts!
Yet not to shame thy Queen hath left thee now,
In this thine end; nor shalt thou die unnamed,
Or rumoured in men's ears as unavenged.
For whosoe'er hath harmed thy sacred limbs
Shall pay deserved death!" A mound of earth,
Dercennus' tomb, Laurentum's ancient King,
Beneath a hill stood screened by ilex shade;
Where first the lovely Goddess, springing swift,
Lighted, and from the tomb spied Arruns out.
Whom when she saw gay-armed and swollen with pride;
"Why step aside?" said she, "Turn here thy feet!
Come here to die, and for Camilla take
Fit prize. Shall Dian's shafts slay such as thou?"

From golden quiver then one flying shaft
The Thracian took, and bent her vengeful bow
And drew it far, till the curved tips were joined
And both hands level, while one touched the barb,
The other touched the bowstring and the breast.
One sound he heard of singing bow and wind

Together, and the steel was in his flesh.
Him dying there, and moaning his last moan,
Heedless in common dust his comrades leave:
To high Olympus Opis wings her way.

  Their leader lost, Camilla's squadron flees:
Atinas flees; the scared Rutulians flee.
Captains dispersed and maniples forlorn
Seek safety, and their horses townward turn.
And none can meet the Trojans' deadly charge,
Nor hold them back by arms. On shoulders spent
They bear the bows unstrung, while all the plain
Crumbles and reels with thud of hurrying hoofs.
Dark clouds of dust are rolling to the walls;
And mothers on the watch-towers beat their breasts,
And to the stars uplift their women's cries.
But they who first have galloped through the gate,
Mixt with the foemen's host are sore beset,
Nor scape their deaths; but on the threshold's edge,
Stabbed in their walls, among their sheltering homes,
Pant out their lives. Part close the gates, nor dare
Give opening to receive their pleading friends;
And piteous carnage springs of those who hold
The approach, and those who plunge upon their points.
Shut out before their weeping parents' eyes,
Some, swept away, roll headlong to the moat;
Some blindly with loose rein their horses spur
To ram the portals and the strong barred gates.
In that sore strait e'en mothers on the walls,
Who saw Camilla, taught by patriot love,
Fling darts with shaking hands, and with hard oak
With sticks and staves burnt hard instead of steel,
Strike, burning to die first their town to save.

  And harshly fell on Turnus in the woods
The news when Acca told of all that rout;
Of Volscian files undone, Camilla's fall,
The foe's fierce onset, that swift flood of war
O'erwhelming all, and panic in the town.
Infuriate he, (so Jove's stern will required,)
Left the hill's ambush and the thorny brakes.
Who scarce from sight had gone, and gained the plain,
When Prince Aeneas, through the pass left bare,

Surmounts the hill, and quits the forest gloom.
So townward both in haste with all their force
Pass, and few paces separate the twain.
And while Aeneas spied from far the fields
Smoking with dust, and saw Laurentum's troops,
Turnus was ware of fierce Aeneas armed,
And heard their coming feet and snorting steeds.

Straight had they clashed, and tried the chance of war,
But in Iberian waves the rose-red Sun
Dipped his tired steeds, and day in darkness sank.
Before the walls they camp, and trench their lines.

Book XII

WHEN TURNUS SAW the Latins foiled in war,
Shattered and spent, his promise claimed, himself
Marked of all eyes, his swelling soul burst out
In quenchless flame. As when on Punic leas
The lion, chased and wounded to the heart,
Shows fight at last, and on his brawny neck
Tosses his mane with joy, and dauntless bites
The spoiler's spear, and roars with bloody jaws:
So fury swelled in Turnus' kindling soul.
Then thus the King, thus headstrong, he bespake:

"Turnus delays not! Cause to waive their words,
Or break their bond, our dastard foe hath none!
I meet him. Sanctify and frame the bond!
This hand to Hell shall send the Dardan down,
Troy's runagate, (let Latins sit and see!)
This single sword refute the blame of all,
Or he may rule, Lavinia's conquering lord!"
To whom Latinus answered, calm in soul.

"O bold! the more thy fiery spirit swells,
More deeply must I ponder, and with fear
Weigh every risk. Thy father Daunus' realms,
And many towns are thine thy hand hath won.

Latinus, too, hath gold and gratitude.
More maids in Latium and Laurentum dwell,
Not meanly born. Thus harshly let me speak
Without disguise, and deeply drink my words!
To none of yore who wooed her might I wed
My child unblamed; so augured gods and men.
Won by my love for thee, by ties of blood,
Won by my sad wife's tears, I broke all bonds,
Stole his betrothed and drew a traitor's sword!
Thou see'st what woes, what wars pursue me since,
What labours, Turnus, thou art chief to bear.
Twice in pitched battle conquered, scarce we save
Italian hopes: the Tiber with our blood
Flows hot; and plains are whitened with our bones.
Where drifts my mind so oft by madness warped?
If I would welcome them with Turnus slain,
Why end I not the strife with Turnus whole?
What will Italians, what will thine own kin,
Rutulians, say, if I (which heaven forfend!)
Give thee to death, the suitor of my child?
Think on war's changes! Pity him who mourns,
Thine age-worn father in his Ardean home
Far hence!"
                    But Turnus by no words is bent:
His fury swells, and sickens at the cure.
At last, when speak he could, he thus began:

   "Thy care for me, good father, for my sake
Lay down, and let me barter life for fame.
We, too, throw spears; no feeble steel our hand
Scatters, and bloodshed follows on our blow.
No mother will be near, in shadows hid,
To cloak his fleeing with her woman's cloud."

   But weeping, awed by that new turn of war,
The death-marked Queen to fiery Turnus clung.

   "O by these tears, if thou regard at all
Amata, O Son, sole hope, sole solace now
Of our sad age! Latinus' pride and power
Lie in thine hand: the House leans all on thee!
I only pray, clash not with Trojan men!
Whate'er await thee, Turnus, in such strife,

Waits me. I, too, shall leave the hateful light,
Nor captured see Aeneas son of mine!"

Lavinia heard her mother, and the tears
Dewed her hot face; a mantling rose of flame
Ran o'er her glowing cheeks; as when a man
Incarnadines the Indian ivory
With crimson stain, or as pale lilies blent
With roses flush; so flushed her maiden cheek.
On her he fixed his gaze, o'erwhelmed by love,
And burning more for battle answered brief:

"O not with tears, not with such omens, pray,
To War's stern field, O Mother, send me forth!
For Turnus is not free to give Death pause.
Haste, Idmon! to the Phrygian despot bear
These words unwelcome. When the morrow's Dawn
Glows from her rosy chariot, let him lead
No troops to war: let Troy's, Rutulia's arms
Rest; let the War be settled by our blood,
And on yon field Lavinia wooed and won!"

Thence homeward speeding for his steeds he calls,
And joys to see them whinnying at his look,
Those snow-bright steeds which Orithyia's self
Gave proud Pilumnus to outrace the winds.
The busy grooms all round with hollow palms
Pat their loud chests and comb the flowing hair.

Then on his back he throws the hauberk rough
With gold and orichalc, and dons in place
His sword and shield and crimson-crested helm, —
The sword of Daunus, which the Fire God's self
Forged white and tempered in the Stygian wave;
Then grasps the spear which stands within his halls
Leaning against a column, Actor's spoil
The Auruncan, and the quivering weapon shakes
Crying, "O Spear, that never failed my call!
Now comes mine hour! Thee greatest Actor bare;
Now Turnus bears thee. Grant me to lay dead
This Phrygian eunuch, and with stalwart hand
Shred his rent mail, and soil in dust his locks
Curled with the heated iron and drenched in myrrh!"

Such madness goads him: all his sparkling face
Flames, and fire flashes from his furious eyes.
As when a bull wakes his dread battle roar,
And calling to his horns the gathering wrath
Butts at a tree, and shocks the air with blows,
Or sheds the scattered sand, preluding war.

And in his mother's armour not less fierce
Aeneas whets with rage his martial soul,
Full glad that proffered truce should lull the war.
He calms his friends and sad Iulus' fear,
Teaching his Doom; and bids men take the King
His firm response, and name the terms of peace.

The morrow morn scarce strewed the hills with light,
And the Sun's horses from the seething sea
Leapt up, and from their nostrils blew the day,
When Trojans and Rutulians measured out
By the great city's wall the field of fight,
And hearths and altars for their common Gods
There made of grass. Some clad in linen bear
Water and fire, with vervain round their brows.
Ausonia's legions from the streaming gates
March out in serried ranks; and all the force
Of Troy and Tuscany diversely armed
Pour forth arrayed in steel, as if grim War
To battle called. In gold and purples proud
Midmost the Captains flash, Asilas bold,
Mnestheus the Assaracan, Messapus fierce,
The Sea God's son, the Tamer of the Steed.

The signal given, both armies take their ground,
And plant their spears in earth and pile their shields;
And eager rushing mothers, unarmed folk,
Old feeble men, fill tower and roof, or stand
By the tall gates.
              But Juno from the Mount
Now Alban named, (no name it had, no praise
Nor glory then,) looked out upon the field,
And saw both Trojan and Laurentine lines,
And the King's city; and thus the Goddess then
To Turnus' sister spake, herself divine, —
Queen of the pools and murmuring streams was she,
Her with such grace the King of Heaven had dowered

For her lost maidenhood.
                          "O Nymph most dear!
O Splendour of the Streams! Thee more than all
The Latin maids who climbed the ungrateful bed
Of high-souled Jove I loved, thou knowest well,
And in thy Heavenly place set thee with joy.
Juturna, learn thy grief, and blame not me.
While Fate and Fortune let the Latian weal
Prosper, I shielded Turnus and thy walls.
Now him I see confronting fate ill-matched:
His day of doom draws near, his stringent foe.
This fight, this league I cannot watch. If more
Thou darest for a brother, 'tis for thee!
Go. Happier days may tread on Sorrow's trail!"

    She scarce had said, when fair Juturna smote
Thrice and four times her bosom, shedding tears.
"No time is this for tears," Saturnia said.
"Speed! Wrest from death thy brother, if thou may'st,
Or waken war, and break the purposed league;
I warrant the bold act!" She urged, but left
Uncertain still her sorrow-clouded mind.

    Now came the Kings with pomp. In four-horsed car
Latinus rode, about whose gleaming brow
Shone twelve gilt rays, the badge of his great Sire
The golden Sun; and drawn by two white steeds
Turnus, whose hand two steel-bound lances shook;
Then, bright with starry Shield and Heaven-sent arms,
Aeneas, Rome's original great Sire,
Fast by Ascanius rode, Rome's second hope.
Then to the altars went the clear-stoled Priests,
With sheep unshorn and young of bristled swine,
And set them by the flame. They turned their eyes
To face the rising sun, and from their hands
Gave the salt meal, and branded with the steel
The victims' foreheads, pouring out the bowls.
And good Aeneas drew his sword and prayed:

    "Be witness now, O Sun! Give ear, O Land!
Land for whose sake such pains I could endure!
Almighty Sire, and Juno thou, his Queen,
Now, Goddess, now more kind! And thou, great Mars,
Whose will sways all men's strife! Rivers and Springs,

Etherial Virtues, and whatever Powers
Dwell in the dark blue Sea, on you I call!
If conquest crown the Ausonian, homeward then
To Evander's walls the vanquished men shall go,
Iulus leave the land, Aeneas' seed
Not draw rebellious swords nor vex this realm
Thereafter. But should Victory, as I ween,
(May heaven confirm it!) give the day to us,
I will not bid Italians bow to Troy,
Nor ask the crown myself. In during league
Let both unconquered nations join as one.
Gods I will give and rites. His arms, his sway
Let my bride's father keep, and Trojans build
My City, which shall bear Lavinia's name."

    Thus first Aeneas: then the King to Heaven
Looked, and his hand uplifting thus rejoined:
"I likewise swear by Earth and Sea and Stars,
Latona's twins, and Janus double-faced,
The Infernal Powers and shrines of loveless Dis.
Hear too, thou Sire, whose thunder seals the bond!
I touch the altars: mediate fires and Gods
I adjure! No day shall break the Italians' bond,
Let come what may; no power of ill shall turn
My purpose, though all Earth in deluge drowned
Merge into sea, and Heaven be fused with Hell!
Surely as this staff," (for staff he bare in hand,)
"No more will break to tender leaf and shade
Since root and branch 'twas sundered by the steel
From its green mother in the shady wood,
A tree no more, but now by craftsman's hand
Fair-bound in brass for Latin Lords to bear!"

    With suchlike words they in their Chieftains' sight
Pledge faith between them; then above the flame
Stabbing the victims, flay the living flesh,
And heap the altars with full-laden plates.

    But to Rutulians long the fight had seemed
Ill-matched; and now their harassed hearts are torn
Yet more, to see more near the unequal strength.
Turnus confirms them by his silent gait,
His looks down-cast in reverence at the shrine,
His faded cheek and youthful body wan.

And when Juturna saw the growing talk,
The hearts that drooped in doubt, she in their midst,
Feigning the form of Camers, (who was sprung
Of lofty line, and of a sire well-named
For valour, and himself of puissant arms,)
She, plunging in their midst, not uninformed,
Shedding the seeds of rumour thus began:

"Think ye not shame, Rutulians, for all these
One life to give? In numbers or in strength
Are we not matched? Lo, all their fates command, —
Arcadia, Troy, and Turnus' Tuscan foes!
Scarce half of us that met would find a match!
He to those Gods to whom he vows himself
Will soar by fame, and live on all men's lips:
We, tamely sitting here, our land must lose,
And pay forced homage to disdainful lords!"

Such words their resolution fired yet more,
And murmurs crept abroad. E'en Laurentines,
E'en Latin men are changed. For they that hoped
For peace and weal unvexed, now choosing war
Pray that the bond may fail, and the hard lot
Of Turnus pity. And yet more to this
Juturna adding, sent from Heaven a Sign
Which more than all perplexed Italian hearts
With portents false. For in the rose-flushed sky
Jove's golden Bird took flight, and drove in chase
A winging troop of clamorous water-fowl.
He sudden dropped, and in his knavish claws
Stole from the wave one swan excelling all.
Intent the Italians watched, while all the birds,
(Wondrous to view!) their flight with clamour turned,
Darkening the sky with wings, and on their foe
Fell, a thick cloud, till beaten down he flagged
From very weight, and flinging to the stream
His talons' booty, fled to skies afar.
Then, then with shouts and spreading hands that sign
Rutulians hail: and first Tolumnius cries,
The Augur: "This, 'twas this I prayed for oft!
I hail, I own the Gods! Take up the sword!
I, I will lead you! whom this foreign knave
Scares like frail birds, O wretches! laying waste
Your coasts. He too shall fly, with sails outspread,

To skies afar! Now one in heart your ranks
Close up, and fight to save your stolen King!"

He spake, and running forth launched on the foe
A spear, and singing through the air it sped,
Shrill, sure; and shouts and clamour and dismay
Filled every line, and hearts in tumult burned.
On sped the spear, till in its path there stood
Nine comely brothers, to Gylippus borne
All by one Tuscan wife in Arcady;
And one it struck, just where the waist is chafed
By the stitched belt and buckles bite the side,
A shapely man in sunbright armour clad,
Struck through his ribs and laid him in the dust.
But fired by grief his brothers' gallant band
Grasped sword or flying lance and blindly sprang
Forward; on whom the legioned Laurentines
Charge, and once more Agyllans, Trojan men,
And gaily-armed Arcadians roll their waves.
One mind rules all, to measure steel with steel.
The altars are despoiled: a storm of darts
Torments the air, and iron showers fall thick.
Bowls, hearths are borne away. Latinus' self,
His Gods defeated and his truce undone,
Takes flight. The others yoke the chariot teams,
Or leap to horse, and with drawn blade stand firm.

Thirsting to break the truce, Messapus turned
His horse to daunt Aulestes, Tuscan King,
Wearing the sign of Kings, who back recoiled,
Striking the altar, and o'er head and neck
Rolled hapless. And Messapus hotly flew,
And from high horseback with his beamy spear
Smote him who cried for mercy, and spake thus,
"He hath it! Gods, this better victim take!"
The Italians throng to strip the life-warm flesh.

Then Corynaeus from the hearth a brand
Seized, and as Ebusus came up to strike
Filled all his face with fire, and his great beard
Blazed, smelling as it burned. He onward came,
And caught the hair of his bewildered foe,
And pressed his knee, and pinning him to earth,

Shared thus his side.

               And Podalirius fell
On peasant Alsus in the van of war,
And towered above him with his naked sword.
But he with swinging axe through brow and chin
The assailer clove, and bathed his arms in blood.
Peace fell upon his eyes, and iron sleep
Closed them in endless night.

                    But with bare head
The good Aeneas stretched his hand unarmed,
And called aloud:

               "Where rush ye? What new broil
Hath crept among you? O restrain your rage!
The bond is struck: each covenant is made.
Mine sole is right of battle! Fear no more;
Give place to me! My hand shall clench your bond!
Now our solemnities make Turnus mine!"

    While thus he cried, lo! whistling on the wing
An arrow came upon him, by what hand
Driven, by what force, none knew, nor whether chance
Or God such honour to Rutulians brought.
Its fame lay buried: no man for that deed
Won praise, or boasted of Aeneas' wound.

    Hope sudden flared in Turnus, when he saw
Aeneas drawing off, the Chiefs confused.
For horse he called, for arms, and on his car
Sprang proudly, and grasped the reins, and flying wide
Struck many brave men dead, and many rolled
Dying, and with his wheels crushed squadrons whole,
Or showered on men in flight quick spear on spear.
As by cold Hebrus' stream when blood-fired Mars
Rides beating on his shield, and slips to war
His madding steeds. They flying leave behind
South Wind and West: the bounds of Thrace cry out
Beaten with hoofs; and the dark face of Fear,
And Fury and Fraud accompany their God.
So Turnus through the fray his smoking steeds
Lashed on, careering o'er the piteous dead.
The flying feet rained blood; the trodden soil
With blood was mixed. Now face to face he slew
Pholus and Thamyrus, and now from far

Speared Sthenelus and Imbrasus' two sons,
Glaucus and Lades, whom their father bred
In Lycia, and had armed alike to fight
Or fly on horseback and outspeed the wind.
Elsewhere Eumedes through the battle rides,
Great Dolon's son, who bore his grandsire's name,
His father's heart and hand, renowned in war,
Who once to spy the Danaan camp durst ask
Achilles' team in payment: other pay
Tydides for such boldness made him take,
And for Achilles' steeds he sighs no more!

Him Turnus marked from far, and with light spear
Pursued him through the gap, then stopped his team,
Sprang from the car, and striding o'er the fallen
And half-dead man, set foot upon his neck,
Wrenched from his hand its sword and in his throat
Bathed deep the flaming blade, and added thus:
"Lie there, and measure these Hesperian fields,
Your Trojans' goal! Who dares draw steel on me
I thus reward; 'tis thus they make their home!"

Him joined Asbutes, Chloreus, Sybaris,
Thersilochus and Dares struck with spear;
Thymoetes too from plunging charger thrown.
As in the Aegean when loud Boreas blows,
Chasing the seas to land, then all the clouds
Scud o'er the sky where'er the stormwind drove,
So squadrons swerved where Turnus cut his way,
So flew their rout. His impulse bears him on,
And the wind meets and waves his streaming plumes.

His haughty onset Phegeus could not brook,
But met the car and with his hand turned off
The horses' foaming mouths, and as he hung
Dragged on the pole, his unprotected side
A broad lance reached, and rent his twofold mail,
And tasted the razed skin. But he with targe
His enemy confronted, and to aid
His dirk was drawing, when the flying wheel
Struck down and flung him headlong to the ground.
And Turnus following 'twixt the helmet's base
And the top rim of mail with sweeping blade
Severed his head and left the trunk in dust.

While thus victorious Turnus strewed the field,
Mnestheus, Ascanius and Achates true
Led to the camp Aeneas dropping blood,
And leaning on his spear each other step.
Enraged he strove to tear away the point
Snapt from the shaft, and begged the nearest aid,
That they should cut the wound, with steel unbare
The barb's retreat, and send him back to war.

Then came Iapis, Phœbus' dearest love,
To whom Apollo once in amorous joy
Offered his own good arts, his very skill,
His augur's power, his harp and flying shafts.
But to prolong his father's life he chose
To know the power of herbs and healing skill,
And live inglorious with the silent arts.

There fretting sore and leaning on his spear,
With grieved Iulus by and many a Chief,
Aeneas stood, immoveable by tears;
And with his robe girt up as Healers use,
With hand, with herbs of Phœbus, the old man
Tried vainly many a cure, and vainly his hand,
Vainly his gripping pincers probed the sore.
No fortune guides his path: the patron God
Aids not; while fiercer swells the roar of war,
Nearer the peril comes. Now heaven appears
All dust; the Horse come nigh, and on mid camp
Thick fall the darts: a dolorous sound goes up
Of men that fight or fall in deadly strife.

Then Venus, stricken by her son's distress,
From Cretan Ida plucked a soft-leaved stem
Of rose-bloom dittany, a herb known well
To mountain goats, whéne'er the flying shaft
Stands in their flesh. She, veiled in viewless cloud,
Down bare it, and within the stream that filled
The shining cauldrons steeped it for a salve
In secret, dropping in the healing juice
Of fragrant heal-all and ambrosia.
So with that lymph Iapis bathed the wound
In ignorance; and suddenly all pain
Fled, and all bleeding of the wound was stanched;
And now the shaft came out upon the hand
Unforced, and all his ancient strength revived.

"Haste! Bring his arms! why loiter?" cries the Leech,
First in their hearts to light the fire of war,
"No human aid, no skill hath ordered thus;
Mine hand preserves thee not. Here rules the God,
Greater, who sends thee back to greater deeds!"

Thirsting for battle then he scorned delay,
And cased each leg in gold, and flashed his spear.
With shield at side and corslet on his back,
He held Iulus fast in mailed embrace,
And kissed him through his vizor, speaking thus:

"Learn, Boy, true toil and manliness from me;
Success from others! Now my hand in war
Will shield and lead thee in the paths of praise.
Thou, when thine age is ripe, forget not this:
Walk in thy fathers' footsteps, where thy sire
Aeneas, where thine uncle Hector calls!"

He said, and through the gate gigantic passed,
Shaking a massy spear. In dense array
Antheus and Mnestheus and the host entire
Stream forth from camp. The land is dark with dusk,
And shakes beneath the trampling of their feet.

Them coming from his ramparts Turnus saw,
The Ausonians saw, and cold through every heart
Ran terror. But Juturna heard them first,
And knew the sound, and shuddering fled away.
He hastes, and throws dark brigads o'er the plain.
As when from sundered heavens a tempest drives
Landward o'er sea: the weary fieldman's heart
Foreboding shivers: it will ruin trees,
And lay the corn, and make the land one waste.
Winds fly before, and bear its voice to land.
Thus on their foes the Trojan led his lines,
Each in thick wedges closed.
                              Then first Thymbraeus
Put to the sword Osiris; Mnestheus slew
Arcetius, and Achates Epulo,
And Gyas Ufens; and the Augur's self
Tolumnius fell, who first had thrown the spear.
Din rose to heaven. Once more in dusty flight
Rutulians turned their backs. The Prince himself

Deigns not to slay the flying, nor on men
Met foot to foot, or levelling the lance
Makes onset. Turnus only through the gloom,
Turnus alone he tracks and calls to fight.

    Fear-struck Juturna then, the Warrior Maid,
Flings down Metiscus, Turnus' charioteer,
Among his reins, and from the pole far fallen
Leaves him and guides herself the streaming thongs,
In all, voice, shape and arms, Metiscus' self.
As when a swallow in some great lord's house
Through the long hall flies black, and gathers bits
And little scraps to feed her chattering brood,
Breaking the silence of the empty courts
And standing pools; so flitting fast her car
Juturna drives through all, and here and there
Displays her conquering brother, yet to close
Permits him not, but wheels their flight aloof.
Not less Aeneas, winding on his trail,
Seeks to confront him, and through squadrons gored
Calls him loud-voiced. Oft as he sights his foe,
And running tries to match his winged steeds,
So oft Juturna whirls away the car.
What can he do? Amid distracting thoughts
He wavered idly swayed. On him the while
Messapus, bearing in his left two spears,
Supple and shod with steel, ran lightly up,
And one cast forward with unerring aim.
Aeneas stopped, and, gathered up in arms,
Sank on one knee, yet the keen missile touched
His helmet's top and shared the feathered crest.
Then rose his rage, when widely he saw the car
Borne from him, moved by treachery at last,
Calling on Jove and on the perjured shrines,
He pierced the press, unsparing, fraught with dread,
And dealt wide havoc, flinging all his wrath
Unbridled, while he swept on victory's stream.

    What God such woes, such divers deaths will tell,
And sing the chieftains' fate, whom Turnus now,
Now o'er the field the Trojan hero drove?
Was it thy will, O Jove! that thus embroiled
Nations should clash foredoomed to lasting peace?

Not long delayed by Sucro, (though that fight
Stayed first the Trojans' rush,) Aeneas smote
His side, and through the ribs, the bosom's fence,
Where death is swiftest, thrust the naked blade.

Turnus on foot, dishorsing Amycus,
Lanced him, and smote his brother with the sword,
Diores. On his car their severed heads
He bore suspended, dropping dews of blood.

Talos, Cethegus, Tanais the other
Slew at one bout; and laid Onites low,
The Echion name, whom Peridia bore.

Turnus the brothers from the Lycian meads
Of Phoebus slew, and vainly hating war
Menoetes, who by Lerna's fishy streams
Had his poor house and craft, nor knew the cares
Of wealth; his father sowed a hireling's soil.

And as two fires from diverse quarters spread
O'er withered woods and brakes of rustling bay;
Or as, down plunging from sheer precipices,
Two foaming rivers roar and run to sea,
Each ruining his road; so fierce to war
Aeneas plunged and Turnus. Now their rage
Boils inly; now their hearts that cannot yield
Burst, and their strength is dealt in every blow.

One with a mighty hurricane of stone
Sheer flung to earth Murranus, of proud race
Boasting and great old names, whose blood was drawn
From Latin Kings. Him under reins and yoke
The wheels rolled o'er, and the horses' beating hoofs,
Unmindful of their master, trod him down.

The other, meeting Hyllus loud in rage,
Lanced through his gilded brows, and in his brain
The spear stood fast. Nor thee, most brave of Greeks,
Cretheus, thy prowess saved from Turnus' arm!
Nor, when Aeneas came, did all his Gods
Protect Cupencus; when his breast met steel,
Nought skilled the brazen targe to stay his pain.
Thee too, O Aeolus! Laurentine plains
Saw fallen, and stretching all thy length on earth;
Struck dead at last, whom Argives could not slay,

Nor Peleus' son who razed the towers of Troy!
Here lay thy goal: neath Ida rose thy home:
Thy home Lyrnesus, Latin soil thy grave.

Now clashed all arms, all Latins, Dardans all,
Mnestheus, Serestus and Asilas bold,
With horse-quelling Messapus, Arcad wings,
Etruria's phalanx. Each man all his strength
Strained without rest or pause: in conflict wild
The battle raged.
                    But on Aeneas' mind
An impulse from his Heaven-sweet Mother fell,
To turn his force, and falling on the town,
With swift and sudden havoc stun the foe.
He through the battle tracking Turnus' steps,
Turns here and there his eyes, and sees the town
Safe from that storm of war in happy peace.
A dream of greater battle fired his soul.
Mnestheus, Sergestus and Serestus brave,
His chiefs, convoking, he ascends a mound,
To which the Trojans, dropping shield nor spear,
Swarm dense; and mid them from the height he spake.

"Let nought delay my charge: God stands with us.
Let none fall slack before a sudden feat.
The town that woke the war, Latinus' home,
If to our yoke they yield not, I this day
Will raze, and level all her smoking towers!
Shall I abide till Turnus choose to bear
Our arms, and meet his vanquisher once more?
There lies the head and sum of this bad war!
Haste! Bring the torch! Reclaim our bond with fire!"

He ceased; and all with eager hearts alike,
Wedging their files, sweep townward in a mass.
Then ladders spring to sight and sudden fire.
Some run to every gate and slay the guards:
Some flinging darts, obscure the heavens with iron.
Among the first Aeneas to the walls
Lifting his hand, Latinus loudly charged,
And bade Heaven witness he is thrust once more
On Latin foes, and twice their bond is riven!
Confusion rends the city: some the gates
Bid open to the Dardans, and their King
Drag to the ramparts: others start in arms

To guard the walls. As when a swain hath tracked
Bees to their pumiced rock, and filled the lair
With bitter smoke. They in their waxen walls
Run to and fro confused and whet their wrath
Loud buzzing: the dark odour through their house
Rolls, and the rock with hidden murmur hums,
While smoke goes upward to the empty sky.

Now one more blow on laboured Latins fell,
Which shook the city to its depths with grief.
The Queen espied their coming, the walls scaled,
Fire leaping roofward; but she saw nowhere
Rutulian ranks opposed, nor Turnus' troops.
Hapless she deemed that in the shock of war
His life was quenched, and wild with sudden woe,
Herself proclaimed disaster's fount and spring;
And in mad anguish wailing, fain to die,
Tore through her purple robes, and from a beam
Wove Death's dark noose. And when the women learned
That she lay dead, her child Lavinia first
Shent her hair's bloom, and tore her rosy cheeks.
Then all the crowd seethe round, and with lament
The great house rings. Thence spreads the rumoured woe
Through all the town. Hearts sink: Latinus goes
With vesture torn, stunned by Amata's doom,
His city's fall; and, soiling his grey hairs
With dust and shame, he blames himself full sore,
That to the Dardan Prince he held not out
Welcome, and for his city gained a son.

Meanwhile bold Turnus in the field's extreme
Chased scattered men more slow, now less and less
Rejoicing in the triumph of his steeds;
And there the breezes bore to him those shouts
Mixt with blind fears, and on his ear the hum
Of the vext city struck with joyless din.
"O what wild sorrow surges in the walls?
What roar sweeps hither from the distant town?"
He said, and lost in wonder drew the rein.
To whom his sister, in Metiscus' shape
Guiding the car and horses, thus returned:

"Here, Turnus, let us chase the sons of Troy,
Where instant victory leads! Others there are
To guard our homes. Aeneas plunged in war

Threats Italy: let us with stroke as fierce
Destroy his Trojans; nor shalt thou withdraw
Less in thy tale of dead, nor less renowned!"
Turnus to her:

"Sister, long since I knew thee, when thy craft
First clouded peace, and plunged thee in this war!
Now too in vain thou hid'st thine Heavenly form.
But who hath sent thee down to bear such pain?
Was it to see thy brother's cruel doom?
What can I do? What saving chance remains?
I saw Murranus fall and heard his cry,
Who left me none so dear, a mighty man
Mightily vanquished: Ufens died in grief
Lest he should see our shame, and Trojan men
Spoil now his armoured corse. And shall I bear,
(What only lacks!) the ruin of our homes,
Nor with mine arm refute all Drances' taunts?
And shall this land see Turnus flinch and flee?
Is death so sad? O Shades, entreat me well,
Since Heaven hath turned away! A soul unstained,
That knows no blame of yours, to you I come,
Not once unworthy of my valiant sires!"

He scarce had said, when lo! on foaming horse
Flew Saces through the foe, an arrow's wound
Full in his face, imploring him by name.

"Turnus, our final hope, O help thine own!
Aeneas, thundering through the battle, threats
To raze and ruin all our topmost towers!
Firebrands are flying at our roofs! To thee,
To thee the Latins look! The King himself
Doubts whom to call his son, whose hand to take.
Yea too, the Queen, thy loyalest, herself
Slain by her hand, hath left the light in fear.
Sole at our gates Messapus holds the war
With bold Atinas, and the troops round each
Stand dense: all iron waves the field of swords,
While o'er deserted grass thou wheel'st thy car!"

Stunned by distracting visions, Turnus stood
Spellbound in silent stare, and in his heart
Surged one great flood of shame and frantic pain,
And love to fury driven and conscious worth.

When shadows left his mind and light returned,
His blazing eyeballs casting on the walls
In turbid rage he scanned the mighty town.
And lo! a spire of flame that streamed to heaven
Eddying between its floors had seized a tower,
A tower himself had built with mortised beams
And set on wheels and on high bridges raised.

"Now, Sister, now Fate triumphs. Stay no more.
Where God, where Fortune calls us, let us go.
I vow to meet Aeneas, and to bear
What sharpness is in death. Thou shalt not see me
Longer in shame! This fury let me wreak
Before the end!" And leaping from the car
He left his sister sad, through shafts, through foes
Plunged, and broke hotly through the ranks of war.
As when a rock falls plunging down a cliff,
Torn off by wind, or if tempestuous rain
Hath washed it out, or lapsing years unloosed.
Sheer with great impulse sweeps the wanton crag,
Bounding along the ground, and with it roll
Woods, herds and men: so Turnus through the rout
Plunged to the walls, where all the earth was wet
With bloodshed, and all air was shrill with spears;
And signing with his hand, thus loudly cried:

"Forbear, Rutulians! Latins, stay the sword!
Whate'er be doomed, 'tis mine! 'Tis I alone
Should purge your bond, and take the steel's award!"
All from the midst retiring gave him room.

But hearing Turnus' name, Aeneas leaves
Rampart and tower, and flings off all delay,
Breaks from all deeds, and with exultant joy
Thunders in armour dread; as Athos great,
Or great as Eryx, or as when he waves
His roaring oaks great father Apennine,
Lifting elate to heaven his snow-crowned head.
And each Rutulian, and each man of Troy,
Each Latin gazed, and all who held the wall,
And all who thrust the ram, and every man
Laid down his arms. Latinus saw amazed
Those men of might, in lands far sundered born,
Meet face to face to try the sword's award.

They, when the field lay vacant, running out
With rapid onrush, cast their spears from far,
Then closed in strife with shields and sounding brass.
Earth groans: the sword-thrusts quicken; chance and skill
Mingle in one. And as on Sila's mount.
Or high Taburnus when two bulls engage
In deadly warfare with confronting brows:
The fearful hinds have fled, and all the beasts
Stand dumb with awe; the lowing heifers doubt
Which bull shall rule the forest and the herd.
They mixt in fury deal each other wounds,
And thrust their goring horns, and with poured blood
Bathe necks and sides; the echoing forest roars.
So clash Aeneas and the Daunian Prince,
And that great shock of shields fills all the sky.
Jove holds the balance true, and in the scales
Lays each man's fate, whom battle's toil shall doom,
Whose weight shall sink with death.

                            Now Turnus springs,
Deeming himself secure, and rises high
With all his body to the uplifted sword,
And strikes. Both armies shout, and strain their gaze,
Trojans and Latins. But the traitor sword
Breaks, and deserts him burning in mid stroke, —
Did flight not aid. He flies more swift than wind,
When that strange hilt he sees, that swordless hand.

He in his haste, 'tis said, his harnessed car
Mounting for battle, left his father's brand,
And hurriedly snatched up Metiscus' sword;
Which long, while Trojans turned their scattered backs,
Served him; but meeting Vulcan's Heavenly arms,
The mortal blade that struck, like brittle ice,
Snapped, and its fragments sparkled on the sand.

Wide o'er the field distracted Turnus flies,
In wayward rings, uncertain, for all round
Trojans have hemmed him close, and on one side
Lies marish waste, on one the high-built wall.

Nor less Aeneas, though the hindering shaft
Clogged oft his halting knees, in eager chase
Pressed step on step to reach the hurrying man.
As when a hound hath caught a hunted stag,

Hemmed by a stream or scarlet-feathered scare,
And barking runs him hard. Then he in dread
Of toils and steepy bank, flies to and fro
A thousand ways. The Umbrian, open-mouthed,
Clings close, and all but holds, and snaps his jaws
As though he held, but baffled bites the air.
Then shouts uprise; the pools and banks around
Echo, and tumult fills the thundering sky.
He while he flies, calling on each by name,
Taunts the Rutulians, and demands his sword.
Swift death and sure Aeneas threatens back,
If any approach, and frightens them with threats
To raze the town, and follows hard, though maimed.
Five rounds they run, and thread as many more,
This way and that; for no light stake is theirs,
No frolic wreath, but Turnus' life and blood.

A wilding olive near with bitter leaves
Sacred to Faunus was revered of yore
By sailors saved from sea, who there would hang
Gifts to Laurentum's God and votive weeds.
Nathless had Trojans lopped its sacred stem,
That those who fought might meet on level field.
Here stood Aeneas' spear: in that tough root
Borne by its flight it stuck. The Dardan stooped
To tear away the steel, and with that lance
Reach whom he could not reach by speed of foot.

Then, wild with terror, Turnus prayed and said;
"Have mercy, Faunus! Keep the steel, O Earth!
Kind Earth! since ever have I kept your faith
Pure, which the Trojans have profaned in war!"

He said, nor vainly prayed the God for help:
For struggling long and lingering o'er the root
With all his strength Aeneas could not loose
The wood's firm bite. And while he strove and strained,
Changed to Metiscus' shape, the Daunian Nymph
Ran forth and to her brother gave his sword.
But Venus, wroth such licence should be hers,
Drew near, and tore the weapon from the root.
Then both erect, in arms and heart renewed,
One with his sword, one bold with lifted spear,
They stood opposed, and drew the breath of war.

Meanwhile to Juno, from a golden cloud
Watching man's strife, thus spake the Olympian King:
"Where shall this end, O Wife? What yet remains?
Thou know'st, thou own'st Aeneas shall be raised
High to the starry Heaven, his country's God.
What plan, what hope detains thee in cold clouds?
Was't well that mortal wound profaned a God?
That Turnus' sword (for had Juturna power
Without thine aid?) be given him and new force
To conquered men? O cease, I prithee, yield!
Nor let such sorrow eat thy silent heart,
And grief so oft from thy sweet lips o'erflow.
The end is reached. On lands and sea thine hand
Might chase the Trojans, wake War's awful flame,
Stain a fair House, and bridals mix with woe.
More I forbid thee try!"
                          Thus Jove began;
Thus answered Juno with submissive mien:

"Because, great Sire, I knew such will was thine,
Turnus and Earth I left against my wish;
Nor wouldst thou see me else, enskied alone,
Bear good and bad, but standing girt with flames
In Trojan ranks and dragging them to fight!
I bade Juturna help her brother's need;
Yea, for his life I sanctioned bolder acts;
But not to aim the arrow nor the bow:
By Styx I swear it, whose unpitying spring
Is Heaven's sole dread. And now I go, and leave
The hated strife. But what no law of Fate
Binds, I conjure thee, grant for Latium's sake,
For thine own people's greatness. When they make
A happy bridal peace, (so let it be!)
And join in laws and leagues, O bid not then
The native Latins change their ancient name,
And take the Teucrian name as Trojan men,
Or change their tongue or dress. Let Latium still
Be Latium! Let the Alban Kings endure!
Let Latin valour make the Roman strong,
And fallen Troy lie nameless where she fell!"

Smiling on her the World's Creator thus:
"Jove's sister art thou, Saturn's other child,

Such waves of wrath are surging in thy breast!
But cease thine idle fury; what thou wilt
I grant: I yield, both conquered and content.
The Ausonian men shall keep their ways and speech,
Their name be as it is; and Troy shall sink
Merged in their flesh, and I will fuse their rites,
And I will make all Latins, all one tongue.
Then from their blended blood a race shall rise
O'erpassing men in worth, o'erpassing Gods;
And none shall pay such honours to thy name!"

Assenting Juno then with altered mind
Descended joyous from the Heavenly cloud;
And musing sole the Father schemes himself
To draw Juturna from her brother's sword.

Twain Plagues there are, the Dread Ones named of men,
Whom with Megaera at one Hellish birth
Night bare untimely, and with serpent coils
Wreathed each alike, and gave them windy wings.
Beside Jove's throne, and at the grim King's door,
These wait, to whet the fears of suffering men,
Whene'er the Lord of Heaven deals pain and death
And terror, or affrights the doomed with war.
One swift from Heaven Jove sent, and bade her meet
Juturna, boding ill; who flew to earth,
Riding the whirlwind, as a bow-shot reed
Cuts through the clouds, which armed with poison juice
Some Parthian wild or some Cydonian launched,
A dart incurable, which hissing leaps
Across the hurrying darkness undiscerned.
So sped Night's Daughter on her earthward way.

When Ilian ranks she espied and Turnus' troops,
Shrunk suddenly in shape to that small bird
Which oft on tombs and ruined roofs by night
Sings late and frets the dark, so changed in shape
Before the face of Turnus to and fro
Shrieking she flew, and beat his shield with wings.

Strange terror froze his limbs; his hair with dread
Rose, and his tongue was tied. But when from far
Joyless Juturna knew the Dread One's wings
And strident hiss, her loosened locks she tore,
Rent her fair face with nails, and beat her breast.

"How can thy sister, Turnus, aid thee now?
What waits my stubborn heart? What skill is mine
Thy life to lengthen, or this bane to fight?
Now, now I leave the field. O birds obscene,
Redouble not my fears! I know your wings,
Beating the sound of death. I know your charge
From generous Jove! Is this a maiden's meed?
Why gave He endless life? Why have I lost
The mortal fate? Now surely could I end
All pain, and share my brother's path of gloom.
I deathless! How can aught of mine be sweet
Without thee, Brother? O could Earth yawn deep,
And plunge my godhead in the depths of Hell!"
She spake, and in grey mantle wrapped her head,
Moaning, and sank within the river pools

Onward Aeneas came, and shook his spear,
The tall tree shaft, and cried with angry soul;
"What hinders still? Why, Turnus, dost thou shrink?
No race is this, but grim debate of war!
Take every shape, and gather all thy strength
Of skill and prowess! Pray for wings to reach
The stars, or in the covering earth to hide!"

He tossed his head: "Not me thy fiery words
Daunt. The Gods daunt me, and the hate of Jove!"
Nor further spake, but one vast stone espied,
A vast and ancient stone, that on the plain
Lay bounding fields to end a suit of lands.
Scarce twelve picked men had borne it on their backs,
Men of such stature as the Earth bears now.
He seized, and rising hurled it on his foe
With shaking hand, hard running; nor himself
Knows if he runs or moves or lifts in hand
Or throws the enormous stone. His knees are slack;
His blood is frozen cold. The stone itself
Spun through the empty void, nor all the gap
Traversed nor struck its blow. And as in sleep,
When quiet Night has sealed the languid lids,
In some long race we seem to strive in vain,
And striving swoon; our tongue is faint; our limbs
Refuse their aid; no voice, no words ensue.
Thus howsoever Turnus strives to make
His way by valour, that dire Goddess still

Denies success. His heart with many a pang
Trembles. He scans his city and his troops,
Falters, and shudders at the threatening spear;
And knows not how to flee nor how attack,
And sees no car, no sister charioteer.
He falters, and Aeneas, with keen eye
Lighting on fortune, shakes and hurls from far
The fatal spear. No stone the Sling hath shot
Clangs on the wall so loud: no thunder bursts
With hoarser peal. Like some black storm it flew,
Laden with death; and pricked the harness joints,
And outmost circles of the sevenfold shield,
And hissing pierced the thigh. The wounded man
Fell huge to earth with knees beneath him bent.

Up sprang Rutulians groaning: all the hill
Re-echoed, and far woods sent back their cry.
But he, with eyes and pleading hand outstretched,
Spake humbly: "I deserved it, nor repine.
Use thou thy chance. If thee a father's pain
Can touch, I pray, (such was thy sire to thee,
Anchises,) pity Daunus in his age.
Me or my life-lorn corse restore to mine.
Thou hast prevailed, and me Ausonia sees
Stretch conquered palms. Lavinia's hand is thine.
No further press thine hate."
                              His armed foe
Stood wroth with rolling eyes and held his hand:
And more and more those words began to bend
Him wavering, when he saw the baldric flash
High on his shoulder with the well-known boss,
Young Pallas' belt, whom Turnus smote and slew,
And round his back that badge of hate he bore.
Then when his eyes drank in the spoils which told
Of bitter grief, in furious wrath he cried
Terrific: "Shalt thou in my dear ones' spoils
Escape me? Pallas, Pallas with this blow
Strikes, and takes vengeance from thy guilty blood!"

He said, and flaming in his heart the steel
Plunged deep. But faint and cold the other grew;
And with one groan indignant life took flight.

WITH SPEED AND VIOLENCE

WITH SPEED AND VIOLENCE

Why Scientists Fear Tipping Points
in Climate Change

FRED PEARCE

BEACON PRESS

Boston

BEACON PRESS
25 Beacon Street
Boston, Massachusetts 02108-2892
www.beacon.org

Beacon Press books
are published under the auspices of
the Unitarian Universalist Association of Congregations.

11 10 09 08   8 7 6 5 4 3 2 1

This book is printed on acid-free paper that meets the uncoated paper
ANSI/NISO specifications for permanence as revised in 1992.

Composition by Wilsted & Taylor Publishing Services

Library of Congress Cataloging-in-Publication Data

Pearce, Fred.
With speed and violence : why scientists fear tipping points in climate change / Fred Pearce.
    p. cm.
Includes index.
ISBN-13: 978-0-8070-8577-6 (pbk. : alk. paper)
ISBN-10: 0-8070-8577-4 (pbk. : alk. paper)   1. Climatic changes.   2. Climatic changes—
History—Chronology.   I. Title.

QC981.8.C5P415 2006
551.6—dc22   2006019901

We are on the precipice of
climate system tipping points
beyond which there is no redemption.

JAMES HANSEN, *director,*
NASA Goddard Institute for Space Studies,
New York, December 2005

CONTENTS

III. Riding the carbon cycle

IV. Reflecting on warming

V. Ice ages and solar pulses

VI. Tropical heat

VII. At the millennium

VIII. Inevitable surprises

CHRONOLOGY OF CLIMATE CHANGE

5 billion years ago   Birth of planet Earth

600 million years ago   Last occurrence of "Snowball Earth," followed by warm era

400 million years ago   Start of long-term cooling

65 million years ago   Short-term climate conflagration after meteorite hit

55 million years ago   Methane "megafart" from ocean depths causes another short-term conflagration

50 million years ago   Cooling continues as greenhouse-gas levels in air start to diminish

25 million years ago   First modern ice sheet starts to form on Antarctica

3 million years ago   First ice-sheet formation in the Arctic ushers in era of regular ice ages

100,000 years ago   Start of most recent ice age

16,000 years ago   Most recent ice age begins stuttering retreat

14,500 years ago   Sudden warming causes sea levels to rise 65 feet in 400 years

12,800 years ago Last great "cold snap" of the ice age, known as the Younger Dryas era, is triggered by emptying glacial lake in North America and continues for around 1,300 years before ending very abruptly

8,200 years ago Abrupt and mysterious return to ice-age conditions for several hundred years, followed by warm and stable Holocene era

8,000 years ago Storegga landslip in North Sea, probably triggered by methane clathrate releases that also bolster the warm era

5,500 years ago Sudden aridification of the Sahara

4,200 years ago Another bout of aridification, concentrated in the Middle East, causes widespread collapse of civilizations

1,200 to 900 years ago Medieval warm period in the Northern Hemisphere; megadroughts in North America

700 to 150 years ago Little ice age in the Northern Hemisphere, peaking in the 1690s

1896 Svante Arrhenius calculates how rising carbon dioxide levels will raise global temperatures

1938 Guy Callendar provides first evidence of rising carbon dioxide levels in the atmosphere, but findings ignored

1958 Charles Keeling begins continuous monitoring program that reveals rapidly rising carbon dioxide levels in the atmosphere

1970s Beginning of strong global warming that has persisted ever since, almost certainly attributable to fast-rising carbon dioxide emissions, accompanied by shift in state of key climate oscillations such as El Niño and the Arctic Oscillation, and increased melting of the Greenland ice sheet

Early 1980s   Shocking discovery of Antarctic ozone hole brings new fears of human influence on global atmosphere

1988   Global warming becomes a front-page issue after Jim Hansen's presentations in Washington, D.C., during U.S. heat wave

1992   Governments of the world attending Earth Summit promise to prevent "dangerous climate change" but fail to act decisively

1998   Warmest year on record, and probably for thousands of years, accompanied by strong El Niño and exceptionally "wild weather," especially in the tropics; major carbon releases from burning peat swamps in Borneo

2001   Government of Tuvalu, in the South Pacific, signs deal for New Zealand to take refugees as its islands disappear beneath rising sea levels

2003   European heat wave—later described as the first extreme-weather event attributable to man-made global warming—kills more than 30,000; a third of the world is reported as being at risk of drought: twice as much as in the 1970s

2005   Evidence of potential "positive feedbacks" accumulates with exceptional hurricane season in the Atlantic, reports of melting Siberian permafrost, possible slowing of ocean conveyor, escalating loss of Arctic sea ice, and faster glacial flow on Greenland

THE CAST

Richard Alley, Penn State University, Pennsylvania. A glaciologist and leading analyst of Greenland ice cores, Alley is one of the most articulate interpreters of climate science. He has revealed that huge global climate changes have occurred over less than a decade in the past.

Svante Arrhenius, a Swedish chemist. In the 1890s, he was the first to calculate the likely climatic impact of rising concentrations of carbon dioxide in the atmosphere, and thus invented the notion of "global warming." Modern supercomputers have barely improved on his original calculation.

Gerard Bond, formerly of Lamont-Doherty Earth Observatory, Columbia University, New York. A geologist, Bond was one of the first analysts of deep-sea cores; until his death, in 2005, he was an advocate of the case that regular pulses in solar activity drive cycles of climate change on Earth, such as the little ice age and the medieval warm period.

Wally Broecker, Lamont-Doherty Earth Observatory, Columbia University. An oceanographer and one of the most influential and controversial U.S. climate scientists for half a century, Broecker discovered the ocean conveyor, a thousand-year global circulation system that begins off Greenland and ends in the Gulf Stream, which keeps Europe warm.

Peter Cox, UK Centre for Hydrology and Ecology, Wareham. Cox is an innovative young climate modeler of aerosols' likely role in keeping the planet cool—and of the risks that land plants will turn from a "sink" for to a "source" of carbon dioxide later in this century.

James Croll, a nineteenth-century Scottish artisan and self-taught academic. After many years of study, he uncovered the astronomical causes of the ice ages, a discovery that was later attributed to the Serbian mathematician Milutin Milankovitch.

Paul Crutzen, Max Planck Institute for Chemistry, Mainz, Germany. An atmospheric chemist who won the Nobel Prize in 1995 for his work predicting the destruction of the ozone layer, Crutzen pioneered thinking about stratospheric chemistry, the role of man-made aerosols in shading the planet, and "nuclear winter," and coined the term "Anthropocene."

Joe Farman, formerly of the British Antarctic Survey, Cambridge. Farman's dogged collection of seemingly useless data was rewarded by discovery of the ozone hole over Antarctica.

Jim Hansen, director of NASA's Goddard Institute for Space Studies, New York. Hansen's unimpeachable scientific credentials have preserved his position as President George W. Bush's top climate modeler (as this book goes to press), despite his outspoken warnings that the world is close to dangerous climate change, which have clearly irked the Bush administration.

Charles David Keeling, formerly of Scripps Institution of Oceanography, La Jolla, California. Until his death, in 2005, Keeling had made continuous measurements of atmospheric carbon dioxide on top of Mauna Loa, in Hawaii, since 1958. The resulting "Keeling curve," the most famous graph in climate science, shows a steady annual rise superimposed on a seasonal cycle as Earth " breathes."

Sergei Kirpotin, Tomsk State University, Russia. Kirpotin is the ecologist who told the world about the "meltdown" of permafrost in the West Siberian peat lands, raising fears that massive amounts of methane would be released into the atmosphere.

Michael Mann, director of the Earth System Science Center, Penn State University, Pennsylvania. A climate modeler and the creator of the "hockey stick" graph, a reconstruction of past temperatures showing that recent warming is unique to the past two millennia, Mann is the butt of criticism from climate skeptics, but gives as good as he gets. He is the co-founder of the RealClimate Web site.

Peter deMenocal, Lamont-Doherty Earth Observatory, Columbia University, New York. A climate historian, deMenocal has charted mega-droughts, the sudden drying of the Sahara, and other major climate shifts of the past 10,000 years, and their role in the collapse of ancient cultures.

John Mercer, formerly of Ohio State University, Columbus. The glaciologist who first proposed that the West Antarctic ice sheet has an Achilles heel, and that a "major disaster" there may be imminent, Mercer also pioneered research on tropical glaciers.

Drew Shindell, NASA's Goddard Institute for Space Studies, New York. An ozone-layer expert and climate modeler, Shindell is doing ground-breaking research on unexpected links between the upper and the lower atmosphere, revealing how the stratosphere can amplify small changes in surface temperature.

Lonnie Thompson, Byrd Polar Research Institute, Ohio State University, Columbus. A geologist, Thompson has probably spent more time above 20,000 feet than any lowlander alive, all in the pursuit of ice cores from tropical glaciers that are rewriting the planet's climate history.

Peter Wadhams, head of polar ocean physics at the University of Cambridge. He rode in British military submarines to provide the first data on thinning Arctic sea ice and discovered the mysterious "chimneys" off Greenland where the global ocean conveyor starts.

PREFACE TO THE PAPERBACK EDITION

The prognosis for climate change just keeps getting worse. But the predictions themselves are becoming less certain. This is a paradox that has worried me for a while. Some people have used it to pour scorn on the scientists trying to come to grips with the consequences of our meddling with the climate—our planet's life-support system. They suggest the uncertainty means we don't need to worry. I take a rather different view.

The central message of this book is that while skeptics about climate change have a valid point when they say that scientists' climate predictions are far less certain than is often claimed, those skeptics are dreadfully wrong to take comfort in this. I take no comfort at all. There is chaos out there, and we should be afraid.

I am a reporter on climate change. I have been following the topic for *New Scientist* magazine in the UK and others for twenty years now. And when I talk to climate scientists during their coffee breaks and at their private conferences—as I have done extensively both before and after completing this book—I hear them warn that the current accepted predictions could be much too optimistic; that their statistical models of climate, sophisticated though they undoubtedly are, badly underestimate the forces of change; that we could be close to triggering sudden lurches in the world's climate. Hence the subtitle of the book: *Why Scientists Fear Tipping Points in Climate Change.*

These tipping points boil down to three things: The first is that manmade warming will release natural stores of gases that will accelerate warming—perhaps creating unstoppable, runaway climate change. The second is that warming will trigger the rapid breakup of the great ice sheets on

Greenland and Antarctica—a vast global version of the annual spring breakup on a river. This would raise the sea level by several meters in a few decades. The third is that warming will disrupt seemingly permanent features of the world's climate such as El Niño and the Asian monsoon, features on which 2 billion people depend for their survival.

These predictions do not appear in the current climate models, and they are only hinted at in the latest predictions made by the UN's Intergovernmental Panel on Climate Change, which reported afresh during 2007. Some people accuse the IPCC of being alarmist. On the contrary, my reading is that the latest report worked so hard to assuage the concerns of its critics that it left out all the things its authors really fear.

For instance, the 2007 IPCC report predicts a likely sea-level rise of 18 to 59 centimeters this century. But Jim Hansen, the top NASA planetary physicist and former IPCC author whose work features prominently in this book, said this summer: "I find it almost inconceivable that business-as-usual climate change will not result in a rise in sea level measured in meters within a century." For him, that is a judgment call, one I think we should heed.

A couple of weeks before writing this preface, I attended a conference of climate modelers at Cambridge University in the UK. I was the only journalist there. It was mid-August, and many of the scientists had broken off their summer vacations to attend. Maybe that loosened their tongues a little; at any rate, the event was close to a confessional. They were debating a series of papers on the reliability of climate models that had been published that week by the Royal Society in London. And the papers all said the same thing: we know less than we think.

The papers' titles were dry. One was called "Confidence, Uncertainty and Decision-Support Relevance in Climate Predictions." But the author of that paper, Lenny Smith, an American statistician now working at the London School of Economics, told the Cambridge meeting: "Our models are being overinterpreted and misinterpreted. We need to drop the pretense that they are nearly perfect."

Did this result in howls of outrage from the assembled modelers? Far from it. They nodded grimly. They knew this realization was far from reassuring. As they have second thoughts about the reliability of their predictions, the modelers are growing ever more fearful about what might really lie out there—maybe only a decade or so in the future.

A group of top European scientists—headed by John Schellnhuber, the chief climate adviser to German chancellor Angela Merkel—has drawn up a list of the most likely tipping points that could wreck the IPCC's predictions. The group says sea ice in the Arctic has already thinned so much that the entire ocean will be ice free in summer by about 2040. And it argues that the ice on top of Greenland, the world's largest island, could also be ready to go. That ice is 2 miles thick, and its melting would raise sea levels worldwide by 23 feet. Tim Lenton from the University of East Anglia told the Cambridge meeting: "We are close to being committed to a collapse of the Greenland ice sheet, but we don't think we have passed the tipping point yet." How long have we got? Maybe less than a decade.

The European study identified eight dangerous tipping points that could be passed this century; they are all discussed in this book. Several could trigger others in a cascade. The now "very likely" collapse of the Greenland ice sheet could halt the Gulf Stream and switch off the Asian monsoon. It would also warm the South Pacific Ocean, which might in turn destabilize a second huge ice sheet in west Antarctica, which would raise sea levels by a further 23 feet.

Nobody is yet sure if such a catastrophic chain of events could occur. But when we dig up and burn carbon that has been buried for tens of millions of years, we are playing with fire. And our uncertainty about the precise outcome doesn't altogether reassure me. How lucky do we feel?

But this is not a book of despair. Far from it. Yes, we face potentially very dangerous tipping points in climate in the coming decades. But I also detect that our society may be close to its own tipping point, the moment where we collectively decide that it makes more sense to generate our energy without burning coal and oil; where we switch instead to a low-carbon economy. And I think that, once under way, that switch could happen very fast.

Why such optimism? Technically, the switch would not be hard; economically, it would be a breeze if oil remains above fifty dollars a barrel. The politics might be the problem. Can we get beyond that tipping point in our global economy before nature triggers runaway climate change and unstoppable sea-level rise? I wish I had an answer to that. But the one certainty is that the faster we act, the better our chances.

PREFACE: THE CHIMNEY

The Greenland Sea occupies a basin between Greenland, Norway, Iceland, and the Arctic islands of Svalbard. It is like an antechamber between the Atlantic and the Arctic Ocean: the place where Arctic ice flowing south meets the warm tropical waters of the Gulf Stream heading north. Two hundred years ago, the sea was a magnet for sailors intent on making their fortunes by harpooning its great schools of bowhead whales. For a few decades, men such as the Yorkshire whaling captain and amateur Arctic scientist William Scoresby sailed north each spring as the ice broke up and dodged the ice floes to hunt the whales that had congregated to devour the spring burst of plankton. Scoresby was the star of the ice floes, landing a world-record thirty-six whales at Whitby Harbour after one trip in 1798. He was the nimblest navigator around a great ice spur in the sea known as the Odden tongue, where the whales gathered.

Scoresby was too clever for his own good, and boom turned to bust when all the whales had been killed. What was once the world's most prolific and profitable whaling ground is still empty of bowheads. But just as the unique mix of warm tropical waters and Arctic ice was the key to the Greenland Sea's whaling bonanza, so it is the key to another hidden secret of these distant waters.

It's called "the chimney." Only a handful of people have ever seen it. It is a giant whirlpool in the ocean, 6 miles in diameter, constantly circling counterclockwise and siphoning water from the surface to the seabed 2 miles below. That water will not return to the surface for a thousand years. The chimney, once one of a family, pursues its lonely task in the middle of one of the coldest and most remote seas on Earth. And its swirling waters may be the switch that can turn the heat engine of the world's climate system on and off. If anything could trigger the climatic conflagration shown in the Hollywood movie *The Day After Tomorrow,* it would be the chimney.

The existence of a series of these chimneys was discovered by a second British adventurer, Cambridge ocean physicist Peter Wadhams. In the 1990s, he began hitching rides in Royal Navy submarines beneath the Arctic ice. Like Scoresby, he was fascinated by his journeys to the Odden tongue—not for its long-departed whales, but because of the bizarre giant whirlpools he found there. He concluded that they were the final destination for the most northerly flow of the Gulf Stream. The waters of this great ocean current, which drives north through the tropical Atlantic bringing warmth to Europe, are chilled by the Arctic winds in the Greenland Sea and start to freeze around the Odden tongue. The water that is left becomes ever denser and heavier until it is entrained by the chimneys and plunges to the ocean floor.

This was a dramatic discovery. The chimneys were, Wadhams realized, the critical starting point of a global ocean circulation system that oceanographers had long hypothesized but had never seen in action. It traveled the world's oceans, passing south of Africa, around Antarctica, and through the Indian and Pacific Oceans, before gradually resurfacing and sniffing the air again as it returned to the Atlantic, joined the Gulf Stream, and moved north once again to complete a circulation dubbed by oceanographers the "ocean conveyor."

But even as he gazed on these dynamos of ocean circulation, Wadhams knew that they were in trouble. For the Arctic ice was disappearing. Sonar data he had collected from the naval submarines revealed that the entire ice sheet that once covered the Arctic was thinning and breaking up. By the end of the 1990s, the Odden tongue was gone. The Gulf Stream water still came north, but it never again got cold enough to form ice. The ice tongue has not returned.

"In 1997, the last year that the Odden tongue formed, we found four chimneys in a single season, and calculate there could have been as many as twelve," says Wadhams. Since then, they have been disappearing one by one—except for one particularly vigorous specimen. Wadhams first spotted it out in the open ocean, at 75° north and right on the Greenwich Mean Line, during a ship cruise in March 2001. By rights, it should not have been there without the ice, he says. But it was, hanging in there, propelled downward perhaps by the saltiness created by evaporation of the water in the wind.

He found the same chimney again later that summer, twice the following year, and a final time in spring 2003, before the British government cut off his research funds. Over the two years he tracked it, the last great chimney had moved only about 20 miles across the ocean, like an underwater tornado that refused to go away. Wadhams measured it and probed it. He sent submersible instruments down through it to measure its motion at depth. It rotated, he said, right to the ocean floor, and such was the force of the downward motion that it could push aside a column of water half a mile high. "It is amazing that it could last for more than a few days," Wadhams says. "The physics of how it did it is not understood at all."

The great chimney had in May 2003 one dying companion, 40 miles to the northwest. But that chimney no longer reached the surface and was, he says, almost certainly in its death throes. That left just one remaining chimney in the Greenland Sea. "It may be many decades old or just a transitory phenomenon," he says. "But either way, it, too, may be gone by now. We just don't know." Like Scoresby's bowheads, it may disappear unnoticed by the outside world. Or we may come to rue its passing.

INTRODUCTION

Some environmental stories don't add up. I'm an environment journalist, and sometimes the harder you look at a new scare story, the less scary it looks. The science is flaky, or someone has recklessly extrapolated from a small local event to create a global catastrophe. Ask questions, or go and look for yourself, and the story dissolves before your eyes. I like to question everything. I am, I hope in the best sense, a skeptical environmentalist. Sometimes it is bad for business. I have made enemies by questioning theories about advancing deserts, by pointing out that Africa may have more trees than it did a century ago, and by condemning the politics of demographic doomsday merchants.

But climate change is different. I have been on this beat for eighteen years now. The more I learn, the more I go and see for myself, and the more I question scientists, the more scared I get. Because this story does add up, and its message is that we are interfering with the fundamental processes that make Earth habitable. It is our own survival that is now at stake, not that of a cuddly animal or a natural habitat.

Don't take my word for it. Often in environmental science it is the young, idealistic researchers who become the impassioned advocates. Here I find it is the people who have been in the field the longest—the researchers with the best reputations for doing good science, and the professors with the best CVs and longest lists of published papers—who are the most fearful, often talking in the most dramatic language. People like President George W. Bush's top climate modeler, Jim Hansen, the Nobel Prize–winner Paul Crutzen, and the late Charles Keeling, begetter of the Keeling curve of rising carbon dioxide levels in the atmosphere. They have seemed to me not so much old men in a hurry as old men desperate to impart their wisdom, and their sense that climate change is something special.

Nature is fragile, environmentalists often tell us. But the lesson of this book is that it is not so. The truth is far more worrying. Nature is strong and packs a serious counterpunch. Its revenge for man-made global warming will very probably unleash unstoppable planetary forces. And they will not be gradual. The history of our planet's climate shows that it does not do gradual change. Under pressure, whether from sunspots or orbital wobbles or the depredations of humans, it lurches—virtually overnight. We humans have spent 400 generations building our current civilization in an era of climatic stability—a long, generally balmy spring that has endured since the last ice age. But this tranquility looks like the exception rather than the rule in nature. And if its end is inevitable one day, we seem to be triggering its imminent and violent collapse. Our world may be blown away in the process.

The idea for this book came while I sat at a conference, organized by the British government in early 2005, on "dangerous climate change" and how to prevent it. The scientists began by adopting neutral language. They made a distinction between Type I climate change, which is gradual and follows the graphs developed by climate modelers for the UN's Intergovernmental Panel on Climate Change (IPCC), and Type II change, which is much more abrupt and results from the crossing of hidden "tipping points." It is not in the standard models. During discussions, this temperate language gave way. Type II climate change became, in the words of Chris Rapley, director of the British Antarctic Survey, the work of climatic "monsters" that were even now being woken.

Later in the year, Jim Hansen spoke in even starker terms at a meeting of the American Geophysical Union, saying: "We are on the precipice of climate system tipping points beyond which there is no redemption." The purpose of this book is to introduce Rapley's monsters and Hansen's tipping points and to ask the question, How much time have we got?

The monsters are not hard to find. As I was starting work on this book, scientists beat a path to my door to tell me about them. I had an e-mail out of the blue from a Siberian scientist alerting me to drastic environmental change in Siberia that could release billions of tons of greenhouse gases from the melting permafrost in the world's biggest bog. Glaciologists, who are more used to seeing things happen slowly, told me of dramatic events in Greenland and Antarctica, where they are discovering huge river systems of meltwater beneath the ice sheets, and of events in Pine Island Bay, one of the most remote spots in Antarctica, that they discussed with a shudder. Soon, they said, we could be measuring sea level rise in feet rather than inches.

Along the way, I also learned about solar pulses, about the "ocean conveyor," about how Indian village fires may be melting the Arctic, about a rare molecule that runs virtually the entire clean-up system for the planet, and above all about the speed and violence of past natural climate change. Some of this, I admit, has the feel of science fiction. On one plane journey, I reread John Wyndham's sci-fi classic *The Kraken Wakes,* and was struck by the similarities between events he describes and predictions for the collapse of the ice sheets of Greenland and Antarctica. It is hard to escape the sense that primeval forces lurk deep in the ocean, in ice caps, in rainforest soils, and in Arctic tundra. Hansen says that we may have only one decade, and one degree of warming, before the monsters are fully awake. The worst may not happen, of course. Nobody can yet prove that it will. But, as one leading climate scientist put it when I questioned his pessimism, how lucky do we feel?

I hope I have retained my skepticism through this journey. One of the starting points, in fact, was a reexamination of whether the climate skeptics—those who question the whole notion of climate change as a threat—might be right. Much of what they say is political hyperbole, of more benefit to their paymasters in the fossil-fuel lobby than to science. Few of them are climate scientists at all. But in some corners of the debate, they have done good service. They have, for instance, provided a useful corrective to the common assumption that all climate change must be man-made. But my conclusion from this is the opposite of theirs. Far from allowing us to stop worrying about man-made climate change, the uncertainties they highlight underline how fickle climate can be and how vulnerable we may be to its capricious changes. As Wally Broecker, one of the high priests of abrupt planetary processes, says, "Climate is an angry beast, and we are poking it with sticks."

This book is a reality check about the state of our planet. That state scares me, just as it scares many of the scientists I have talked to—sober scientists, with careers and reputations to defend, but also with hopes for their own futures and those of their children, and fears that we are the last generation to live with any kind of climatic stability. One told me quietly: "If we are right, there are really dire times ahead. Having a daughter who will be about my present age in 2050, and will be in the midst of it, makes the issue more poignant."

WITH SPEED AND VIOLENCE

I

Welcome to the Anthropocene

THE PIONEERS

The men who measured the planet's breath

This story begins with a depressed Swedish chemist, alone in his study in the sunless Nordic winter after his marriage to his beautiful research assistant, Sofia, had collapsed. It was Christmas Eve. What would he do? Some might have gone out on the town and found themselves a new partner. Others would have given way to maudlin sentiment and probably a few glasses of beer. Svante Arrhenius chose neither release. Instead, on December 24, 1894, as the rest of his countrymen were celebrating, he rolled up his sleeves, settled down at his desk, and began a marathon of mathematical calculations that took him more than a year.

Arrhenius, then aged thirty-five, was an obdurate fellow, recently installed as a lecturer in Stockholm but already gaining a reputation for rubbing his colleagues the wrong way. As day-long darkness gave way to months of midnight sun, he labored on, filling book after book with calculations of the climatic impact of changing concentrations of certain heat-trapping gases on every part of the globe. "It is unbelievable that so trifling a matter has cost me a full year," he later confided to a friend. But with his wife gone, he had few distractions. And the calculations became an obsession.

What initially spurred his work was the urge to answer a popular riddle of the day: how the world cooled during the ice ages. Geologists knew by then that much of the Northern Hemisphere had for thousands of years been covered by sheets of ice. But there was huge debate about why this might have happened. Arrhenius reckoned that the clue lay in gases that could trap heat in the lower atmosphere, changing the atmosphere's radiation balance and altering temperatures.

He knew from work half a century before, by the French mathematician Jean Baptiste Fourier and an Irish physicist called John Tyndall, that some gases, including carbon dioxide, had this heat-trapping effect. Tyndall had measured the effect in his lab. Put simply, it worked like this: the gases were transparent to ultraviolet radiation from the sun, but they trapped the infrared heat that Earth's surface radiated as it was warmed by the sun. Arrhenius reasoned that if these heat-trapping gases in the air decreased for some reason, the world would grow colder. Later dubbed "greenhouse gases," because they seemed to work like the glass in a greenhouse, these gases acted as a kind of atmospheric thermostat.

Tyndall, one of the most famous scientists of his day and a friend of Charles Darwin's, had himself once noted that if heat-trapping gases were eliminated from the air for one night, "the warmth of our fields and gardens would pour itself unrequited into space, and the sun would rise upon an island held fast in the iron grip of frost." That sounded to Arrhenius very much like what had happened in the ice ages. Sure enough, when he emerged from his labors, he was able to tell the world that a reduction in atmospheric carbon dioxide levels of between a third and a half would cool the planet by about 8 degrees Fahrenheit—enough to cover most of northern Europe, and certainly every scrap of his native Sweden, in ice.

Arrhenius had no idea if his calculations reflected what had actually happened in the ice ages. There could have been other explanations, such as a weakening sun. It was another eighty years before researchers analyzing ancient air trapped in the ice sheets of Greenland and Antarctica found that ice-age air contained just the concentrations of carbon dioxide that Arrhenius had predicted. But as he reached the end of his calculations, Arrhenius also became intrigued by the potential of rising concentrations of greenhouse gases, and how they might trigger a worldwide warming. He had no expectation that this was going to happen, but it was the obvious counterpart to his first calculation. And he concluded that a doubling of atmospheric carbon dioxide would raise world temperatures by an average of about 10°F.

How did he do these calculations? Modern climate modelers, equipped with some of the biggest supercomputers, are aghast at the labor involved. But in essence, his methods were remarkably close to theirs. Arrhenius started with some basic formulae concerning the ability of greenhouse gases to trap heat in the atmosphere. These were off the shelf from Tyndall and Fourier. That was the easy bit. The hard part was deciding how much of the solar radiation Earth's surface absorbed, and how that proportion would alter as Earth cooled or warmed owing to changes in carbon dioxide concentrations.

Arrhenius had to calculate many things. The absorption capacity of different surfaces across the globe varies, from 20 percent or less for ice to more than 80 percent for dark ocean. The capacities for dark forest and light desert, grasslands, lakes, and so on lie between these two extremes. So, armed with an atlas, Arrhenius divided the surface of the planet into small squares, assessed the capacity of each segment to absorb and reflect solar radiation, and determined how factors like melting ice or freezing ocean would alter things as greenhouse gas concentrations rose or fell. Eventually he produced a series of temperature predictions for different latitudes and seasons determined by atmospheric concentrations of carbon dioxide.

It was a remarkable achievement. In the process he had virtually invented the theory of global warming, and with it the principles of modern climate modeling. Not only that: his calculation that a doubling of carbon dioxide levels would cause a warming of about 10°F almost exactly mirrors the Intergovernmental Panel on Climate Change's most recent assessment, which puts 10.4°F at the top of its likely warming range for a doubling of carbon dioxide levels.

Arrhenius presented his preliminary findings, "On the Influence of Carbonic Acid in the Air upon the Temperature of the Ground," to the Stockholm Physical Society in December 1895 and, after further refinements, published them in the *London, Edinburgh and Dublin Philosophical Magazine and Journal of Science.* There he offered more predictions that are reproduced by modern computer models. High latitudes would experience greater warming than the tropics, he said. Warming would also be more marked at night than during the day, in winter than in summer, and over land than over sea.

But he had cracked an issue that seemed to interest no one else. The world forgot all about it. Luckily for Arrhenius, this labor was but a sideshow in his career. A few years after completing it, he found fame as the winner of the 1903 Nobel Prize for Chemistry, for work on the electrical conductivity of salt solutions. Soon, too, he had a new wife and a child, and other interests—he dabbled in everything from immunology to electrical engineering. He was an early investigator of the northern lights and a popular proponent of the idea that the seeds of life could travel through space.

But after the First World War, his mood changed. The optimism of his generation, which believed that science and technology could solve every problem, crumbled in the face of a war that killed so many of its sons. He railed against the wastefulness of modern society. "Concern about our raw materials casts a dark shadow over mankind," he wrote, in an early outburst of twentieth century environmental concern. "Our descendants surely will censure us for having squandered their just birthright." His great fear was that oil supplies would dry up, and he predicted that the United States might pump its last barrel as early as 1935. He advocated energy efficiency and proposed the development of renewable energy, such as wind and solar power. He sat on a government commission that made Sweden one of the first countries to develop hydroelectric power.

Many Swedes today see Arrhenius as an environmental pioneer and praise his efforts to promote new forms of energy. He would have been bemused by this appreciation. For one thing, he never made the connection between his work on the greenhouse effect and his later nightmares about disappearing fossil fuels. He knew from early on that burning coal and oil generated greenhouse gases that would build up in the air. But he rather liked the idea, writing in 1908: "We may hope to enjoy ages with more equable and better climates, especially as regards the colder regions of the Earth, ages when the Earth will bring forth much more abundant crops for the benefit of a rapidly propagating mankind." But he had concluded with some sadness that it would probably take a millennium to cause a significant warming. And when he later began to perceive the scale of industrial exploitation of fossil fuels, his fear was solely that the resources would run out.

For half a century after Arrhenius's calculations, the prevailing view continued to be that man-made emissions of carbon dioxide were unlikely to

have a measurable effect on the climate anytime soon. Nature would eas-
ily absorb any excess. From time to time, scientists did measure carbon
dioxide in the air, but local variability was too great to identify any clear
trends in concentrations of the gas.

The only man to take the prospect of greenhouse warming seriously was
a British military engineer and amateur meteorologist, Guy Callendar. In
a lecture at the Royal Meteorological Society in 1938, he said that the few
existing measurements of carbon dioxide levels in the atmosphere sug-
gested a 6 percent increase since 1900, that this must be due to fossil fuel
burning, and that the implication was that warming was "actually occur-
ring at the present time." Like Arrhenius, Callendar thought this on bal-
ance rather a good thing. And like Arrhenius, he saw his findings pretty
much ignored.

The next person to make a serious effort was Charles David Keeling, a
young student at the Scripps Institution of Oceanography, in La Jolla, Cal-
ifornia. He began monitoring carbon dioxide levels in the mid-1950s, first
in the bear-infested hills of the state's Yosemite National Park, where he
liked to go hiking, and later, in the hope of getting better data, in the clean
air 14,000 feet up on top of Mauna Loa, a volcano in Hawaii. Keeling took
measurements every four hours on Mauna Loa, in the first attempt ever to
monitor carbon dioxide levels in one place continuously. He was so serious
about his measurements that he missed the birth of his first child in order
to avoid any gaps in his logbook.

The results created a sensation. Keeling quickly established that in
such a remote spot as Mauna Loa, above weather systems and away from
pollution, he could identify a background carbon dioxide level of 315 parts
per million (ppm). The seasonal cycling of carbon dioxide caused an an-
nual fluctuation around this average between summer and winter. Plants
and other organisms that grow through photosynthesis consume carbon
dioxide from the air, especially in spring. But during autumn and winter,
photosynthesis largely stops, and the photosynthesizers are eaten by soil
bacteria, fungi, and animals. They exhale carbon dioxide, pushing at-
mospheric levels back up again. Because most of the vegetation on the
planet is in the Northern Hemisphere, the atmosphere loses carbon diox-
ide in the northern summer and gains it again in the winter. Earth, in ef-
fect, breathes in and out once a year.

But Keeling's most dramatic discovery was that this annual cycle was superimposed on a gradual year-to-year rise in atmospheric carbon dioxide levels—a trend that has become known as Keeling's curve. The background concentration of 315 ppm that Keeling found on Mauna Loa in 1958 has risen steadily, to 320 ppm by 1965, 331 ppm by 1975, and 380 ppm today.

The implications of Keeling's curve were profound. "By early 1962," he later wrote, "it was possible to deduce that approximately half of the CO_2 from fossil fuel burning was accumulating in the air," with the rest absorbed by nature. By the late 1960s he had noticed that the annual cycling of carbon dioxide was growing more intense. And the spring downturn in atmospheric levels was beginning earlier in the year—strong evidence that the slow annual increase in average levels was raising temperatures and creating an earlier spring.

Keeling personally supervised the meticulous measurements on Mauna Loa until his death, in 2005. In his final year, this generally mild man picked up the public megaphone one last time to warn that, for the first time in almost half a century, his instruments had recorded two successive years, 2002 and 2003, in which background carbon dioxide levels had risen by more than 2 ppm. He warned that this might be because of a weakening of the planet's natural ability to capture and store carbon in the rainforests, soils, and oceans—nature's "carbon sinks." He feared that nature, which had been absorbing half the carbon dioxide emitted by human activity, might be starting to give it back—something that, in his typically understated way, he suggested "might give cause for concern."

On his death, Keeling's bosses at Scripps were kind enough to call the Keeling curve "the single most important environmental data set taken in the 20th century." Nobody disagreed. One writer called him the man who "measured the breathing of the world."

Thanks to Keeling's curve, the ideas of Arrhenius and Callendar were rescued from the dustbin of scientific history. It seemed he was right that people could tamper with the planetary thermostat. Climatologists, many of whom had predicted in the 1960s that natural cycles were on the verge of plunging the world into a new ice age, began instead to warn of imminent man-made global warming. As late as the early 1970s, U.S. government officials had been asking their scientists how to stop the Arctic sea ice from becoming so thick that nuclear submarines could not break through. But by the end of the decade, President Jimmy Carter's Global 2000 Report on the environment had identified global warming as an urgent new issue, and the National Academy of Sciences had begun the first modern study of the problem.

A vast amount of research has been conducted since. For the past decade and a half, the IPCC has produced regular thousand-page updates just to review the field and pronounce on the scientific consensus. But in some ways, mainstream thinking on how climate will alter as carbon dioxide levels rise has not advanced much in the century since Arrhenius. Thanks to Keeling, we know that those levels are rising; but little else has changed.

Only in the past five years, as researchers have learned more about the way our planet works, have some come to the conclusion that changes probably won't be as smooth or as gradual as those imagined by Arrhenius—or as the scenarios of gradual change drawn up by the IPCC still suggest. We are in all probability already embarked on a roller-coaster ride of lurching and sometimes brutal change. What that ride might feel like is the central theme of this book.

TURNING UP THE HEAT

A skeptic's guide to climate change

Ever since the rise of concern about climate change during the 1980s, the scientists involved have been dogged by a small band of hostile critics. Every time they believe they have seen them off, the skeptics come right back. And in some quarters, their voices remain influential. One leading British newspaper in 2004 called climate change a "global fraud" based on "left-wing, anti-American, anti-West ideology." And the best-selling author Michael Crichton, in his much-publicized novel *State of Fear,* portrayed global warming as an evil plot perpetrated by environmental extremists.

Many climate scientists dismiss the skeptics with a wave of the hand and return to their computer models. Most skeptics, they note, fall into one of three categories: political scientists, journalists, and economists with little knowledge of climate science; retired experts who are aggrieved to find their old teachings disturbed; and salaried scientists with overbearing bosses to serve, such as oil companies or the governments in hock to them. If the skeptics are to be believed, the evidence for global warming and even the basic physics of the greenhouse effect are full of holes. The apparent scientific consensus exists only, they say, because it is enforced by a scientific establishment riding the gravy train, aided and abetted by politicians keen to play the politics of fear. Much of this may sound hysterical. But could the skeptics be on to something?

First, the basic physics. As we have seen, much of this goes back almost two centuries. Fourier and Tyndall both knew that the atmosphere stays warm because a certain amount of the short-wave radiation reaching Earth

from the sun is absorbed by the planet's surface and radiated at longer infrared wavelengths. Like any radiator, this warms the surrounding air. They knew, too, that this heat is trapped by gases—such as water vapor, carbon dioxide, and methane—that have a "greenhouse effect," without which the planet would be frozen, like Mars. But you can have too much of a good thing. Our other planetary neighbor, Venus, has an atmosphere choked with greenhouse gases and is broiling at around 840°F as a result. And that is a worry. For, thanks to Keeling's curve, there can be no doubt now that human activity on planet Earth is raising carbon dioxide in the atmosphere to roughly a third above pre-industrial levels.

The effect this has on the planet's radiation balance is now measurable. In 2001, Helen Brindley, an atmospheric physicist at Imperial College London, examined satellite data over almost three decades to plot changes in the amount of infrared radiation escaping from the atmosphere into space. Because what does not escape must remain, heating Earth, this is effectively a measure of how much heat is being trapped by greenhouse gases—the greenhouse effect. In the part of the infrared spectrum trapped by carbon dioxide—wavelengths between 13 and 19 micrometers—she found that less and less radiation is escaping. The results for the other greenhouse gases were similar.

These findings alone should be enough to establish for even the most diehard skeptic that man-made greenhouse gas emissions are making the atmosphere warmer. Climate models developed by the U.S. government's space agency, NASA, estimate that Earth is now absorbing nearly one watt more than it releases per 10.8 square feet of its surface. This is a significant amount. You could run a 60-watt light bulb off the excess energy supplied to the area of the planet that a modest house occupies.

More contentious is whether we can actually feel the heat. Direct planet-wide temperature records go back 150 years. They suggest that nineteen of the twenty warmest years have occurred since 1980, and that the five warmest years have all been since 1998. Could the thermometers be misleading us? That has to be a possibility. The records, after all, are not a formal planetary monitoring system; they are just a collection of all the data that happen to be available.

Two important criticisms are made. One is that satellite sensors and instruments carried into the atmosphere aboard weather balloons do not back up the surface thermometers. The instrument data suggest that if air close to the surface is warming, that warming is not spreading through the bottom 6 miles of the atmosphere, known as the troposphere, in the way that climate scientists predict. If true, this is very worrying, says Steve Sherwood, a meteorologist at Yale University and author of a study of the problem: "It would spell trouble for our whole understanding of the atmosphere."

Not surprisingly, skeptics have given great play to the suggestion that satellites "prove" the surface thermometers to be at fault. Not so fast, says Sherwood. The satellite data are untrustworthy, because they measure the temperature in the air column beneath a satellite and cannot easily distinguish between the troposphere, which is expected to be warming, and the stratosphere, which should be cooling as less heat escapes the lower atmosphere. Further, satellites do not provide direct measurements in the way that thermometers do. Temperatures have to be interpreted from other data, which creates errors. The scientists running the instruments accept that the results "drift." Every week, says Sherwood, they recalibrate their satellite measurements according to data from weather balloons. In effect, therefore, the long-term average data from satellites are creatures of the balloon data.

So how good is the balloon data? Here Sherwood found a surprisingly obvious flaw—obvious, at any rate, to anyone who has left an ordinary thermometer out in the sun. The sun's ultraviolet rays shining on the bulb force the temperature reading continuously upward so that it no longer measures the air temperature. The true air temperature can be captured only in the shade, unmolested by the sun's direct rays. Thermometers on weather balloons, it turns out, are no different. They are "basically cheap thermometers easily read by an electric circuit," says Sherwood. They, too, show spurious readings when in the sun.

Meteorologists have recently fixed the problem by shielding the thermometers attached to weather balloons inside a white plastic housing. But this was rarely done thirty years ago. Sherwood concludes that "back in the 1960s and 1970s especially, the sun shining on the instruments was making readings too high." And that, he says, is the most likely explanation for why balloon measurements do not reveal a warming trend.

Two further observations back up this interpretation. First, spurious readings should not be a problem when the sun goes down, so 1960s and 1970s readings at night should be reliable. And sure enough, nighttime balloon data over the past thirty years show a warming trend. Second, the data from both balloons and satellites show a strong cooling in the stratosphere—which is likely only if more heat is truly being trapped beneath it, in the troposphere.

Another serious criticism of the surface-temperature trends is that measurements by surface thermometers have been biased by the growth of cities. The concrete and tarmac of cities retain more heat than rural areas, especially at night. The argument is that over the decades, more and more temperature-measuring sites have become urban, so the temperature trends reflect the urbanization of thermometers rather than real warming. The "urban heat island," as researchers call it, is undoubtedly real. Cities do hang on to heat. But is it skewing the global data?

This seems unlikely. The largest areas of warming have been recorded over the oceans, and the greatest magnitude of warming is mainly in polar regions, distant from big centers of population. The skeptics should finally have been silenced by a neat piece of research in 2004 by David Parker, of the Hadley Centre for Climate Prediction, part of Britain's Met Office in Exeter. He figured that the urban heat island effect should be most intense when there is no wind to disperse the urban heat. So he divided the historical temperature data into two sets: one of temperatures taken in calm weather, and the other of temperatures taken in windy weather. He found no difference. So, while nobody denies that the urban heat island effect exists, it is not sufficient to upset the reliability of global trends in thermometer readings.

There are other disputes, which we might call "second order," because they are about circumstantial evidence of climate change. Is it true, for instance, that temperatures at the end of the twentieth century were really hotter than at any other time in the past millennium? That is the claim made by U.S. researcher Michael Mann. He produced a controversial graph dubbed the "hockey stick," which used data from tree rings and other "proxy" sources to show that the millennium comprised 950 years of stable temperatures and a sudden upturn at the end. The arguments, which we will look at in more detail later, continue as to whether Mann's data are correct. And in the end, we may simply never know enough about past temperatures to be sure. But however the dispute goes, it doesn't change the basic science of the greenhouse effect. And in any event, it should be no part of the case for future climate change that past climate did not vary. It rather obviously did. As this book will argue, there is no comfort in past variability. Quite the contrary.

Similarly, there is room for uncertainty about the cause of the rise in temperature over the past 150 years, which is, depending on how you draw your average for recent years, put at a global average of between 1.1 and 1.4°F. The warming itself is real enough, but that doesn't necessarily mean that humans are to blame. It could be natural.

One argument is that more radiation reaching us from the sun can account for most of the warming of the past 150 years. This case was made best by the Danish scientists Knud Lassen and Eigil Friis-Christensen in 1991. They found a correlation between sunspot activity, which historically reflects the energy output of the sun, and temperature changes on Earth from 1850 onward. Time-based statistical correlations are notoriously tricky, because they can happen by chance; but the Danes' correlation looked convincing, and prominent skeptics took up the case. However, newer data have convinced Lassen that solar activity cannot explain more recent climate change. Declining sunspot activity since 1980 should have reduced temperatures on Earth. Instead, they have been rising faster than ever.

Overall, this particular dispute has been good for science, and the skeptics can claim a tie. Climate scientists who once put all global warming since 1850 down to the greenhouse effect now concede that up to 40 percent was probably due to the sun. Solar changes may have been the main cause of the substantial global warming in the first half of the twentieth century, for instance. But there is no way the sun's activity can explain the dramatic warming since 1970.

Both sides play one last trick. Web sites run by skeptics regularly publish temperature graphs from particular places that show no warming, suggesting that the whole idea of global warming is a myth. But climate scientists are almost as guilty when they indiscriminately attribute every local warming to global trends, whereas well-understood local climate cycles may be the more likely cause. The case for setting up local climate "watchtowers" in parts of the planet known to be sensitive to climate change, such as the Arctic, remains strong. But they will never provide unambiguous proof of global change, because global warming has not canceled out natural variations in local climate systems. What is so remarkable about recent trends is not local events but the global reach of warming. Virtually no region of the planet is spared. This is in contrast to natural oscillations that mostly just redistribute heat. The greenhouse effect is putting more energy into the entire climate system. Occasionally that causes cooling and other weird weather, but mostly it causes strong warming.

To summarize the current state of affairs: the global trends are real. No known natural effect can explain the global warming seen over the past thirty years. In fact, natural changes like solar cycles would have caused a marginal global cooling. Only some very convoluted logic can avoid the conclusion that the human hand is evident in climate change. Indeed, to think anything else would be to flout one of the central tenets of science. The fourteenth-century English philosopher William Ockham coined the principle of Ockham's razor when he argued that, if the evidence supported them, the simplest and least convoluted explanations for events were the best. Changes in greenhouse gases are the simple, least convoluted explanation for climate change. And those changes are predominantly man-made.

This is not the end of the story, however. While we can be fairly certain that more greenhouse gases in the air will push the atmosphere to further warming, big uncertainties remain about how the planet will respond. An assessment of the sensitivity of global temperatures to outside forcing —whether to changes in sunlight or the addition of greenhouse gases— mostly revolves around disentangling the main feedbacks: the things changed by an altered climate that influence the climate in turn. Positive feedbacks reinforce and amplify the change, and run the risk of producing a runaway change—the climatic equivalent of a squawk on a sound system. Negative feedbacks work in the other direction, moderating or even neutralizing change.

The current climate models concur with Arrhenius that the planet will amplify the warming. But skeptics believe that nature has strong stabilizing forces that will act as negative feedbacks and head off climate change. They don't by any means agree on how this will work. Some say a warmer world will be a cloudier world, providing us with more shade from the sun. Others, like the respected Massachusetts Institute of Technology meteorologist Richard Lindzen, have argued that the higher reaches of the troposphere might actually become drier, reducing the greenhouse effect of water vapor. Many of these arguments reflect legitimate uncertainty among climate scientists, though some of the negative feedbacks proposed by the skeptics, such as cloud processes, could equally turn into major positive feedbacks and make the IPCC projections too small.

Where does this leave us? Actually, with a surprising degree of scientific consensus about the basic science of global warming. When the science historian Naomi Oreskes, of the University of California in San Diego, reviewed almost a thousand peer-reviewed papers on climate change published between 1993 and 2003, she found the mainstream consensus to be real and near universal. "Politicians, economists, journalists and others may have the impression of confusion, disagreement or discord among climate scientists, but that impression is incorrect," she concluded. The disagreements were mainly about detail. The consensus, stretching from Tyndall through Arrhenius to the IPCC, lived on.

For hard-line skeptics, of course, any scientific consensus must, by definition, be wrong. As far as they are concerned, the thousands of scientists behind the IPCC models have either been seduced by their own doom-laden narrative or are engaged in a gigantic conspiracy. For them, the greater the consensus, the worse the conspiracy. The maverick climatologist Pat Michaels, of the University of Virginia in Charlottesville, says we are faced with what the philosopher of science Thomas Kuhn called a "paradigm problem." Michaels, who is also the state meteorologist for Virginia, one of the United States' largest coal producers, and a consultant to numerous fossil fuel companies, says: "Most scientists spend their lives working to shore up the reigning world view—the dominant paradigm—and those who disagree are always much fewer in number." The drive to conformity, he says, is accentuated by peer review, which ensures that only papers in support of the paradigm appear in the research literature, and by public funding of research into the prevailing "paradigm of doom."

Even if you accept this cynical view of how science is done, it doesn't mean that the orthodoxy is always wrong. The fact that scientists universally agree that the world is round does not make it flat. Many of the same claims that are now made against the global warming "paradigm" were once made about the "AIDS industry" by people who disputed that HIV caused AIDS. Some governments took their side for a long time, and their citizens are now living with the consequences. Where are those skeptics now? Some of them can be heard making the case against climate change.

But all that said, I do think the skeptics are important to the arguments about climate science. The desire for consensus is always likely to lead the mainstream scientific community to don blinkers. This has not only blotted out the arguments of skeptics but also sidelined results from the handful of "rogue" climate models that keep turning up tipping points that could tumble the world into much worse shape than what is currently predicted by the mainstream. One scientist told me in the corridors of a conference in early 2005: "By ignoring these outliers, IPCC has failed for ten years to investigate the possible effects of more extreme climate change."

So, despite their sometimes cynical motives, the skeptics have served a purpose in picking away at the IPCC orthodoxy. As in politics, every good government needs a good opposition. And though their arguments have often been opportunistic and personal, the skeptics have spotted the stifling impact of consensus-building. They are, if nothing else, helping to keep the good guys honest. The pity is that they have not done a better job, by engaging in more real science and less empty rhetoric. And in their enthusiasm to debunk climate change, they have failed to grasp one alarming possibility: that the IPCC could be underestimating, not overestimating, the threat that the world faces.

3

THE YEAR

How the wild weather of 1998 broke all records

Lidia Rosa Paz was at a loss. She caught my arm and pointed despairingly into the raging river. Out there, about 50 yards into the water, was the spot where, until days before, she had lived. On the night of October 28, 1998, her shantytown of Pedro Dias, in the town of Choluteca, in Honduras, had been washed away, taking more than a hundred people to their deaths. Lidia had survived, but every one of her possessions was gone. "What will I do now?" she asked. I didn't have an answer.

Hers was one story from a night when floods and landslides ripped apart the small Central American country's geography, leaving more than 10,000 Hondurans dead and 2 million homeless. It was the night that Hurricane Mitch, the most vicious hurricane to hit the Americas in 200 years, came calling, and dumped a year's rain in just a few hours. Choluteca is in southern Honduras, on the Pacific coast, far from the normal track of Caribbean hurricanes. When the radio issued storm warnings that night, neither Lidia nor any of her neighbors took much notice. "Hurricanes never come here," she told me. Or at least they never had.

I was in Honduras a couple of weeks after the hurricane had struck. The devastation was appalling. Huge floods had rushed down rivers and into the capital, Tegucigalpa, in the mountainous heart of the country, ripping away whole communities. A thousand people lost their lives beneath a single slide that landed on the suburb of Miramesi. Another stopped just short of the American embassy in the capital. Rivers changed their paths right across the country, obliterating towns. And flash floods on steep hillsides buried whole communities under mud. Sixty percent of the country's bridges were destroyed, along with a quarter of its schools and half its agricultural productivity, including nearly all its banana plantations. The first visitors to the southern town of Mordica reported, "All you can see is the top of the church." Ministers said the country's economic development had been put back twenty years.

For tens of millions of people across the world, the violence of Mitch is an omen. Many climatologists believe that Mitch, a ferocious hurricane made worse by the warm seas that allowed it to absorb huge amounts of water from the ocean, was a product of global warming—and a sign of things to come for the hundreds of millions of inhabitants of flood-prone river valleys and coastal plains across the world; for those living on deforested hillsides prone to landslips; and for many millions more who do not yet know that they are vulnerable in a new era of hyperweather. People like Lidia before Mitch hit.

Those who do not believe that global warming is a real and dangerous threat should visit places like Choluteca and talk to people like Lidia. It may not convince them that climate change is making superhurricanes and megafloods. But it will show them the forces of nature untamed and the human havoc caused when weather breaks its normal shackles. For hundreds of millions of people, these issues are no longer a matter for computer modeling or debate in the corridors of Congress or future forecasts. They are about real lives and deaths. The question is not: Can we prove that events like Mitch are caused by climate change? It is: Can we afford to take the chance that they are?

The year 1998 was the warmest of the twentieth century, perhaps of the millennium. It was also a year of exceptionally wild weather, and few doubt that the two were connected. That year, besides the storms, the rainforests got no rain. Forest fires of unprecedented ferocity ripped through the tinder-dry jungles of Borneo and Brazil, Peru and Tanzania, Florida and Sardinia. New Guinea had the worst drought in a century; thousands starved to death. East Africa saw the worst floods in half a century—during the dry season. Uganda was cut off for several days, and much of the desert north of the region flooded. Mongol tribesmen froze to death as Tibet had its worst snows in fifty years. Mudslides washed houses off the cliffs of the desert state of California. In Peru, a million were made homeless by floods along a coastline that often has no rain for years at a time. The water level in the Panama Canal was so low that large ships couldn't make it through. Ice storms disabled power lines throughout New England and

Quebec, leaving thousands without power or electric light for weeks. The coffee crop failed in Indonesia, cotton died in Uganda, and fish catches collapsed in the Pacific off Peru. Unprecedented warm seas caused billions of the tiny algae that give coral their color to quit reefs across the Indian and Pacific Oceans, leaving behind the pale skeletons of dead coral.

All a coincidence? Not according to the IPCC. Some of the damage was caused by an intense outbreak of a natural climate cycle in the Pacific known as El Niño. Every few years, this causes a reversal of winds and ocean currents across the equatorial Pacific, for a few months taking rains to drought regions and droughts to normally wet areas. But as we shall see in Chapter 30, there is growing evidence that El Niños are becoming stronger and more frequent under the influence of global warming. This is probably part of a pattern identified by the IPCC, in which, all around the world, the weather is becoming more extreme and more unpredictable as the world warms. And 1998, the warmest year yet, was the epitome of the trend.

The heat is intensifying the hydrological cycle. Globally, average annual rainfall increased by up to 10 percent during the twentieth century, because warming has increased evaporation. Locally, the trends are even stronger. The floods that inundated Mozambique in 2000 occurred because maximum daily rainfall there had risen by 50 percent. In the eastern U.S., the proportion of rain falling in heavy downpours has increased by a quarter. In Britain, winter rain falls in intense downpours twice as often as it did in the 1960s. There are similar patterns in Australia, South Africa, Japan, and Scandinavia. Even the Asian monsoon has become more intense but less predictable. At the same time, dry areas in continental interiors have become drier, causing deserts to spread. The year 1998 was the first in a run of years of intense drought that stretched from the American West through the Mediterranean to Central Asia.

At the time of this writing, no other year has been as hot as 1998—and no other year so climatically violent. Unless, that is, you were caught in one of the record number of tropical storms in the North Atlantic in 2005. But if you want to know what the first stage of climate change is shaping up to be like, look no further than 1998.

4

THE ANTHROPOCENE

A new name for a new geological era

Welcome to the Anthropocene. It's a new geological era, so take a good look around. A single species is in charge of the planet, altering its features almost at will. And what more natural than to name this new era after that top-of-the-heap anthropoid, ourselves? The term was coined in 2000 by the Nobel Prize–winning Dutch atmospheric scientist Paul Crutzen to describe the past two centuries of our planet's evolution. "I was at a conference where someone said something about the Holocene, the long period of relatively stable climate since the end of the last ice age," he told me later. "I suddenly thought that this was wrong. The world has changed too much. So I said: 'No, we are in the Anthropocene.' I just made up the word on the spur of the moment. Everyone was shocked. But it seems to have stuck."

The word is catching on among a new breed of scientists who study Earth systems—how our planet functions. Not just climate systems, but also related features, such as the carbon cycle on land and at sea, the stratosphere and its ozone layer, ocean circulation, and the ice of the cryosphere. And those scientists are coming to believe that some of these systems are close to breakdown, because of human interference. If that is true, then the gradual global warming predicted by most climate models for the next centuries will be the least of our worries.

The big new discovery is that planet Earth does not generally engage in gradual change. It is far cruder and nastier, says Will Steffen, an Australian expert on climate and carbon cycles who from 1998 to 2004 was director of the International Geosphere Biosphere Programme, a research agency dedicated to investigating Earth systems. A mild-mannered man not given to hyperbole, Steffen nonetheless takes a hard-nosed approach to climate change. "Abrupt change seems to be the norm, not the exception," he says. We have been lured into a false sense of security by the relatively quiet climatic era during which our modern complex civilizations have grown and flourished. It may also have left us unexpectedly vulnerable as we stumble into a new era of abrupt change.

We have also been blind, he says, to the extent of the damage we are doing to our planetary home. We often see our impact as limited to individual parts of the system: to trashed rainforests, polluted oceans, and even raised air temperatures. We rarely notice that by doing all these things at once, we are undermining the basic planetary systems. Something, Steffen says, is going to give: "The planet may have an Achilles heel. And if it does, we badly need to know about it." Without that knowledge and the will to act, he says, the Anthropocene may well end in tears.

A report from the U.S. National Academy of Sciences in 2002, under the chairmanship of Richard Alley, of Penn State University—a glaciologist with the slightly manic appearance of an ex-hippie, who has become a regular on Capitol Hill for his ability to talk climate science in plain language—sounded a similar warning. "Recent scientific evidence shows that major and widespread climate changes have occurred with startling speed," the report began. "The new paradigm of an abruptly changing climate system has been well established by research over the last decade, but this new thinking is little known and scarcely appreciated in the wider community of natural and social scientists and policymakers." Or, Alley might have added, among the citizens of this threatened planet.

We have already had one lucky break. It happened twenty years ago, when a hole suddenly opened in the ozone layer over Antarctica, stripping away the continent's protective shield against ultraviolet radiation. We were lucky that it happened over Antarctica, and lucky that we spotted it before it spread too far.

Many of the scientists who worked to unravel the cause of the ozone hole—including Crutzen, who won his Nobel Prize in this endeavor—are among the most vehement in issuing the new warnings. They know how close we came to disaster. Glaciologists like Alley are another group who take the perils of the Anthropocene most seriously. In the past decade, they have analyzed ice cores from both Greenland and Antarctica to map the patterns of past natural climate change. The results have been chilling.

It has emerged, for instance, that around 12,000 years ago, as the last ice age waned and ice sheets were in full retreat across Europe and North America, the warming abruptly went into reverse. For a thousand years the world returned to the depths of the ice age, only to emerge again with such speed that, as Alley puts it, "roughly half of the entire warming between the ice ages and the postglacial world took place in only a decade." The world warmed by at least 9 degrees—the IPCC's prediction for the next century or so—within ten years. This beggars belief. But Alley and his co-researchers are adamant that the ice cores show this happened.

Similar switchback temperature changes occurred regularly through the last glaciation, and there were a number of other "flickers" as the planet staggered toward a new postglacial world. Stone Age man, with only the most rudimentary protection from a climatic switchback, must have found that tough. Heaven knows how modern human society would respond to such a change, whereby London would have a North African climate, Mexican temperatures would be visited on New England, and India's billion-plus population would be deprived of the monsoon rains that feed them.

The exact cause of the rise and fall of the ice ages still excites disputes. But it seems that the 100,000-year cycles of ice ages and interglacials that have persisted for around a million years have coincided with a minor wobble in Earth's orbit. Its effect on the solar radiation reaching the planet is minute, and it happens only gradually. But somehow Earth's systems amplify its impact, turning a minor cooling into an abrupt freeze or an equally minor warming into a sudden defrost. The amplification certainly involves greenhouse gases, as Arrhenius long ago surmised. The extraordinary way in which temperatures and carbon dioxide levels have moved in lockstep permits no other interpretation. It also probably involves changes to ocean currents and the temperature feedbacks from growing and melting ice.

We will return to this conundrum later. What matters here is that a minor change in the planet's heating—much less, indeed, than we are currently inflicting through greenhouse gases—could cause such massive changes worldwide. The planet seems primed to leap into and out of glaciations and, perhaps, other states too.

Some see this hair trigger as rather precisely organized. Will Steffen says that for a couple of million years, Earth's climate seems to have had just two "stable states": glacial and interglacial. There was no smooth transition between them. The planet simply jumped, at a signal from the orbital wobble, from the glacial to the interglacial state, and made the jump back again with a little, but not much, more decorum. "The planet jumps straight into the frying pan and makes a bumpy and erratic slide into the freezer," Steffen says. The glacial state seems to have been anchored at carbon dioxide levels of around 190 ppm, while the interglacial state, which the modern world occupied until the Industrial Revolution, was anchored at about 280 ppm. The rapid flip between the two states must have involved a reallocation of about 220 billion tons of carbon between the oceans, land, and the atmosphere. Carbon was buried in the oceans during the glaciations and reappeared afterward. Nobody knows quite how or why. But the operation of the hair-trigger jump to a much warmer state raises critical questions for the Anthropocene.

In the past two centuries, humanity has injected about another 220 billion tons of carbon into the atmosphere, pushing carbon dioxide levels up by a third, from the stable interglacial level of 280 ppm to the present 380 ppm. The figure continues to rise by about 20 ppm a decade. So the big question is how Earth will respond. Conventional thinking among climate scientists from Arrhenius on predicts that rising emissions of carbon dioxide will produce a steady rise in atmospheric concentrations and an equally steady rise in temperatures. That's still the IPCC story. But Steffen takes a different view: "If the ice age seemed to gravitate between two steady states, maybe in future we will gravitate to a third steady state." Nature might, he concedes, fulfill the expectations of climate skeptics and push back down toward 280 ppm; but if it was going to do that, we would already see evidence of it. And we don't.

Other scientists, including Alley, are not convinced by Steffen's sense of order in the system. Sitting in his departmental office, Alley likens the climate system to "a drunk—generally quiet when left alone, but unpredictable when roused." When he is writing scientific papers or committee reports, his language is not so vivid. He talks of a "chaotic system" vulnerable to "forcings" from changes in solar radiation or greenhouse gases. "Abrupt climate change always could occur," he says. But "the existence of forcings greatly increases the number of possible mechanisms [for] abrupt change"; and "the more rapid the forcings, the more likely it is that the resulting change will be abrupt on the timescale of human economies or global ecosystems." Drunks, in other words, may be unpredictable, but if you shout at them louder or push them harder, they will react more vehemently. Right now, moreover, we are offering our drunk one more for the road.

The past 10,000 years, since the end of the last ice age, have not been without climate change. The Asian monsoon has switched on and off; deserts have come and gone; Europe and North America have flipped from medieval warm period to little ice age. None of these events has been as dramatic as the waxing and waning of the ice ages themselves. But most were equally abrupt, and civilizations have come and gone in their wake. Even so, human society in general has prospered, learning to plant crops, domesticate animals, tame rivers, create cities, develop science, and ultimately industrialize the planet.

But in the Anthropocene, the rules of the game have changed. Alley and Steffen agree that humanity is today pushing planetary life-support systems toward their limits. The stakes are higher, because what is happening is global. "Before, if we screwed up, we could move on," says Steffen. "But now we don't have an exit option. We don't have another planet."

5

THE WATCHTOWER

Keeping climate vigil on an Arctic island

A chill wind was blowing off the glacier. Small blue chunks of ice occasionally split from its face and floated down the fjord toward the ocean. A strange green ribbon of light flashed across the sky above from an anonymous building on the foreshore. And on the snow behind, a polar bear wandered warily around a strange human settlement that had grown up on this remote fjord at the seventy-ninth parallel.

I had come to Ny-Alesund, an international community of scientists that, in the darkening days of autumn, numbered fewer than thirty people. The hardy band was there to man this Arctic watchtower on the northwest shores of Spitzbergen, the largest island of a cluster of Arctic islands called Svalbard, because it is reckoned to be one of the most likely places to witness firsthand any future climatic conflagration. Hollywood directors may have chosen New York as the place that would descend into climatic chaos first. But while the scientists here heartily enjoy watching their DVD of *The Day After Tomorrow,* they are convinced that Ny-Alesund is the place to be. The place where our comfy, climatically benign world might begin to end. Where nature may start to take its revenge.

Ny-Alesund is a tiny town of yellow, red, and blue houses two hours' flight from the northernmost spot on mainland Europe. It is nearer Greenland and the North Pole than Norway, which administers Svalbard under an international treaty signed in 1920. It has history. This was where great Norwegian Arctic explorers such as Roald Amundsen and Graf Zeppelin set out for the North Pole, by ship, seaplane, and even giant airship assembled here. More recently, the High Arctic was famous for its military listening posts, where the staff sat in the cold silence, waiting for the first sign of a Russian or American nuclear missile streaking over the ice to obliterate New York or Moscow or London. But today the biggest business is climate science—waiting for the world to turn. Says Jack Kohler, of the Norwegian Polar Institute, down south in Tromso: "If you want to see the world's climate system flip, you'd probably best come here to see it first."

Spitzbergen is already one of the epicenters of climate change. For a few days in July 2005, the scientists put aside their instruments, donned T-shirts and shorts, and sipped lager by the glaciers in temperatures that hit a record 68°F—just 600 miles from the North Pole. Even in late September, as the sun hovered close to the horizon and the long Arctic night beckoned, the sea was still ice-free, and tomatoes were growing in the greenhouse behind the research station kitchens. Old-timers like the British station head Nick Cox, who has visited Ny-Alesund most years since 1978, marvel at the pace of change. "It stuns me how far the glaciers have retreated and how the climate has changed," Cox says. "It used to be still and clear and cold. Now it is a lot warmer, and damper, too, because the warmer air can hold more moisture."

Photographs in the town's tiny museum show families who used to work in coal mines here in the 1930s, huddled in warm clothes down by the shore. Looming behind them are glaciers that are barely visible today, having retreated about 3 miles back up the fjord. The glaciers and ice sheets that still cover two thirds of Svalbard are some of the best-studied in the world. And visiting glaciologists leave each time with worsening news. In the summer of 2005, British glaciologists discovered that the nearby Midtre Lovenbreen glacier had lost 12 inches of height in a single week as it melted in the sun. The Kronebreen glacier may be dumping close to 200,000 acre-feet of ice into the fjord every year.

Jack Kohler is attempting a "mass balance" of the ice of Svalbard. He reckons that 20 million acre-feet melts and runs off into the ocean each year now. Another 3 million acre-feet is lost from icebergs slumping into the sea from 620 miles of ice cliffs. At most, half of this loss is being replaced with new snow. That is an annual net loss of around 11 million acre-feet— a staggering volume for a small cluster of islands, and probably second in the Arctic only to the loss from the huge ice sheet covering Greenland.

And there is more to come, Kohler says. Many of Svalbard's glaciers and ice caps are close to the freezing point and "very sensitive to quite small changes" in temperature. Boreholes drilled into the permafrost show a staggering 0.7°F warming in the past decade. A few more tenths of a degree could be catastrophic, he says.

Ny-Alesund is a cosmopolitan community, especially in summer, with Norwegians and Germans, Swedes and British, Spanish and Finns, Italians and French, Russians and Americans, Japanese and Chinese and Koreans. It is also quirky. Checking some equipment in the empty Korean labs, I found a pair of Spanish scientists hiding there. They said they couldn't afford the accommodation fees in the main compound, but couldn't bear to give up their work measuring glaciers. The Chinese had departed for the winter, but left behind a pair of two-ton granite lions to guard the entrance to their building. The week before, a shipload of Scotsmen, dressed in kilts and offering whiskey galore, showed up at the quayside for some R&R while investigating the sediments on the bottom of the fjord; and since then some Yorkshiremen had flown a remote-controlled helicopter the size of a small dog over glaciers to map them in 3D.

At Ny-Alesund there are magnetometers and riometers and spectrophotometers probing the upper atmosphere; there are weather balloons aplenty, a decompression chamber for divers, and even a big radio telescope that measures the radiation from distant quasars with such accuracy that it helps correct global positioning systems for the effects of continental drift. The scientists here measure chlorofluorocarbons (CFCs) and carbon dioxide, mercury and ozone, water vapor and radon; they fingerprint the smoke and dust brought in on the breeze to find out where they came from; they photograph the northern lights and sniff for methane from the melting tundra. On some cloudless nights, the German researcher Kai Marholdt sends that green shaft of laser light into the sky to probe the chemistry of the stratosphere. There is so much scientific equipment littering the tundra that nobody is sure what is still in use and what has been abandoned by long-since-departed researchers. There are plans for a cleanup, because passing reindeer keep getting tangled in the cables.

Meanwhile, the bears are coming. As the sea ice disappears, polar bears that live out on the ice and hunt for seals are being forced ashore. They are becoming bold. They break into the huts dotting the island, which are maintained for scientists spending a night out on the ice. They are looking for meat, but will sink their teeth into anything soft—bed mattresses and even inflatable boats have been torn to shreds. Anyone moving out of Ny-Alesund has to carry a gun.

Svalbard has long been recognized as extremely sensitive to climate variations. In the early twentieth century, during a period of modest warming in much of the Northern Hemisphere, temperatures rose here by as much as 9°F—a figure probably not exceeded anywhere on the planet. In the 1960s they fell again by almost as much, but the rise since has taken them back to the levels of the 1920s, with no end in sight. Climatologists warn against seeing warming here as an unambiguous sign of man-made climate change. But Ny-Alesund does seem uniquely sensitive to nudges on the planetary thermostat. It is a place where climate feedbacks like melting sea ice and changes in winds and ocean currents work with special force. And who knows what the future will hold? Only about a hundred miles out to sea, Wadhams's last chimney may be living out its final days.

Svalbard is a place to watch like a hawk, and not just for changing climate. The ozone layer is on a hair trigger here, too. Many researchers expect a giant ozone hole to form over the Arctic one day soon, just as it did in the Antarctic twenty-five years ago. And so, on the roof of the Norwegian Polar Institute, the largest research station in Ny-Alesund, pride of place goes to a gleaming steel instrument with a grand embossed nameplate announcing that you are in the presence of Dr. Dobson's Ozone Spectrophotometer No. 8—Dobson Meter No. 8, for short. The British meteorologist Gordon Dobson, one of the earliest researchers into the ozone layer, built the first of his spectrophotometers in 1931, in a wooden hut near Oxford. His eighth, built in 1935, came north to Ny-Alesund and ever since has been pointing to the sky, measuring the ultraviolet radiation pouring through the atmosphere, and thus indirectly measuring the thickness of the ozone layer.

Dobson eventually produced 150 machines. They still form the core of the world's ozone-layer monitoring network. Their work was considered routine, even dull, until one of them discovered an ozone hole over Antarctica in the early 1980s. Now Dobson Meter No. 8 and its minder, research assistant Carl Petter Niesen, are looking into the skies above Ny-Alesund for a repeat here. The most northerly and among the oldest in continual service, the instrument needs a little help these days to keep going. It has a duvet and a small heater to keep it from seizing up in the winter cold. Uniquely here, it is not connected to a computer logger. Even in the depths of winter, Niesen goes up on the roof to write down its reading with a pencil in a large logbook. Not much science happens that way anymore, but the Dobson meter, with its idiosyncratic but continuous record for more than half a century, is irreplaceable.

Dobson Meter No. 8 hasn't spotted a full-blown hole in the ozone layer yet. But as the researchers have waited, they have discovered other strange things happening to the chemistry of the atmosphere. Svalbard, it turns out, is on the flight path of acid fogs from Siberia that get trapped in thin, pancakelike layers of air close to the ice and turn the clear, still air into a yellow haze. Sometimes it rains mercury here, as industrial pollution cruises north and suddenly, within a matter of minutes, precipitates onto the snow.

Pesticides, too, have arrived in prodigious quantities, apparently from the fields of Asia. They condense in the cold air and become absorbed in vegetation. They work their way up the food chain to fish and polar bears and birds. But the very highest concentrations occur in a lake on Bear Island, in the south of the Svalbard archipelago, beneath a huge auk colony. The chemicals that have become concentrated in the Arctic air, and then concentrated again in the Arctic food web, are concentrated one more time in the urine of the auks. What at first sight might seem to be just about the least polluted place on Earth turns out to be a toxic sump.

Ny-Alesund is the most northerly permanent settlement on Earth. And the summit of Mount Zeppelin, 1,600 feet above the settlement, is the top of the top of the world—the ultimate watchtower for the world's climate. I went to the summit in the world's most northerly cable car with Carl Petter Niesen, who was taking his daily journey to tend the huge array of instruments designed to sniff every molecule of passing Arctic air. Recently, he says, carbon dioxide levels in the air on Mount Zeppelin have increased more sharply than at other monitoring stations around the world. Some days he measures levels approaching 390 ppm—fully 10 ppm above the global average. There is always some scatter in the readings. But it seems, he says, as if fast-rising emissions from power plants and cars in China and India are traveling north on the winds with the mercury and the pesticides and the acid haze. Not for the first time, he has caught a whiff of the future here at the top of the world.

II

FAULT LINES IN THE ICE

6

NINETY DEGREES NORTH

Why melting knows no bounds in the far North

"Has anybody in history ever got to 90° north, to be greeted by water and not ice?" That was the question posed by a group of scientists after returning from a cruise to the North Pole in August 2000. Sailing north from Svalbard on one of the world's most powerful icebreakers, the *Yamal*, the researchers found very little ice to break. And when they got to their polar destination, they were amazed to find not pack ice but a mile-wide expanse of clear blue water.

The story went around the world. For some, it revived the tales of ancient mariners, who said that beyond the Arctic ice there was an open ocean, and beyond that a mystical land, an Atlantis of the North. The proprietors of the *Yamal* were quick to cash in, offering summer cruises to "the land beyond the pole." But for the less romantically inclined, the story of the ice-free North Pole ignited panic about Arctic melting. By chance, the scientists on board the *Yamal* had included James McCarthy, a Harvard oceanographer on summer vacation from chairing an IPCC working group on the impacts of climate change. He didn't want to be alarmist, he said on his return. The Arctic ice sheet is made up of shifting plates, so there are bound to be gaps. But there were more and more gaps. So the unexpected discovery was "a dramatic punctuation to a more remarkable journey, in which the ice was everywhere thin and intermittent, with large areas of open water."

The whole Arctic was remarkably ice-free that summer. And that included the Holy Grail of generations of Arctic explorers, the Northwest Passage. The search for a route from the Atlantic to the Pacific and the riches of the Orient excited early explorers almost as much as El Dorado.

But it was a deadly pursuit. The ice swallowed up hundreds of them, most notably Sir John Franklin, whose 1845 expedition disappeared with all 128 hands. But in 2000, a Canadian ship made the journey through the Northwest Passage without touching ice. Its skipper, Ken Burton, said: "There were some bergs, but we saw nothing to cause any anxiety."

Inuit whalers the previous June told glaciologists meeting in Alaska that the ice had been disappearing for some years. "Last year it stayed over the horizon the whole summer; we had to go thirty miles just to hunt seals," said Eugene Brower, of the Barrow Whaling Captain's Association. Recently declassified data from U.S. and British military submarines had revealed that the Arctic ice in late summer was on average 40 percent thinner in the 1990s than in the 1950s. And NASA satellites, which had been photographing the ice for a quarter century, offered the most incontrovertible evidence. Their analyst-in-chief is Ted Scambos, of the National Snow and Ice Data Center, in Boulder, Colorado, a wannabe astronaut who turned to exploring the polar regions as a second best. He reports annually on how the retreat of ice is turning into a rout. In 2005, just 2 million square miles of ice were left in mid-September, the usual date of minimum ice cover. That was 20 percent less than in 1978.

The Arctic is a place without half measures. There is no mid point between water and ice. Melting and freezing are, in the jargon of the systems scientists, threshold processes. Melting takes a lot of solar energy, but once it is complete, the sun is free to warm the water left behind. And, because it is so much darker, that water is also far better at absorbing the solar energy and using it to heat the ambient air. "This makes the whole ice sheet extremely dynamic," says Seymour Laxon, a climate physicist at University College London. "The concept of a slowly dwindling ice pack in response to global warming is just not right. The process is very dynamic, and it depends entirely on temperature each summer."

"Feedbacks in the system are starting to take hold," Scambos says. The winter refreeze is less complete every year; the spring melt is starting ever earlier—seventeen days earlier than usual in 2005. "With all that dark, open water, you start to see an increase in Arctic Ocean heat storage." The Arctic "is becoming a profoundly different place." Most glaciologists agree with Scambos that the root cause of the great melt is Arctic air temperatures that have risen by about 3 to 5°F in the past thirty years—several times the global average. Global warming, it seems, is being amplified here. This is partly because the feedbacks of melting ice create extra local warming. And partly, too, because of a long warm phase in a climatic variable called the Arctic Oscillation, which brings warm winds farther north into the Arctic. The Arctic Oscillation is a natural phenomenon, but there is growing evidence that it is being accentuated by global warming, as we shall see in Chapter 37.

There is another driver for the melting, again probably connected to global warming. Warmer air above the ice is being accompanied by warmer waters beneath. Weeks before Scambos published his 2005 report, Igor Polyakov, of the International Arctic Research Center, in Fairbanks, Alaska, reported on an "immense pulse of warm water" that he had been tracking since it entered the Arctic in 1999. It had burst through the Fram Strait, a narrow "throat" of deep water between Greenland and Svalbard that connects the Greenland Sea and the Atlantic to the Arctic Ocean. And since then, it had been slowly working its way around the shallow continental shelves that encircle the Arctic Ocean. One day in February 2004, the pulse reached a buoy in the Laptev Sea north of Siberia. A thermometer strapped to the buoy recorded a jump in water temperature of half a degree within a few hours. The warm water stayed, the rise proved permanent, and the Laptev Sea rapidly became ice-free. "It was as if the planet became warmer in a single day," Polyakov told one journalist.

Pulses of warm water passing through the Fram Strait may be a regular feature of the Arctic. They were known to the Norwegian explorer and oceanographer Fridtjof Nansen, who a century ago used a specially strengthened ship called the *Fram* to float with the ice and monitor currents in the Arctic. But as the Atlantic itself becomes warmer, the pulses appear to become bigger, and their impact on the Arctic is growing. One theory is that some of the water that once disappeared down the chimneys in the Greenland Sea now comes farther north into the Arctic.

"The Arctic Ocean is in transition toward a new, warmer state," says Polyakov. And most glaciologists working in the Arctic agree. Writing in the journal of the American Geophysical Union, *Eos,* in late 2005, a group of twenty-one of them began in almost apocalyptic terms: "The Arctic system is moving to a new state that falls outside the envelope of glacial-interglacial fluctuations that prevailed during recent Earth history." Soon the Arctic would be ice-free in summer, "a state not witnessed for at least a million years," they said. "The change appears to be driven largely by global warming, and there seem to be few, if any, processes within the Arctic system that are capable of altering the trajectory towards this 'super-interglacial' state."

What would the world be like with an ice-free Arctic? Oil and mineral companies and shipping magnates long for the day when they can prospect at will, build new cities, and navigate their vessels in all seasons from Baffin Island to Svalbard and Greenland and Siberia. But it would be a world without polar bears and ice-dwelling seals, a world with no place for the Inuit way of life. And the influence of such a change would spread around the world. Without the reflective shield of ice, the whole world would warm several more degrees; ocean and air currents driven by temperature differences between the poles and the tropics would falter; on land, methane and other gases would break out of the melting permafrost, raising temperatures further; and as the ice caps on land melted, sea levels would rise so high that much of the world's population would have to move or drown. If the Arctic is especially sensitive to climate change, the whole planet is especially sensitive to changes in the Arctic.

7

ON THE SLIPPERY SLOPE

Greenland is slumping into the ocean

We are on "a slippery slope to hell." That is not the kind of language you expect to read in a learned scientific paper by one of the top climate scientists in the U.S., who is, moreover, the director of one of NASA's main science divisions, the Goddard Institute for Space Studies, in New York. Not even in a picture caption. But Jim Hansen, President George W. Bush's top in-house climate modeler, though personally modest and unassuming, calls it as he sees it.

I've followed Hansen's work for a long time. He began his career investigating the greenhouse effect on Venus, and was principal investigator for the *Pioneer* space probe to that planet in the 1970s. But he soon switched to planet Earth. He was the first person to get global warming onto the world's front pages, during the long, hot U.S. summer of 1988. Half the states in the country were on drought alert, and the mighty Mississippi had all but dried up. The Dust Bowl, it seemed to many, was returning. Hansen picked that moment to turn up at a hearing of the Senate's Energy and Natural Resources Committee in Washington and tell the sweating senators: "It is time to stop waffling so much. We should say that the evidence is pretty strong that the greenhouse effect is here." He didn't quite say that greenhouse gases were causing the drought across the country—a claim that would have been hard to substantiate. But everybody assumed he had.

Sixteen years later, Hansen was the senior U.S. government employee who, seven days before the 2004 presidential election, began a public lecture with the words "I have been told by a high government official that I should not talk about dangerous anthropogenic interference with climate, because we do not know how much humans are changing the earth's climate or how much change is dangerous. Actually, we know quite a lot." And he went on to describe what we know in some detail. Most of his fellow researchers thought that would be the end for Hansen as a government employee. But a year later this outwardly diffident man—who couldn't stop apologizing for keeping me waiting when we met in his large, paper-strewn office—was still at his post. To the astonishment of many of his colleagues. "He is saved by his science; he is just too good to be fired," said one. "Also, he is one of the good guys. He doesn't have enemies. If he needed saving, there are a lot of people who would volunteer for the job."

And now Hansen says the world, or more particularly Greenland, is on a slippery slope to hell. We had better listen.

The world's three great ice sheets—one over Greenland and the other two over Antarctica—contain vast amounts of ice. Leftovers from the last ice age, they are piles of compressed snow almost 2 miles high. Glaciologists divide the sheets into two parts. On the high ground inland, where snowfall is greatest and melting is least, they accumulate ice. But on the edges and on lower ground, where snowfall is usually less and melting is greater, they lose ice. The boundary between the two zones is known as the equilibrium line.

For many centuries these great ice sheets have been in balance, with ice loss at the edges matched by accumulation in the centers, and the equilibrium line remaining roughly stationary. Glaciologists have regarded this balance as rather secure, since such huge volumes of ice can change only very slowly. Glacially. This image of stability and longevity is reassuring. If the ice sheets all melted, or slumped into the ocean, they would make a big splash. They contain enough ice to raise sea levels worldwide by 230 feet. That would drown my house, and probably yours, too. Luckily, as glaciologists have been telling us for years, this won't happen. Not even if there is fast global warming. Large ice sheets, they say, tend to maintain their own climate, keeping the air above cold enough to prevent large-scale melting. And even if warming did take hold at the surface, it could penetrate the tightly packed ice only extremely slowly.

The scariest suggestion, made by the IPCC in 2001, was that beyond a warming of about 5°F, Greenland might gradually start to melt, with a wave of warmth moving down through the ice. Once under way, the process might be unstoppable, because as the ice sheet melted, its surface would lower and become exposed to ever-warmer air. But the melting would take place very slowly, "during the next thousand years or more." Now, that is not a nice legacy to leave to future generations, but a thousand years is forty or so generations away. So maybe it is not something to worry us today.

That used to be the scientific consensus. But Hansen is the spokesperson for a growing body of glaciologists who say that things could happen much faster. Because ice sheets, even the biggest and slowest and most stable-looking, have a secret life involving dramatic and dynamic change. And their apparent stability could one day be their undoing. The story is told best in a single picture. Hansen's "slippery slope" caption accompanied a photograph of a river of water flowing across the Greenland ice sheet and pouring down a hole. The photo has an apocalyptic feel, and in the top right-hand corner a couple of researchers look on from a distance, giving an awesome sense of scale.

What is going on here? The water is not entirely new. Small lakes have always formed on the surface of Greenland ice in the summer sun. And sometimes those lakes empty down flaws in the ice—whether crevasses or vertical shafts, which are known to glaciologists as moulins. But what is new is the discovery that as the surface warms, more and more water is pouring into the interior of the ice sheet. Waterfalls as high as 2 miles are taking surface water to the very base of the ice, where it meets the bedrock. "The summer of 2005 broke all records for melting in Greenland," says Hansen. And such melting threatens to destabilize large parts of the ice sheet on timescales measured in years or decades, not millennia.

Jason Box, of Ohio State University, is a young researcher who knows more about this than most. Every year, he visits Swiss Camp, a research station set up in 1990 on Greenland ice. The name was chosen by the camp's founder, Konrad Steffen, of Zurich, so that he felt more at home. The station was originally sited on the equilibrium line, where the ice melt in summer exactly matches the accumulation of new snow in winter. But the equilibrium line has since moved many miles north, as ever-larger chunks of Greenland find themselves in the zone of predominant melting. These

days, Box goes boating in an area close to Swiss Camp dubbed the "Green-
land Lake District." "Some of these lakes are three or four miles across and
have lasted for a decade or more now," he says. "You wouldn't think it was
Greenland at all."

The lakes are more than just symptoms of melting. They are also reser-
voirs for the destruction of the ice sheet. "These lakes keep growing and
growing until they find a crevasse, into which they drain," Box says. "Down
there are extensive river systems, between the ice and the hard rock, that
eventually emerge at the glacier snout. There may be great lakes, too."

Another regular visitor to Swiss Camp is the glaciologist Jay Zwally,
one of Hansen's colleagues at NASA. He made the alarming discovery that
during warm years the half-mile-thick ice lifts off the bedrock and floats
on the water—rising half a yard or more at times. And it floats toward the
ocean. Ice sheets are never entirely still, of course. But Swiss Camp is al-
ready more than a mile west of where it started. And Zwally found that in
summer, when the surface is warmer and more water pours down the cre-
vasses, the velocity of the ice sheet's flow increases. Acceleration starts a
few days after the melting begins at the surface. It stops when the melting
ceases in the autumn.

This discovery is a revelation, glaciologists admit. "These flows com-
pletely change our understanding of the dynamics of ice-sheet destruc-
tion," says Richard Alley, of Penn State. "We used to think that it would
take 10,000 years for melting at the surface to penetrate down to the bot-
tom of the ice sheet. But if you make a lake on the surface and a crack opens
and the water goes down the crack, it doesn't take 10,000 years, it takes
ten seconds. That huge lag time is completely eliminated."

As ever, Alley has a good analogy. "The way water gets down to the base
of glaciers is rather the way magma gets up to the surface in volcanoes—
through cracks. Cracks change everything. Once a crack is created and
filled, the flow enlarges it and the results can be explosive. Like volcanic
eruptions. Or the disintegration of ice sheets." The lakes on the surface of
Greenland are, he says, the equivalent of the pots of magma beneath vol-
canoes. "More melting will mean more lakes in more places, more water
pouring down crevasses, and more disintegration of the ice." No wonder,
in a paper in *Science,* Zwally called the phenomenon "a mechanism for
rapid, large-scale, dynamic responses of ice sheets to climate warming."

Could such processes be close to triggering a runaway destruction of the Greenland ice sheet? It is hard to be sure, but Greenland does have past form, says David Bromwich, Box's colleague at Ohio State. There is good evidence that the ice sheet lost volume around 120,000 years ago, during the warm era between the last ice age and the previous one. "Temperatures then were very similar to those today," he says. "But the Greenland ice sheet was less than half its present size." He believes that the Greenland ice sheet is a relic of the last ice age whose time may finally have run out. "It looks susceptible, and with the drastic warming we have seen since the 1980s, the chances must be that it is going to melt, and that water will go to the bottom of the ice sheet and lubricate ice flows."

Greenland melting seems to have set in around 1979, and has been accelerating ever since. The interior, above the rising equilibrium line, may still be accumulating snow. But the loss of ice around the edges has more than doubled in the past decade. The NASA team believes that "dynamic thinning" under the influence of the raging flows of meltwater may be responsible for more than half of the ice loss. In early 2006, it reported the results of a detailed satellite radar study of the ice sheet showing that it was losing 180 million acre-feet more of ice every year than it was accumulating through snowfall. That was double the estimated figure for a decade before. And all this gives real substance to the evidence accumulating from Greenland's glaciers, the ice sheet's outlets to the ocean.

Swiss Camp is in the upper catchment of a glacier known as Jakobshavn Isbrae. It is Greenland's largest, flowing west from the heart of the ice sheet for more than 400 miles into Baffin Bay. It drains 7 percent of Greenland. Jakobshavn has for some decades been the world's most prolific producer of icebergs. From Baffin Bay they journey south down Davis Strait; past Cape Farewell, the southern tip of Greenland; and out into the Atlantic shipping lanes. Jakobshavn was the likely source of the most famous iceberg of all—the one that sank the *Titanic* in 1912. But it has been in overdrive since 1997, after suddenly doubling the speed of its flow to the sea. It is now also the world's fastest moving glacier, at better than 7 miles a year.

Jason Box has installed a camera overlooking the glacier to keep track. It takes stereo images every four hours throughout the year. As well as flowing ever faster toward the sea, he says, the glacier is becoming thinner, and in 2003 a tongue of ice 9 miles long that used to extend from its snout into the ocean broke off. "What is most surprising is how quickly this massive volume of ice can respond to warming," says Box. There seems to be a direct correlation between air temperatures in any one year and the discharge of water from glaciers into the ocean. Long time lags, once thought to be a near-universal attribute of ice movement, are vanishing. Jakobshavn, he estimates, could be shedding more than 40 million acre-feet a year, an amount of water close to the flow of the world's longest river, the Nile. Half of that volume is water flowing out to sea from beneath the glacier, and half is calving glaciers.

Other Greenland glaciers are getting up speed, too. The Kangerdlugssuaq glacier, in eastern Greenland, which drains 4 percent of the ice sheet, was flowing into the sea three times faster in the summer of 2005 than when last measured in 1988. At an inch a minute, its movement was visible to the naked eye. Meanwhile, its snout has retreated by three miles in four years. This familiar pattern of faster flow, thinning ice, and rapid retreat of the ice front has also shown at the nearby Helheim glacier, where Ian Howat, of the University of California in Santa Cruz, concludes that "thinning has reached a critical point and begun drastically changing the glacier's dynamics."

Most of these great streams of ice are exiting into the ocean beneath the waterline, in submarine valleys, via giant shelves of floating ice that buttress them. But as the oceans warm, these ice shelves are themselves thinning. It is, says Hansen, a recipe for rapid acceleration of ice loss across Greenland.

The picture, then, is of great flows of ice draining out of Greenland, lubricated by growing volumes of meltwater draining from the surface to the base of the ice sheet and uncorked by melting ice shelves at the coast. All this is new and frightening. "The whole Greenland hydrological system has become more vigorous, more hyperactive," says Box. "It is a very nonlinear response to global warming, with exponential increases in the loss of ice. I've seen it with my own eyes. Even five years ago we didn't know about this." Alley agrees: "Greenland is a different animal from what we thought it was just a few years ago. We are still thinking it might take centuries to go, but if things go wrong, it could just be decades. Everything points in one direction, and it's not a good direction."

"Building an ice sheet takes a long time—many thousands of years," says Hansen. "It is a slow, dry process inherently limited by the snowfall rate. But destroying it, we now realize, is a wet process, spurred by positive feedbacks, and once under way it can be explosively rapid."

8

THE SHELF

Down south, shattering ice uncorks the Antarctic

Over three days in March 2002, there occurred one of the most dramatic alterations to the map of Antarctica since the end of the last ice age. It happened on the shoreline of the Antarctic Peninsula—a tail of mountains 1,200 miles long and more than a mile high pointing from the southern part of the continent toward the tip of South America. A shelf of floating ice larger than Luxembourg and some 650 feet thick, which had been attached to the peninsula for thousands of years, shattered like a huge pane of glass. It broke into hundreds of pieces, each of them a huge iceberg that floated away into the South Atlantic.

There were no casualties, except the self-esteem of Antarctic scientists who believed that after a century of studying the continent's ice, they knew how it behaved. Their subsequent papers revealed their shock. "The catastrophic break-up of the Larsen B ice shelf is remarkable because it reveals an iceberg production mechanism far different from those previously thought to determine the extent of Antarctic ice shelves," wrote Christina Hulbe, a peace activist and glaciologist from Portland State University, in Oregon. Rather than the normal "infrequent shedding of icebergs at the seaward ice front," this time "innumerable icebergs were created simultaneously through the entire breadth of the shelf."

The demise of the Larsen B ice shelf was not in itself a surprise. Both the air and the water around the Antarctic Peninsula had been warming since the 1960s. It had become one of the hot spots of global warming. Warm currents had been gradually eating away at the underside of the floating shelf, while warmer air produced pools of melting water on the surface. It was obvious that the sheet was under strain. Some cracks

formed across the surface in 1994; a chunk around the edge of the shelf
broke off in 1998. But nothing had prepared glaciologists for what was
about to happen. During January 2002, the height of the southern sum-
mer, temperatures hit a new high and the heavy winter snow on the shelf's
surface began to melt. By the end of the month, satellite pictures showed
dark streaks across the shelf. Some were ponds, but others were crevasses
that had filled with water.

Water is denser than ice. So, once inside the crevasses, it created pres-
sure that levered them ever wider. There were, in effect, thousands of
mechanical wedges pushing ever deeper into the ice shelf. Then, in three
climactic days at the start of March, the entire structure gave way. Some
500 billion tons of ice burst into the ocean. In many ways, says Richard
Alley, what happened at Larsen B mirrored the processes under way in
Greenland. "Water-filled cracks more than a few tens of yards deep can be
opened easily by the pressure of water. Ponding of water at the ice surface
increases the water pressure wedging cracks open." In their enthusiasm to
study ice, glaciologists had forgotten about water.

Larsen B was one of a series of floating shelves formed by ice draining
from the mountains of the Antarctic Peninsula. The shelves are the float-
ing front edges of glaciers, and where they meet the ocean, icebergs regu-
larly break off. In recent years, Larsen B had been moving forward by about
a yard a day. Despite this constant movement, the ice shelf itself, at more
than 650 feet thick, was a surprisingly permanent structure. After its col-
lapse, study of the diatoms in the sediment beneath the former shelf sug-
gested that Larsen B had been there for the entire 12,000 years since the
end of the last ice age, when a single ice sheet covered the whole region.

Larsen B wasn't alone; nor has it been alone in disappearing. In all, more
than 500 square miles of ice shelves have been lost from around the Antarc-
tic Peninsula in the past half century. The Larsen A ice shelf, the other side
of an ice-covered headland called Seal Nunatak, broke up in a storm in
1995. And before that, the Wordie shelf, on the west side of the peninsula,
disappeared between 1974 and 1996, triggering a dramatic thinning of
the glaciers that fed it. But both were much smaller than Larsen B, and
neither disappeared in the catastrophic manner of Larsen B.

"Really we don't think there is much doubt that the collapse of the Larsen B shelf was caused by man-made climate change," says John King, chief climatologist at the British Antarctic Survey (BAS), the inheritor of the great tradition of explorers such as Robert Scott and Ernest Shackleton. From their base at Rothera, on Adelaide Island, BAS researchers have mapped in detail how a pulse of warmer air temperatures has pushed south across the peninsula over the past fifty years, lengthening the summer melt season, sending glaciers into retreat, and destabilizing ice shelves as it goes.

Armed with the evidence of Larsen B, glaciologists are reassessing the stability of dozens of peninsula ice shelves—starting with Larsen C, immediately to the south, which is thinning and widely expected to be the next to go. Eventually, they say, the warming will reach the Ronne ice shelf, a slab of ice the size of Spain at the south of the peninsula. And on the other side of the continent is the Ross ice shelf, the continent's largest. It, too, now seems to be vulnerable, says Hulbe.

Disappearing ice shelves do not contribute to sea level rise because their ice is already floating. Their loss no more raises sea levels than an ice cube melting in a drink causes the glass to overflow. But their disappearance does change what happens inland. Ice shelves buttress the glaciers that feed them. After Larsen B disappeared, it was "as if the cork had been removed from a bottle of champagne," says the French glaciologist Eric Rignot, who works at NASA's Jet Propulsion Laboratory, in California. The glaciers that once discharged their ice onto the Larsen B shelf are now flowing into the sea eight times faster than they did before the shelf collapsed. Similar acceleration has happened after other ice sheet collapses. And that faster discharge of ice from land into the ocean is raising sea levels. With the Ross Sea being the main outlet for several of the largest glaciers on the West Antarctic ice sheet, which contains enough ice to raise sea levels by six yards, the stakes are rising.

9

THE MERCER LEGACY

An Achilles heel at the bottom of the world

John Mercer was an English eccentric and, frankly, somewhat disreputable. The list of charges against him is long. He had a penchant for doing his fieldwork in the nude, and was once convicted for jogging naked near his campus at Ohio State University, in Columbus. He regularly fell out with colleagues, and once abandoned two graduate students, including his acolyte and eventual successor Lonnie Thompson, high in the Andes after the money ran out on a field trip. Thompson thought it was something he'd said, until he realized that "those kinds of things kept happening to John; he was the same with everyone."

Mercer, who died of a brain tumor in 1987, is now a largely forgotten figure outside the glaciology community. But within it he is regarded by many, not least Thompson himself, as a genius. In the late 1940s, he set off alone to explore the ice in distant Patagonia, mapping much of the area, and came to realize that tropical glaciers might hold clues to the history of the world's climate. He is credited with inventing the term "greenhouse effect" during a symposium at Ohio State in the early 1960s. But probably his greatest legacy is in Antarctica, where back in the 1960s he made a prophetic warning that may one day ensure the revival of his memory.

At a time when everyone else saw Antarctic ice as just about the most dependable glacial feature on the planet, Mercer began to argue that much of it may have entirely disintegrated during the last interglacial era, about 125,000 years ago. And, though it took him a decade to get his warning into print, he feared that it might be about to happen again. In 1978, in *Nature,* he published a paper declaring: "I contend that a major disaster— a rapid deglaciation of West Antarctica—may be in progress... within about 50 years."

The two ice sheets covering Antarctica are vast. The smaller of them, the West Antarctic ice sheet, covers around 1.5 million square miles. It is vulnerable because, unlike its larger eastern neighbor, it does not sit on dry land. Instead, like a giant ship that has foundered in shallows, it is perched precariously on an archipelago of largely submerged mountains. Ocean currents are swirling beneath its giant ice shelves. The sea temperatures today are close to freezing, but the risk is that as they rise, melting will loosen the ice sheet's moorings.

The heart of the West Antarctic ice sheet has some protection from the ocean. On two sides it is buttressed by mountains, and on the other two sides it is held in place by the Ronne and Ross ice shelves. But Mercer warned that if the ice shelves gave way, the entire sheet could lift off and float away: "Climate warming above a critical level would remove all ice shelves, and consequently all ice grounded below sea level, resulting in the deglaciation of most of West Antarctica." Once under way, the disintegration would "probably be rapid, perhaps catastrophically so." Most of the ice sheet would be gone within a century. He reckoned that a warming of 9 degrees would be enough to set the process in train. Parts of the continent have already experienced more than 3.6 degrees of warming. "One warning sign that a dangerous warming is beginning will be the break-up of ice shelves in the Antarctic Peninsula," he said. Like Larsen B.

Another old acolyte of Mercer's is Terry Hughes, of the University of Maine. Back in 1981, he suggested that the West Antarctic ice sheet might have another vulnerability—a "weak underbelly" in Pine Island Bay, a large inlet on the Amundsen Sea, west of the Antarctic Peninsula. This is one of the most remote places on Earth. Head north from Pine Island Bay, and you don't hit land until Alaska. These are dangerous waters—deep, with unusually tall icebergs breaking off the glaciers and being blown fast across the bay by fierce winds. There is a constant danger of getting trapped by the ice if the wind changes. Onshore, the terrain is rugged, and its weather is violent, with intense snowstorms steered inland by the Antarctic Peninsula. Even Antarctic researchers have given Pine Island Bay a wide berth. There are no bases here.

Hughes's "weak underbelly" theory was, like Mercer's warnings a decade before, roundly ignored at the time. When I first wrote about it, a few years later, other glaciologists warned me off, suggesting that it had been discredited. But today, just mentioning Pine Island Bay is enough to send a shudder through the hearts of many glaciologists. Hughes, they now believe, was right on the mark.

The bay is the outlet for two of Antarctica's top five glaciers: Pine Island and Thwaites. Together, they drain about 40 percent of the West Antarctic ice sheet. They were already the fastest-flowing glaciers in Antarctica when, in the 1990s, Pine Island began to accelerate sharply, and Thwaites, while traveling at the same speed, doubled its flow by becoming twice as wide. The glaciers were responding to a rapid melting of their own ice shelves. The melting was in turn caused by warmer seawater circling into the bay.

The discovery of the accelerating glaciers has, once again, turned conventional thinking about the dynamics of ice on its head. The old view holds that events on the coast, where a glacier meets the ocean, have little bearing on what happens inland. But at Pine Island Bay, the impacts of coastal melting are swiftly being felt throughout the glaciers' network of tributaries across the ice sheet. In the past decade, the flow of the two glaciers has speeded up, not just at the coast but for 125 miles inland. The NASA glaciologist Eric Rignot reported in 2004 that the two glaciers are dumping more than 200 million acre-feet of ice a year into Pine Island Bay. This dwarfs even the very heavy snowfall, which adds about 130 million acre-feet a year. The net "mass loss" of ice from the Pine Island Bay catchment has tripled in a decade.

Since Rignot's paper was published, the news has become even grimmer. Studies of the Pine Island glacier show that its ice shelf is thinning fast. As it thins, ever more warm seawater penetrates beneath the glacier. The "grounding line," the farthest point downstream where the ice makes contact with solid rock, has been retreating by more than a mile a year. Once under way, the retreat of the grounding line is "theoretically self-perpetuating and irreversible, regardless of climate forcing," says Rignot. The glacier is primed for runaway destruction.

In 2005, British and Texas researchers flew more than 45,000 miles on more than a hundred flights back and forth across the Pine Island and Thwaites glaciers, using ice-penetrating radar to map the rocks beneath an area of ice the size of France and sometimes nearly 2 miles high. They found that inland along its major tributaries the Pine Island glacier sat on great lakes of meltwater. There seemed to be remarkably little to hold back its flow. Meanwhile, the Thwaites glacier, which is a stream of ice flowing through a wider area of ice sheet, could be about to widen again, says David Vaughan, of the BAS, who masterminded the survey.

If the Pine Island and Thwaites glaciers are on a one-way trip to disaster, the implications are global. Together they drain an area containing enough ice to raise sea levels worldwide by 1–2 yards. In all probability, the Pine Island and Thwaites glaciers are already the biggest causes of sea level rise worldwide. Hughes believes their collapse could destabilize the entire West Antarctic ice sheet, and potentially parts of the East Antarctic ice sheet, too. "The well-documented changes happening just within the past decade are a numbing prospect," he told me. "And we have only hints about exactly what is going on."

Days after Vaughan presented the first findings of the survey to a conference in the U.S., I met Richard Alley. He had been in the audience and had been astounded by the findings. "Thwaites just taps right into the vast reservoirs of ice in the middle of the ice sheet, and the question is whether it will drag them along with it," he said. "I think Thwaites could be absolutely critical. If you pull the plug, the ice goes faster and there is thinning. The only question is whether the plug can re-form a bit further back, or whether the ocean will deliver enough heat for it to just blowtorch its way to the center. I don't think we know the answer to that yet." There was, he said, "a possibility that the West Antarctic ice sheet could collapse and raise sea levels by 6 yards in the next century."

The East Antarctic ice sheet is the biggest, highest slab of ice on the planet. In the unlikely event that it all melted, sea levels would rise by 50 yards or more. But it has been in place for some 20 million years. And in 2005, Curt Davis, of the University of Missouri, reported, after analyzing satellite data, that extra snowfall linked to global warming is raising the height of the ice by almost three quarters of an inch a year—enough to shave current rates of sea level rise by 10 percent. All seemed well, then, with the East Antarctic ice sheet.

But there was a slight problem. Davis's study could cover only the flat interior. Satellite instruments are not yet good enough to establish altitude trends near the coasts, where there is sloping terrain. A footnote to his paper mentions that "mass loss in areas near the coast could be even greater than the gains in the interior." Unfortunately, other researchers say that is precisely what may be happening.

Exhibit A in this case is the Totten glacier. It is a biggie—62 miles wide at its mouth, where it calves icebergs into the Indian Ocean. Totten's network of tributary glaciers drains an area containing more ice than the whole of the West Antarctic. And since the early 1990s, says Andy Shepherd, of the Scott Polar Research Institute, in Cambridge, England, that catchment has been losing enough ice to lower its height by more than 10 yards a year. Another giant of the East Antarctic ice sheet, the Cook glacier, is doing the same.

The last bastion of glacial stability suddenly looks much less safe. And Shepherd points out that Totten and Cook have something else in common with Pine Island, Thwaites, and the other troublesome glaciers on the west side—something suggesting that worse could be ahead. Both Totten and Cook have grounding lines in the ocean that are below sea level—more than 300 yards below in the case of Totten. That is, its contact with the continental land mass is so tenacious that the glacier slides 300 yards under water before the ice gives up contact with the rock and begins to float. That sounds like good news: evidence of stability. The problem is that warmer waters appear to be weakening that contact. Should the grounding line start to retreat, we can expect the glacier to begin the familiar process of thinning and accelerating. The retreat would, in other words, remove the cork from a very large bottle.

Nobody is yet saying that the East Antarctic ice sheet is vulnerable in the way that the western sheet appears to be. It remains very big and, by and large, extremely stable. But, as Rignot puts it, "it is not immune." And every new discovery seems to raise the stakes for the fate of the Antarctic ice. As recently as 2001, the IPCC reported a scientific consensus that it was "very unlikely" that Antarctica would produce any significant rise in sea levels during the twenty-first century. Few glaciologists are repeating that claim with any confidence now. Most would agree with Alley that "major changes are taking place in the Antarctic, on much shorter time scales than previously anticipated."

The British Antarctic Survey now employs a mathematician full time to apply chaos and complexity theory to the fate of the continent's ice—a topic once considered to be of the utmost simplicity. The BAS is using the language of fractals, phase space, and bifurcations to work out what might happen next to the ice sheets of the Antarctic Peninsula and the glaciers of Pine Island Bay. Its scientists have seen Larsen B shatter in three days; they believe they are seeing the soft underbelly of the West Antarctic ice sheet ripped open before their eyes. What next?

RISING TIDES

Saying "toodle-oo" to Tuvalu

The Carteret Islands are to be abandoned. Life is simply too hard for their 2,000 inhabitants, huddled on a clutch of low-lying coral islands in the South Pacific, with a total surface area of just 150 acres, and rising sea levels threatening to wash them away. The islands, named after an eighteenth-century English explorer of the South Seas, Philip Carteret, have been under nearly constant erosion since the 1960s, and the current guess is that they will be wholly submerged by 2015. Already their fields have been invaded by salt water, and the breadfruit crops have died. The people, refugees in their own land, depend on handouts.

In 2001, when strong winds and rough seas cut off the atoll and prevented them from going to sea to catch fish, many resorted to eating seaweed. One resident on the island of Han pleaded by radio for rescue: "Erosion is occurring from both sides, and the island is getting narrow. In Piul, many families are leaving. Huene Island is divided in half, and four families only are left. On Iolasa, Iosela, and Iangain, when high seas occur, they stand below sea level. This is very frightening." Indeed. In November 2005, the central government in Papua New Guinea, of which the Carteret Islands form a part, agreed that the islanders should all be moved to Bougainville, a four-hour boat ride to the southwest. Ten families at a time will journey over the next few years, relinquishing their ancestral homes forever.

For most people around the world, stories of a rise in sea level remain a matter of academic interest, if that. The risks seem remote. But for the inhabitants of low-lying islands like the Carterets, it is happening now and devastating their lives.

The 10,000 citizens of the nine inhabited South Pacific islands of Tuvalu are also abandoning ship. High tides regularly wash across the main street in the capital, Funafuti; sea salt is poisoning their fields and killing their coconuts. Tuvalu is a full-fledged nation-state. Formerly the British Ellice Islands, it won independence in 1975. But just thirty years on, it seems destined to be the first modern nation-state to disappear beneath the waves. A twenty-first-century Atlantis. "In fifty years, Tuvalu will not exist," says the prime minister. His government has signed a deal with New Zealand, 1,800 miles away, that will allow the entire population to move there in the coming years, as rising tides and worsening storms destroy their homes.

One by one, the island nations of the South Pacific are drowning. Kiribati, formerly the British Gilbert Islands, won its independence on the same day as Tuvalu. It, too, is going under. Two uninhabited islands disappeared in 1999. The following year, Nakibae Teuatabo, a resident of Kiribati, explained its plight to me at a climate-change conference in Bonn, where he had been sent to plead for his country's survival. "Eight or nine house plots in the village that my family belongs to have been eroded. I remember there was a coconut tree outside the government quarters where I lived. Then the beach all around it was eroded, and eventually the tree disappeared. It might not sound a lot to you. But the atolls are just rings of narrow islands surrounding a lagoon, with the open ocean on the outside. Some of the islands are only a few yards wide in places. Imagine standing on one of these islands with waves pounding on one side and the lagoon on the other. It's frightening."

Villagers on some outer islands have already moved away as the sea gobbles up their land, he said. "Apart from causing coastal erosion, higher tides are pushing salt water into the fields and into underground freshwater reservoirs. In some places, it just bubbles up from the ground." It was a heart-rending story—good for journalists, but of no interest to most government negotiators at the conference. Such nations, it seems, are expendable.

The world's sea levels have been largely stable for the past 5,000 years, since the main phase of melting of ice sheets after the end of the last ice age abated. Some residual ice loss continued to raise sea levels at less than one hundredth of an inch a year. But around 1900, the rise began to increase. At first, this was most likely owing to the melting of glaciers after the little ice age ended, in the mid-nineteenth century. That should have diminished during the twentieth century. But instead it has accelerated in the past fifty years, to around 0.08 inches a year. About half of this increase is probably due to the process known to physicists as thermal expansion. And the rest is probably due to the resumed melting of the world's glaciers and ice caps, doubtless largely a result of man-made climate change.

The first signs of a further acceleration emerged in the early 1990s, when satellite data suggested a sudden rise of 0.11 inches a year. Since 1999, it may have risen further, to 0.14 inches. At the time of this writing, these figures had failed to gain much attention, because glaciologists remained worried about their reliability. Some think there may be a problem calibrating the satellite data; others that it may simply be a natural fluctuation. But, with every year that passes, more researchers are concluding that we are seeing the first effects of the dramatic changes apparently under way on the ice sheets of Greenland and Antarctica.

The planet has a history of startling sea level rise that cannot be explained by the conventional models used by glaciologists to predict future change. Consider events toward the end of the last ice age. Around 20,000 years ago, at what glaciologists call the "glacial maximum," so much water was tied up in ice on land that sea levels were around 400 feet lower than they are today. Then a thaw began. Sea levels initially rose by around 0.4 inches a year. That is four or five times faster than today, but within the traditional expectations of glaciologists. Then something happened. About 14,500 years ago, the tides went haywire. Within 400 years, sea levels rose by 65 feet. That's an average rate of just over a yard every twenty years.

It is worth thinking about those numbers. If such a rise happened today, you could say "toodle-oo" to Tuvalu by 2010; most of Bangladesh would be under water by 2020; millions of people on the Nile Delta would be looking for new homes by 2025; London would need a new Thames Barrier immediately. New Orleans? Well, forget New Orleans, and Florida, and most of the rest of the U.S. seaboard, too. Lagos, Karachi, Sydney, New

York, Tokyo, Bangkok: you name your coastal megacity, and it would be abandoned by midcentury. It sounds unbelievable, but we know the rise happened. The evidence is in tidemarks on ancient cliffs and in the remains of coral that can live only close to sea level.

How could such a thing have happened? It required the transfer into the oceans of about 13 billion acre-feet of ice every year throughout the 400-year period. That is a huge amount of ice. Glaciologists believe that the West Antarctic ice sheet, which was much larger then, was the most likely source. But wherever it came from, it could have reached the oceans in such quantities and at such speed only by some process in addition to melting. Such discharges required the physical collapse of ice sheets on a grand scale. That can have happened only if the ice sheets were lubricated at their base by great rivers of meltwater, and destabilized at the coasts by the shattering of ice shelves.

Go back further. In the last interglacial period, about 120,000 years ago, evidence such as wave-cut notches along cliffs in the Bahamas show sea levels 20 feet higher than they are today. During a previous interglacial, some 400,000 years ago, they may have been even higher. In neither period were temperatures significantly higher than they are today. On the face of it, either the West Antarctic ice sheet, or the Greenland ice sheets, or both, succumbed at temperatures close to our own. We can expect that temperatures will rise by about 3 to 5 degrees within the coming century. That, says Hansen, would make them as high as they were 3 million years ago, before the era of ice ages started. What were sea levels then? About 25 yards higher than today, plus or minus 10 yards, he says.

A first guess is that we will very soon have set the world on a course for reaching such levels again. The models of glaciologists suggest that, if this happens, it will take thousands of years. Jim Hansen doesn't believe it. "I'm a modeler, too, but I rate data higher than models," he says. He already sees evidence of the start of runaway melting in Greenland and Antarctica, and anticipates that "sea levels might rise by a couple of yards this century, and several more the next century."

Some see this prognosis as alarmist. Where, they say, is the evidence of big sea level rises so far? Hansen says that much of the extra melting has been camouflaged by increased snowfall on the ice sheets: "Because of this, sea level changes slowly at first, but as global warming gets larger, as summer melt extends higher up the ice sheet, and as buttressing ice shelves melt away, multiple positive feedbacks come into play, and the nonlinear disintegration wins the competition, hands down."

The world's ice sheets are "a ticking time bomb," he says. There is no reason why the events of 14,000 years ago should not be repeated in the twenty-first century. "The current planetary energy imbalance is now pouring energy into the Earth system at a rate sufficient to fuel rapid deglaciation." Hansen's hunch is that an increasing amount of global warming will be harnessed to melting the ice sheets. That could slow the heating of the atmosphere, but at the price of faster-rising sea levels. Within a few decades, vast armadas of icebergs could be breaking off the Greenland ice sheet, making shipping lanes impassable and cooling ocean surfaces like the ice in a gin and tonic. Sea level rise, he concludes, is "*the* big global issue." He believes it will transcend all others in the coming century.

It is easy to forget the plight of the people of the Carteret Islands and Tuvalu. Few of us could even find these places on the map. But as the tides rise ever higher, and as the precarious state of the big ice sheets becomes more apparent, we might want to heed those people's fate. It could be that of our own children.

III

RIDING THE CARBON CYCLE

IN THE JUNGLE

Would we notice if the Amazon went up in smoke?

The Amazon rainforest is the largest living reservoir of carbon dioxide on the land surface of Earth. Its trees contain some 77 billion tons of carbon, and its soils perhaps as much again. That is about *twenty* years' worth of man-made emissions from burning fossil fuels. The rainforest is also an engine of the world's climate system, recycling both heat and moisture. More than half of the raindrops that fall on the forest canopy never reach the ground; instead they evaporate back into the air to produce more rain downwind. The forest needs the rain, but the rain also needs the forest.

But as scientists come to understand the importance of the Amazon for maintaining climate, they are also discovering that it may itself be under threat from climate change. We are familiar enough with the damage done to the world's biggest and lushest jungle by farmers armed with chain saws and firebrands. But, hard as they try, they can destroy the rainforest only slowly. Despite many decades of effort, most of this jungle, the size of western Europe, remains intact. Climate change, on the other hand, could overwhelm it in a few years.

Until recently, many ecologists have thought of the Amazon rainforest much as their glaciologist colleagues conceived of the Greenland ice sheet: as big and extremely stable. The Greenland ice maintained the climate that kept the ice securely frozen, while the Amazon rainforest maintained the rains that watered the forest. But, just as with the Greenland ice sheet, the idea that the Amazon is stable has taken a knock: some researchers believe that it is in reality a very dynamic place, and that the entire ecosystem may be close to a tipping point beyond which it will suffer runaway destruction in an orgy of fire and drought. Nobody is quite sure what would happen if the Amazon rainforest disappeared. It would certainly give an extra kick to climate change by releasing its stores of carbon dioxide. It would most likely diminish rainfall in Brazil. It might also change weather systems right across the Northern Hemisphere.

One man who is trying to find out how unstable the Amazon rainforest might be is Dan Nepstad, a forest ecologist nominally attached to the Woods Hole Research Center, in Massachusetts, but based for more than two decades in the Amazon. He doesn't just watch the forest: he conducts large experiments within it. In 2001, Nepstad began creating a man-made drought in a small patch of jungle in the Tapajos National Forest, outside the river port of Santarem. Although in most years much of the Amazon has rain virtually every day, Tapajos is on the eastern fringe of the rainforest proper, where weather cycles can shut down the rains for months. The forest here is, to some extent, adapted to drought. But there are limits, and Nepstad has been trying to find out where they lie.

He has covered the 2.5-acre plot with more than 5,000 transparent plastic panels, which let in the sunlight but divert the rain into wooden gutters that drain to canals and a moat. Meanwhile, high above the forest canopy, he has erected gantries linked by catwalks, so that he can study the trees in detail as the artificial drought progresses. The work was all done by hand to avoid damaging the dense forest, and the scientists soon found they were not alone. The canals became "congregating places for every kind of snake you can imagine," says Nepstad. Caimans and jaguars cruised by, just, it seemed, to find out what was going on.

The results were worth the effort. The forest, it turns out, can handle two years of drought without great trouble. The trees extend their roots deeper to find water and slow their metabolism to conserve water. But after that, the trees start dying. Beginning with the tallest, they come crashing down, releasing carbon to the air as they rot, and exposing the forest floor to the drying sun. By the third year, the plot was storing only about 2 tons of carbon, whereas a neighboring control plot, on which rain continued to fall, held close to 8 tons. The "lock was broken" on a corner of one of the planet's great carbon stores. The study shows that the Amazon is "headed in a terrible direction," wrote the ecologist Deborah Clark, of the University of Missouri, discussing the findings in *Science*. "Given that droughts in the Amazon are projected to increase in several climate models, the implications for these rich ecosystems are grim."

Everywhere in the jungle, drought is followed by fire. So, in early 2005, Nepstad started an even more audacious experiment. He set fire to another stretch of forest with kerosene torches. "We want to know if recurring fire may threaten the very existence of the forest," he says. The initial findings were not good: the fires crept low along the forest floor, and no huge flames burst through the canopy. The fire may even have been invisible to the satellites that keep a constant watch overhead. But many trees died nonetheless, as their bark scorched and the flow of sap from their roots was stanched.

Nepstad's experiments are part of a huge international effort to monitor the health of the Amazon, called the Large-scale Biosphere-Atmosphere Experiment in Amazonia. From planes and satellites and gantries above the jungle, researchers from a dozen countries have been sniffing the forest's breath and assessing its survival strategies. The current estimate is that fires in the forest are releasing some 200 million tons of carbon a year—far more than is absorbed by the growing forest. The Amazon has become a significant source of carbon dioxide, adding to global warming. More worrying still, the experiment is discovering a drying trend across the Amazon that leaves it ever more vulnerable to fires. Nepstad's work suggests that beyond a certain point, the forest will be unable to recover from the fires, and will begin a process of rapid drying that he calls the "savannization" of the Amazon.

And even as he concluded his drought experiment, nature seemed to replicate it. The rains failed across the Amazon through 2005, killing trees, triggering fires, and reducing the ability of the forest to recycle moisture in future—thus increasing the risk of future drought. Nepstad's experiments suggest that the rainforest is close to the edge—to permanent drought, rampant burning, savannization, or worse. In the final weeks of 2005, the rains returned. The forest may recover this time. But if future climate change causes significant drying that lasts from one year to the next, feedbacks in the forest could realize Nepstad's worst fears.

The 2005 drought was caused by extremely warm temperatures in the tropical Atlantic—the same high temperatures that are believed to have caused the record-breaking hurricane season that year. The rising air that triggered the hurricanes eventually came back to earth, suppressing the formation of storm clouds over the Amazon. And, as I discovered at Britain's Hadley Centre for Climate Prediction, that is precisely what climate modelers are forecasting for future decades.

The Hadley Centre's global climate model is generally regarded as one of the world's top three. And it predicts that business-as-usual increases in industrial carbon dioxide emissions worldwide in the coming decades will generate warmer sea temperatures, subjecting the Amazon to repeated droughts, and thus creating "threshold conditions" beyond which fires will take hold. The Amazon rainforest will be dead before the end of the century. Not partly dead, or sick, but dead and gone. "The region will be able to support only shrubs or grass at most," said a study published by the Hadley Centre in 2005.

Not all models agree about that. But the Hadley model is the best at reproducing the current relationship between ocean temperatures and Amazon rainfall, so it has a good chance of being right about the future, too. Nepstad himself predicts that a "megafire event" will spread across the region. As areas in the more vulnerable eastern rainforest die, they will cease to recycle moisture back into the atmosphere to provide rainfall downwind. A wave of aridity will travel west, creating the conditions for fire to rip through the heart of the jungle.

With the trees gone, the thin soils will bake in the sun. Rainforest could literally turn to desert. The Hadley forecast includes a graph of the Amazon's forest's future carbon. It predicts that the store of a steady 77 billion tons over the past half century will shrink to 44 billion tons by 2050 and 16.5 billion tons by the end of the century. That, it calculates, would be enough to increase the expected rate of warming worldwide by at least 50 percent.

The Amazon rainforest does not just create rain for itself. By one calculation, approaching 6 trillion tons of water evaporates from the jungle each year, and about half of that moisture is exported from the Amazon basin. Some travels into the Andes, where it creates clouds that swathe some mountains so tightly that their surfaces have never been seen by satellite. Some blows south to water the pampas of Argentina, some east toward South Africa, and some north toward the Caribbean. The forest is a vital rainmaking machine for most of South America. As much as half of Argentina's rain may begin as evaporation from the Amazon.

But the benefits of the great Amazonian hydrological engine extend much further, and are not restricted to rainfall. The moisture also carries energy. A lot of solar energy is used to evaporate moisture from the forest canopy. This is one reason why forests stay cooler than the surrounding plains. And when the moisture condenses to form new clouds, that energy is released into the air. It powers weather systems and high-level winds known as jets far into the Northern Hemisphere. Nicola Gedney and Paul Valdes, two young climate researchers at the University of Reading, have calculated that this process ultimately drives winter storms across the North Atlantic toward Europe. "There is a relatively direct physical link between changes over the deforested region and the climate of the North Atlantic and western Europe," they say. If the rainforest expires, the hydrological engine, too, is likely to falter, and the link will be cut.

I 2

WILDFIRES OF BORNEO

Climate in the mire from burning swamp

The smoke billowed through Palangkaraya. One of the largest towns in Borneo was engulfed in acrid smog denser even than one of London's old pea-soupers. It blotted out so much sun that there was a chill in the air of a town more used to the dense, humid heat of the rainforest that encircled it. This was late 1997, and the rainforest was burning. The most intense El Niño event on record in the Pacific Ocean had stifled the storm clouds that normally bring rain to Borneo and the other islands of Indonesia. Landowners took advantage of the dry weather to burn the forest and carve out new plantations for palm oil and other profitable crops. The fires got out of control, and the result was one of the greatest forest fires in human history. The smoke spread for thousands of miles. Unsighted planes crashed from the skies, and ships collided at sea; in neighboring Malaysia and distant Thailand, hospitals filled with victims of lung diseases, and schools were closed. The fires became a global news story. The cost of the fires in lost business alone was put at tens of billions of dollars.

But it was not just the trees that were burning. The densest smoke was in central Borneo, around Palangkaraya, where the fires had burrowed down, drying and burning a vast peat bog that underlay the forest. The peat, 60 feet deep in many places, was the accumulated remains of wood and forest vegetation that had fallen into the swamps here over tens of thousands of years. Even after the rains returned, the peat continued to smolder for months on end. When the smoke finally cleared, most of the swamp forest was burned and black, and skeletons of trees poked from charred ground that had shrunk in places by a yard or more.

The burning of the Borneo swamp was part of a wider global assault on tropical rainforests—for timber and for land. But there were aggravating factors here. Until recently, the swamps were empty of humans. Local tribes and modern farmers alike had found them inhospitable and inaccessible. But in the early 1990s, Indonesia's President Suharto decreed that an area of the central Borneo swamp forest half the size of Wales should be drained and transformed into a giant rice paddy to make his country self-sufficient in its staple foodstuff. Some 2,500 miles of canals were dug to drain the swamp. Some 60,000 migrant farmers were brought in from other islands to cultivate the rice. The soils proved infertile, and virtually no rice was ever grown. The megaproject was abandoned. But its legacy lingers, as the canals continue to drain the swamps, and the desiccated peat burns every dry season. Especially during El Niños.

This is no mere local environmental disaster. Jack Rieley, a British ecologist with a love of peat bogs who has adopted the central Borneo swamps for his field studies, says the disaster is of global importance. At least half of the world's tropical peat swamps are on the Indonesian islands of Borneo, Sumatra, and West Papua. And the largest, oldest, and deepest of them are in central Borneo, where they cover an area a quarter the size of England and harbor large populations of sun bears and clouded leopards, as well as the world's largest surviving populations of orangutans. They also contain vast amounts of carbon—perhaps 50 billion tons of the stuff. That is almost as much as in the entire Amazon rainforest, which is more than ten times as large. One acre of Borneo peat swamp contains 880 tons of carbon.

Tropical peat swamps are a major feature of the planet's carbon cycle. They are important amplifiers of climate change, capable of helping push the world into and out of ice ages by capturing and releasing carbon from the air. For thousands of years, they have been keeping the world cooler than it might otherwise be, by soaking up carbon from the air. For that carbon to be released now, as the world struggles to counter global warming, would be folly indeed. But that is what is happening. Rieley estimates that during the El Niño event of 1997 and 1998, as Palangkaraya disappeared for months beneath smoke, the smoldering swamps lost more than half a yard of peat layer, and released somewhere between 880 million and 2.8 billion tons of carbon into the atmosphere: the equivalent of up to 40 percent of all emissions from burning fossil fuels worldwide that year.

At first there was some skepticism about his figures. Few other researchers had been to Borneo to see what was going on. But in 2004, U.S. government researchers published a detailed analysis of gas measurements made around the world. It showed that roughly 2.2 billion tons more carbon than usual entered the atmosphere during 1998—and two thirds of that excess came from Southeast Asia. The Borneo fires must have contributed most of that, and burning peat was almost certainly the major component. "We are witnessing the death of one of the last wilderness ecosystems on the planet, and it is turning up the heat on climate change as it goes," says Rieley. "What was once one of the planet's most important carbon sinks is giving up that carbon. The whole world is feeling the effect."

Every year, farmers continue burning forest in Borneo to clear land for farming. And whenever the weather is dry, those fires spread out through the jungle and down into the peat. Satellite images suggest that 12 million acres of the swamp forests were in flames at one point during late 2002. And 2002 and 2003 were the first back-to-back years in which net additions to the atmosphere's carbon burden exceeded 4.4 billion tons. Rieley reckons that the burning swamp forests contributed a billion tons of that.

It looked as if smoldering bogs in remote Borneo were single-handedly ratcheting up the speed of climate change. They show, says David Schimel, of the National Center for Atmospheric Research (NCAR), in Boulder, Colorado, how "catastrophic events affecting small areas can have a huge impact on the global carbon balance." Fire in Borneo and the Amazon may be turning the world's biggest living "sinks" for carbon dioxide into the most dynamic new source of the gas in the twenty-first century.

13

SINK TO SOURCE

Why the carbon cycle is set for a U-turn

It seemed too good to be true. Throughout the 1980s and 1990s, evidence grew that wherever forests survived around the world, they were growing faster. And as they did so, they were soaking up ever more carbon dioxide from the air. Despite deforestation in the tropics, the world's forests overall were a strong carbon sink. Most researchers assumed that the extra growth happened because rising concentrations of carbon dioxide in the atmosphere made it easier for trees to absorb the gas from the air. Provided that the other ingredients for photosynthesis, such as water and nutrients, were available, the sky was the limit for growing plants. The "CO_2 fertilization effect" entered the climate scientists' lexicon.

In 1998, at the height of this enthusiasm, a group of carbon modelers at Princeton University scored what looked like a political as well as a scientific bull's-eye. Song-Miao Fan and colleagues claimed in a paper in *Science* to have discovered "a large terrestrial carbon sink in North America." The U.S. and Canada, they said, had become a hot spot for carbon absorption, as trees grew on abandoned farmland and previously logged forests, and carbon dioxide in the air boosted growth. They calculated the sink at a stunning 2.2 billion tons a year—more than enough to offset the two countries' total annual emissions from power plants, cars, and the rest. Thanks to their trees, the biggest polluters on the planet were "carbon neutral."

To many, it seemed an outrageous claim. And on examination, it turned out to involve some fairly heroic assumptions about where carbon dioxide in the atmosphere was coming from, where it was going, and how it moved around. Carbon-cycle specialists poured cold water on the notion. The figure of 2.2 billion tons was not far off the total amount of carbon that North America's trees absorbed in a year in order to grow. If it was accurate, it meant that no North American trees were dying; they weren't even breathing out—because both processes release carbon dioxide back into the air. But the findings came less than a year after the Clinton administration had signed up for tough carbon-dioxide-emissions targets at Kyoto, without any clear idea of how it was going to achieve them. They seemed like manna from heaven.

And yes, it was too good to be true. The authors agreed that their data were sparse and their analytical techniques largely untried. Nobody, it turned out, could repeat the results. A plethora of researchers demonstrated that U.S. forests could never have stashed away more than a fifth of the nation's emissions. After a while, nobody stood up to defend the original results, and they disappeared from view as fast as they had arrived.

The final nail entered the coffin when it emerged later that 1998, when the report was published, was just about the worst year on record for nature's ability to soak up carbon dioxide from the air. Forests and peat bogs had burned from the Amazon to Borneo. If there had been a big sink, it was disappearing even as it was uncovered. And it wasn't just in the tropics that carbon had been seeping out of the biosphere. There were major forest fires from Florida to Sardinia, and from Peru to Siberia—where Russian foresters revealed that a conflagration on a par with Borneo's had been taking place virtually unnoticed. The world's largest stretch of forest, which for 200 years had been soaking up a fraction of Europe's industrial emissions as they poured east on the prevailing winds, was giving up what it had previously absorbed. As 1998 closed, the idea of a huge carbon sink in the U.S. or anywhere else seemed absurd.

The next episode in the story of the amazing disappearing carbon sink came in the summer of 2003, when Europe suffered a massive heat wave. Temperatures averaged 10°F above normal during July. In France, the mercury soared above 104°F. With the high temperatures accompanied by less than half the usual rainfall, Europe's beech trees and cornfields, grasslands and pine forests, were expiring.

Philippe Ciais, a Paris-based environmental scientist, followed events.

He was a key player in CarboEurope, a project begun a couple of years earlier to measure Europe's carbon sink. It was launched in the aftermath of the purported discovery of the large North American carbon sink. European politicians, like their U.S. counterparts, were keen to discover if nature was helping them meet their own Kyoto Protocol targets. Ciais's initial assessment was that, thanks to warmer temperatures, higher carbon dioxide levels in the air, and a longer growing season, Europe's ecosystems were absorbing up to 12 percent of its man-made emissions.

But in 2003, the carbon sink blew a fuse. During July and August that year, when Europe's ecosystems would normally have been in full bloom and soaking up carbon dioxide at their fastest, around 550 million tons of carbon escaped from western European forests and fields. This was roughly equivalent to twice Europe's emissions from burning fossil fuels during those two months. All the carbon absorbed in recent years was being dumped back into the atmosphere in double-quick time. The rapid exhaling of the continent's ecosystems was "unprecedented in the last century," said Ciais. But he judged that it was likely to be repeated "as future droughts turn temperate ecosystems from carbon sinks into carbon sources."

Europe seemed to have fast-forwarded into a nightmare future strapped to a runaway greenhouse effect. And it soon emerged that Europe's carbon crisis was part of a more general story of summer stress across the Northern Hemisphere. Ning Zeng, of the University of Maryland, found an area of drought stretching from the Mediterranean to Afghanistan. It had lasted from 1998 to 2002, and had eliminated a natural carbon sink across the region that had averaged 770 million tons a year over the previous two decades.

Alon Angert, of the University of California at Berkeley, explained the big picture. Through the 1980s and into the early 1990s, the "CO_2 fertilization effect" had been working rather well, with increased photosynthesis in the Northern Hemisphere soaking up ever more carbon dioxide. But sometime around 1993 that had tailed off, probably because of droughts and higher temperatures. And since the mid-1990s, the carbon sink had been in sharp decline. From the Mediterranean to central Asia, and even in the high latitudes of Siberia and northern Europe, the added uptake of carbon by plants in the early spring was canceled out by the heat and water stress of hotter, drier summers. The findings, Angert said, dashed widespread expectations of a continuing "greening trend" in which warm summers would speed plant growth and moderate climate change. Instead, "excess heating is driving the dieback of forests, accelerating soil carbon loss and transforming the land from a sink to a source of carbon to the atmosphere."

And further north, beyond the tree line, where some of the fastest warming rates in the world are currently being experienced, fear is growing about the carbon stored in the thick layers of permanently frozen soil known as permafrost. The carbon comprises thousands of years' accumulation of dead lichen, moss, and other vegetation that never had a chance to rot before it froze. David Lawrence, of the NCAR, reported in 2005 that he expected the top 3 yards of permafrost across most of the Arctic to melt during the twenty-first century. This will leave a trail of buckled highways, toppled buildings, broken pipelines, and bemused reindeer; it will also unfreeze tens and perhaps hundreds of billions of tons of carbon. As the thawed vegetation finally rots, most of its carbon will return to the atmosphere as carbon dioxide. In those bogs and lakes where there is very little oxygen, most of the carbon will be converted into methane—which, as we will see in the next chapter, is an even more potent greenhouse gas.

We should not write off the carbon sink entirely. It won't die altogether. Especially in higher latitudes, warmer and wetter conditions will sometimes mean that trees grow faster and farther north than before—at least where plagues of insects don't get them first. Right now, the best guess is that, on average, forests are still absorbing more carbon dioxide than they release. Up to a fifth of the carbon dioxide emitted by burning fossil fuels may still be being absorbed by soils and forests. But the sink is diminishing, not rising as many anticipated. And many believe that the sink is doomed as we face more and more years like 1998 and 2003.

One of those who fear the worst is Peter Cox, a top young British climate modeler who left the Hadley Centre to spend more time investigating the carbon cycle at the Centre for Ecology and Hydrology, at Winfrith, in Dorset. He believes he is on the trail of the disappearing carbon sink, and is prepared to put a date on when it will disappear. "Basically, we are seeing two competing things going on," he says. "Plants absorb carbon dioxide as they grow through photosynthesis; but they give back the carbon dioxide as they die and their wood, leaves, and roots decompose. The speed of both processes is increasing."

First, the extra carbon dioxide in the atmosphere encourages photosynthesis to speed up. So plants grow faster and absorb more carbon dioxide. But that extra carbon dioxide is also warming the climate. And the warming encourages the processes that break down plant material and release carbon dioxide back into the air. Because it takes a couple of decades for the extra carbon dioxide to bring about warmer temperatures, we have seen the fertilization effect first. Now the process of decay is starting to catch up.

The processes do not involve plants alone. Soils have their own processes of inhaling and exhaling carbon. And they, too, will switch from being a net sink to a net source—eventually releasing what carbon they have absorbed in recent decades. Ultimately, "you can't have the one without the other," Cox says. "If you breathe in, eventually you have to breathe out." And soon, most of the rainforests and soils of the world will be breathing out, pouring their stored carbon back into the air. If the climate gets drier and more fires occur, then the release of the carbon dioxide will happen even more quickly. But it will happen anyway.

The entire land biosphere—the forests and soils and pastures and bogs—has been slowing the pace of global warming for some decades. Soon the biosphere will start to speed it up. The day the biosphere turns from sink to source will be another tipping point in Earth's system. Once under way, the process, like collapsing ice sheets, will be unstoppable. Potentially, hundreds of billions of tons of carbon in the biosphere could be destabilized, says Pep Canadell, a carbon-cycle researcher for the Australian government research agency CSIRO.

Nobody is quite sure when the tipping point might occur. "It is possible," says Cox, "that the 2003 surge of carbon dioxide into the atmosphere is the first evidence." But while some parts of the biosphere may now be irrevocably stuck as carbon sources, the entire system is likely to take a few decades to switch. But of course, much will probably depend on how fast we allow temperatures to rise.

Cox suggests that 2040 is probably when the biosphere will start taking its revenge on us for relying on its accommodating nature. He calculates that by the end of the century, the biosphere could be adding as much as 8 billion tons of carbon to the atmosphere each year. That is roughly the amount coming each year from burning fossil fuels today, and probably enough to add an extra 2 or 3°F to global temperatures—degrees that are not yet included in the IPCC forecasts.

Only one country, so far as I am aware, has completed anything like a national study of the current impact of these changes on its carbon budget. Perhaps understandably, such studies have a lower priority since nature was shown to be unlikely to offer a helping hand in meeting Kyoto targets. But Guy Kirk, of the National Soil Resources Institute, part of Cranfield University, has done the job for Britain. He surveyed 6,000 test plots across forest and bog, heath and farmland, scrub and back gardens, to see how much carbon dioxide is leaving the biosphere and how much is entering it. His conclusion is that the British biosphere is releasing about 1 percent of its carbon store into the atmosphere every year. Enough, in other words, to turn the whole country into desert in one century.

Kirk rules out altered methods of farming or land use as the predominant cause. The increase is so universal that it can only be owing to climate change. He puts the national release at around 14 million tons a year. That, he points out, is roughly the amount of carbon dioxide the British government has kept from the atmosphere each year in its efforts to comply with the Kyoto Protocol. As the German researcher Ernst-Detlef Schulze, of CarboEurope, puts it—rather gloatingly, I think—this "completely offsets the technological achievements of reducing carbon dioxide emissions, putting the UK's success in reducing greenhouse gas emissions in a different light." True enough. But Britain is not alone.

I4

THE DOOMSDAY DEVICE

A lethal secret stirs in the permafrost

One of my favorite films is *Dr. Strangelove.* It was made back in 1964, when the biggest global threat was nuclear Armageddon. Directed by Stanley Kubrick, and starring Peter Sellers as Dr. Strangelove, a wheelchair-bound caricature of Henry Kissinger, the film was a satire of the military strategy known as Mutual Assured Destruction—or MAD, for short. The plot involved the Soviet Union's building the ultimate defense, a doomsday device in the remote wastes of Siberia. If Russia were attacked, the device would shroud the world in a radioactive cloud and destroy all human and animal life on earth. Unfortunately, the Soviet generals forgot to tell the Americans about this, and, needless to say, Dr. Strangelove and the American military attacked. The film ends with a deranged U.S. officer (played by Slim Pickens) sitting astride a nuclear bomb as it is released into the sky above Siberia. The end of the world is nigh, as the credits roll.

Now our most feared global Armageddon is climate change. But reason to fear truly does lurk in the frozen bogs of western Siberia. There, beneath a largely uninhabited wasteland of permafrost, lies what might reasonably be described as nature's own doomsday device. It is primed to be triggered not by a nuclear bomb but by global warming. That device consists of thick layers of frozen peat containing tens of billions of tons of carbon.

The entire western Siberian peat bog covers approaching 400,000 square miles—an area as big as France and Germany combined. Since its formation, the moss and lichen growing at its surface have been slowly absorbing massive amounts of carbon from the atmosphere. Because the region is so cold, the vegetation only partially decomposes, forming an ever-thickening frozen mass of peat beneath the bog. Perhaps a quarter of all the carbon absorbed by soils and vegetation on the land surface of Earth since the last ice age is right here.

The concern now is that as the bog begins to thaw, the peat will decompose and release its carbon. Unlike the tropical swamps of Borneo, which are degrading as they dry out, and producing carbon dioxide, the Siberian bogs will degrade in the wet as the permafrost melts. In fetid swamps and lakes devoid of oxygen, that will produce methane. Methane is a powerful and fast-acting greenhouse gas, potentially a hundred times more potent than carbon dioxide. Released quickly enough in such quantities, it would create an atmospheric tsunami, swamping the planet in warmth. But we have to change tense here. For "would create," read "is creating."

In the summer of 2005, I received a remarkable e-mail from a man I had neither met nor corresponded with, a young Siberian ecologist called Sergei Kirpotin, of Tomsk State University, in the heart of Siberia. A collaborator of his at Oxford University had suggested me as a Western outlet for what Kirpotin in his e-mail called an "urgent message for the world." He had recently undertaken an expedition across thousands of miles of the empty western Siberian peatlands between the bleak wind-swept towns of Khatany-Mansiysk, Pangody, and Novy Urengoi. Nobody, barring a few reindeer herders, lives out here. It was an area that Kirpotin and his colleagues had visited several times in the past fifteen years, observing the apparently unchanging geography and biology of the tundra. This time they had found a huge change.

"We had never seen anything like it, and had not expected it," he said. Huge areas of frozen peat bog were suddenly melting. The former soft, spongy surface of lichens and moss was turning into a landscape of lakes that stretched unbroken for hundreds of miles. He described it as an "ecological landslide that is probably irreversible and is undoubtedly connected to climate warming." Most of the lakes had formed, he said, since his previous visit, three years before. There was clearly a huge danger that the melting peatland would begin to generate methane.

I had come across Russian scientists before who had been left out in the tundra too long with their crackpot theories. But Kirpotin did not fit that

category. He had only recently been appointed vice-rector of his univer-
sity. And the more I checked it, the more likely his story seemed. Larry
Smith, of the University of California at Los Angeles, told me that the
western Siberian peat bog was warming faster than almost any other place
on the planet. Every year, he said, the spring melt was starting earlier and
the rainfall was increasing, making the whole landscape wetter.

Others were finding big methane emissions in the region. Katey Wal-
ter, of the University of Alaska in Fairbanks, had told a meeting of the U.S.
Arctic Research Consortium just a few weeks before about "hot spots" of
methane releases from lakes in eastern Siberia that were "unlike anything
that has been observed before." Peat on the bottom of lakes was convert-
ing to methane and bubbling to the surface so fast that it kept the lakes
from freezing over in winter. And Euan Nisbet, of London's Royal Hol-
loway College, who oversees a big international methane-monitoring pro-
gram that includes Siberia, said his estimate was that methane releases
from the western Siberian peat bog were up to 100,000 tons a day, which
meant a warming effect on the planet greater than that of all the U.S.'s
man-made emissions. "This huge methane flux depends on temperature,"
he said. "If peatlands become wetter with warming and permafrost degra-
dation, methane release from peatlands to the atmosphere will dramati-
cally increase."

So I wrote up Kirpotin's story for *New Scientist* magazine, emphasizing
the methane angle. It went around the world. The London *Guardian* re-
produced much of it the day after the story was released, under the front-
page banner headline "Warming hits 'tipping point.'" In *Dr. Strangelove,*
one nuclear device dropped on Siberia unleashed a thousand more. Here,
in the real world of melting Arctic permafrost, one degree of global warm-
ing could unleash enough methane to raise temperatures several more
degrees.

I had visited western Siberia a few years before, traveling with Western for-
est and oil-industry scientists to Noyabr'sk, a large oil town on the south
side of the great peat bog. On a series of helicopter rides, I had seen thou-
sands of square miles of still-intact swamp sitting on top of permafrost.
The landscape was terribly scarred by human activity: divided into frag-
ments by oil pipelines, roads, pylons, and seismic-survey routes; smeared

with spilled oil; littered with abandoned drums, pipes, cables, and the remains of old gulags and half-built railways; and shrouded in black smoke from gas flares. The reindeer had fled, and the bears had been hunted almost to extinction. But the peat bog and the permafrost had survived. The helicopter landed frequently, and we jumped out without so much as getting our feet wet on the spongy surface.

No longer. On my way to meet Kirpotin's colleagues at their research station at Pangody, on the Arctic Circle, I flew for two hours over a vast bog that was seemingly going into solution. In place of the green carpet of moss and lichen, as Kirpotin had told me, numberless lakes stretched to the horizon. From the air, they did not look like lakes that form naturally in depressions in the landscape. They were generally circular, looking more like flooded potholes in a road. The lakes had formed individually from small breaches in the permafrost. Wherever ice turned to water, a small pond formed. Then surrounding lumps of frozen peat would slump into the water, and the pond would grow in an ever-widening circle, until mile after mile of frozen bog had melted into a mass of lakes.

"Western scientists cannot imagine the scale of the melting," Kirpotin told me. But I could see it beneath me as I flew east. It seemed to me that a positive feedback was at work, much as in the accelerated melting of Arctic sea ice. The new melted surface, darker than the old frozen surface, absorbed more heat and caused more warming. Kirpotin agreed. There seemed to be a "critical threshold" beyond which "the process of warming would be essentially and suddenly changed," he said. "Some kind of trigger hook mechanism would come into play, and the process of permafrost degradation would start to stimulate itself and to urge itself onwards." His imperfect English somehow made the events he was describing sound even more awful. "The problem concerned does not have only a scientific character: it has passed to the plane of world politics. If mankind does not want to face serious social and economic losses from global warming, it is necessary to take urgent measures. Obviously we have less and less time to act."

I was defeated in my efforts to see these processes in the Siberian bogs at first hand. Landing at Novy Urengoi with all the necessary paperwork, I was nonetheless refused admission. "You need a special invitation from an organization in the city," a fearsome policewoman at the airport told me as she confiscated my passport and put it in a safe. This was a company town. I later discovered that the mayor, a gas-company nominee, had won approval from Moscow some months earlier for special rules to keep out unwanted foreigners. Novy Urengoi was one of Russia's few surviving closed cities.

It was also rather disorganized. Unsupervised, I wandered into town anyhow, and looked around one of the most desolate and inhospitable places I have ever been to. No wonder its name means "godforsaken place" in the language of the local reindeer herders. I briefly met with the scientists I had come halfway across the world to see, before being rounded up and driven back to the airport by a spook wearing a double-breasted suit and a smile like Vladimir Putin's. He seemed to think I was a terrorist, and the fact that I was meeting scientists investigating the tundra only made him more suspicious. I can at any rate say I have been thrown out of Siberia.

Back home, concern has grown about the role of methane in stoking the fires of global warming. In early 2006, a dramatic study suggested that all plants, not just those in bogs, are manufacturing methane—something never previously considered by scientists. That led to headlines about trees causing global warming, which seemed a bit hard on them. If they do make methane, they also absorb carbon dioxide. And since trees have been around for millions of years, and there are probably fewer of them now than for the majority of that time, any role for them in recent warming seems unlikely. They are simply part of the natural flux of chemicals into and out of the atmosphere. Though if evidence emerged that they were emitting more methane than before, as a result of warming, that would be a big worry. And that is precisely what seems to be happening with peat bogs in the Arctic permafrost.

There is a critical line around the edge of the Arctic that marks the zone of maximum impact from global warming. It is a front line of climate change, marking the melting-point isotherm, where the average year-round temperature is 32°F, the melting point of ice. To the north of this line lie ice and snow, frozen soil and Arctic tundra. To the south lie rivers and lakes and fertile soils where trees grow. The line runs through the heart of Siberia and Alaska—where huge blocks of frozen soil, stable for thousands of years, are now melting—and across Canada, skirting the southern shore of Hudson Bay, through the southern tip of Greenland, and over northern Scandinavia.

Having failed to visit Kirpotin's field station to see the melting of the Siberian bogs close up, I went instead to northern Sweden to visit what is almost certainly the longest continually monitored Arctic peat bog in the world. In 1903, scientists took over buildings erected near Abisko during the construction of a railway to take iron ore from the Swedish mine of Kiruna to the Norwegian port of Narvik. They have been out there ever since, through the midnight sun and the long dark winters, measuring temperatures and dating when the ice came and went on Tornetrask, an adjacent lake; plotting movements of the tree line; examining the bog ecosystems; reconstructing past climates from the growth rings of logs in the lake, and investigating the cosmic forces behind the area's spectacular northern lights.

So they are on solid ground when they say it is getting dramatically warmer here. The lake freezes a month later than it did only a couple of decades ago—in January rather than mid-December. It used to stay frozen till late May, but several times in recent years an early breakup has forced the cancellation of the annual ice-fishing festival on the lake in early May. The average annual temperature here over the past century has been 30.7°F, but in recent years it has sometimes crept above 32°.

Just east of Abisko is the Stordalen mire. This is not a large bog, but it is old, and probably the best-monitored bog in the best-monitored Arctic region in the world. It has withstood numerous periods of natural climate change during the past 5,000 years. But suddenly it seems doomed. For here, as Kirpotin has found across the western Siberian wetland, the evidence of what happens to a bog that finds itself straddling the melting-point isotherm is obvious at every step. Apart from scientists, the bog's main visitors are birdwatchers. A couple of years ago, the local authorities built a network of duckboards for them. But already the boards are capsizing, because the mounds of permafrost on which they were built are melting and slumping into newly emerging ponds of water.

Arriving rather spectacularly aboard a helicopter hired to remove some equipment from the site, I found a dry hummock on which to talk to Torben Christensen, a Danish biochemist who heads the research effort here. "The bog is changing very fast," he said. Below our feet, the permafrost was still as deep as 30 feet, but a step away it was gone. We examined a crack in the peat, where another chunk was preparing to slide into the water. "Of all the places in the world, it is right here on the melting-point isotherm, on the edge of the permafrost, that you'd expect to see climate change in action," Christensen said. "And that is exactly what we are seeing. Of course, they are seeing it on a much bigger scale in the Siberian bogs, but here we are measuring everything."

Out on the mire, Christensen has some of the most sophisticated equipment in the world for measuring gas emissions in the air. In one area, individual bog plants grow inside transparent plastic boxes whose lids open and shut automatically as monitoring equipment captures and measures the flux of gases between plant and atmosphere. Pride of place goes to an eddy-correlation tower. This logs every tiny wind movement in the ambient air, vertical as well as horizontal, and uses a laser to measure passing molecules of methane and other gases. Combining the two sets of data, the tower can produce a constant and extremely accurate readout of the flux of methane coming off the mire.

There is a regular loss of methane from the bog now, says Christensen. Some of the gas seeps out of the boggy soil, some bubbles up through the pond water, and some is brought to the surface by plants. The figures sound small: an average of 0.0002 ounces of methane is released per 10 square feet of mire per hour. But scaled up, this packs a greenhouse punch. Combining the flux data with satellite images that show the changing vegetation on the Stordalen mire, Christensen estimates that in the past thirty years, methane emissions have risen by 30 percent and increased this small bog's contribution to global warming by 50 percent.

There is nothing unusual about Stordalen. It was not chosen to give dramatic results. Monitoring began back when researchers were intent only on tracking what they believed to be unchanging processes. Other local mires are faring far worse as the melting-point isotherm moves north. Out in the nearby birch forest, the Katterjokk bog has gone in just five years from being an area largely underlain by permafrost to being an ice-free zone. Rather, Stordalen looks to be typical of bogs across northern Scandinavia and right round the melting-point isotherm. Individually they are only a pinprick on climate change, but taken together they threaten an eruption.

Back in the warmth of the Abisko library, Christensen found a study showing that half the bog permafrost in the north of Finland has disappeared since 1975. The rest will be gone by 2030. Christensen himself has coordinated a study of methane emissions from peatlands at sites right around the Arctic, using temporarily deployed equipment for measuring gas fluxes. North of the melting-point isotherm, the study shows little change. Little methane bubbles out of the tundra in northeastern Greenland, for instance, where the average temperature is still around 14°F. But, he says, "as temperatures rise, methane emissions grow exponentially." The highest emissions are in western Siberia and Alaska, where big temperature rises are taking place.

What is happening out on these Arctic mires is, at one level, quite subtle. On many of them, temperatures remain cold enough to limit the decomposition of vegetable matter, and so carbon is still accumulating as it has done ever since the bogs began to form, at the end of the last ice age. But the decomposition rates are rising. And critically, because the melting permafrost is making the bogs ever wetter, more and more of the carbon is released not as carbon dioxide but as methane. That dramatically changes the climate effect of the bogs. Methane being such a powerful greenhouse gas, the warming influence of its release overwhelms the cooling influence of continued absorption of carbon dioxide. Thus "mires are generally still a sink for carbon, while at the same time being a cause of global warming," Christensen says. "This can be a hard point for people to grasp, but it is absolutely crucial for what is happening right around the Arctic."

There are still so few good data that it is hard to say for sure how much the Arctic peat bogs are contributing to global warming today. Current emissions of methane are probably still below 50 million tons a year. But that is still the warming equivalent of more than a billion tons of carbon dioxide. And with lakes forming everywhere, and climate models predict-

ing that 90 percent of the Arctic permafrost will have melted to a depth
of at least three yards by 2012, there is "alarming potential for positive
feedback to climate from methane," says Christensen.

Larry Smith, of UCLA, estimates that the northern peat bogs of Siberia,
Canada, Scandinavia, and Alaska could contain 500 billion tons of carbon
altogether, or one third of all the carbon in all the world's soils. If all that
carbon were released as carbon dioxide, it would add something like 5°F
to average temperatures around the world. But if most of it were released
as methane instead, it could provide a much bigger short-term kick. How
much bigger would depend on how fast the methane was released, because
after a decade or so, methane decomposes to carbon dioxide. If the methane
all came out at once, it could raise temperatures worldwide by tens of de-
grees. That may be an unlikely scenario. Even so, the odds must be that
melting along the melting-point isotherm is destined to have a major
impact on the twenty-first-century climate. From Stordalen to Pangody,
these bogs are primed.

I 5

THE ACID BATH

What carbon dioxide does to the oceans

The oceans are the ultimate sink for most of the heat from the sun and also for most of the greenhouse gases we are pouring into the atmosphere. The atmosphere may be the place in which we live and breathe, but for long-term planetary systems it is just a holding bay. At any one time, there is fifty times as much carbon dioxide dissolved in ocean waters as there is in the atmosphere. Given time, the oceans can absorb most of what we can throw into the atmosphere. But time is what we do not have, and the oceans' patience with our activities may be limited.

Carbon dioxide moves constantly between the oceans' surface and the atmosphere, as the two environments share out the gas. And, because of ever-rising concentrations in the atmosphere, the oceans currently absorb in excess of 2 billion tons more a year than they release. Much of that surplus eventually finds its way to the ocean floor after being absorbed by growing marine organisms—a process often called the biological pump. Sometimes there are so many skeletons falling to the depths that biologists call it marine snow.

Though they are the ultimate sink for most carbon dioxide, the oceans do not simply absorb any spare carbon dioxide left in the atmosphere. The relationship is much more dynamic—and much less reliable. In the long run, carbon dioxide seems to seesaw between the oceans on the one hand and the atmosphere and land vegetation on the other. Plants on land generally prefer things warm. Certainly the carbon "stock" on land is greater during warm interglacial eras like our own, and less during ice ages. By contrast, ocean surfaces absorb more carbon dioxide when the waters are cold. This seems to be partly because the plankton that form the basis of life in the oceans prefer cold waters, and partly because when the land is cold and dry, dust storms transport large amounts of minerals that fertilize the oceans.

During the last ice age, some 220 billion tons of carbon moved from the land and atmosphere to the oceans. This process didn't cause the ice ages, but it was a very powerful positive feedback driving the cooling. And that is a worry. For if the ice-age pattern holds, future generations can expect the oceans' biological pump to decline as the world warms. The story of the oceans' exchanges of carbon dioxide with the atmosphere may turn out to be rather like that of the carbon sink on land. In the short term, the extra carbon dioxide in the air has fertilized the biological pump and encouraged greater uptake. But in the longer term, warmer oceans are likely to weaken the biological pump and release large amounts of carbon dioxide into the air.

Is something of the sort likely? Very much so, said Paul Falkowski, of Rutgers University, in New Jersey, in a long review of the carbon cycle in *Science*. "If our current understanding of the ocean carbon cycle is borne out, the sink strength of the ocean will weaken, leaving a larger fraction of anthropogenically produced carbon dioxide in the atmosphere." With tens of millions of tons of carbon moving back and forth between the atmosphere and the oceans each year, it would take only a small change to turn the oceans from a carbon sink into a potentially very large carbon source. This may already be happening. In 2003, the NASA scientist Watson Gregg published satellite measurements suggesting that the biological productivity of the oceans may have fallen by 6 percent since the 1980s. It could be part of a natural cycle, he said, but it could also be an early sign that the biological pump is slowing as ocean temperatures rise.

So far, since the beginning of the Industrial Revolution, the oceans have absorbed from the atmosphere something like 130 billion tons of carbon resulting from human activities. While much of it has fallen to the seabed, a considerable amount remains dissolved in ocean waters—with a singular and rather remarkable effect: it is making the oceans more acid.

The carbonic acid produced by dissolving carbon dioxide is corrosive and especially damaging to organisms that need calcium carbonate for their shells or skeletons. These include coral, sea urchins, starfish, many shellfish, and some plankton. Besides eating away at the organisms, the acid reduces the concentration of carbonate in the water, depriving them of the chemicals they need to grow.

Acidity, measured as the amount of hydrogen ions in the water, is already up by 30 percent. To put it another way, the pH has dropped by 0.1 points, from 8.2 to about 8.1. If the oceans continue to absorb large amounts of the atmosphere's excess carbon dioxide, acidification will have more than tripled by the second half of this century, badly damaging ocean ecosystems. The most vulnerable oceans are probably the remote waters of the Southern Ocean and the South Pacific. They are distant from land, and so are already short of carbonate—in particular a form known as aragonite, which seems to be the most critical.

"Corals could be rare on the tropical and sub-tropic reefs such as the Great Barrier Reef by 2050," warned a report from Britain's Royal Society. "This will have major ramifications for hundreds of thousands of other species that dwell in the reefs and the people that depend on them." Other species may suffocate or die for want of energy. High-energy marine creatures like squid need lots of oxygen, but the heavy concentrations of carbon dioxide will make it harder for them to extract oxygen from seawater.

"It is early days," says Carol Turley, of the Plymouth Marine Laboratory, a world authority in this suddenly uncovered field of research. "The experiments are really only getting under way." But one set of results is already in. James Orr, of the Laboratoire des Sciences du Climat et de l'Environnement, in France, put tiny sea snails called pteropods into an aquarium and exposed them to the kind of ocean chemistry expected later in this century. These creatures turn up all around the world and are vital to many ecosystems. They are the most abundant species in some waters around Antarctica, where a thousand individuals can live in 300 gallons of seawater. As well as being a major source of food for everything from fish to whales, pteropods are the biggest players in the biological pump there.

Orr found that within hours, the acid pitted the pteropods' shells. Within two days, the shells began to peel, exposing the soft flesh beneath. In the real world, predators would break through the weakened shells. "The snails would not survive," he concluded. The demise of the pteropods would cause a "major reduction in the biological pump," the Royal Society agreed. Within a few decades, it could leave the oceans more acid than at any time for 300 million years.

Whatever the outcome, we are seeing the start of an unexpected and frightening side effect of rising atmospheric carbon dioxide levels. Perhaps the nearest parallel to the current situation was 55 million years ago—the last time a major slug of carbon was released into the atmosphere over a short period . . .

16

THE WINDS OF CHANGE

Tsunamis, megafarts, and mountains of the deep

It was Earth's biggest fart ever. Fifty-five million years ago, more than a trillion tons of methane burst from the ocean, sending temperatures soaring by up to 18°F extinguishing two thirds of the species in the ocean depths, and causing a major evolutionary shock at the surface. The story, while from long ago, is a reminder that methane lurks in prodigious quantities in many parts of the planet—not just in frozen bogs—and that one day it could be liberated in catastrophic quantities.

The first whiff of this prehistoric megafart was unearthed in 1991, from a hole drilled about a mile into a submarine ridge just off Antarctica. Examining the different layers of the ancient sediment removed from the hole, the geologists James Kennett, of the University of California at Santa Barbara, and Lowell Stott, of the University of Southern California in Los Angeles, found evidence of a sudden mass extinction of organisms living on the sea floor 55 million years ago. They had apparently disappeared from the ocean within a few hundred years—perhaps less. Kennett and Stott soon discovered that other researchers had detected evidence of similar extinctions from the same era, in Caribbean and European marine sediments. This was clearly a global event—one of the largest extinctions in the history of the planet.

What happened? Looking at the chemistry of fossils in the drilled sediment, the two geologists found some intriguing clues. There was, for instance, a sudden change in the ratio of two oxygen isotopes, known as oxygen-18 and oxygen-16. The ratio in the natural environment is very sensitive to temperature, and this isotopic "signature" in sediments and ice cores is a widely used indicator of past temperatures. Kennett and Stott concluded that after rising gradually for several million years, ocean temperatures had soared much more dramatically about 55 million years ago. The change happened at the same time as the extinctions.

The sediments also revealed a second isotopic shift, this time between isotopes of carbon. Earth's organic matter suddenly contained a lot more carbon-12. From somewhere, trillions of tons of the stuff had been released into the environment. Clearly a greenhouse gas, either carbon dioxide or methane, had caused both changes. The problem was finding a likely source with sufficient capacity to do the job.

Jerry Dickens, a biochemist at James Cook University, in Townsville, Australia, set himself the task of working out where this carbon-12 might have come from. The first suggestion was carbon dioxide in volcanic eruptions, which are a rich source of carbon-12 in the modern atmosphere. But, says Dickens, that would have required volcanic eruptions at an annual rate a hundred times the average over the past billion years. Fossil fuels like coal, oil, and natural gas were possible sources. But they are mostly buried out of harm's way, sealed in rocks. Given that there were no creatures digging them up and burning them at the time, that, too, seemed implausible. The same was true for methane from swamps and wetlands like those found today in Borneo and Siberia. About three times as many of them existed then, but even so, they could not have delivered the amount of carbon-12 required. Only one last source—big enough and accessible enough to unleash a climatic eruption—was left. That, Dickens suggested, had to be the vast stores of methane that geologists have recently been discovering frozen in sediment beneath the oceans: methane clathrates.

Methane clathrates are an enigma. They have until recently escaped the attention of oil and gas prospectors, because they don't turn up in the kind of deep and confined geological formations where prospectors traditionally look for fossil fuels. Nor are they the product of current ecosystems, such as tropical and Arctic bogs. They are generally close to the surface of the ocean floor but frozen—confined not by physical barriers but by high pressures and low temperatures, in a lattice of ice crystals rather like a honeycomb. Scientists still debate exactly how and when they were formed, but they seem to arise when cold ocean water meets methane created by microbes living beneath the seabed. Seismic surveys have revealed these structures in the top few hundred yards of sediments beneath thousands of square miles of ocean. They exist unseen, usually just beyond the edge of continental shelves. Many of these frozen clathrate structures trap even larger stores of gaseous methane beneath, where heat from Earth's core keeps them from freezing.

Dickens estimates that between 1 and 10 trillion tons of methane is tied up today in or beneath clathrates. But its confinement may not be permanent. Release the pressure or raise the temperature, and the lattices will shatter, pouring methane up through the sediment into the ocean and finally into the atmosphere. It seems that some such event must have happened 55 million years ago. Moreover, if this was the source of the great release of carbon-12, it would also explain why the extinctions appeared to be most serious in the ocean depths, where extensive acidification would have been almost certain. "Right now, most everybody seems to accept that the release of methane clathrates is the only plausible explanation for what happened 55 million years ago," says Dickens.

His chronology goes like this. For several million years, the world was warming, probably because of extraterrestrial influences such as the sun. The warming gradually heated sediments on the seabed until the clathrates started to shatter and release methane. Perhaps it happened in stages, with warming releasing methane that caused further global warming that released more methane. But at any rate, over a few centuries, or at most a few thousand years, trillions of tons of methane were eventually released into the atmosphere—enough to cause the observed global shift in carbon isotopes and a large and long-lasting hike in temperatures.

"The world just went into chaos," as Dickens puts it. Life on Earth was transformed almost as much as by the asteroid hit 10 million years before that wiped out the dinosaurs. Once the methane releases had ended, the planet's ecosystems gradually absorbed the remainder of the great fart, the climate recovered its equilibrium, and the oceans settled down again. But the evolutionary consequences of that long-ago event have lasted to this day. By the time the climate had recovered, many land and ocean species had become extinct, while others evolved and flourished.

"At the same time as the great warming, there was a major evolution and dispersal of new kinds of mammals," says Chris Beard, a paleontologist at the Carnegie Museum of Natural History, in Pittsburgh. It was "the dawn of the age of mammals." Among those on the evolutionary move were all kinds of ungulates—including the ancestors of horses, zebras, rhinos, camels, and cattle—and primates. And among the new primates evolving in the balmy conditions were the omomyids, the ancestors of simians, who in turn spawned humans.

Could such a cataclysm happen again? Maybe in the twenty-first century? Certainly there is still enough methane buried beneath the oceans. But could current global warming provide the trigger for its release? Some say that is unlikely; modern seawater is still much colder than it was 55 million years ago. But Deborah Thomas, of the University of North Carolina, who has analyzed the event in detail, is not so sanguine. The oceans may still be cooler, but they are also warming faster than they were 55 million years ago. And the pace of change may be as dangerous as the extent. If so, she says, "the trigger on the clathrate gun will be a lot touchier than it was 55 million years ago."

Apparently seaworthy ships can disappear from the ocean without warning for many reasons. They can be hit by giant waves, upturned by submarines, punctured by icebergs, or dashed onto rocks in storms. Could huge slugs of methane bursting from the ocean depths be another cause? Some say so. Take the strange case of Alan Judd and Witch Hole.

Judd is a British marine geologist at the University of Newcastle with a long interest in methane clathrates. In the late 1990s, he persuaded a French oil company to fund work in the North Sea to map giant pockmarks on the seabed. Geologists regard these otherwise inexplicable pockmarks as the aftermath of past methane eruptions from clathrates deep in the sediment. One day, about 90 miles off Aberdeen, Judd's remote-controlled probe was exploring a particularly large crater, about a hundred yards across and known to mariners as Witch Hole, when it crashed into something. Something large, metal, and unidentified, which destroyed the probe.

In the summer of 2000, Judd returned to try to find out what his probe had struck. This time he had money from a television company and a tiny remote-controlled submarine equipped with a video camera. He found the culprit. It was the steel hull of an 80-foot trawler dating, judging by its design, from the early twentieth century. The ship sat upright on the seabed, in the middle of the crater, apparently unholed. "The boat didn't go in either end first; it went down flat," Judd said later. "It looks as though it was just swamped." The ship could have gone down in a storm, but "for the boat to have randomly landed within Witch Hole would be an amazing coincidence," he said. "It is tempting to suggest that it is evidence of a catastrophic gas escape."

Efforts to identify the ship and find contemporary reports of why it went to the bottom have so far yielded nothing. And funds for another survey have failed to materialize. But the story remains an intriguing mystery to set beside other stories of ships that apparently disappeared in calm waters. Some say methane emissions from the depths could explain the mysterious loss of ships in the area of the Atlantic known as the Bermuda Triangle, for instance. Certainly, methane clathrates have been found in the area. So, while there is much mythology and misinformation about the Triangle, it may contain some truth. "When the gas bubbles to the surface, it lowers the density of the water and therefore its buoyancy," says Judd. "Any ship caught above would sink as if it were in a lift shaft." Any people jumping overboard to save themselves would sink, too. No trace would remain—at the surface.

Meanwhile, pockmarks are turning up on the seabed almost everywhere that clathrates are found: from the tropics to the poles, from the Atlantic, the Pacific, and the Arctic to the Indian and Southern Oceans. Evidence of when methane was released from the ocean floor remains sketchy, but the signs are of major releases. At Blake Ridge, off the eastern U.S., marine geologists have found pockmarks 700 yards wide and up to 30 yards deep, like huge moon craters. And drilling studies suggest that the ridge may still have around 15 billion tons of frozen methane hidden beneath the craters, with at least as much again trapped as free gas in warmer sediments beneath the frozen zone. European researchers have found pockmarks just as big in the Barents Sea southeast of Svalbard. The widely quoted estimate that 1 to 10 trillion tons of methane is trapped down there remains a bit of a stab in the dark, but the scale sounds right.

The lattice structures that hold methane clathrates survive only at low temperatures and high pressures, so sightings are rare. Occasionally they survive briefly at the ocean surface. Fishing nets bring lumps to the surface from time to time. They fizz away on the ship's deck, releasing their methane. Alarmed fishermen usually throw them back fast. Researchers have found white clathrate chunks "the size of radishes" sitting in the mud on the bottom of the Barents Sea; sometimes they track small plumes of methane rising from the seabed to the surface. Russian researchers have reported clathrates bursting out of the Caspian Sea and igniting "like a huge blowtorch, producing flames that rise several hundred metres high." But these events are mild curiosities compared with the evidence being pieced together of major catastrophic events caused by methane releases from beneath the ocean—including events that occurred much more recently than 55 million years ago.

On the east coast of Scotland, cliff faces often show a mysterious layer of gray silt about 4 inches thick sandwiched between layers of peat. The silt seems unremarkable, except that it extends right up the coast for hundreds of miles, and is full of the remains of tiny marine organisms that are normally found only on the ocean floor. The silt was deposited about 8,000 years ago by a tsunami that surged across the North Sea after the collapse of an underwater cliff on the edge of the continental shelf west of Norway. This was a huge event. The 250-mile-long cliff slumped more than 1.5 miles vertically down the slope onto the floor of the deep ocean, taking with it a staggering 1 billion acre-feet of sediment. It spread across an area of seabed almost the size of Scotland.

The scars left by this huge submarine slide were first spotted in 1979 by Norman Cherkis, of the Naval Research Laboratory in Washington, D.C. Cherkis was using sonar equipment to scour the ocean bed for hiding places for military submarines. He assumed at first that the slide had been caused by an underwater earthquake, though there was little seismological evidence for this. That presumption was shaken by a Norwegian marine geologist, Juergen Mienert, of the University of Tromso, who saw that the area of seabed that had slumped, known as Storegga, also contained large numbers of pockmarks associated with bursts of clathrates.

Mienert suggested that the slide coincided with a rise of 11°F in ocean temperatures off Norway as currents carrying the warm tropical waters of the Gulf Stream became much stronger in the aftermath of the last ice age. The strong wash of warm water over a previously cold seabed would have been enough, he said, to melt clathrates. Since just 100 cubic feet of clathrate contains enough methane to produce 16,000 cubic feet of gas at normal atmospheric pressure, the releases would have had explosive force, stirring up the seabed sediments over a huge area, and creating more releases and a cataclysmic slide.

Mienert estimated that this undersea eruption released between 4 and 8 billion tons of methane—enough to heat the global atmosphere by several degrees. His theory gained dramatic support when analysis of Greenland ice cores showed a big rise in methane concentrations in the air at that time. Some argue that the methane surge came from tropical wetlands that grew as the world warmed and became wetter. Mienert disagrees, but the argument has yet to be resolved.

The tsunami certainly had a huge impact. A 40-foot wave crashed into the Norwegian coast and deposited silt 20 feet above the shoreline in Scotland. The Shetland Islands took the brunt, receiving at least two waves that left a slimy trace 65 feet above what was then sea level. In the hours after Storegga slipped, many Stone Age people must have died on the shores of Europe. And it wasn't an isolated event. There appear to have been several earlier slips at Storegga. The fear must be that it could happen again here. "There is still a lot of methane on the north side of the slide," Mienert says.

Since the discovery of the Storegga slip, the remains of a number of other, similar slips have been discovered in areas of the ocean known to harbor methane clathrates. They have turned up off British Columbia, off both the East and West Coasts of the U.S., and at the mouths of great rivers like the Amazon and the Congo, where huge offshore fans of sediment contain methane generated by rotting vegetation from the rainforests upstream. Exactly when these slips occurred is not yet certain, but Mienert believes that the thermal shock caused by Storegga may have had a domino effect, releasing other clathrates stocks already made vulnerable by the warming postglacial oceans.

Some researchers postulate a "clathrate gun" theory of climate change, in which, at the end of the ice ages and perhaps at other times, successive releases of methane instigated a worldwide warming. They see the catastrophic event 55 million years ago as just the biggest in a whole family of methane-related climate disasters.

When I met Juergen Mienert in his lab, on a hill overlooking a fjord on the edge of Tromso (suitably raised, we joked, in case of a tsunami), he was planning a major new European research project to find more remains of slides and clathrate blowouts. The Euromargins project, which he chairs, "will be targeting areas where there are both pockmarks, indicating past clathrate releases, and warm ocean currents, indicating a risk of destabilization," he said.

He is already on the trail of an ancient slip high in the Arctic, off the north coast of Spitzbergen. This area is currently warming fast and is bathed periodically in warm waters from the Gulf Stream that break through the Fram Strait into the Arctic. "Some of the world's richest methane deposits lie right below that current," he said. He showed me new survey images of the seabed there, taken on a cruise two months before, in an area known as Malene Bay. They reveal another huge event. "Look at this," he enthused. "Look at the height of the cliff that fell. It was 1,500 yards high.

The prognosis, Mienert says, is worrying. Current conditions are disturbingly similar to those in which the great methane releases of the past happened—fast-rising sea temperatures penetrating the sediment and defrosting the frozen methane. Global warming, he believes, "will cause more blowouts and more craters and more releases." The risk of a giant tsunami blasting into Europe, the most densely populated continent on Earth, at the same time that a huge outburst of methane pushes climate change into overdrive is disturbing, to say the least.

Some argue that such concerns are exaggerated. It would take decades or even centuries for a warming pulse from the ocean to penetrate sediment to the zones where methane clathrates generally cluster. But Mienert counters that clathrates are being found ever closer to the surface, particularly in the Arctic. In any event, there is a second and much faster route downward for the heat. The U.S. naval researcher Warren Wood has discovered that seabed sediments often contain cracks that extend into the frozen clathrate zone. Warm water takes no time to penetrate the cracks and can quickly unleash the methane. As Richard Alley said of the crevasses inside ice caps, "Cracks change everything."

Methane is only the third most important greenhouse gas, after water vapor and carbon dioxide. But, says Euan Nisbet, "arguably it is the most likely to cause catastrophic change." This is "because the amount needed to change climate is smaller than for carbon dioxide, and because the amount of the gas available, in soils and especially methane clathrates, is so large." Methane has clearly had catastrophic effects in the past. In the dangerous world of sudden and unstoppable climate change, methane is the gunslinger.

IV

REFLECTING ON WARMING

I7

WHAT'S WATTS?
Planet Earth's energy imbalance

Jim Hansen knows about the atmosphere from top to bottom. He began his career as an atmospheric physicist, studying under James van Allen, after whom the Van Allen Belts of the upper atmosphere are named. He published papers on the Venusian atmosphere before he moved on to our own. So when Hansen stops talking about degrees of temperature and starts counting how many watts of energy reach Earth's atmosphere and how many leave it, I recognize that we are getting down to the nitty-gritty of what sets Earth's thermostat.

I know about watts. I have a 60-watt bulb in the lamp over my desk. At school almost forty years ago, my physics teacher had a stock line for any lesson on electricity. "It's the watts what kill," he said, meaning that they are what matters. When Hansen says the sunlight reaching the surface of Earth in recent centuries has been about 240 watts for every 10.8 square feet, I can visualize that. It is four 60-watt bulbs shining on a surface area the size of my desk. That figure ever changes only slightly, because the sun itself is largely unchanging. If the sun were to grow stronger, more radiation would reach Earth, and we would warm up. But only so much. A warmed surface also releases more energy, so eventually a new equilibrium would be reached. Similarly, as additional greenhouse gases trap more solar energy, Earth warms until a new equilibrium is reached, with as much energy leaving as arriving. Put another way, Earth's temperature is whatever is required to send back into space the same amount of energy that the planet absorbs.

So what is happening today? Thanks to our addition of greenhouse gases to the atmosphere, the planet is suffering what Hansen calls "a large and growing energy imbalance" that "has no known precedent." The planet is warming, but it has not yet reached a new equilibrium.

The net warming effect of man-made pollutants is about 1.8 watts per 10.8 square feet. Most of this goes into heating either the lower atmosphere or the oceans. Ocean surfaces and the atmosphere share heat fairly freely, constantly exchanging energy. Because the oceans have a greater heat capacity than the atmosphere, they take the lion's share of the extra energy. But there are time lags in this exchange system. It takes some time to heat the oceans to their full depth. The warming of recent decades has created a pulse of heat that so far has gone as deep as 2,500 feet into the oceans in some places. As this pulse progresses, the oceans are draining more heat out of the atmosphere than they will once they return to a long-term balance with the atmosphere. It is rather like using a central heating system to warm a house. We have to heat all the water in all the radiators before the full effect of heating air in the house is felt. Likewise, the full impact of global warming will be felt in Earth's atmosphere only after the oceans have been warmed.

The best guess is that about 1°F—representing about 0.8 watts per 10.8 square feet—is currently lopped off the temperature of the atmosphere by the task of warming the oceans. That is warming "in the pipeline," says Hansen. Whenever we manage to stabilize greenhouse gases in the atmosphere, there will still be that extra degree to come. Half of it, Hansen reckons, will happen within thirty to forty years of stabilization, and the rest over subsequent decades or perhaps centuries.

While most of the extra heat being trapped by greenhouse gases is currently going into heating the oceans and the atmosphere, there is a third outlet: the energy required to melt ice. At present, no more than 2 percent is involved in this task. But Hansen believes that percentage is likely to rise substantially. Recent surging glaciers and disintegrating ice shelves in Greenland and Antarctica suggest that it may already be increasing. Melting could in future become "explosively rapid," Hansen says, especially as icebergs begin to crash into the oceans in ever-greater numbers.

There would be a short-term trade-off. Extra energy going into melting would raise sea levels faster but leave less energy for raising temperatures. But in the longer term, that would be of no help. For as more ice melts, it will expose ocean water, tundra, or forest. Those darker surfaces will be able to absorb more solar energy than the ice they replace. So we may get accelerated melting *and* more warming.

The critical term here is "albedo," the measure of the reflectivity of the planet's surface. Anything that changes Earth's albedo—whether melting ice or more clouds or pollution itself—will affect Earth's ability to hold on to solar energy just as surely as will changes in greenhouse gases. On average, the planet's albedo is 30 percent—which means that 30 percent of the sunlight reaching the surface is reflected back into space, and 70 percent is absorbed. But that is just an average. In the Arctic, the albedo can rise above 90 percent, while over cloudless oceans, it can be less than 20 percent.

During the last ice age, when ice sheets covered a third of the Northern Hemisphere, the vast expanses of white were enough to increase the planet's albedo from 30 to 33 percent. And that was enough to reduce solar heating of Earth's surface by an average of 4 watts per 10.8 square feet. It was responsible for two thirds of the cooling that created the glaciation itself. And just as more ice raised Earth's albedo and cooled the planet back then, so less ice will lower its albedo and warm the planet today.

According to the albedo expert Veerabhadran Ramanathan, of the Scripps Institution of Oceanography, if the planet's albedo dropped by just a tenth from today's level, to 27 percent, the effect would be comparable to a fivefold increase in atmospheric concentrations of carbon dioxide." To underline the importance of the issue, Ramanathan is organizing a Global Albedo Project to probe the albedo of the planet's clouds and aerosols. Lightweight robotic aircraft began flying from the Maldives, in the Indian Ocean, in early 2006. The project could prove as important as Charles Keeling's measurements of carbon dioxide in the air.

The prognosis for albedo cannot be good. We have already seen how the exposure of oceans in the Arctic is triggering runaway local warming and ice loss that can only amplify global warming. The same is also happening on land. Right around the Arctic, spring is coming earlier. And such is the power of the warming feedbacks that it is coming with ever-greater speed. As lakes crack open, rivers reawaken, and the ice and snow disappear, the landscape is suddenly able to trap heat. The "cold trap" of reflective white ice is sprung, and temperatures can rise by 18°F in a single day. No sooner have the snowsuits come off than travelers are sweltering in shirtsleeves.

Stuart Chapin, of the Institute of Arctic Biology, in Fairbanks, says that the extra ice-free days of a typical Alaskan summer have so far been enough to add 3 watts per 10.8 square feet to the average annual warming there. As a result, he says, the Arctic is already absorbing three times as much extra heat as most of the rest of the planet. And there are other positive feedbacks at work in the Arctic tundra. In many places, trees and shrubs are advancing north, taking advantage of warmer air and less icy soils. Trees are darker than tundra plants. And because snow usually falls swiftly off their branches, they provide a dark surface to the sun earlier than does the treeless tundra. Chapin estimates that where trees replace tundra, they absorb and transfer to the atmosphere about an extra 5 watts per 10.8 square feet.

This creates a surprising problem for policymakers trying to combat climate change. Under the Kyoto Protocol, there are incentives for countries to plant trees to soak up carbon dioxide from the atmosphere. They can earn "carbon credits" equivalent to the carbon taken up as the trees grow, and use these credits to offset their emissions from power stations, car exhausts, and the like. The idea is to promote cost-effective ways to remove greenhouse gases from the atmosphere—the presumption being that that will cool the planet. But in Arctic regions, the effect will usually be the reverse, because although new trees will indeed absorb carbon dioxide, they will also warm the planet by absorbing more solar radiation than the tundra they replace.

Clearly there is a balance between cooling and warming. But Richard Betts, of Britain's Hadley Centre, says that in most places in the Arctic, the warming will win. In northern Canada, he estimates, the warming effect of a darker landscape will be more than twice the cooling effect from the absorption of carbon dioxide. And in the frozen wastes of eastern Siberia, where trees grow even more slowly, the warming effect will be five times as great. Every tree planted will hasten the spring, hasten the Arctic thaw, and hasten global warming.

18

CLOUDS FROM BOTH SIDES

Uncovering flaws in the climate models

The graph flashed up on the screen for only a few seconds, but it set alarm bells ringing. Had I read it right? The occasion was a workshop on climate change at the Hadley Centre for Climate Prediction, held in Exeter in mid-2004. The room was packed with climate modelers from around the world. Even they raised a collective eyebrow when the graph sank in. If carbon dioxide in the atmosphere doubled from its pre-industrial levels, the graph suggested, global warming would rise far above the widely accepted prediction of 2.7 to 8.1°F. The real warming could be 18°F or even higher. Surely some mistake? Too much wine at lunch? No. This was for real.

Till now, climate modelers have graphed the likely effect of doubling carbon dioxide levels using what is known in the trade as a bell graph: the best estimate—about 5°—falls in the middle, and probabilities fall symmetrically on either side. So the chance that the real warming will be 8.1°, for instance, is the same as that it will be 2.7°. But the graph of likely warming that James Murphy, of the Hadley Centre, was displaying on an overhead screen that morning looked very different. The middle point of the prediction was much the same as everybody else's. But rather than being bell-shaped, the graph was highly skewed, with a long "tail" at the top end of the temperature range. It showed a very real chance that warming from a doubling of carbon dioxide would reach 10, 14, 18, or even 21°F.

Carbon dioxide is widely expected to reach double its pre-industrial levels within a century if we carry on burning coal and oil in what economists call a business-as-usual scenario. But nobody has seriously tried to work out what 18 degrees of extra warming would mean for the planet or for human civilization. It would certainly be cataclysmic.

Let's be clear. Murphy was not making a firm prediction of climatic Armageddon. But neither was this a Hollywood movie. The high temperatures on the display, he said, "may not be the most likely, but they cannot be discounted." Nor was Murphy alone with his tail. The meeting also saw a projection by David Stainforth, of Oxford University, that suggested a plausible warming of 21°F. Six months later, this new generation of scarily skewed distributions started turning up in the scientific journals. Unless the editors take fright, these figures will probably become part of the official wisdom, incorporated into the next report of the IPCC.

So what is going on? For one thing, modelers have for the first time been systematically checking their models for the full range of uncertainty about the sensitivity of the climate system to feedbacks that might be triggered by greenhouse gases. Assessing those efforts for the IPCC was the main task of the Exeter meeting. And what has emerged very strongly is that clouds, which have always been seen as one of the weakest links in the models, are even more of a wild card than anyone had imagined. The old presumption that clouds will not change very much as the world warms is being turned on its head. There may be more clouds. Or fewer. And their climatic impact could alter. It is far from clear whether more clouds would damp down the greenhouse effect, as previously thought, or intensify it. Being mostly of an age to remember 1970s Joni Mitchell songs, the climate scientists in Exeter mused over coffee that they had "looked at clouds from both sides now." And they didn't like what they saw.

An assessment of the sensitivity of global temperatures to outside forcing —whether changes in sunlight or the addition of greenhouse gases—has been central to climate modeling ever since Svante Arrhenius began his calculations back in the 1890s. This assessment mostly revolves around disentangling the main feedbacks.

The three biggest feedbacks in the climate models are ice, water vapor, and clouds. We have already looked at the effect of melting ice on the planet's albedo. It explains why the Arctic is warming faster than elsewhere and giving an extra push to global warming. Water vapor, like carbon dioxide, is a potent greenhouse gas, without which our planet would freeze. The story of what will happen to water vapor is a little less clear-cut. A warmer world will certainly evaporate more water from soils and oceans, and this process is already increasing the amount of water vapor in the atmosphere, amplifying warming. In the standard climate models, extra water vapor in the air at least doubles the direct warming effect of carbon dioxide. But it's when we come to clouds that the calculations get sticky.

A lot of water vapor in the air eventually forms clouds. At first guess, you might say that clouds would have the opposite effect of water vapor, shading us from the sun's rays and keeping air temperatures down. They do that on a summer's day, of course. But at night they generally keep us warm, acting like a blanket that traps heat. Globally, these two effects— or, rather, their absence—are most pronounced in deserts. Where there are no clouds, the days are boiling, but the nights can get extremely cold, even in the tropics.

The temperature effects of clouds turn out also to depend on the nature of the clouds. Their height, depth, color, and density can be vital, because different clouds have different optical properties. The wispy cirrus clouds that form in the upper atmosphere heat the air beneath, because they are good at absorbing the sun's rays and re-radiating the heat downward, whereas the low, flat stratus clouds of a dreary summer's day are good at keeping the air below cool.

Researchers still know surprisingly little about how many and what sort of clouds are above our heads. For instance, it has only recently emerged that there may be many more cirrus clouds than anyone had thought. Many are almost invisible to the naked eye, but nonetheless seem to be highly effective at trapping heat. Some studies suggest that, taken globally, the cooling and warming effects of clouds currently largely cancel each other out, with perhaps a slight overall cooling effect. But nobody is sure. And even small changes in cloudiness could affect planetary albedo substantially. If a warmer world tipped clouds into causing greater warming, the effects could be considerable.

So what is the prognosis? Again, a first guess is that extra evaporation will make more clouds, because a lot of the water vapor will eventually turn into cloud droplets. But even that may not be so simple. Evaporation doesn't just lift water vapor into the air to create more clouds; it also burns off clouds, leaving behind blue skies. And greater evaporation can also make clouds form faster, so that they fill with moisture faster, make raindrops faster, and dissipate faster. So, in a greenhouse world, fluffy cumulus clouds that we are used to seeing scudding across the sky all day could instead boil up into dark cumulonimbus clouds and rain out, leaving behind more blue skies.

Bruce Wielicki has been trying to figure out the answer to such questions during more than twenty years of cloud-watching at NASA's Langley Research Center, in Hampton, Virginia. He says that satellite data suggest that clouds probably still have an overall cooling effect on the planet; but, especially in the tropics, there is a trend toward clearer skies. Since the mid-1980s, the great tropical convection processes that cause air to rise where the sun is at its fiercest have intensified. As a result, storm clouds are forming and growing more quickly in those areas. This may be increasing the intensity of hurricanes across the tropics. Less obvious is Wielicki's discovery that the storm clouds not only form more quickly but also rain out more quickly. That leaves the tropics drier and less cloudy as a whole.

Many researchers see the phenomenon as strong evidence of an unexpected positive feedback to global warming. But Wielicki is cautious about what is behind his discovery of clearer tropical skies. We need to know, because the tropics are where an estimated two thirds of the moisture in the atmosphere evaporates—an important element in the planet's thermostat. "Since clouds are thought to be the weakest link in predicting future climate change, these new results are unsettling—the models may be more uncertain than we had thought," says Wielicki. His own guess is that clouds may be two to four times more important in controlling global temperatures than previously thought.

And that takes us back to the graphs on display in Exeter, where Murphy and Stainforth reached much the same conclusion as Wielicki in their new modeling projections of possible future warming. To make his graph, Murphy took a standard climate model and tweaked it to reflect the new range of uncertainties for cloud cover, lifetime, and thickness. His model responded by delivering much higher probabilities of greater-than-expected warming. "Variations in cloud feedback played a major role in the predictions of higher temperatures," he said. Susan Solomon, who as chair of the IPCC's science working group will be the final arbiter of what goes into its 2007 assessment of climate change, concurs. The biggest difference between models that give high estimates of global warming and those that give lower ones, she says, is how they handle cloud feedbacks.

Who is right? Are fears about a strong positive feedback from clouds warranted or not? One way of finding out is to test how the different models reflect the real world today. The IPCC is currently using this approach more widely to help weed out poor models from its analysis. Murphy has no doubt about what the outcome will be. The models that predict low warming "have a lot of unrealistic representations of clouds," he says. "The weeding process suggests higher temperatures." That is not proof, but it is worrying.

Clouds are not the only thing changing the reflectivity of Earth's atmosphere. Planet Earth is becoming hazier; the wild blue yonder is not so blue. The problem is pollution spreading across the Northern Hemisphere and much of Asia, blotting out the sun. The issue is not just aesthetic. Nor is it just medical, though millions of people die from the toxic effects of this pollution every year. It is also climatic. While some parts of the world are seeing temperatures soar, some of the world's most densely populated countries have seen temperatures drop. Climatologists who have spent many years warning about global warming are reaching the conclusion that we may need to be at least as concerned about the effects of this localized cooling.

The pollutants of concern here are normally lumped together under the name aerosols, but they are of many types and come from many sources. The culprits include operators of power stations in Europe, farmers burning crop stubble in Africa and trees in the Amazon, steel manufacturers in India, and millions of women cooking dinner over millions of open cooking stoves across the tropics. Most of these activities produce greenhouse gases, but they also produce aerosols in the form of smoke, soot, dust, smuts of half-burned vegetation, and much tinier but highly reflective sulfate particles. Depending on their characteristics, these aerosols reflect or absorb solar radiation. In fact, most do both, in varying quantities. But with one important exception that we shall return to, the dominant effect is cooling. The result is that some parts of the planet, from central Europe to the plains of India and the Amazon jungle to eastern China, have missed out on global warming either permanently or at certain times of the year.

A global cooling to counteract global warming might seem a good idea. Sadly, things are not so simple. The competing forces are pulling the climate system in two different directions that may not so much counteract as inflame each other. Certainly they introduce a new element of uncertainty in atmospheric processes. But although many countries are trying to reduce their emissions of smog-making aerosols, for excellent public-health reasons, the cleanup will lift the "parasol of pollution" over those countries. The likely result will be a burst of warming that could happen within days of the pollution's clearing.

We can see evidence of this already in central Europe. Fifteen years ago, countries like Poland, Czechoslovakia, and East Germany reeked with the smell of burning fossil fuels from the old Soviet-style heavy industries. Chimneys belched, and smog was endemic. The region where the three countries met became known as the "black triangle." The pollution was having a local cooling effect more than twice as great as the warming effect of greenhouse gases. Since the fall of the Berlin Wall, the old polluting industries have mostly shut down, and the air has cleared. More sun penetrates the smog-filled landscape, and central Europe has warmed correspondingly. In the past fifteen years, temperatures there have risen at three times the global average rate.

This real-world experiment shows clearly the power of aerosols to cool Earth's surface. And it raises another question for the future: How much warming is being suppressed globally by aerosols? "We are dealing with a coiled spring, with temperatures being held back by aerosols," says Susan Solomon, chief scientist for the IPCC. "If you shut off aerosols today, temperatures would increase rapidly, but we don't yet know exactly how much, because we don't know how coiled the spring is." The best guess until recently was that aerosols were holding back a quarter of the warming, or about 0.36°F. In other words, a greenhouse warming of 1.4 degrees since

pre-industrial times has been reduced by aerosols to a current warming of
1 degree. But critics say this calculation is little more than a guess, and the
first efforts at a more direct measurement of radiation changes caused by
aerosols suggest that the spring may be much more tightly coiled.

I was present at one of the first meetings where these ideas were discussed
in detail. The occasion was a workshop of climate scientists held at
Dahlem, a quiet suburb of Berlin, in 2003. The meeting was discussing
"earth system analysis," and the man who brought the issue to the table
was the distinguished Dutch atmospheric chemist Paul Crutzen, whose
brilliant and creative mind first divined many of the secrets of chemical
destruction of the ozone layer. Back in the 1980s, Crutzen had stumbled
on the notion that during a nuclear war, so many fires would be burning
that the smoke "would make it dark in the daytime" and "temperatures
would crash." That insight has led to continued analysis of the role of
everyday aerosols in climate and to his conclusion, argued in Dahlem, that
aerosols could be disguising not a quarter but a half to three quarters of
the present greenhouse effect. "They are giving us a false sense of security,"
he said. Past calculations of the cooling effect of aerosols, he said, had been
inferred by comparing the warming predicted by climate models with ac-
tual warming. The aerosol cooling effect was reckoned as the warming that
had "gone missing." But as the modeler Stephen Schwartz, of the Brook-
haven National Laboratory, put it on another occasion, "that approach as-
sumes that we know that the climate model is accurate, which of course is
what needs to be tested."

After dinner in Dahlem—over a few Heinekens, as I remember—Pe-
ter Cox, a hard-thinking, hard-drinking climate modeler then at the Met
Office in England, did some back-of-the-coaster calculations about what
Crutzen's conjecture might mean for future climate. He became rather ab-
sorbed. A couple of bottles later, he had come to the conclusion that, if
Crutzen was right, the true warming effect of doubling carbon dioxide
could be more than twice as high as existing estimates, at 12 to 18°F. The
following morning, his more sober colleagues registered agreement. I
went home and wrote a story for *New Scientist,* quoting Cox's numbers and
the workshop's conclusion that the findings had "dramatic consequences

for estimates of future climate change." I was rather excited by it, but the story decidedly failed to interest the rest of the world.

Later Cox, his Hadley Centre colleague Chris Jones, and Meinrat Andreae, of the Max Planck Institute for Chemistry, in Mainz, tested the guesses in more detail, and reached the same conclusions that Cox had on his coaster. They did it by running climate models that assumed either a low greenhouse warming moderated by a small cooling from aerosols, or a bigger greenhouse warming held back by a bigger aerosol cooling. They reported in *Nature* that the "best fit" involved a warming from doubling greenhouse gases that, without the moderating effect of aerosols, would be "in excess of" 10.8 degrees and "may be as high as" 18 degrees.

"Such an enormous increase in temperatures would be greater than the temperature changes from the previous ice age to the present," wrote the three researchers. "It is so far outside the range covered by our experience and scientific understanding that we cannot with any confidence predict the consequences for the Earth."

Still the world didn't take much notice. I asked Andreae about this strange indifference. "It's always amazing," he e-mailed me, "how many people don't see how important this issue is for the future development of the climate system." The discussion at the Dahlem meeting had rather changed his worldview, he said. "Before the Dahlem meeting, I was becoming kind of climate complacent, in the sense that I was convinced of coming global warming, but felt that it was going to be a couple of degrees and we could deal with that. Also, I felt that the aerosols were doing us a favor in slowing and reducing warming. But after it, I came to realize that the aerosols brake will come off global warming, and also that the aerosol cooling introduces a great uncertainty about climate sensitivity. I'm now in a situation where, as a human being, I hope that I'm wrong as a scientist. If we are right with our current assessment, there are really dire times ahead."

Models are only models, of course. But whatever the precise scale of the current aerosol effect, it would be quite wrong to imagine that it can carry on protecting us from the worst as global warming gathers momentum. That is because aerosols and greenhouse gases have very different life spans in the atmosphere. Aerosols stay for only a few days before they are washed to the ground in rain. By contrast, carbon dioxide has a life span of a century or more. If, for the sake of argument, we stuck with current emission levels of both aerosols and carbon dioxide, the aerosol levels in the air would stay the same. There would be no accumulation and no increase in the cooling effect. But carbon dioxide levels would carry on rising and produce ever greater warming.

Probably. The trouble is that scientific knowledge is, if anything, even poorer about aerosols than it is about the effects of clouds. Says Stephen Schwartz: "There are many different kinds of aerosols, lots of interactions among them, and unknown issues of cloud microphysics—all of which need to be better understood. This is hard science which I am afraid nobody has come to grips with yet." There is no dispute that some aerosols, such as sulfate particles from coal-fired power stations, predominantly scatter sunlight and reflect it back into space. They increase albedo and cool the planet for sure. Others, though, have some scattering effect but also absorb solar radiation and then re-radiate it, warming the ambient atmosphere. And with them it is harder to be sure where the balance between the two effects lies.

Here the biggest concern is soot, the black carbon produced from the incomplete burning of coal, biomass, or diesel. Scientific understanding of the role of soot is, to be frank, all over the place, as a quick scan of the major scientific journals makes clear. In March 2000, a paper in *Science* said soot was "masking global warming"; eleven months later another, in its chief rival, *Nature,* said soot was "generating global warming." Ten months later, presentations at a big U.S. conference of the American Geophysical Union called it variously "a cooling agent" and "the biggest cause of global warming after carbon dioxide." These can't both be right.

The truth seems to be this. A cloud of soot—whether from a forest fire, a cooking stove, or an industrial boiler—shields Earth from the sun's rays, thus cooling the ground beneath. But it also absorbs some of that radiation and converts it to heat, which it radiates into the surrounding air. So soot cools the ground but warms the air. The ground doesn't move, but the air does. The cooling effect, though intense, is mostly located near the pollution source; while the warming effect, though less intense, extends much farther.

There is still great uncertainty about the precise role of soot in global climate. Jim Hansen suggests that it could be responsible for up to a quarter of warming over parts of the Northern Hemisphere. He believes that soot may be the third most important man-made contributor to the greenhouse effect, behind carbon dioxide and methane, and that controlling it offers one of the cheapest, most effective, and quickest ways of curbing global warming. Even so, in those parts of the world where it is produced in large quantities, it is undoubtedly cooling the land. Those parts of the world are mainly in Asia. And now there is a new concern. Could aerosol emissions in India and China turn off the Asian monsoon?

19

A BILLION FIRES

How brown haze could turn off the monsoon

I have been traveling to India for twenty years now—not regularly, but often enough to notice that every time I go, the air seems to be dirtier and more choked with black smoke and fumes. In the cities, much of this comes from the exhaust pipes of the millions of ill-maintained diesel-burning buses and two-stroke rickshaws that ply the gridlocked streets. The haze also contains natural sea salt and mineral dust, a fair amount of fly ash and sulfur dioxide from India's coal-burning power stations, and huge amounts of organic material and soot from the countryside. For in India's million villages, where most of its billion-strong population still live, the air is often scarcely better than it is in the cities, with smoke billowing from a hundred million cooking stoves, all burning wood, dried cow dung, and crop residues.

This smoke is becoming a major climatic phenomenon. It is merging into one giant cloud that climate researchers call India's "brown haze." Its heart is over the northern Indian plain, one of the world's most densely populated areas, which suffers near-constant smog during the winter months. This is a giant version of the old pea-soup smog that used to hit London in the days when the city was heated by coal fires. As I complete this chapter, Delhi's air is reportedly worse than ever, with thick smog preventing flights from its airport. But the haze spreads more widely, shrouding the whole of India and beyond.

The term "brown haze" was coined by scientists during the first investigation of the phenomenon. In 1999, some two hundred scientists taking part in the Indian Ocean Experiment (INDOEX) assembled in the Maldives for a three-month blitz of measuring the air over India and the Indian Ocean from aircraft and ships. The results were a surprise, even to those who had planned the project. Every winter, from November to April, a pall of smog more than a mile thick occupied a huge area south of the Himalayas, stretching from Nepal through India and Pakistan, out over the Arabian Sea and the Bay of Bengal, and even south of the equator as far as the Seychelles and the Chagos Islands. It covered 4 million square miles, an area seven times the size of India.

"To find thick brown smog 13,000 feet up in the Himalayas, and over the coral islands of the Maldives, was a shock," says Paul Crutzen, one of the masterminds of the project. Crutzen, who won a Nobel Prize for predicting a dramatic thinning of the ozone layer fifteen years before it happened, said the haze had a similar potential to cause "unpleasant environmental surprise" in India and beyond. The haze could, he said, have "very major consequences" for the atmosphere.

The INDOEX findings proved controversial in India, which felt singled out for criticism. Why pick on us? locals asked. Indian government scientists issued a detailed and largely spurious "rebuttal." The INDOEX scientists quickly switched to discussing the "Asian brown haze"—and quite rightly, for the haze is an Asia-wide phenomenon. But when I used that term at a meeting in India in mid-2005, I was quietly hissed. Even mentioning an Asian haze is considered politically incorrect today. Why single out Asia? people ask. In fact, antagonism has become so great that many Indian scientists now refuse to discuss the subject with foreigners like me, for fear of getting into political hot water.

India has been the focus of attention because its aerosol pollution is of genuinely global importance. Dorothy Koch, of Columbia University, estimates that a third of the soot that reaches the Arctic, sending pollution meters soaring from Mount Zeppelin, in Svalbard, to northern Canada, comes from South Asia. The soot is falling onto the snow and ice, making the white surface darker and so triggering melting. When her findings were published, in April 2005, one headline read: "Home fires in India help to melt the Arctic icecap half a world away." No wonder the Indians are twitchy. Suddenly a country with one of the lowest per capita emissions of greenhouse gases in the world was being fingered as a prime cause of climate change.

But, wary though they may be in public, India's scientists have been at work finding out where all the pollution comes from. At first, they assumed that most must be the product of India's fast-growing and undoubtedly polluting industries. But at the Indian Institute of Technology, in Mumbai, they mocked up rural kitchens to check emissions from cooking stoves of the kind found across the Indian countryside. They fueled the fires with wood, crop waste, and dried cattle manure; on the stoves, they boiled kettles and even cooked lunch. They concluded that smoke emissions from India's domestic cooking fires produce between 1 and 2 million tons of aerosols a year, including a quarter of a million tons of soot. That makes them responsible for some 40 percent of India's aerosol emissions.

Discussion about the climatic impact of the Asian brown haze has become a statistical minefield. The "headline figure," widely quoted, is that in winter the haze reduces the amount of solar radiation reaching the ground in India by an average of about 22 watts per 10.8 square feet. That is a reduction of about a tenth, and would be enough to cause massive cooling. The statistic is literally true, but only part of the story. For only about 7 watts of that radiation is lost entirely, "backscattered" into space. The other 15 watts is absorbed by the soot in the aerosols and re-radiated, heating the atmosphere. Thus, though the radiation budget is much altered, the cooling effect is much less than it might otherwise be. Even so, in winter it is sufficient both to counteract global warming and to cool the air across much of India by an average of about 0.9°F. In summer, when the pollution is rained out in the monsoon and the skies are clearer, temperatures have risen in recent decades by about the same amount, in line with the global average.

The consequences don't end there, says Veerabhadran Ramanathan, the Indian scientist who, with Crutzen, masterminded INDOEX from the Scripps Institution of Oceanography. In particular, the cooling impact of the haze over the Indian land surface delays the heating of the land that stimulates the monsoon winds. It thus threatens the lifeblood of India: the monsoon rains.

There seems to be some confusion among scientists about the Indian monsoon. Scientists investigating the brown haze all claim that the monsoon has weakened in recent decades, and they see this as a likely effect of the haze. But researchers investigating global warming are equally certain that it has increased in intensity. What undisputed evidence there is suggests that the monsoon rains have become more intense in the traditionally wetter south of India, where the haze is thinner, but have diminished in the north, where the haze is thickest. How those trends develop is obviously of vast importance for a country entirely dependent on just a hundred days of monsoon rains to water the crops that feed a billion people. A wider collapse of the monsoon in South Asia would be a global calamity of immense proportions. It could happen.

East Asia could be in the same boat—a situation that would threaten food production for the world's most populous nation, China. North of the Himalayas, there is a similar intense brown haze in winter, though it is composed less of the smoke from burning cow dung and more of the sulfur dioxide and other fumes from burning coal. And it is interrupting the sun's rays. When Yun Qian and Dale Kaiser, of the U.S. government's Northwest National Laboratory, in Richmond, Washington, studied the records of Chinese meteorological sunshine recorders over the past fifty years, they found a decline in sunshine since 1980 of 5 or 6 percent in the most polluted south and east of the country.

And this decline is lowering temperatures. While global warming is evident across much of China, daytime temperatures in the most polluted regions have fallen by about 1°F. That, in turn, is altering rainfall patterns. In the south of the country, the monsoon rains are becoming stronger, with flooding in the great southern river, the Yangtze; whereas farther north, in the catchment of the Yellow River, there is now less rainfall. Chinese records, which are among the most meticulous in the world, suggest that this shift is the biggest alteration in the country's rainfall patterns in a thousand years. To some extent, links between the rainfall trends and the increasing brown haze are conjecture. But when climate models are programmed to include a strong Asian brown haze, many of them produce extra rainfall in southern China, coupled with near-permanent droughts in the north. So if the models are right, while the haze lingers, these major calamities are set to continue.

Meinrat Andreae estimates that about 8 billion tons of biomass is burned in the tropics each year—approaching 1 ton for every inhabitant of Earth. All of it produces aerosols that billow into the air.

Asian countries, with their huge populations, have the worst smog. But parts of Africa and the Brazilian Amazon are also shrouded when farmers clear land for crops by burning grasslands and forests. Hundreds of thousands of fires burn across the Brazilian Amazon each year, covering the area with billowing dense smoke. During the weeks of burning, the amount of sunshine reaching the ground typically drops by 16 percent. In Zambia, studies have found a 22 percent drop in sunlight as the savannah is burned.

The changes are "causing all sorts of havoc with the atmospheric circulation," says Dale Kaiser, of the Northwest National Laboratory, who is the author of the Amazon study. Over the Amazon, he says, the smoke causes cooling and suppresses the formation of raindrops. That both reduces rainfall and keeps the aerosols in the air longer. Meanwhile, the buildup of water vapor results in the upper atmosphere's becoming wetter, according to Daniel Rosenfeld, of the Hebrew University, who flew research planes through the smoke over the Amazon. It eventually forms a few extremely intense thunderstorms, known in the trade as "hot towers," which cause hailstorms. Hail falls in the Amazon only when fires have been burning.

Some of these changes could have impacts far beyond the regions where the smoke forms. Condensation in Amazon hot towers releases very large amounts of heat into the upper atmosphere, influencing jet streams and other wind patterns across the tropics and beyond. And more water vapor may reach the stratosphere, where it could increase ozone destruction. Meanwhile, modeling studies supervised by Jim Hansen suggest that soot emissions over India and China may trigger drought in the African Sahel and even warming in western Canada—though exactly how remains unclear.

These impacts are, of course, only the predictions of climate models. It is hard to prove whether they reflect events in the real world. But the models are based on real physical processes in the atmosphere. So at the least, they suggest the potential for a worldwide climatic change from the effect of aerosol emissions in the tropics. Cooking stoves in India, it seems, could have global consequences.

2 0

HYDROXYL HOLIDAY

The day the planet's cleaner didn't show up for work

It could be the doomsday that creeps up on us unawares: the day the atmosphere's cleaning service fails to show up for work. For one of the most disturbing secrets of our planet's metabolism is that just one chemical is responsible for cleaning most of the pollution out of the atmosphere. If it took a day off, we would be in serious trouble, with smog spreading unchecked across the planet.

The chemical in question is called hydroxyl. Its molecules are made up of one atom of oxygen and one atom of hydrogen. They are created when ultraviolet radiation bombards common gases such as ozone and water vapor. But it is the most ephemeral of chemicals. Almost as soon as it is created, it reacts with some other molecule, mostly some polluting substance, and is gone again. It has an average lifetime of about a second. Because it comes and goes so fast, it is also rather rare, with an average concentration in the atmosphere of less than one part per trillion. You could pack every last molecule of the stuff into the Great Pyramid of Egypt and still have room for two more atmospheres' worth.

Yet it is crucial to life on Earth. For hydroxyl is, more or less literally, the atmosphere's detergent. It transforms all manner of gaseous pollutants so that they become soluble in water and wash away in the rain. The process is called oxidation. To take one example, hydroxyl converts sulfur dioxide, which would otherwise clog up the air for months, to acid rain, which soon falls to the ground. Much the same happens to carbon monoxide and methane (both of which are oxidized to carbon dioxide), nitrogen oxide, and many others. The one major pollutant it doesn't neutralize is carbon dioxide, which, partly as a result, has a much longer lifetime in the atmosphere than most other pollutants.

Concentrations of hydroxyl are generally much higher in the warm air over the tropics, where ultraviolet radiation is most intense, but are close to nonexistent in the Arctic, where, despite ozone holes, there is usually little ultraviolet around to make more hydroxyl. As a result, "toxic chemicals that might survive for only a few days in the tropics will last for a year or more in Arctic air," says Frank Wania, of the University of Toronto. That is one reason, he says, why pollutants like acid hazes and pesticides accumulate in the Arctic, poisoning polar bears and much else.

Hydroxyl has a hard life keeping up with our polluting gases, especially since it is destroyed in the process of oxidizing them. Fears that the atmosphere's janitor could be overworked and in trouble go back a few years. But because the chemical is so transient and rare, it is virtually impossible to measure hydroxyl concentrations directly. All the estimates are indirect, based on measuring chemicals with which it reacts. So when Joel Levine, a NASA chemist, suggested back in the 1980s that hydroxyl in the air could have declined by 25 percent over the previous thirty years, his argument didn't make much headway, because he couldn't prove it. There was no chance of his producing something definitive like the Keeling curve on carbon dioxide.

In 2001, a brief forecast in the IPCC report of a possible 20 percent decline in hydroxyl by 2100, because of excess demands placed on it by a rising tide of pollution, met much the same fate. So did a report the same year by Ronald Prinn, a leading atmospheric chemist from the Massachusetts Institute of Technology, of a possible decline in global hydroxyl levels during the 1990s.

But we should be concerned. Hydroxyl spends more energy oxidizing one chemical than any other. That chemical is carbon monoxide. Emitted mostly from forest fires, fossil fuel burning, and small domestic stoves, it has for many years been the Cinderella pollutant. Dangerous to humans in confined spaces, it has been largely ignored as an environmental pollutant threat. The biggest concern has been that it oxidizes to carbon dioxide. But its concentration in the air tripled worldwide during the twentieth century. That suggests a bottleneck that could be the prelude to a wider breakdown of the cleaning service.

In the absence of good data on hydroxyl and its works, probably the best hope of finding a problem ahead of time is through modeling. Sasha

Madronich, of the National Center for Atmospheric Research, in Boulder, Colorado is one of the few researchers who have attempted to model how hydroxyl might respond to changing pollution levels. He says that the atmospheric cleaning service could have a breaking point: "Under high pollution, the chemistry of the atmosphere becomes chaotic and extremely unpredictable. Beyond certain threshold values, hydroxyl can decrease catastrophically." Many urban areas, he says, "are already sufficiently polluted that hydroxyl levels are locally suppressed." This is partly because the sheer volume of pollution consumes all the available hydroxyl, but also because the smog itself prevents ultraviolet radiation from penetrating into the air to create more.

"The oxidation processes that should clean the air virtually shut down in smog-bound cities like Athens and Mexico City," he says. It takes a breath of fresh air from the countryside to revive them. "If, in future, large parts of the atmosphere are as polluted as these cities are today, then we could anticipate the collapse of hydroxyl on a global scale." With large areas of Asia becoming submerged beneath a cloud of brown haze every year, it may be that the atmosphere is approaching just such a crisis. Nobody knows.

But the doomsday scenario may require another element. If the cleanup chemical is under pressure from too much dirt, the worst thing to happen would be a decline in supply of the chemical. So the critical question may be: What might reduce the amount of hydroxyl produced by the atmosphere? Clearly smog is a problem, because it reduces ultraviolet radiation in the lower atmosphere. But a thicker ozone layer, nature's protective filter against ultraviolet, could have the same effect. And the world is currently working quite hard to repair the damaged ozone layer and make it thicker. Our efforts to solve one environmental problem could exacerbate another.

The worry is that over the past thirty years or so, we have been living on borrowed time with hydroxyl. Pollutants like CFCs have thinned the ozone layer, and so let more ultraviolet radiation into the lower atmosphere. And while that is bad for marine ecosystems, and probably causes more skin cancers, it has ensured a beefed-up supply of hydroxyl to cleanse the air of many other pollutants. Arguably, it has helped the planetary cleaning service keep on top of a rising tide of pollution. Over the next half century, we should succeed in healing the ozone layer once again. There are good ecological, human-health, and even climatic reasons for doing this. But it could have a downside for hydroxyl.

So here is the doomsday scenario. If we repair the ozone layer, we will reduce hydroxyl production to the levels of the mid-twentieth century. But we will be doing it at a time when the demands on hydroxyl's services are considerably higher than they were then. That could be the moment when Madronich's threshold is crossed, and oxidation processes in the atmosphere go into sharp decline. I have no data, no models, and no peer-reviewed papers to justify this scenario. It is just that: a scenario and not a prediction. But it is plausible speculation. It could conceivably happen.

V

ICE AGES AND SOLAR PULSES

GOLDILOCKS AND THE THREE PLANETS

Why Earth is "just right" for life

Our sun has an inner ring of planets, starting with Mercury and moving out to Venus, Earth, and Mars. Right from their birth 5 billion years ago as cosmic debris, these planets have been more than lumps of rock. For one thing, they are hot, with thin solid crusts hiding large molten cores. Turbulent chemistry in their depths releases gases through the crusts. Although Mercury was too small, and its gravity too weak to capture these gases, the other three have held on to at least some of them, creating atmospheres. These atmospheres contain greenhouse gases such as carbon dioxide, water vapor, and methane that trap solar heat and create climates.

The three atmospheres of the three planets were initially probably rather similar. But they have evolved in very different ways. Today, Venus has a thick atmosphere with enough greenhouse gases to hold temperatures at around 850°F. Mars appears once to have had a considerable atmosphere and a climate that supported rainfall. It may have had life, as well. But somewhere along the way, it lost much of its atmosphere and dried up, and any life is now presumed extinguished. The demise of the life-support system on Mars is a conundrum, because the planet has plenty of carbon at its surface. It was probably once floating in the form of carbon dioxide in the atmosphere, where it would have formed a blanket sufficiently warm for liquid water and for life. But most of that carbon has ended up in rocks.

Earth, by contrast, has a rich and chemically very active atmosphere, and a sufficiency of greenhouse gases to maintain equable temperatures and lots of liquid water—and it is very much alive. Some planetary scientists have dubbed Earth the "Goldilocks planet." When, in the children's story,

Goldilocks tasted porridge at the house of the three bears, she found one bowl (Venus) too hot, one (Mars) too cold, and one (Earth) just right. At first, this seems the purest chance. Earth must have been just the right distance from the sun. And yet, since in the early days the three planets had very similar atmospheres, the theory has developed that their different fates had as much to do with the fates of those atmospheres as with the planets' distance from the sun.

Earth's atmosphere has certainly endured, and has proved a congenial place for the development of myriad life forms. Things were often difficult in the early days, it is true. At various points, the planet seems to have been entirely covered by ice and snow, with life surviving only in warm crevasses beneath the frozen exterior. The fate of Mars threatened. "It was a close call," says Joe Kirschvink, of the California Institute of Technology, in Pasadena, who coined the term "Snowball Earth" to describe this condition, which last occurred some 600 million years ago. He believes that the planet escaped a fate similar to that of Mars only because of a buildup of carbon dioxide emitted from volcanoes beneath the ice: "If the Earth had been a bit further from the Sun, the temperature at the poles could have dropped enough to freeze the carbon dioxide, robbing us of this greenhouse escape from Snowball Earth."

Despite such difficulties, Earth came through, and for the past half-billion years at least, it has maintained a surprisingly constant temperature. Not, as we shall see, completely constant, but surprisingly so given the cosmic forces being played out around it. In particular there was the sun. It is the main source of most of the energy and warmth at Earth's surface, of course. By comparison, the contribution of the heat from Earth's core is minute. But the sun has changed a great deal over the lifetime of Earth. Back in the early days—for about the first billion years of Earth's existence—it was a weak beast. It emitted about a third less energy than it does today. Even 500 million years ago, it was as much as 10 percent weaker than it is today. Yet, with Snowball Earth a distant memory, the world then seems to have been warmer than it is now, and ice-free. This is because the atmosphere was rich in methane, carbon dioxide, and water vapor, all forming a thick blanket that kept the planet and its growing armies of primitive life warm. Volcanic activity was still strong, so new releases of carbon dioxide topped up any leakage from the atmosphere, keeping concentrations around twenty times higher than they are today.

But as the planet has aged, the emissions from volcanoes have lessened, and carbon dioxide has gradually started to disappear from the atmosphere. Its decline may at various times have threatened a return of Snowball Earth, and a Martian relapse into a cold, lifeless world. But it may ultimately have saved the planet from a fate similar to that of Venus. This raises an interesting question. Did this happy Goldilocks outcome occur entirely by chance? Or could the planet have developed some kind of crude thermostat? The surprising answer is that it seems to have done just that.

Carbon dioxide, then as now, was removed from Earth's atmosphere largely by being dissolved in rain to form dilute carbonic acid. That acid ate away at rocks on the ground, which were made primarily of calcium silicate, creating calcium carbonate, which ended up as sediment on the ocean floor. This process has a temperature control built in, because the amount of rain depends on the temperature. So erosion rates rise when it is warm, but faster erosion removes more carbon dioxide from the air and lowers temperatures again. If the thermostat overshoots, and temperatures get too cold, then the rate of weathering slows, and temperatures recover. This is a negative feedback operating through the carbon cycle. It won't save us today, because it takes millions of years to have a serious impact. But over geological timescales, it was probably rather good at moderating temperatures and keeping the planet's climate convenient for life.

Very convenient. Suspiciously so, thought the charismatic British chemist and maverick inventor Jim Lovelock, back in the 1980s. Lovelock wondered if life itself might be controlling this process; and soon afterward two of his acolytes, Tyler Volk and David Schwartzman, suggested that he was right by demonstrating that basalt rocks erode a thousand times faster in the presence of organisms such as bacteria. This introduces a new and extremely dynamic negative feedback. More bacteria will keep the planet cool. But if the air gets too cool, the planet becomes covered by ice, the bacteria die, the erosion slows, and the atmosphere warms again. This process is potentially an extremely powerful thermostat for planet Earth, and is one of the foundation stones of Lovelock's grand vision of Earth as a self-regulating system called Gaia. It may also explain why the carbon cycle feedback did not save Mars: perhaps, at some critical moment, the red planet did not have enough life to make it work properly.

Lovelock is a controversial character. Now in his eighties, he first devised his idea of Gaia while working for NASA and trying to think of ways to decide if other planets had life. He figured that the best way was to look for signs of gases that could be made or maintained in the air only by life forms. And he began to realize that life could evolve quite naturally in ways that would maintain an environment that suited it. He argues that since the early days, life on Earth has evolved sophisticated strategies for stabilizing climate over long timescales. For him, the temperature of life on Earth was "just right" because life made it so by taking control of key planetary life-support systems like the carbon cycle.

For many years, Lovelock was virtually cast out of the scientific community, and Gaia was often seen as quasi-religious mumbo-jumbo. Major journals like *Nature* and *Science* would not publish his work. He made his living as a freelance inventor of scientific devices. But his idea of Earth as, metaphorically at least, a single living organism has made him the spiritual father of a whole generation of Earth system scientists. Whether or not you buy the notion of a living Earth, his way of thinking about Earth as a single system with its own feedbacks has been extremely influential.

The thermostat, whether run by life or by geology, is pretty crude. For some 400 million years, planet Earth has been getting cooler. Some see this as a refutation of Gaian ideas. But others, like Greg Retallack, a soil scientist at the University of Oregon, argue that the cooling happened because life, or at any rate large parts of it, wanted it that way. Plants in particular, he says, like it cool. And plants have proved extremely efficient at capturing carbon dioxide and burying it permanently where it cannot return to the atmosphere. Some 7 trillion tons of old vegetable carbon has been stored for tens of millions of years in the form of fossil fuels beneath Earth's surface. In addition, probably as much methane is captured in frozen clathrates beneath the ocean bed. That is a lot of warming stored away, as we are currently in danger of discovering the hard way.

The cooling of Earth has been a long, slow, and fitful process. Around 55 million years ago, as we saw earlier, Earth experienced the "biggest fart in history," a vast surge of methane into the atmosphere from the under-sea clathrate store, which pushed air temperatures up by around 9°F. That was clearly no part of a Gaian grand plan. But Gaians would argue that life-mediated feedbacks resumed control. The methane eventually decayed to carbon dioxide, which was in turn absorbed back into the oceans. But even after normality had been resumed, levels of carbon dioxide in the at-mosphere were still about five times as high as they are today—at around 2,000 parts per million. Within a million years or so, however, those con-centrations began to fall sharply. (Sharply, that is, on geological timescales: the average pace of decline was less than one ten-thousandth of the rate of increase in recent decades.) By 40 million years ago, they had subsided to 700 ppm. And by around 24 million years ago, they were below 500 ppm, probably for the first time since the planet's earliest days.

It was around then that an ice sheet spread across Antarctica—the first permanent ice to form on the planet for hundreds of millions of years. And by about 3 million years ago, another surge of cooling had begun, result-ing in ice sheets forming in the Northern Hemisphere, too. Explanations for this general cooling range from continental drift in the western Pacific to another turn of the Gaian thermostat. But we can leave that to one side. Because the ice ages themselves—the geologically brief but extremely vicious cold snaps within the general cooling trend—happened on time-scales of much more interest in our current climatic predicament. Un-raveling the causes of the ice ages may, many climate scientists believe, provide vital clues to our fate in the coming decades.

THE BIG FREEZE

How a wobble in our orbit triggered the ice ages

The discovery that the world had once been plunged into an ice age was one of the great scientific revelations of the nineteenth century. It was to the earth sciences what Charles Darwin's theories on evolution were to the life sciences. It changed everything. The story emerged gradually, but the first man to perceive the scale of the glaciation that had overtaken so much of the Northern Hemisphere was a Swiss naturalist called Louis Agassiz. While Agassiz was summering in the Alps in 1836, his host pointed out giant scratch marks on the mountainsides that showed, he said, how the glaciers must once have extended much farther down their valleys.

Agassiz pondered the significance of this. He realized that he had seen similar marks in the landscape in many parts of Europe that were distant from present-day glaciers. He heard similar reports of glacial scratch marks from across North America. And he read contemporary newspaper stories of perfectly preserved mammoths being dug from the snow in Siberia, their meat so fresh that it was fed to local dogs and scavenged by polar bears. The only explanation, he concluded, was that much of the Northern Hemisphere must once have been covered by ice, and that the event happened very suddenly, in a vast, icy apocalypse. "The land of Europe, previously covered with tropical vegetation and inhabited by herds of great elephants, enormous hippopotami and gigantic carnivores, was suddenly buried under a vast expanse of ice," he wrote. "The movement of a powerful creation was supplanted by the silence of death."

Agassiz's vision was like a creation myth in reverse. Advances in geology soon revealed that not one ice age but a whole series of glaciations had occurred, separated by warm periods like our own. But his picture has otherwise survived remarkably intact. Indeed, recent evidence has revived his original idea that the onset of the last ice age must have been rather fast, with temperatures crashing in a couple of hundred years at most, and very probably much less.

We now know that two main ice sheets formed. One stretched from the British Isles across the North Sea and Scandinavia, and then west through Russia and western Siberia, and north across the Barents Sea as far as Svalbard. A second, even larger sheet covered the whole of Canada and southern Alaska, with a spur extending over Greenland. A smaller sheet sat over Iceland, and the seas around were full of thick floating ice. Strangely, northern Alaska and eastern Siberia, though deep-frozen, were never iced over. But, combined with the older ice covering Antarctica, these ice sheets contained three times as much ice as is present on Earth today—enough to keep sea levels worldwide some 400 feet lower than they are now—and covered 30 percent of Earth's land surface. The ice sheets were high as well as broad, rising up to 2.4 miles above the land surface. They chilled the air above and acted as a barricade for the prevailing westerly winds, which were forced south, skirting the ice sheets. This perpetuated the ice sheets, since the winds would have been the likeliest source of warmth to melt them.

Temperatures fell by around 9°F as a global average, but were 36 degrees lower than they are today in parts of Greenland, and just 5.4 degrees lower in the western Pacific Ocean. The world beyond the ice sheets became dry and cold. Deserts covered the American Midwest, France, and the wide lands of Europe and Asia between Germany and the modern-day Gobi Desert, in Mongolia. Farther south, the Sahara Desert expanded, the Asian monsoon was largely extinguished, and the tropical rainforests of Africa and South America contracted to a few refuges surrounded by grasslands. At the low point, around 70,000 years ago, even the grasslands were largely extinguished, leaving huge expanses of desert, from which winds whipped up huge dust storms. Humans lived by hunting on the plains and hunkering down in the small areas where lush vegetation persisted despite the cold and arid conditions.

It was clear from the start that something drastic must have triggered all this. Astronomical forces were suggested early on—in particular, the idea that the gravitational pull of other planets in the solar system, such as Jupiter, could influence the steady changing of the seasons, and in that way cause glaciers and ice sheets to grow. Many scientists of the day played with this idea. But the first man to subject it to detailed analysis was the son of a Scottish crofter with virtually no formal learning, but a passion for self-education and an extraordinary streak of diligence. James Croll was a shy, large-framed man with big ambitions. He stumbled on the idea of an astronomical cause for the ice ages while reading in libraries; transfixed, he spent most of the 1860s and 1870s pursuing the idea. He took numerous jobs, from insurance salesman to school caretaker to carpenter, in order to finance his passion.

Astronomical forces, he discovered, have three principal effects on Earth, all of which slightly alter the distribution of the solar radiation that reaches it. The effects are greatest in polar regions, where they can alter the amount of sun by as much as 10 percent. First, they change the shape of Earth's annual orbit around the sun. The orbit is not circular but slightly elliptical, and the shape of this ellipse changes according to the gravitational pull on Earth of the other orbiting planets. This "eccentricity" in Earth's orbit has a cycle that repeats itself about every 100,000 years.

As well as orbiting the sun once every year, Earth spins, making one revolution every day. But the axis around which it spins is not quite at a right angle to the direction of its orbit around the sun. So looked at from space, Earth appears to be spinning on a slight tilt. The combination of the orbit around the sun and the tilt of Earth's axis is what gives us our seasons, because it means that at certain times of the year the Northern and Southern Hemispheres see more or less of the sun. But this situation is not static. Astronomical forces also gradually alter the tilt of the axis. This change in Earth's "inclination" causes a difference in the intensity of the seasons. It has a 41,000-year cycle.

Finally, there is a further wobble in the axis around which Earth rotates, called the precession. This is exactly like the wobble that affects a spinning top. It influences the time of year when the different hemispheres are farthest from or nearest to the sun. It is complicated by its relationship with the other two effects, but it repeats on a cycle of 19,000 to 23,000 years. Currently the Northern Hemisphere has its summer, and the Southern

Hemisphere has its winter, when Earth is farthest from the sun; 10,000 years ago, it was the other way around.

It turns out that the eccentricity of Earth's orbit around the sun drives the 100,000-year cycles into and out of ice ages. Meanwhile, the other two effects, especially the precession, seem to trigger the short warm episodes that punctuate each ice age.

Croll realized that, averaged over a year, these changes made little difference to the amount of solar radiation reaching Earth. The overall effect was probably less than 0.2 watts per 10.8 square feet. But the changes did alter where and when the sun hit. Croll calculated in great detail how these influences waxed and waned over tens of thousands of years. And he established, at any rate to his own satisfaction, that they coincided with what geologists were then discovering about the timing of Earth's progress into and out of ice ages.

Taken together, the changing orbital shape, planetary tilt, and rotational wobble alter the strength of seasonality, making summers and winters more or less intense. And it was this that triggered the growth of ice sheets on land in the Northern Hemisphere, he said. Ice sheets would grow when northern winters were coldest. That would be when Earth was farthest from the sun, and when changing tilt ensured that it received the least sunlight. Once ice sheets started to grow, they would reflect ever more sunlight back into space, intensifying the cooling. Croll realized, too, that there was much less room for ice sheets to spread in the Southern Hemisphere, because they were confined to the continent of Antarctica. So the Northern Hemisphere would dominate events, driving the overall heat budget of the planet. But, he suggested, other feedbacks, such as changes to winds and ocean currents, could help drive the world further into an ice age.

In fact it turned out that Croll was wrong in assuming that it was cold winters that were critical. Later research proved that cold summers gave the world a bigger kick into ice ages, by providing little chance for winter accumulations of snow to melt. Nonetheless, Croll's work was a breathtaking piece of sustained cogent analysis that opened up a new field —much as Arrhenius did later with his examination of the impact of changing carbon dioxide levels on climate.

Croll's theory won him a few medals. But, being of low birth and of a taciturn disposition, he never fitted into the scientific salons of the day. They quickly tired of him and his ideas. Croll spent the last decade of his working life as the resident surveyor and clerk at the Scottish Geological Survey, in Edinburgh. To the last, he had to do his research in his own time. By the end of the nineteenth century, Croll and his ideas were largely forgotten. Even Arrhenius, who might have been expected to understand the importance of his work, dismissed it as an unwelcome rival to his own ideas, though in fact it complemented them.

Today, the idea that astronomical forces influence the formation of ice sheets is back in vogue and probably here to stay. Proof of its worth finally came in the 1970s. The British geophysicist Nick Shackleton carried out painstaking isotopic analysis of sediments on the ocean floor and in the process finally dated the glacial cycles sufficiently accurately to make clear their association with astronomical events. But even as the textbooks have been rewritten, Croll has been largely lost from the story. The orbital changes that he analyzed so painstakingly are known universally as the Milankovitch wobbles, after Milutin Milankovitch, a balding, monocled mathematician from Serbia who revived and elaborated Croll's ideas in the early twentieth century.

While Croll and Milankovitch have established to most people's satisfaction that orbital changes are the pacemaker of the ice ages, they did not by any means clear up the processes involved. How did a small change in the distribution of solar heating get amplified into a global freeze on a scale probably not seen since Snowball Earth thawed 600 million years before? And why, among a series of different wobbles, was it just one, with a return period of 100,000 years, that had much the greatest impact on global climate? A wobble, moreover, with an apparently weaker effect than the others on solar radiation reaching Earth. It seems, in the words of Dan Schrag, a geochemist at Harvard University, that Earth's system contains "powerful embedded amplifiers that can make it highly sensitive to relatively small forcings." Or, as Richard Alley would put it, we have a drunk on our hands. Identifying those amplifiers is important, not least because it should help answer how Earth's climate system might respond to our interference in its actions today.

Croll believed strongly in the power of growing ice itself to amplify cooling, and there is plenty of evidence to support the strength of this ice-albedo feedback. Once snow began to accumulate in the Canadian highlands around Hudson Bay, the ice sheet tended to grow of its own accord by cooling the area around it. Jim Hansen calculates that at the height of the last glaciation, it reduced the amount of heat absorbed by the planet's surface by some 4 watts per 10.8 square feet. What has troubled researchers rather more is exactly what limited it. Why, after reaching their greatest extent about 21,000 years ago, did the ice sheets begin to retreat?

Given the power of the ice-albedo feedback, it is far from clear why the ice sheets did not continue to grow until they had covered the entire planet and created a comeback for Snowball Earth. Even a change in the wobble to end the change in seasonality that started the ice growth might not have been enough. And it certainly would not explain the extremely fast collapse of the ice sheets at the end of the last glaciation. They disappeared more than ten times as quickly as they had arrived. Some fast feedback must have taken hold. One suggestion is that the sheer size of the ice sheets shut down further growth and eventually caused their rapid destruction. The main theory is that ice sheets are vulnerable to attack by heat rising from the interior of the planet. Trapped beneath the ice, it would have become of increasing importance as the sheets grew. Eventually, the theory goes, some threshold was passed, and the ice sheets melted from their base, creating a giant, continent-wide version of one of Hansen's "slippery slopes," with great chunks of ice skating into the ocean.

The second feedback that converted a planetary wobble into an ice age was greenhouse gases. Anyone who doubts the role of carbon dioxide in climate change should look at the graphs of atmospheric temperatures and of carbon dioxide levels in ice cores taken from the Greenland and Antarctic ice sheets. They cover the past half-million years, a period that includes several glaciations. Throughout, the two graphs are in lockstep. As carbon dioxide levels fall, so do temperatures, and vice versa. That does not determine which leads, but it clearly shows that they are engaged in a very intimate dance, in which carbon dioxide must amplify temperature changes even where it does not initiate them.

As temperatures fell at the start of each glaciation, around 220 billion tons of carbon left the atmosphere, returning during the brief interglacial periods. Its disappearance was enough to directly reduce Earth's uptake of solar energy by about 2 watts per 10.8 square feet. But what triggered this big shift in the planet's carbon cycle, and where did the carbon go? It certainly did not end up in vegetation on land, since that was shrinking as the world cooled. The obvious answer is the oceans. There are today about 44 trillion tons of carbon dissolved in the oceans—fifty times as much as in the atmosphere. So a minor uptake of carbon by the oceans could have had a huge effect on the atmosphere.

How might this have happened? Physics will help. Colder water (as long as it has not frozen) dissolves carbon dioxide better than warmer water. But most researchers believe that there must be some more dynamic feedback involved. To take a cue from Gaia, life is the obvious force here. One idea is that the initial cooling made the oceans more biologically productive. Plankton, the meadows of the oceans, do like colder temperatures. That is why the Southern Ocean around Antarctica is today one of the most productive. As the plankton grew, they drew more carbon dioxide out of the atmosphere. This strengthening of the biological pump would probably have been encouraged by enhanced dust storms, created by stronger winds and spreading deserts, which would have distributed mineral dust across the oceans. Even today, iron and other minerals are the limiting factor on the fecundity of much of the ocean food chain.

There may have been other feedbacks at work to push the planet into ice ages and drag it back out again. Methane may have been important. Its atmospheric concentration is in lockstep with temperature apparently as fixedly as that of carbon dioxide. One likely explanation is that the arid ice ages dried up wetlands and reduced their emissions of methane. Likewise, a colder atmosphere would have contained less water vapor—which would also have amplified the cooling.

A final amplifier may have been the ocean circulation system, with its huge ability to move heat around the planet. There is good evidence that the circulation system slows down during ice ages, and may have shut down entirely at the coldest point in the last glaciation. This is the province of a legend in the climate debate, Wally Broecker, and we will return to it in the next chapter.

The study of the ice ages suggests that over the past couple of million years at least, the natural climate system has constantly returned to one of two conditions. One is glaciated; the other is interglacial. The former has an atmosphere containing around 440 billion tons of carbon dioxide; the latter has an atmosphere containing about 660 tons. The planet oscillates between the two states regularly, repeatedly, and rapidly. But it doesn't hang around in any in-between states.

The evidence, says Berrien Moore III, the director of the Institute for the Study of Earth, Oceans, and Space, at the University of New Hampshire, "suggests a tightly governed control system with firm stops." There must be negative feedbacks that push any small perturbation back to the previous position. But there must also be strong positive feedbacks. Once things go too far, and the system seems to cross a hidden threshold, those positive feedbacks kick it to the other stable state. Each time, the guiding feedback seems to have rapidly moved about 220 billion tons of carbon between the atmosphere and the ocean.

That appears to have been the story for about the past two million years —until now. For the first time in a very long time, the system is being pushed outside this range. In the past century or so, human activity has moved another 220 billion tons of carbon into the atmosphere, in addition to the high concentrations of the interglacial state. The atmosphere now contains twice as much carbon as it did during the last ice age, and a third more than in recent interglacial eras, including the most recent. And we are adding several billion tons more each year. This extra carbon in the atmosphere has not been part of recent natural cycles. It comes mainly from fossilized carbon, the remains of swamps and forests that grew tens of millions of years ago.

This addition of carbon to the atmosphere is perhaps the biggest reason why Earth-system scientists feel the need to talk about the Anthropocene era. We are in uncharted territory. And the big question is: How will the system respond to this vast injection? Where will the carbon end up? There seem to be three possibilities. First, as some optimists hope, the system may deploy negative feedbacks to suppress change. Perhaps an accelerating biological pump in the ocean might remove the carbon from the atmosphere. It is possible. But the oceans generally like it cold. And there is no sign of such negative feedbacks kicking in yet, nor any obvious reason why they might. If anything, the biological pump has slowed in recent years.

The second possibility is the one broadly embraced by most climate models and the scientific consensus of the IPCC. It is that the system will carry on operating normally, gradually accumulating the carbon and gradually raising temperatures. There will be no abrupt thresholds that launch the climate system into a new state. This is moderately comforting, and fits the standard computer models, but it is contrary to experience over the past two million years.

And that raises a third possibility. Many Earth-system scientists think that their climate-modeling colleagues have not yet got the measure of the system. They fear that we may be close to a threshold beyond which strong positive feedbacks take hold, as they do when Earth begins to move between glacial and interglacial eras. The feedbacks may flip the system into a new, as-yet-unknown state. Most likely it would be one with much higher atmospheric concentrations of carbon dioxide and methane—more like the early days on planet Earth. That state might mean an era of huge carbon releases from the soil, or massive methane farts from the ocean floor, or wholesale changes to the ocean circulation system, or the runaway melting of the ice caps. That is conjecture. We simply don't know. But hold on to your hat: we could be in for a bumpy ride.

23

THE OCEAN CONVEYOR

The real day after tomorrow

Wally Broecker is a maverick—a prodigious and fearless generator of ideas, and one of the most influential figures in climate science for half a century. Sometimes he can be more. Amid the admiration for his science, you hear some harsh words about him in the science community. A bully, some say, especially to young scientists; a man who will use his influence to suppress ideas with which he disagrees. For a man in his seventies, he certainly comes on strong and relishes conflict. Here are his unprompted, on-the-record remarks to me about one of the U.S.'s leading climate modelers, who incurred the wrath of some Republican senators: "I think the senators were well out of line, but if anyone deserves to get hit, it was him. The goddamn guy is a slick talker and superconfident. He won't listen to anyone else. I don't trust people like that. A lot of the data sets he uses are shitty, you know. They are just not up to what he is trying to do."

Broecker is not a man to cross lightly. And to be honest, I thought a bit before writing the above. Much as I like his vigor, I'd hate to be caught in his crosshairs. Some believe he has earned the right to sound off about young colleagues he thinks don't pass muster. Some worry that Broecker seems to save his invective for people who resemble him in his younger years. But he is a man in a hurry. When I met him late in 2005, at Columbia's Lamont-Doherty Earth Observatory, his distinguished friend and collaborator Gerard Bond, a man a decade younger than Broecker, had recently died.

Broecker is a geochemist with an unimpeachable track record in pioneering the use of isotopic analysis to plot ocean circulation. He has been writing and thinking for more than three decades about what he calls the ocean conveyor, which more traditional scientists call the meridional overturning circulation or the thermohaline circulation. Whatever you call it, it is the granddaddy of all ocean currents, a thousand-year circulation with "a flow equal to that of a hundred Amazon rivers," as he puts it.

The conveyor begins with the strong northward flow of the Gulf Stream pouring warm, salty water from the South Atlantic across the tropics and into the far North Atlantic. In the North Atlantic, the water is cooled, particularly in winter, by the bitter winds blowing off Canada and Greenland. This cooling increases the density of the water, a process amplified by the formation of ice, which takes only the freshwater and leaves behind increasingly saline and dense water. Eventually the dense water sinks to the bottom of the ocean, generally in two spots: one to the west of Greenland, in the Labrador Sea, and the other to the east, down Wadhams's vertical chimneys. From there the water begins a journey south along the bed of the far South Atlantic, where a tributary, formed from cold, saline water plunging to the ocean bed around Antarctica, joins up. The conveyor then heads east through the Indian and Pacific Oceans before resurfacing roughly a thousand years later in the South Atlantic and flowing north again as the Gulf Stream to the far North Atlantic—where it goes to the bottom once more.

The circulation has many roles: distributing warm water from the tropics to the polar regions, mixing the oceans, and aiding the exchange of carbon dioxide between the atmosphere and the oceans. Along the way, it keeps Europe anomalously warm in winter. In Richard Alley's words, it "allows Europeans to grow roses farther north than Canadians meet polar bears." On the face of it, the circulation is self-sustaining. The operation of the chimneys draws Gulf Stream water north, which provides more water for the chimneys. But it is also temperamental, prone to switching on and off abruptly. That switch, says Broecker, is a vital component of the entire global climate system. Not everyone agrees on the nature of the switch and how much it matters, but he makes a persuasive case.

Broecker's picture of the ocean conveyor is disarmingly simple. Too simple, some say. He admits it had its origins in a cartoon. Asked by *Natural History* magazine to produce a diagram to illustrate a complicated argument about ocean-water movement, he drew a map with a few arrows suggesting likely "rivers" of intense flow within the circulation. "They sent it to an artist; he drew something, and I made a couple of corrections. I didn't realize it was going to be that important, but it was a popular magazine, and suddenly the diagram became a kind of logo for climate change."

Broecker is quite candid about the crudeness of the cartoon. But while some scientists might have disowned it, he recognizes its power and has embraced it. Its origins lie in Broecker's pioneering work using chemical tracers to identify movements of water in the oceans. He noticed that water in the Pacific and Indian Oceans appeared to be a mixture of water that had plunged to the depths in the North Atlantic and lesser amounts of water that had done the same thing around Antarctica. He could also see that water that had reached the ocean floor in the North Atlantic was largely made up of water that, prior to that, had made its way north as the Gulf Stream. To some extent, he filled in the rest. "The conveyor is clearly real," he insists. "But of course it's not as highly organized as it appears in the diagram." It is more a trend than a current—"a combination of random motions." And yet his cartoon has proved to be one of the most important concepts to emerge from climate science in the past quarter century.

Broecker chose the term "conveyor" because, he says, "I think names are very powerful, and that was much better than the proper scientific term. Some scientists say it is stupid, but laypeople can imagine a conveyor belt much more easily." He certainly has a way with words. Broecker was the first scientist to use the term "global warming," in a paper in the 1970s.

I first discovered the conveyor back in the late 1980s, while researching a book on environmental change. I was fascinated by the simplicity of the idea; by the fact that the conveyor might have two natural states, on and off; and by the scary possibility that climate change might shut the conveyor down if the ocean off Greenland became so flooded with freshwater that the dynamics of dense saline water formation around the chimneys broke down. For me, that idea was the first real inkling that climate change might not be as it was in the mainstream models—that the greenhouse effect might unleash something altogether nastier.

Early on, Broecker was often ambivalent about the potential for truly disastrous events. But by 1995, he felt confident enough to title a lecture on the conveyor to a big science conference "Abrupt Climate Change: Is One Hiding in the Greenhouse?" In it he outlined how evidence from sea-floor and lake sediments, ice cores, coral, and glacier records "demonstrates unequivocally" that an on-off switch on the global conveyor operated at the beginning and the end of the last ice age. The suggestion was that the conveyor had shut down and single-handedly started the ice ages, lowering temperatures by "4 degrees C [7.2°F] or more . . . often within the life-span of a generation"—a claim he inflated soon afterward, in the pages of *Scientific American*, to "10 degrees C [18°F] over the course of as little as a decade."

Broecker's picture, then, is of a powerful but fickle ocean conveyor with an on-off switch functioning in the far North Atlantic. Switched on, it warms the world, especially the Northern Hemisphere, and is typical of periods between ice ages. Switched off, it cools the Northern Hemisphere, and is typical of glaciations. But the system flickers at other times, too, he says. It triggered warm episodes that punctuated the depths of the last ice age, and perhaps drove more recent events such as Europe's medieval warm period and the little ice age. Broecker accepts that the ultimate forcing for these dramatic changes may lie in a celestial event like the slow movements of the Milankovitch cycles. But when a threshold is crossed and sudden climate change occurs, it is the conveyor that throws the switch.

These claims remain extremely controversial. Most would accept that Broecker is right that the conveyor slowed during the ice ages and probably shut down at various points. But most researchers believe that it was a consequence, and not a cause, of the glaciation. The big forces behind the cooling were the shift of carbon dioxide into the oceans and the spread of ice. And how important the ocean conveyor was in those processes has yet to be demonstrated. While the conveyor may have intensified cooling in the North Atlantic region, where the Gulf Stream is an acknowledged important feature in keeping the region warm, it is far less clear whether its global effects are anything like as big as Broecker claims.

But Broecker has rarely been bogged down in detail. Two years after making his claims for the ocean conveyor and the ice ages—and just a week before the world met in Japan to agree to the Kyoto Protocol—he was

warning that climate change could trigger a future shutdown of the con-
veyor. "There is surely a possibility that the ongoing buildup of green-
house gases might trigger yet another of those ocean reorganizations," he
said. If it did, "Dublin would acquire the climate of Spitzbergen in ten
years or less... the consequences would be devastating." He called the
conveyor the "Achilles heel of the climate system."

Broecker was also, I think, making a wider point. He wants to gener-
ate a change in the way we think about the planet. Climate systems work,
he suggests, rather as Stephen Jay Gould said evolution worked: not grad-
ually, through constant incremental change, but in sudden bursts. Gould's
phrase "punctuated equilibrium" sounds right for Wally's world of cli-
mate, too. And his new paradigm also fits the science of chaos theory, in
which his ocean conveyor is an "emergent property" in the wider Earth
system.

But the crux of the public debate on Broecker's ocean conveyor remains
a very simple question: Could global warming shut the conveyor down?
Broecker seems rarely to have doubted it. And the claim has in recent years
seemed almost to have a life of its own. This struck me most strongly at a
conference on "dangerous" climate change held at the Hadley Centre for
Climate Prediction, in Exeter in 2005. There I met Michael Schlesinger,
of the University of Illinois at Urbana-Champaign. He is a sharp-suited
guy sporting a pastiche of 1950s clothes and hairstyle. But if there were
serious doubts in Exeter about whether his style sense would ever come
back into fashion, there was no doubt that his ideas about climate change
had found their moment.

For more than a decade, Schlesinger has been making Broecker's case
that a shutdown of the ocean conveyor could be closer than mainstream
climate modelers think. Some critics feel that he just doesn't know when
to give up and move on. But he has stuck with it, criticizing the IPCC and
its models for systematically eliminating a range of quite possible dooms-
day scenarios from consideration. "The trouble with trying to reach a con-
sensus is that all the interesting ideas get eliminated," he said at the
conference. Science by committee ends up throwing away the good stuff—
like the idea of the conveyor's shutting down. But in Exeter, Schlesinger

was back in vogue. He had been invited to present his model findings that a global warming of just 3.6°F would melt the Greenland ice sheet fast enough to swamp the ocean with freshwater and shut down the conveyor. The risk, he said, was "unacceptably large."

Although he had been saying much the same for a decade, he was now considered mainstream enough to be invited across the Atlantic to expound his ideas at a conference organized by the British government. And he was no longer alone. Later in the day, Peter Challenor, of the British National Oceanography Centre, in Southampton, said he had shortened his own odds about the likelihood of a conveyor shutdown from one in thirty to one in three. He guessed that a 3-degree warming of Greenland would do it. Given how fast Greenland is currently warming, that seems a near certainty.

But all this is models. What evidence is there on the ground for the state of the conveyor? The truth is that dangerous change is already afoot in the North Atlantic. And, whatever the skepticism about some of Broecker's grander claims, the conveyor may already be in deep trouble. Since the mid-1960s, says Ruth Curry, of the Woods Hole Oceanographic Institution, the waters of the far North Atlantic off Greenland—where Wadhams's chimneys deliver water to the ocean floor and maintain Broecker's conveyor—have become decidedly fresher.

In fact, much of the change happened back in the 1960s, when some 8 billion acre-feet of freshwater gushed out of the Arctic through the Fram Strait. Oceanographers called the event the Great Salinity Anomaly. To this day, nobody is quite sure why it happened. It could have been ice breaking off the great Greenland ice sheet, or sea ice caught up in unusual circulation patterns, or increased flow from the great Siberian rivers like the Ob and the Yenisey. Luckily, most of the freshwater rapidly headed south into the North Atlantic proper. Only 3 billion acre-feet remained. Curry's studies of the phenomenon, published in *Science* in June 2005, concluded that 7 billion acre-feet would have been enough to "substantially reduce" the conveyor, and double that "could essentially shut it down." So it was a close call.

With the region's water still substantially fresher than it was at the start of the 1960s, the conveyor remains on the critical list. Another single slug of freshwater anytime soon could be disastrous. In the coming decades, some combination of increased rainfall, increased runoff from the land surrounding the Arctic, and faster rates of ice melting could turn off the conveyor. And there would be no turning back, because models suggest that it would not easily switch back on. "A shift in the ocean conveyor, once initiated, is essentially irreversible over a time period of many decades to centuries," as Broecker's colleague Peter deMenocal puts it. "It would permanently alter the climatic norms for some of the most densely populated and highly developed regions of the world."

As I prepared to submit this book to the publisher, new research dramatically underlined the risks and fears for the conveyor. Harry Bryden, of the National Oceanography Centre, had strung measuring buoys in a line across the Atlantic, from the Canary Islands to the Bahamas, and found that the flow of water north from the Gulf Stream into the North Atlantic had faltered by 30 percent since the mid-1990s. Less warm water was going north at the surface, and less cold water was coming back south along the ocean floor. This weakening of two critical features of the conveyor was, so far as anyone knew, an unprecedented event.

Probing further, Bryden found that the "deep water" from the Labrador Sea west of Greenland still seemed to be flowing south. But the volume of deep water coming south from the Greenland Sea, the site of Wadhams's chimneys, had collapsed to half its former level. The implication was clear: the disappearing chimneys that Wadhams had watched with such despair were indeed hobbling the ocean circulation. Broecker seemed on the verge of being proved right that the ocean conveyor was at a threshold because of global warming.

None of this demonstrated that Broecker's bleaker predictions of what would happen if the conveyor shut down were about to come true—that "London would experience the winter cold that now grips Irkutsk in Siberia." Something more like the little ice ages was the worst that most climate modelers feared. But there did seem to be a real possibility that many of Broecker's ideas were about to be put rather dramatically to the test.

2 4

AN ARCTIC FLOWER

Clues to a climate switchback

It must have felt like the springtime of the world. Anybody living on Earth 13,000 years ago could only have felt elation. An ice age of some 80,000 years was coming to an end. Temperatures were rising; ice was melting; rivers were in flood; and permafrost was giving way to trees and meadows across Europe and North America. In the Atlantic Ocean, the Gulf Stream was pushing north again, bringing warm tropical water and re-establishing an ocean circulation system that had shut down entirely in the depths of the ice age. Westerly winds blowing across the ocean were picking up the heat and distributing it across Europe and deep into Asia.

Meanwhile, in the tropics, the deserts were in retreat, the rainforests were expanding again from their ice-age refuges, and the Asian monsoon was kicking back in. Most spectacularly, the Sahara was bursting with life, covered in vegetation and huge lakes. This was the dawn of the age of *Homo sapiens,* who had supplanted the last of the Neanderthals during the long glaciation. If there had been a Charles Keeling around, he would have measured rising atmospheric levels of carbon dioxide and methane that were amplifying the thaw. He might even have invented the term "global warming" to describe it.

Then the unthinkable happened: the whole thing went into reverse again. Almost overnight, the thaw halted and temperatures plunged. Temperatures became as cold as they had been in the depths of the ice age. The forests returning to northern climes were wiped out; the permafrost extended; and ice sheets and glaciers started to regain their former terrain.

The springtime seemed to be over almost before it began. But this reversal was not the first. The previous 5,000 years had been full of them.

Some 18,000 years before the present, there was still a full-on ice age. By 16,000 years ago, the world was warming strongly. But by 15,000 years ago, it was cold again, with ice sheets reforming. At 14,500 years ago, it became so warm that within 400 years the ice caps melted sufficiently to raise sea levels worldwide by 65 feet. The cold gained the upper hand once more, only to give way to the pronounced warming of 13,000 years ago, which crashed again 12,800 years ago.

Today we can see this extraordinary climatic history recorded in ice cores extracted from the ice of Greenland and Antarctica. Graphs of the temperatures back then look like seismic readings during a big earthquake—or cardiac readouts during a heart attack. They show a climate system in a protracted series of spasms. Looking back, we recognize the death throes of the ice age. But that is with hindsight. At the time, there was little evidence that the climate system had any sense of direction at all. It lurched between its glacial and interglacial modes. The one thing it didn't do was settle for a happy medium.

The last great cold snap of the ice age, 12,800 years ago, is known today as the Younger Dryas era. The dryas is a white Arctic rose with a yellow center that suddenly reappeared in European sedimentary remains, indicating that the old cold reasserted itself. The era is called the Younger Dryas to distinguish it from the Older Dryas, the climate reversal of a thousand years earlier, and the Oldest Dryas, which came before that. The Younger Dryas, like the others, was swift and dramatic. Within about a generation, temperatures fell worldwide—perhaps by as little as 3 to 5°F in the tropics, but by an average of as much as 28 degrees farther north, and, according to ice cores analyzed by George Denton, of the University of Maine, by 54 degrees in winter at Scoresby Sound, in eastern Greenland.

Not only temperatures crashed. Records of Chinese dust and African lakes and tropical trade winds and South American river flows and New Zealand glaciers all reveal dramatic changes happening in step 12,800 years ago. The world was much drier, windier and dustier. But in the Southern Hemisphere, temperatures may have gone in the opposite direction. Marine sediment cores show dramatic warming in the South Atlantic

and the Indian Ocean—as do temperature records in most Antarctic
ice cores.

The Younger Dryas freeze lasted for fifty or so generations: 1,300 years.
One can imagine tribes of *Homo sapiens* desperately relearning the crafts
that got their ancestors through the ice ages. But it may also have trig-
gered innovation. Some believe that dry conditions in the Middle East at
the time may have encouraged the first experiments with crop cultivation
and the domestication of animals. And then the freeze ended, and tem-
peratures returned to their former levels even faster than they had fallen.
Analysts of the Greenland ice-core chronology say publicly that the warm-
ing must have happened within a decade. But that is the minimum time
frame for the change of which they can be certain, given the resolution of
the ice cores. Richard Alley, who was there handling the ice cores, says:
"Most of that change looks like it happened in a single year. It could have
been less, perhaps even a single season. It was a weird time indeed." Like
The Day After Tomorrow, only in reverse.

All this is doubly strange, because the Younger Dryas cooling went against
the grain of all the long-term trends for the planet. The orbital changes
that had triggered the glaciation had faded by then; astronomical forces
were pushing the planet toward the next interglacial era. Of course, the
real work was being done by feedbacks like melting ice, the return of
greenhouse gases like carbon dioxide and methane into the atmosphere,
and the revival of the ocean conveyor. These feedbacks would have turned
a smooth progression into a series of jumps. But they would not easily have
altered the direction of change. So why the backward flip? What made cli-
mate plunge back into the icy abyss when all the forcings and all the feed-
backs should have been kicking the world into warmer times?

Chaos theory may help here. Alley says that it is just when conditions
are changing fastest that the chances for seemingly random, unexpected,
and abrupt change are greatest. The system is stirred up and vulnerable.
The drunk is on a rampage. And there is a reasonable chance that some of
the abrupt changes will be in the opposite direction to that expected. This
is what, in the clever subtitle to his 2001 report on abrupt climate change,
Alley called "inevitable surprise." What is equally clear is that at the time,

the entire planetary climate system had just two possible states: glacial and interglacial. It knew no third way. And so, during the several thousand years when it was on the cusp between the two, it flickered between them.

On the ground, one element was a sudden switch in Broecker's ocean conveyor. It would be going too far to say that the Younger Dryas proves that the global conveyor is the great climate switch that Broecker claims. But the event makes a compelling case that events in the far North Atlantic can, without help from astronomical or any other forces, sometimes have dramatic and long-lasting effects on global climate.

The unexpected switch of the ocean conveyor was almost certainly triggered by melting ice. In the final millennia of the ice age, as melting made fitful but sometimes dramatic progress, a very large amount of liquid water was produced. Often it did not pour directly into the oceans but formed giant lakes on the ice or on land around the edges. The largest known of these is called Lake Agassiz, after the discoverer of the ice ages. It stretched for more than 600 miles across a wide area of the American Midwest, from Saskatchewan to Ontario in Canada, and from the Dakotas to Minnesota in the U.S., generally moving with the advancing front of warming.

In the early stages of the deglaciation, the lake drained south, down the Mississippi River into the Gulf of Mexico. But about 12,800 years ago, it seems, something stopped this and forced the lake to drain east. Perhaps the route south was blocked by land gradually rising after the weight of the ice was removed. Perhaps the lake simply passed over a natural watershed as it moved north with the retreating face of the ice sheet. But at any rate, there was eventually a huge breakout of freshwater from the heart of North America into the basin now occupied by the Great Lakes, and on into the North Atlantic.

The vast inrush of cold freshwater would have drastically cooled and freshened the ocean. High salinity was critical for sustaining the newly revived, and perhaps still precarious, ocean conveyor. So a fresher ocean shut down the conveyor once more. The warm Gulf Stream was no longer drawn north. Temperatures crashed across the North Atlantic region, and probably particularly around Greenland. The entire global climate system would have been shaken, and may have lurched back from its interglacial to its glacial mode.

Little of this narrative is cut-and-dried. The evidence is patchy. Some doubt whether even a vast eruption of freshwater down the Saint Lawrence Seaway would have had much influence on ocean salinity on the other side of Greenland. And others, hard-line opponents of the Broecker hypothesis, wonder exactly how important the ocean conveyor is to global climate. Even Broecker admits that parts of the story are "a puzzle."

But new evidence is emerging all the time. One compelling rewrite of the Broecker narrative has come from John Chiang, of the University of California at Berkeley. His modeling studies of the North Atlantic suggest that the most critical event at the start of the Younger Dryas may have been not the shutdown of the ocean conveyor itself but the impact of the freshwater invasion on the formation of sea ice in the North Atlantic. He says that an invasion that diluted the flow of warm water from the Gulf Stream would have rapidly frozen the ocean surface. The freeze itself would have flipped a climate switch, preventing further deepwater formation, sealing out the Gulf Stream, and, through the ice-albedo feedback, dramatically chilling the entire region.

Broecker has adopted this idea as an elaboration of his conveyor scenario. Some others see it as a replacement or even a refutation. Alley says: "It looks like this is the real switch in the North Atlantic. In the winter, does the water sink before it freezes, or freeze before it sinks? Sink or freeze. There are only two possible answers. That's the switch." Fresher, colder water will freeze; warmer, more saline water will sink. If the water sinks, the conveyor remains in place and the Northern Hemisphere stays warm. If it freezes, the circulation halts and the westerly winds crossing the ocean toward Europe and Asia stop being warmed by the Gulf Stream and instead are chilled by thousands of miles of sea ice. "The difference between the two is the difference in places between temperatures at zero degrees Celsius [32°F] and at minus 30 degrees [-22°F]," says Alley.

And that switch flipped, Alley argues, at the start and the finish of the Younger Dryas. At the start, freshwater invaded the North Atlantic; the ocean froze, and within a decade "there were ice floes in the North Sea and permafrost in the Netherlands." The westerly winds would have picked up the cold of the Atlantic ice and blown it right across Europe and into Asia. They would have cooled the heart of the Eurasian landmass, preventing it from warming enough to generate the onshore winds that bring the monsoon rains to Asia. This revised narrative also explains the concurrent warming in the Southern Hemisphere. If the Gulf Stream was not flowing north, the heat that it once took across the equator stayed in the South Atlantic. So as the North of the planet froze, the South warmed. A freshwater release in northern Canada had become a global climatic cataclysm. One, moreover, that went against all the long-term trends of the time.

It took about 1,300 years before the North Atlantic water switched back to sinking rather than freezing in winter. There is no consensus on what finally flipped the switch. But when it happened, it was at least as fast as the original freeze. The North Atlantic no longer froze; instead, the water was salty and dense enough to sink. The ocean warmed; the winds warmed; temperatures were restored in a year; nature returned to reclaim the tundra; and deglaciation got back on track.

For some, this story is encouraging. If it takes huge volumes of cold water flowing out of a lake to switch off the ocean conveyor, they say, we should be safe. There are no unstable lakes around of the kind created by the melting of the ice sheets. In any case, the world is warmer today than it was even at the start of the Younger Dryas. It may be, says Alley, that the world climate system is much more stable in warm times than in cold times. But equally it may not. For one thing, the superwarm world we are creating may contain quite different perils. For another, even the old perils may not have been neutralized as much as optimists think.

There is a cautionary tale in what happened 8,200 years ago. Despite large amounts of warming after the demise of the Younger Dryas cold event, the ice had one last hurrah. Again there was a large intrusion of cold freshwater into the North Atlantic. Again there was a big freshwater release; again the ocean was covered by ice; and again there seems to have been a disruption to the global conveyor. This was a lesser event than the Younger Dryas—probably only regional in its impact on climate, and lasting for only about 350 years. But it was nonetheless one of the biggest climate shifts of the past 10,000 years. And perhaps most significant for us today, says Alley, it happened in a world markedly more like our own than that of the Younger Dryas. Temperatures were generally rather close to those of today, and the ice sheets were quite similar. The event suggests, if nothing else, that if sufficient freshwater were to invade the North Atlantic today, it could have a similar impact.

As we have seen, in recent decades large slugs of freshwater have poured into the far North Atlantic. They may have come close to triggering a shutdown of the ocean conveyor. This trend is unlikely to end. As the climate warms and the permafrost melts in Siberia, river flows from there into the Arctic Ocean are rising strongly. And there is always the prospect of future catastrophic melting of the Greenland ice sheet, where glaciers are accelerating and lakes are forming.

Gavin Schmidt, one of Hansen's climate modelers at the Goddard Institute for Space Studies, says that the event 8,200 years ago is a critical test for today's climate models. "If we are to make credible predictions about the risks we run today of catastrophic climate change, those models need to be able to reproduce what happened 8,200 years ago," he says. "If we could do that, it would be really good. It could tell us a lot about processes highly relevant for the climate of the twenty-first century."

$2\,5$

THE PULSE

How the sun makes climate change

The Arctic pack ice extended so far south that Eskimo fishing boats landed on the northern coast of Scotland. They didn't meet much opposition, because the hungry Highlanders had abandoned their crofts after grain harvests had failed for seven straight years, and had gone raiding for food in the lowlands to the south. In the 1690s temperatures in Scotland were more than 3°F below normal; snow lay on the ground long into the summer. Those who stayed behind were reduced to eating nettles and making bread from tree bark. The political repercussions of this Scottish turmoil are still with us today. The king became so worried by fears of insurrection that he shipped off angry clansmen and their starving families to set up Presbyterian colonies in Catholic Northern Ireland. And eventually, after widespread famine in the 1690s brought despair about the future for the Scots as a nation, the clan chiefs forged a union with England.

This was the little ice age: a climatic affair that began early in the fourteenth century and flickered on and off before peaking in the late seventeenth century and finally releasing its grip some 150 years ago. Like a mild echo of the ice ages, it spread its icy fingers from the north across Europe, pushing Alpine glaciers down valleys, creating spectacular skating scenes for the Dutch painters Breugel and Van der Neer, and allowing Londoners to enjoy the frolics of regular frost fairs on the frozen River Thames. On one occasion, Henry VIII traveled by sleigh down the river to Greenwich, and on another an elephant was led across the ice near Blackfriars Bridge.

There were some warm periods amid the cold. In the 1420s, an armada of Chinese explorers is reputed to have sailed around the north coast of

Greenland, a journey that would be impossible even in today's reduced Arctic ice. Between about 1440 and 1540, England was mild enough for cherries to be cultivated in the northeastern Durham hills. Much of Europe was exceptionally warm in the 1730s. But at the height of the little ice age, the Baltic Sea froze over, and there was widespread famine across northern Europe. Some suggest that half the populations of Norway and Sweden perished. Iceland was cut off by sea ice for years on end, and its shoals of cod abandoned the seas nearby for warmer climes. Some say the cold was the hidden hand behind the famine, rising grain prices, and bread riots that triggered the French Revolution in 1789.

In North America, tribes banded together into the League of the Iroquois to share scarce food supplies. The Cree gave up farming corn and went back to hunting bison. But the era was symbolized most poignantly by the collapse of a Viking settlement founded in the balmy days of the eleventh century by Leif Erikson. The Viking king had a real-estate broker's flair for coining a good name: he called the place Greenland to attract settlers. The settlement on the southern tip of the Arctic island thrived for 400 years, but by the mid-fifteenth century, crops were failing and sea ice cut off any chance of food aid from Europe.

If the Viking settlers had followed the ways of their Eskimo neighbors and turned to hunting seals and polar bears, they might have survived. But instead, they stuck to their hens and sheep and grain crops, and built ever-bigger churches in the hope that God would save them. He did not. When relief finally arrived, nobody was left alive in the settlement. Creeping starvation had cut the average height of a Greenland Viking from a sturdy five feet nine inches to a stunted five feet. The last women were so deformed that they were probably incapable of bearing a new generation. We know all this because their buried corpses were preserved in the spreading permafrost.

The little ice age, first documented in the 1960s by the British climate historian Hubert Lamb, is now an established part of Europe's history. It has often been seen as just a historical curiosity—a nasty but local blip in a balmy world of European climatic certainty. But it is increasingly clear that what Europe termed the little ice age was close to a global climatic convulsion, which took different forms in different places.

Because it came and went over several centuries, the task of attributing different climate events around the world to the influence of the little ice age is fraught with difficulties. But reasonable cases have been made that it blanketed parts of Ethiopia with snow, destroyed crops and precipitated the collapse of the Ming dynasty in seventeenth-century China, and spread ice across Lake Superior in North America. In the tropics, temperatures were probably largely unchanged, but rainfall patterns altered substantially. In the Amazon basin, the centuries of Europe's little ice age were so dry that fires ravaged the tinderbox rainforests. In the Sahara, which often seems to experience climate trends opposite to those in the Amazon, repeated floods in the early seventeenth century washed away the great desert city of Timbuktu.

The little ice age is not the only climate anomaly in recorded history. Another, known because of its influence on European climate as the medieval warm period, ran from perhaps 800 to 1300, ending just as the little ice age began. Because it is rather more distant than the little ice age, its history and nature are rather less clear. Certainly, at various times grains grew farther north in Norway than they do today, and vineyards flourished on the Pennines, in England. Warmth brought Europe wealth. There was an orgy of construction of magnificent Gothic cathedrals. The Vikings, as we have seen, set up in Greenland at a time when parts of it could certainly be described as green. Some claim that the medieval warm period may have been warmer even than the early twenty-first century. But most researchers are much more cautious.

Reconstructions of past temperatures come mainly from looking at the growth rings of old trees. There are exceptions, but generally, the wider the rings, the stronger the annual growth and the warmer the summer. Keith Briffa, a British specialist in extracting climate information from tree rings, says: "The seventeenth century was undoubtedly cold. The evidence that the period 1570 to 1850 was also cold seems pretty robust. But the medieval warm period is still massively uncertain. There is not much data, and so much spatial bias in the data. We think there was a warm period around AD 900, certainly at high northern latitudes in summer, where we have the tree-ring evidence. But we have virtually nothing else." It looks likely that much of Europe was between 1.8 and 3.6°F warmer in the medieval warm period than it was in the early twentieth century, while the little ice age was a similar amount cooler in Europe. But any global trends were almost certainly much smaller.

In any case, to talk about a medieval warm period at all is, in the view of many, a very Eurocentric view. Tree rings from the Southern Hemisphere show no sign of anything similar there. Indeed, away from the North Atlantic, those centuries were, if anything, characterized by long superdroughts that caused the collapse of several major civilizations. In Central America, the Mayans had thrived for 2,000 years and built one of the world's most advanced and long-lasting civilizations. Theirs was a sophisticated, urbanized, and scientific and technologically advanced society of around 10 million people, with prolific artistic activities and strong trade links with its neighbors, and seemingly every resource necessary to carry on thriving—strikingly like our own in many respects. Yet faced with three decades-long droughts between the years 800 and 950, which may have been the worst in the region since the end of the ice age, the entire society crumbled, leaving its remains in the jungle. A few hundred miles north, a number of advanced native North American societies collapsed under the impact of sustained droughts through the American West. Best documented are the Anasazi people, ancestors of the modern Pueblo Indians. They had built elaborate apartment complexes in the canyons of New Mexico, and had developed sophisticated irrigation systems for growing crops, but were forced to flee into the wilderness after a long drought that peaked in the 1280s.

The little ice age and the medieval warm period appear to have been recent natural examples of climate change. Though the warming and cooling implied in their names may have been restricted largely to the North Atlantic region, they seem to have left a signature in glaciers and megadroughts across the planet. So what caused them? And does it have anything to tell us about our own future climate? Many theories have been advanced.

The pendulum moves too fast for any orbital cycles. Some theorists have suggested a role for volcanic eruptions, which shroud the planet with aerosols that can cool it. It is true that at certain times during the little ice age, there were major eruptions. The year after the eruption of Tambora, in Indonesia, in 1815, crops failed from India to Europe and North America. It became known as "the year without a summer." But volcanic dust clouds cool temperatures for only a few years at most. They may from time to time have exacerbated the cooling, but they were not sufficiently frequent or unusual to explain a cold era that lasted on and off for almost half a millennium.

Most climatologists believe that the sun should get the blame. The coldest part of the little ice age, in the mid-to-late seventeenth century, is known as the Maunder Minimum. The popularizing of the telescope by Galileo a few decades before meant that astronomers of the day were able to note the virtual disappearance between 1645 and 1715 of the by-then-familiar spots on the surface of the sun. This is now recognized as a good indicator of a reduced output of solar energy. The best guess is that solar radiation reaching Earth's surface during the Maunder Minimum fell by perhaps half a watt per 10.8 square feet, or around 0.2 percent. But climatologists find it perplexing that such a widespread effect could result from such a modest change.

Enter an idiosyncratic, larger-than-life researcher working at the Lamont-Doherty Earth Observatory, just down the corridor from Wally Broecker. His name was Bond, Gerard Bond. Like Broecker, he hated getting bogged down in detail, and liked seeing the big picture. Like Broecker, he was willing to fly a kite, trusted his intuition, and had the confidence to propose an idea in public just to see if anyone could shoot it down. And, again like his compatriot, he had the intellectual reputation to get his kite-flying published in the often conservative scientific literature.

Bond argued forcefully until his death, in 2005, that the little ice age and the medieval warm period were the most recent signs of a pervasive pulse in the world's climatic system. This pulse, he said, had a cycle that recurred once every 1,500 years or so. It was a pulse, moreover, that seemed largely unaffected by other, apparently bigger influences on global climate, like the Milankovitch orbital cycles that triggered the major glaciations. Ice age or no ice age, he argued, the pulse just kept on going. Bond didn't invent the pulse out of thin air. Other researchers had unwittingly been on its trail for years. But, like his friend down the corridor, Bond was the man who had the confidence to compose a big picture out of the scattered fragments of evidence.

In the early 1980s, a graduate student in Germany made the first breakthrough. While at the University of Göttingen, Hartmut Heinrich was examining cores of sediment drilled from the bed of the North Atlantic. He found a number of curious layers of rock fragments that showed up in cores drilled as far apart as the east coast of Canada, the waters west of the British Isles, and around Bermuda. Radiocarbon dating revealed that these rock fragments were laid down in at least six bands over the 60,000 years before the end of the last glaciation, at intervals of roughly 8,000 years.

I looked at some of these rock fragments in the marine sediment store at Bond's old laboratory in New York. They are enormously distinctive. A browse among the trays of sediment revealed fairly subtle differences among the different cores: a change of color here, a slightly different consistency of dust there. Almost everything in these sediments has gone through the mill of being eroded from Earth's surface, discharged down rivers, and dumped in tiny bits on the seabed. But then there are Heinrich's layers. These are a mass of stones the size of gravel or pebbles, but sharp-edged and clearly untouched by the normal processes of erosion and deposition. Researchers soon gave the events that produced them their own name: Heinrich events. There was nothing like them in the sediment record.

Apart from their size and shape, something else was odd about these rock fragments. Though they had been found way out in the middle of the Atlantic Ocean, geologists swiftly established that they came from the Hudson Bay area of northern Canada. How could they have got so far offshore and so far south? What took them there? The only logical explanation, given that all the Heinrich events took place during the last glaciation, was that they had been ripped from the bedrock by great glaciers and carried south on the underside of icebergs. They traveled a long way because the North Atlantic was extremely cold, and were eventually dumped onto the ocean floor as the icebergs melted. That raised other questions. What climatic events would send vast armadas of icebergs sailing south into the tropics? And why the apparent 8,000-year cycle?

The next clue came a few years later, in the early 1990s, when a distin-guished Danish glaciologist, Willi Dansgaard, of the University of Co-penhagen, discovered in the Greenland ice-core record a series of large and sudden temperature changes that again punctuated the last glaciation. Several times, temperatures leaped up by 3.6 to 18°F within a decade or so, before recovering after a few hundred years. So far, more than twenty of these warm phases have been identified in the ice-core record. During many of them, temperatures in Europe at least may have been as warm as today.

These warming events, too, seemed to have some kind of periodicity or pulse. Temperatures moved from cold to warm and back again repeatedly, with a cycle ranging between 1,300 and 1,800 years. It was a recogniza-ble pulse, just as a human pulse that races and then slows is recognizable, and averaged a full cycle roughly every 1,500 years. This pulse also swiftly got a name, the rather cumbersome Dansgaard-Oeschger cycle, after Dans-gaard and his Swiss colleague, Hans Oeschger. Some interpret the data as showing a continuous background temperature cycle that on most but not all occasions triggered a more substantial warming episode during its warm phase, and on rather fewer occasions triggered a Heinrich event dur-ing its cold phase.

The connection between Heinrich events and the Dansgaard-Oeschger cycle wasn't recognized immediately—understandably enough. They had different time signatures, and one was revealed in the sediments of the mid-Atlantic, while the other emerged from the Greenland ice cores. Both, in any case, seemed at first to be minor local curiosities confined to the last glaciation, and therefore of no relevance to modern climate. But Bond had a hunch that the two were linked in some way, and that they had a global significance. Both, he noted, appeared to coincide with other cli-mate changes, such as the advances and retreat of glaciers in Europe and North America. Like the Younger Dryas event and the climate flip 8,200 years ago, they seemed either to push the world into a different climate mode or to be part of such a process. Down the corridor, Bond's buddy Broecker was on hand to suggest a possible link to the ocean conveyor. The story began to take on a life of its own. But first the pair needed evidence to back up their hunch.

Bond began to re-examine trays of sediment cores from the bed of the North Atlantic that were assembled in his New York archive. Some were old cores, taken years before by the Lamont-Doherty research vessel *Vema* from beneath the waters off Ireland and the channel between Greenland and Iceland. Others were new, drilled off Newfoundland under Bond's supervision.

As expected, Bond found further evidence of Heinrich's rock fragments roughly every 8,000 years or so through the last glaciation. But the marine sediment cores also revealed lesser layers of materials normally alien to the seabed of the North Atlantic. Most exciting of all, these lesser layers occurred roughly every 1,500 years, and appeared to coincide with the cold phase of the Dansgaard-Oeschger cycle in the Greenland ice cores. This was pay dirt. Doubly so when it became clear that the iceberg armadas of the Heinrich events occurred during unusually cold phases of the Dansgaard-Oeschger cycle. The pattern seemed to involve a large Heinrich event, followed by five less and less severe 1,500-year Dansgaard-Oeschger cycles, and then another big Heinrich event. Sometimes this stately progression is influenced by other cycles, such as a solar precession, but otherwise it seems to hold.

Most remarkable of all, perhaps, Bond found that although there have been no Heinrich events during the 10,000 years since the end of the last ice age—the last was 15,000 years ago—the marine imprint of the underlying 1,500-year pulse has not missed a beat. "The oscillations carry on no matter what the state of the climate," he said.

Bond died in 2005, at the age of sixty-five. His longtime colleague Peter deMenocal has continued his work, looking for more signs of the pulse. Examining seabed sediments off Africa's west coast, he has found that every 1,500 years or so there were huge increases in dust particles in the sediments, suggesting big dust storms on land. The sediments also revealed dramatic increases in the remains of temperature-sensitive marine plankton, suggesting a temperature switchback in tropical Africa of as much as 9°F. "The transitions were sharp," deMenocal says. "Climate changes that we thought should take thousands of years to happen occurred within a generation or two."

Bond's final claim, that the pulse can be seen in recurrent climatic events right through to the present, seems to be vindicated, especially by temperatures in Europe and North America. There was an especially strong cooling event in the Northern Hemisphere that ended around 2,000 years ago; it was replaced by the medieval warm period that reached its height perhaps 1,100 years ago, and then by another cold era that bottomed out around 350 years ago, during the Maunder Minimum—when temperatures fell by up to 3.6°F in northern Europe, and the Eskimos reached Scotland in their kayaks.

Bond's study was an extraordinary piece of detective work. But it raises more questions than it answers. Two stand out. What, if any, is the relationship between these cycles and other parts of the climate system, such as Broecker's ocean conveyor? And, of course, what causes the mysterious pulse?

Heinrich originally argued that his ice armadas must be the result of some instability in the North American ice sheet that caused periodic collapses into the North Atlantic. There might thus be some link to big freshwater breakouts like that which triggered the Younger Dryas event. Certainly they involved huge amounts of ice. But the timing is fuzzy. Bond argued that while instabilities in the ice sheet could explain Heinrich events, only some of his pulses produced Heinrich events. So instability in ice sheets is unlikely to explain the pulses themselves, which in any case seem to have been unaffected by glaciations. By 2001, Bond believed he had confirmed the answer that many suspected all along.

He went back to the Greenland ice cores to look for evidence of solar cycles. There is no known direct marker for solar cycles in the cores. But other researchers had discovered that isotopic traces of cosmic rays bombarding the atmosphere were left in the ice cores—and that when solar radiation is at its most intense, cosmic rays are literally blown away from the solar system. Thus fewer "cosmogenic" isotopes, like carbon-14 and beryllium-10, are left in the ice cores during periods of strong solar radiation.

Bond came up trumps again. The evidence tallied. Over the past 12,000 years, fluctuations in detritus from the iceberg armadas in the Atlantic coincided with changes in cosmogenic isotopes in the ice cores. Thus there was a solar pulse that translated into a pulse in icebergs, global temperatures, and recurrent climatic events found through both the glacial and the postglacial eras.

Bond was convinced before his death that most climate change over the past 10,000 years had been driven by his solar pulse, amplified through feedbacks such as ice formation and the changing intensity of the ocean conveyor. He worried that people might interpret this as showing that global warming was natural. "But that would be a misuse of the data," he told me in an interview shortly before his death. Rather, he said, the most important lesson from his research is what it shows about the sensitivity of the system itself: "Earth's climate system is highly sensitive to extremely weak perturbations in the sun's energy output." And if it is sensitive to weak changes in solar forcing, it is likely to be sensitive also "to other forcings, such as those caused by human additions of greenhouse gases to the atmosphere."

What, exactly, drives the amplifications is another matter, however. For years, as Bond worked on his ideas, Broecker had declared that the Dansgaard-Oeschger temperature cycle in Greenland was linked to fluctuations in his ocean conveyor. Certainly the geography seemed right. Both appeared to originate in the far North Atlantic. It seemed clear, too, that during the periods when ice armadas were floating south in the Atlantic, temperatures in the North Atlantic were cold, and the amount of deep water being formed around Greenland declined. In extreme cases—perhaps during full-scale Heinrich events—the conveyor probably shut down. Perhaps a reduction in solar radiation triggered the entire sequence. But the evidence of what caused what was largely circumstantial. And as we will see later, there is another explanation, producing a large amplification from another quarter entirely.

But whatever the amplifier, the pulse is real and extremely pervasive. In the postglacial era, perhaps only in the past fifty years has something come along with greater power to disrupt climate.

VI

TROPICAL HEAT

2 6

THE FALL

The end of Africa's golden age

If there was a golden age for humans on Earth—a Garden of Eden that flowed with milk and honey—then it was the high point of the Holocene, the era that followed the end of the last ice age. From around 8,000 to around 5,500 years ago, the world was as warm as it is today, but there appear to have been few strong hurricanes and few disruptive El Niños; and it was certainly a world in which the regions occupied today by great deserts in Asia, the Americas, and especially Africa were much wetter than they are now. Optimists suggest that such conditions might await us in a greenhouse world. As we shall see, there are celestial reasons why that might not happen. But the Holocene era, and its abrupt end, may still offer important lessons about our future climate in the twenty-first century.

No place on Earth exemplifies the fall from this climatically blessed state better than the Sahara. The world's largest desert was not always so arid. Where seas of sand now shimmer in the sun, there were once vast lakes, swamps, and rivers. Lake Chad, which today covers a paltry few hundred square miles, was then a vast inland sea, dubbed Lake Megachad by scientists. It was the size of France, Spain, Germany, and the UK put together. Today, the lake evaporates in the desert sun; but then, it overflowed its inland basin and, at different times, drained south via Nigeria into the Atlantic Ocean, or east down a vast wadi to the Nile.

The difference is that back then, the Sahara had assured rains. The whole of North Africa was watered by a monsoon system rather like the one that keeps much of Asia wet today. Rain-bearing winds penetrated deep into the interior. From Senegal to the Horn of Africa, and from the shores of the Mediterranean to the threshold of the central African rainforest, vast rivers flowed for thousands of miles. Along their banks were swamps, forests, and verdant bush.

Beneath the Algerian desert, archaeologists have found the sand-choked remains of wadis that once drained some 600 miles from the Ahaggar Mountains into the Mediterranean. And in southern Libya, a region so waterless that even camel trains avoid it, archaeologists are finding the bones of crocodiles and hippos, elephants and antelope. If there was a vestige of true desert at the heart of North Africa, it was very much smaller than the desert is today. And, of course, there were people—shepherds and fishers and hunters—and some of the earliest known fields of grains like sorghum and millet. Archaeologists digging in the sands of northern Chad, currently the dustiest place on Earth, have found human settlements around the shores of the ancient Lake Megachad. Paintings in caves deep in the desert depict the lives of the inhabitants of the verdant Sahara of the Holocene.

There are other remains from this time. Rocks beneath the Sahara contain the largest underground reservoir of freshwater in the world. They were filled mostly by leaking wadis in the early Holocene. Some desert settlements today tap these waters at oases. Colonel Gadhafi has constructed pumps and a huge pipeline network to take this water from beneath southern Libya to his coastal farmers. He calls the network his Great Man-made River, though it is a feeble imitation of the real rivers that once ran here.

The wet Sahara and the era known more generally as the African Humid Period began around 13,000 years ago, as the ice age abated; and, except for the Younger Dryas hiatus, it lasted right through to the end of the golden age. It coincided with a time when Earth's precession ensured that the sun was blazing down on the Sahara with full intensity in summer. The land cooked, and convective air currents were strong. As the warm air rose, wet air was drawn in from over the Atlantic to replace it. The process was the same one that creates today's monsoon-rain system in Asia. Meanwhile, the monsoon rains were recycled by the rich vegetation across North Africa. Rather as in the Amazon today, the rain nurtured lush vegetation that ensured that much of it evaporated back into the air. The continually moistened winds took rain to the heart of the Sahara.

But the African Humid Period came to an end very suddenly. In the space of perhaps a century, the rivers of the Sahara emptied, the swamps dried up, the bush died, and the monsoon rain clouds were replaced by clouds of wind-blown sand. The climate system had crossed a threshold that triggered massive change. What happened? The first answer is that the sun moved. Or, rather, the precession continued its stately progress and gradually took away the extremely favorable conditions for Saharan rains. And as summer solar heating lessened, the warm air rose a little less and the monsoon winds from the ocean penetrated a little less far inland some years. The process was gradual, and went on without any appreciable effect on rainfall in most of the Sahara for more than 3,000 years. The vegetation feedback ensured that, at least in most years, the rain kept falling. If Lake Megachad was retreating, we have no evidence of it.

But at some point, the feedback began to falter. Perhaps there was a chance variation in rainfall that dried out the bush for a year or two. The sun was no longer strong enough to make good and revive the rains. Suddenly, what had been a feedback that kept the Sahara watered became a feedback that dried it out. The system as a whole had passed a threshold, and it never recovered. The green Sahara had become a brown Sahara. The North African monsoon rains had died.

Not everybody agrees that the vegetation feedback was the only trigger for the drying of the Sahara. One of Gerard Bond's solar pulses may have had some influence. But climate models show that in all probability, this flip in the Saharan climate was extremely sudden. Martin Claussen, of the Potsdam Institute for Climate Impact Research, in Germany, has played out this tragedy in detail in his model. He turns time forward and backward, recreates the subtle orbital changes, and fine-tunes the vegetation feedbacks. More or less whatever he does to mimic the conditions of 5,500 years ago, the result is the same. The system flips abruptly, turning bush to desert, and seas of water to seas of sand.

Other researchers have replicated his findings. Peter deMenocal, of Lamont-Doherty, calculates that the system flipped when solar radiation in the Sahara crossed a threshold of 470 watts per 10.8 square feet. Jon Foley, of the University of Wisconsin, found that a reduction in Holocene summer sun sufficient to reduce temperatures by just 0.72°F would have cut rainfall across the Sahara by a quarter, and by much more in the farthest interior of the continent. He says that once a region like the Sahara becomes dry and brown, it requires exceptional rains to break the feedback and trigger a regreening. Beyond a certain point—such as that reached 5,500 years ago—virtually no amount of extra rain is likely to be enough. The lack of vegetation "acts to lock in and reinforce the drought."

Back then, the people of the Sahara couldn't have known whether the droughts that suddenly afflicted them were permanent or not. But as the desert asserted control across the region, and the lakes and waterways dried up, they had no alternative but to leave. As part of the exodus, lakeside settlements near the Sudanese border in Egypt were all abandoned at about the same time. One was Nabta, famous now as the site of the world's earliest known stone structures with an astronomical purpose. They predate Stonehenge, in England, by about a thousand years. The key stones point to where the sun would have set at the summer solstice 6,000 years ago. Beneath some of the stones are burial sites for the cattle that the people tended. Nobody can be sure what the precise purpose of the structures was, but it is intriguing to suppose that they were used in an attempt to track the celestial changes that were disrupting the rains and turning their pastures to desert.

It may have been from such places that the myths and legends of past golden ages, and of the Garden of Eden, first emerged. The people who departed from the Sahara to set up new homes on the Nile or even farther afield would have taken their memories of a golden past. Researchers who have tried to date events in the Bible calculate mankind's expulsion from the Garden of Eden at around 6,000 years ago, when kingdoms across the Sahara would have been collapsing. But the Garden of Eden need not have been in the Sahara, because similar stories were played out elsewhere. Arabia dried out at the same time, leaving behind a huge underground reservoir of water not much smaller than that beneath the Sahara. Claussen calculates that the desertification of Arabia could have been caused by the same combination of gradual orbital change and a dramatic vegetation feedback.

The evidence is as yet sketchy, but the dramatic drying of the Sahara and Arabia appears to coincide with other climate changes around the world. In the Pacific Ocean, El Niño appeared to switch into a more active mode at around this time. There were cold periods from the Andes to the European Alps. In both cases, glaciers advanced strongly down their valleys; many of them are only today returning to their former positions. In the Austrian Tyrol, one victim of the advance was the "ice man" named Otzi, whose freeze-dried remains emerged from melting ice in 1991. In Ireland, a 7,000-year temperature record held in tree rings shows a cold era that included the coldest summers in the entire record, at about this time.

All this is particularly intriguing because—unlike during previous great climatic events of the era of the ice ages—there is little evidence that the primary action had much to do with the polar regions. It seems to have been an abrupt climate change formed in the tropics, with its major impacts there, and only ripples beyond. One in the eye for Wally Broecker, some of its investigators have been heard to say—a point to which we will return.

But what does this say about the future of the Sahara? Could warming in the twenty-first century trigger a greener, wetter Sahara? It is an intriguing idea, with plenty of adherents. Reindert Haarsma, a climate modeler at the Royal Netherlands Meteorological Institute, says the Sahara could be destined for a 50 percent increase in rainfall—enough to trigger a return to the golden age, in which crocodiles floated through swamps where today locusts swarm. Claussen, whose model first stimulated the idea, is more skeptical. He points out that the orbital situation now is very different, so summer solar radiation is not great enough to create a revived African monsoon. DeMenocal says solar radiation is currently 4 percent lower in the Sahara than it was when the Holocene flip occurred. But on the other hand, he admits, much higher levels of carbon dioxide in the air might compensate for this by stimulating an earlier recovery of Sahara vegetation.

Optimists point out that on a very modest scale, something of a revival is going on in Saharan rains and vegetation—albeit from the depths of the droughts that afflicted the region in the 1970s and 1980s. It hasn't happened everywhere, and some places have since slipped back. But, according to Chris Reij, of the Free University, in Amsterdam, improved farming methods, such as digging terraces and holding water on the land, may have

encouraged a modest greening of parts of the Sahara, and the resulting veg-
etation feedback could be one reason for the revived rains. But it would be
a big step to predict from that a reversion to the "Garden of Eden" days.

While some in the Sahara may conceivably be able to look forward to
greener, wetter times, the prognosis for many other arid regions around
the world is not so good. The big fear, from the American West to north-
ern China, and from southern Africa to the Mediterranean, is of a twenty-
first century dominated by longer and fiercer droughts.

Again, history is the first guide. DeMenocal has been looking at the
history of droughts and civilization in the Americas, and finds strong ev-
idence of periods of drought much longer than any known in modern
times. "There is good scientific evidence that vast regions of North Amer-
ica witnessed several such periods during the last millennium, with dev-
astating cultural consequences," he says. "These megadroughts can persist
for a century or more."

The six-year Dust Bowl of the 1930s, which caused mass migrations
westward, was "pale by comparison" with its predecessors. Droughts in the
nineteenth century devastated many Native Americans as well as their bi-
son. At the end of the sixteenth century, a twenty-two-year drought de-
stroyed an early English colony at Roanoke, in Virginia. It became known
as the Lost Colony after all its inhabitants disappeared between their ar-
rival, in 1587, and the return of a supply ship four years later. Going back
earlier, tree rings show there was near permanent drought from 900 to
1300 west of the Mississippi and through Central America, which de-
stroyed the Mayan and Anasazi civilizations. DeMenocal concludes that
complex, organized societies can get by in short droughts. They have
stocks of food and water, and know how to trade their way out of trouble
in the short term. But few of them can deal with megadroughts. If hunger
doesn't get them, the strife and turmoil caused by trying to survive does.

And the signs are that worsening droughts are becoming the norm in
regions that have suffered megadroughts in the past. In the American
West, the biggest river, the Colorado, is a shadow of its former self. Early
in the twentieth century, the average flow was 13 million acre-feet a year.
From 1999 to 2003, the average sank to 7 million acre-feet—worse even

than the Dust Bowl years. In 2002, it fell to just 3 million acre-feet. In 2005, the drought was continuing. In Central Asia, the Afghan war of 2002 was fought against a backdrop of drought as debilitating as any Taliban tyranny. The Hamoun wetland, which covers 1,500 square miles on the remote border between Afghanistan and Iran, has for millennia been a place of refuge for people from both countries in times of trouble. But that year it dried out and turned to salt flats. The water has not returned. Southern Europe is increasingly beset by forest fires and desiccated crops.

Richard Seager, of Lamont-Doherty, says that there is a long-standing correlation between drought in the western U.S. and drought in South America, parts of Europe, and Central Asia. And that is a pattern we see reasserting itself in the twenty-first century, as the Arizona desert creeps north, southern Europe increasingly resembles North Africa, and Central Asia takes on the appearance of Iraq or the Arabian Peninsula. Kevin Trenberth, of the National Center for Atmospheric Research, reports that the percentage of Earth's land area stricken by serious drought has more than doubled in thirty years. In the 1970s, less than 15 percent of the land was drought-stricken, but by the first years of the twenty-first century, around 30 percent was. "The climate models predict increased drying over most land areas," he says. "Our analyses suggest that this may already have begun."

That seems to be a common view. Mark Cane, a specialist in Pacific weather at Lamont-Doherty, says scarily: "The medieval warm period a thousand years ago was a very small forcing compared to what is going on with global warming now. But it was still strong enough to cause a 300- to 400-year drought in the western U.S. That could be an analogue for what will happen under anthropogenic warming. If the mechanisms we think work hold true, then we'll get big droughts in the West again." The Garden of Eden it is not.

Many believe that El Niño and the pattern of ocean temperatures in the Pacific are heavily implicated in the historical megadroughts, perhaps as part of a global reorganization of climate systems linked to Gerard Bond's pulses. And this should set modern alarm bells ringing, says Ed Cook, a leading tree-ring expert at Lamont-Doherty: "If warming over the tropical Pacific promotes drought over the western U.S. . . . any trend toward warmer temperatures could lead to a serious long-term increase in aridity over western North America." Martin Hoerling, of the National Oceanic and Atmospheric Administration, thinks that such a process is already under way. He blames the increasing droughtiness of the tropics on a persistent ocean warming in the Pacific that, he says, is "unsurpassed during the twentieth century." The pattern of dryness is beginning to look less like a local, short-term aberration and more like a long-term trend, he says, and he predicts that global warming "may be a harbinger of future severe and extensive droughts."

It won't happen everywhere, of course. Climate models predict that a warmer world will, on average, have more moisture in the atmosphere, and that, in general, the wet places will get wetter and the dry places will get drier. They predict that areas of uplift, where rising air will trigger storm clouds and abundant rain, will see the uplift become more intense. But areas of sinking air, which are the traditional desert lands of the world, will see more-intense sinking and drying. In many parts of the world, this "hyperweather" is likely to set competing forces against each other. Stronger storms will blow off the oceans, and monsoon-type rains may begin again in some places. But the rain-bearing winds will often be confronted by intensifying arid zones of descending air in the continental interiors. It is not obvious which force will win, and where.

Will the Sahara Desert expand and intensify, as drought theorists argue? Or will North Africa be reclaimed by a revived African monsoon? Megadrought or Garden of Eden? Nobody can answer that question yet. Perhaps the greatest likelihood is that in many places, from the Sahara to the American West and Arabia, there will be more and longer droughts, interspersed with brief but devastating outbreaks of intense storms and floods.

SEESAW ACROSS THE OCEAN

How the Sahara Desert greens the Amazon

Two of the world's largest and most fragile ecosystems face each other across the Atlantic. On one side is the Amazon rainforest; on the other the Sahara. They seem to be ecological opposites, and unconnected. The Sahara is rainless and largely empty of vegetation. The Amazon is one of the wettest places on Earth, and certainly the most biologically diverse, with perhaps half of the world's species beneath its canopy. But these two opposites are not so far apart. For one thing, the physical gap is surprisingly small. The Atlantic is narrow near the equator, and the two ecosystems are less than half as far apart as London and New York. For another, many believe they have a surprising symbiosis. Their fates may be intertwined in a rather unexpected way—and one that could have important consequences in the coming decades.

The key to the symbiosis lies in the remote heart of the Sahara, a region called Bodele, in northern Chad. Few people go here. It is littered with unexploded bombs and land mines left behind during Libya's invasion of Chad in the 1980s. And it is by far the dustiest place on Earth. Satellite images show year-round dust storms raging across Bodele and entering the atmospheric circulation. According to Richard Washington, of Oxford University, two fifths of the dust in the global atmosphere comes from the Sahara, and half of that comes from Bodele.

Some of this dust stays local. But much of it is carried on the prevailing winds, which cross the desert wastes of Niger, Mali, and Mauritania before heading out across the Atlantic. The red dust clouds can grow almost 2 miles high as they approach America. They cause spectacular sunrises over Miami, before falling in the rains of the Caribbean and the

Amazon. And there have been a lot of good sunrises in recent decades. The amount of dust crossing the Atlantic grew fivefold between the wet 1960s and the dry 1980s.

The Sahara dust has a series of unexpected effects on the Americas. According to hurricane forecasters in Florida, during dry, dusty years in the Sahara, there are fewer hurricanes on the other side of the Atlantic. It seems that dust in the air interrupts the critical updrafts of warm, moist air that fuel the storms. Equally surprisingly, desert bacteria caught up in the winds are being blamed for bringing new diseases to Caribbean coral reefs, and even for triggering asthma among Caribbean children.

And there is another important link. Saharan dust storms carry huge amounts of minerals and organic matter that enrich soils widely in the Americas. Bodele dust seems especially valuable. Its dunes are the dried-out remains of the bed of the vast Lake Megachad, which covered the central Sahara until its abrupt demise. Most of the dunes are made not of sand or broken rock but of the remains of trillions of diatoms, microscopic fresh-water creatures that once lived in huge numbers in the lake. These fragments blow freely in the wind. That's why they make such plentiful dust storms. And they also make great fertilizer. If Bodele had any rain, the diatoms would make rich farmland. Instead, Chad's loss is the Americas' gain, says Hans Joachim Schellnhuber, a German physicist turned Earth-system scientist, who, as director of Britain's Tyndall Climate Centre, in Norwich, has made a study of the unlikely connection. "Bizarre as it may seem, the arid, barren Sahara fertilizes the Amazon rainforest. This process has been going on for thousands of years, and is one reason why the Amazon basin teems with life."

The two unique habitats are on a kind of seesaw, he says. When the Sahara is dry, as it has been for much of the past quarter century, its dust crosses the Atlantic in huge quantities and fertilizes the Amazon, making the rainforest superabundant. When the Sahara is wet, the dust storms subside and the Amazon goes hungry. That the Sahara seems to have only two basic modes, wet and dry, suggests that there may be two distinct modes in the Amazon, too. The last big change in the Sahara came 5,500 years ago, when the region lurched from wet to dry, probably within a few decades. As yet we know little about how the Amazon changed at that time. But if Schellnhuber is right, the Sahara's loss at that time may have been the Amazon's gain. There may have been a major change for the better in the rainforests.

In the twenty-first century, the seesaw could be on the move again. There are hints that the Sahara may become wetter, says Schellnhuber. And if the wetting turns to greening, and the vegetation feedback kicks in, the whole of North Africa could change dramatically. That would be good news for the Sahara, of course. But it might be bad news for the Amazon, which already seems to be close to its own tipping point, as the climate dries and rainforests give up their carbon. Could a wetter Sahara be the final nail in the Amazon's coffin? Schellnhuber believes it could.

2 8

TROPICAL HIGH

Why an ice man is rewriting climate history

There are two special things about Lonnie Thompson. First, doctors reckon that he has spent more time on mountains above 20,000 feet than any other lowlander on the planet. And second, in his freezer back home in Columbus, Ohio, he has probably the most detailed physical record anywhere of the climate of planet Earth over the past 20,000 years. Not bad for the sixty-year-old son of a hick from Gassaway, a tiny railroad town in West Virginia.

Make that three things. Because Thompson is, in a mild-mannered but determined way, a revolutionary in the world of glaciology. For four decades now, climate scientists have been drilling ice cores in the polar regions to find the secrets of climates past. They have found a lot, and they have developed some impressive theories about how the world's climate system is driven from these cold wastelands. But thirty years ago, Thompson, then still a graduate student in the geology of coal with a temporary post drilling ice cores in Antarctica, set out to prove them wrong about the origins of climate.

With his early mentor, the legendary British glaciologist John Mercer, Thompson ignored the poles and began drilling ice cores in glaciers high in the Andes, the Himalayas, and other mountain regions of the tropics. This was unheard of at the time. Finding funding was hard, because nobody had a budget for such work. But in the years since, he has uncovered a new, entirely unexpected world of tropical climate change. And now, after fifty expeditions to five continents, and with 20,000 feet of ice cores stored in his freezer, he believes he is on the path to proving that the true triggers and drivers and Achilles heels and thresholds and tipping points for the world's climate lie in the tropics.

For men like Broecker, this is sacrilege. But although Thompson's case is not yet proven, he has found some unexpected fans. Richard Alley, a career member of the "polar school," is an admirer of the senior from Gassaway. He told me with a smile: "Lonnie is a legend, and he may well turn out to be right." Whether he is right or not, Thompson's ice cores and the data he has painstakingly extracted from them are the lifeblood of an emerging debate between the polar and tropical schools—a debate that might not be happening at all without him.

Thompson is a loner. He has always avoided the big organizations and funding bodies that dominate so much climate science. Sometimes that has been out of necessity; now he sees it as a virtue. It has given him the freedom to do and think things his way. With his researcher wife, Ellen Mosley-Thompson, he set up a small team at the Byrd Polar Research Institute, part of Ohio State University. "We started small and we try to be self-contained," he says. "That makes us flexible. We don't have to stand in line for analysis of cores, or for supplies. And we have our own workshops to make everything."

The Thompsons build their own lightweight drills and photovoltaic generators, because these are the only means of getting the right gear by horseback onto the high slopes of the world's tallest mountains. And they have their own four automatic mass spectrometers, working 24 hours a day 365 days a year to analyze the samples brought back from around the world. Thompson doesn't even trust the big science institutions to look after his ice cores when he's gone. With the prize money that has come his way in recent years, he has created a trust fund to keep the freezers going in perpetuity.

Being independent means he can pack his bags and head around the world on a whim if he thinks there is an ice core to be had. Back in 1997, he took advantage of a brief thaw in diplomatic relations between Moscow and Washington to fly to Franz Josef Land, in the Siberian Arctic. There he extracted a thousand feet of ice from near an old Russian nuclear bomber base, and persuaded the bomber pilots to fly it back to Moscow for him. More recently, after years of stonewalling by the Tanzanian authorities, he took his drilling kit on a tourist flight to Dar es Salaam and smooth-talked his way up Kilimanjaro to extract vital evidence of the demise of its ice cap.

Thompson has spent half a lifetime taking his ice pick, crampons, and drilling gear to the Andes and the Himalayas, Tibet and the Russian Arctic, Alaska and East Africa. Back in Columbus, he has interrogated the ice and the bubbles of air trapped inside for signs of dust, metals, salts, and isotopes of oxygen and carbon to discover not just temperatures and rainfall but the comings and goings of El Niño events, forest fires, droughts, and monsoons.

His first love, he says, is Quelccaya, the first ice cap he scaled in Peru with John Mercer. It is the one he keeps going back to. He can see the whole world evolve there, he says, from the revival of El Niños in the Pacific around 5,500 years ago to the decades of drought that finished off the pre-Columbian Moche empire; from the first record in the tropics of the little ice age to the recent isotopic signature of global warming. Here and elsewhere across the tropics, he has also found a dust "spike" in the ice that shows that dust storms were sweeping across the tropics 4,200 years ago—evidence, it seems, of a sudden near-global megadrought.

Most intriguing for glaciologists, Thompson's collection of worldwide ice cores has revealed a previously unknown pattern in the formation of glaciers across the tropics. The pattern seems to be independent of the great glaciations that waxed and waned in the polar regions. It seems instead to follow latitude, starting in the Southern Hemisphere close to the Tropic of Capricorn, where he has found evidence that glaciers began to form in Bolivia 25,000 years ago. Then, as if by clockwork, other glaciers began to form and grow farther north. One by one, they started through Peru and Ecuador. Then, 12,000 years ago, a continent to the east but following the same northward trajectory, an ice cap began to form at the summit of Kilimanjaro, on the equator. Skipping north again to the Himalayas, around 8,000 years ago, glaciers started to grow near the Tropic of Cancer. Across three continents, glacier formation was oblivious of longitude or the equator or anything else. Latitude ruled.

Why? Thompson has tied this extraordinary progression to the precession, the wobble in Earth's orbit that gradually alters the line of latitude where the most intense solar heating occurs. This is the same wobble that sustained the African monsoon over the Sahara when the sun was overhead there in the early Holocene, but snuffed out the rains as the sun moved on. In the mountains of the tropics, glaciers generally started where the sun was fiercest. The sun was most intense over the Tropic of Capricorn 25,000 years ago and then moved north, becoming most intense over the Tropic of Cancer. It appears to have triggered the formation of glaciers all the way.

On the face of it, this seems odd. Why would the harshest sun and hottest temperatures create glaciers? Thompson has a simple explanation. The zone of maximum sun in the tropics is also the zone of maximum rainfall, which in the highest mountains means the zone of maximum snow. Up there, he says, it has always been cold enough for glaciers to form. So temperature is not an issue. What the high valleys have often lacked is moisture to feed the growth of glaciers. The sun brought the moisture, and with it the snow and the glaciers.

Many would argue that all the natural variability in climate that Thompson is uncovering offers a soothing reminder that the planet and human society are no strangers to climate change. Not Lonnie. His analysis is uncovering invisible thresholds in the climate system, he says. Cross them, and the whole system goes into a spin, with dramatic cooling or warming, great droughts and the El Niño flip, turned full on or full off for centuries at a time. Should we not be just as concerned that carbon dioxide might send us above a threshold? If that happens, he says, "we won't get gradual climate change, as projected; we will instead get abrupt change."

And, of course, Thompson is tracking with concern the role of modern climate change in melting his glaciers. Back in 1976, he took a core of the ice at the summit of Quelccaya. It showed layers of ice laid down annually for 1,500 years. In 1991, when he returned to update the record, he found that the annual accumulation had stopped and the top 20 yards of ice had melted away—dramatic evidence of a recent and sudden shift in an ancient ice cap's fortunes. In the valley below, Quelccaya's largest glacier, the Qori Kalis, is retreating by 500 feet a year and has lost a fifth of its area since 1963. Across Peru, a quarter of the ice surface has disappeared in thirty years. Elsewhere in the Andes, Bolivia's Chacaltaya lost two thirds

of its ice in the 1990s, and Venezuela has lost four of its six glaciers since
1975.

In Africa, where 80 percent of the ice on Mount Kilimanjaro has melted
away in ninety years, Mount Kenya has lost seven of its eighteen glaciers
since 1900; and most of the ice on the Rwenzori Mountains between
Uganda and Congo has gone, too. Across the Indian Ocean, on New
Guinea, the West Meren glacier vanished altogether in the late 1990s, and
its neighbor Carstensz has shrunk by 80 percent in sixty years. Thompson
has seen the same trends in the Himalayas and Tibet. Glacial retreat, he
says, "is happening at virtually all the tropical glaciers." In some places,
there may be local factors. Occasionally, declining snowfall will do the
damage. But he insists that while snowfall in high altitudes may be criti-
cal to getting a glacier started, it is rarely critical to the glacier's demise,
which starts lower down the slopes. Globally, he says, there can be no ex-
planation for the universal disappearance of glaciers other than global
warming.

Thompson believes that he has only begun to explore the potential of his
ice cores to answer questions about the tropics. He wants to take cores from
ice still attached to the Nevado del Ruiz volcano, in northern Colombia.
The mountain exploded in 1985, engulfing 20,000 people in a landslide
of ash. "I think we could get a record of how often that volcano erupts," he
says, apparently oblivious of the risk for researchers in such an expedition.
He believes that the ice of Quelccaya can offer a history of fires and drought
in the nearby Amazon. And he is looking at dust from China that has col-
lected in ice in Alaska. It is already providing a history of pesticide use in
China, and may eventually reveal whether dust out of Asia, as well as that
from the Sahara, could have fertilized the soils of the Americas.

Thompson believes that by uncovering the secret climate history of the
tropics, he is helping to strip climatology of an unhealthy fixation with
what happens close to the homes of the researchers—in the North At-
lantic: "An important reason why we think that Greenland and those
places are so important is because so much research has been done there—
and that is mainly because it is more convenient than going to Tibet or
Patagonia." He believes that that fixation is diverting researchers from

where the real climatic action is—in the tropics, in the world of El Niño and the Asian monsoon and megadroughts and the dramatic feedbacks that dried up the Sahara, which he sees as "at least as important as anything Wally Broecker has cooked up on the North Atlantic."

To Thompson, it has always seemed obvious that "the global climate is driven from the tropics." Most of the surface of Earth is in the tropics, he says. "It is where the majority of the heat reaches Earth, and from where it is distributed around the globe. It is where the great climate systems like the monsoon and El Niño are based." He argues that truly global climatic events can start only where heat and moisture can be delivered both north and south around the globe. There may be feedbacks operating in the North Atlantic or around Antarctica. But the big drivers must be in the tropics.

Thompson has his own heroes. Mercer is one. Another is James Croll, the lowly Victorian Scot who worked his way through life as a waiter, a school caretaker, and a carpenter so that he could research the astronomical forces behind the ice ages. And Thompson has simple advice for young scientists: plow your own furrow. "Go somewhere or do something that nobody else has even thought about working on." Some academics from the wrong side of the tracks would have settled quietly into faculty life, thankful for their social advance. Not Lonnie. He does research the hard way. "On one trip we were up on Quelccaya for three months. We had to cut the ice cores by hand into 6,000 samples, take them downhill on our backs, and then melt them and put the water in bottles sealed with wax." On another occasion, he found himself in New Zealand dangling on a rope above 2,000 feet of empty space.

Years ago, a student in the field with Thompson died of the aftereffects of altitude sickness. His father sued. That still hurts. Thompson would be the last professor on Earth to send his students somewhere he wasn't prepared to go himself. He is still prepared to live for months under canvas in freezing cold and lung-achingly thin air. Just turning sixty when we met, he was recently back from his biannual trip to the Andes, and his calendar included upcoming trips to Kilimanjaro and central Africa's "mountains of the moon." He had tentative plans for expeditions to the last glaciers in

New Guinea and a Siberian island near where the last mastodon froze to death 5,000 years ago.

He told me he reckoned that his techniques could one day help uncover the remains of life in the ice caps of Mars. And I swear that his eyes lit up when I suggested he might be on the first flight to the red planet.

THE CURSE OF AKKAD

The strange revival of environmental determinism

Around 4,200 years ago, the world's top empire was run by Sargon, the despotic but otherwise unexceptional ruler of the Akkadian empire. Some have called this the first true empire in the world. Certainly it seemed to be a new form of society, created out of a number of previously autonomous city-states on the floodplains of the Tigris and Euphrates Rivers in Meso-potamia. Its rule extended all the way from the headwaters of the two rivers, in Turkey, across much of Syria and as far south as the Persian Gulf. But Sargon's empire had been in business for only a century or so when it suddenly collapsed. Archaeologists initially put this down to an invasion of barbarian hordes from the surrounding mountains. But an energetic field archaeologist called Harvey Weiss, of Yale, changed that rather lazy assumption—and with it changed much else about our perceptions of the rise and fall of past civilizations.

In the late 1970s, while working in Syria, Weiss discovered a "lost city" beneath the desert sands, close to the Iraqi border. Over more than a decade he excavated the remains of the settlement, named Tell Leilan. He pieced together the story of a highly organized city that had grown over several thousand years from a small village to a prosperous outpost of the Akkadian empire. But there was a mystery. It appeared that for some 300 years, the city had been abandoned and its streets had filled with wind-blown dust.

Weiss tied the events at Tell Leilan to a contemporary cuneiform text titled "The Curse of Akkad," which recorded a great drought in which the fields of most of northern Mesopotamia were abruptly abandoned. The granaries emptied, the fruit trees died in the orchards, and even the fish departed as the great rivers dried up. Refugees flooded south. The people of southern Mesopotamia built a hundred-mile wall to keep them out. Archaeologists had previously dismissed "The Curse of Akkad" as mythology. The idea that climatic and other environmental change determined the progress of societies had been hugely out of fashion. The prevailing view was that politics, economics, wars, and dynasties made and broke empires, and that climate was just a more or less benign backdrop.

But Weiss was convinced that only a massive shift in climate could explain a 300-year collapse, after which the climate apparently recovered enough for the northern plains to be settled once more. When he published his findings, they provoked consternation in the archaeological community but huge interest among climate scientists—not least Peter deMenocal, of Lamont-Doherty. "After Weiss's publication, environmental determinism had a huge revival," deMenocal says. Especially after it emerged that the dust storms of Mesopotamia were part of a wider process of aridification right across the Middle East and beyond, which had seen off other societies, too.

In New York, deMenocal was working with a student, Heidi Cullen, on analyzing a core of marine sediment drilled from beneath the Gulf of Oman, 1,500 miles south of Tell Leilan. They decided to look for evidence of dust storms in the core. "We thought the dust might be visible there, and Heidi started to go through it," he told me. "It was very painstaking work, and to be honest, she was about to give up. Then boom. One day she found it. The 300-year layer of dust, dated at 4,200 years ago, and much of it clearly derived from Mesopotamia. We sent it to Harvey, and he was ecstatic."

The news spread. Lonnie Thompson and his team went back to their tropical ice cores and found similar layers of black dust. "It was a huge global dust spike," he said. In the ice on the summit of Kilimanjaro, in East Africa, there is only one dust "spike" in the 12,000-year record. And it occurs right at 4,200 years ago, he said. On the other side of the planet from Syria, at Quelccaya, in Peru, the same period produced "the biggest dust event in the ice core in a 17,000-year record." Fallout of dust onto the glacier was a hundred times as much as normal levels. "And it shows up in the Asian monsoon region of the Himalayas, too," says Thompson's dust analyst, Mary Davis.

From Lake Van, in eastern Turkey, to the Dead Sea, in Palestine, and in Africa from Kenya to Morocco, water levels fell by tens or even hundreds of yards 4,200 years ago. Civilizations were ending everywhere. In Egypt, those years produced a collapse of order that marked the break between the Old and Middle Kingdoms. "On the tombs of the Pharaohs, their histories talk of expansion until 4,200 years before the present, when there were droughts and mass migrations and sand dunes crossing the Nile," says Thompson. In Palestine, the situation was even worse, according to Arie Issar, an Israeli hydrologist and the author of a detailed study of climate change and civilization in the region. The level of the Dead Sea dropped a hundred yards. "All the urban centers were abandoned, and the cities, which had existed for several hundred years, remained only as large heaps of ruins. They were not resettled until nearly half a millennium later." Farther east, in the Indus Valley of modern-day Pakistan, the urban centers of the Harappan civilization collapsed at the same time.

What caused all this? Nobody is sure. Jeffrey Severinghaus, of the Scripps Institution of Oceanography, has found tantalizing evidence of a dust signal in the Greenland ice cores 4,200 years ago. But instead of more dust than before, he found less. There was also a decline in sea ice in the North Atlantic. This has been interpreted as evidence of a change in the ocean conveyor. Did Broecker's conveyor drive things once again? On the face of it, that interpretation looks unlikely. For on this occasion, rather as during the great climatic disruption of 5,500 years ago, events in the North look like mere ripples flowing out from much bigger events in the tropics.

It is more evidence, says deMenocal, that climate switches may lurk in the tropics at least as much as at the poles. Richard Alley again reaches for common ground. Perhaps, he says, the Arctic feedbacks were at their height during and immediately after the ice ages, but lost their influence once most of the ice had gone. During the height of the Holocene, at least, perhaps the tropics ruled. But if so, what is driving the feedbacks in the tropics? Where are the tropical equivalents of Broecker's conveyor, Alley's "sink or freeze" switch, and Juergen Mienert's clathrate gun?

A CHUNK OF CORAL

Probing the hidden life of El Niño

Some researchers have a way of combining business with pleasure. Not for Dan Schrag, the Harvard geochemist, the arduous journeys into thin, cold air on tropical glaciers. Back in 1997, he was on his fourth trip to the paradise islands of the East Indies in search of ancient coral. One day, he was sauntering along a beach on Bunaken Island, a speck of old atoll off the Indonesian island of Sulawesi. "We had had a glorious dive, during which we saw a huge school of barracuda," he remembers. "We stopped for lunch, and I took a walk down the beach, behind the mangrove swamp. It was the last day of the trip. We had failed to find anything useful, and I was preparing to go home. Then I saw this massive coral head on the beach, incredibly well preserved." He chiseled out a piece and headed for the plane.

Back in the lab at Harvard, Schrag discovered that this fossilized piece of coral was 125,000 years old and contained sixty-five years' worth of growth rings that gave a brief window on the climate of the western Pacific back before the last ice age. It was a "fantastic discovery," he says. "I guess I got really, really lucky." The coral he had found was the first piece ever located that was large enough and well enough preserved to give a good snapshot of ancient El Niños. What's more, says Schrag, it came from a region that is in the "bull's-eye" of El Niño, in the heart of Indonesia. His preprandial discovery is helping transform our understanding of El Niño's place in the climate system.

Until recently, climatologists looked on El Niño as a minor aberration in the tropical Pacific, of only passing interest to the wider world. But in the past two decades it has become the fifth horseman of the Apocalypse, a bringer of devastating floods, fires, and famine from Ethiopia to Indonesia to Ecuador, and a sender of weird weather around the world. It has been appearing more frequently, and with effects that are much more violent and last longer. Its current level of activity is unparalleled in the historical record. Yet the historical record doesn't go back far, so nobody has been sure whether this is a perfectly normal upturn or an alarming consequence of global climate change. Schrag's coral has helped provide some answers. It makes a strong case that global warming is already having a profound effect on what climatologists are coming to regard as the flywheel of the world's climate.

El Niño is a periodic reversal of ocean currents, winds, and weather systems that stretches across the equatorial Pacific Ocean, halfway around the planet at its widest girth. It is a redistributor of heat and energy in the hottest part of the world's oceans, which kicks in when the regular circulation systems can no longer cope. In normal times, the winds and surface waters of the tropical Pacific, driven by Earth's rotation, flow from the Americas in the East to Indonesia in the West. In the tropical heat, the water warms as it goes. The result is the gradual accumulation of a pool of hot water on the ocean surface around Indonesia. This pool can be up to 13°F warmer than the water on the other side of the ocean, and can contain more heat energy than the entire atmosphere. All that heat generates storm clouds that keep the rainforests of Southeast Asia wet.

But the constant flow to the west also piles up water. Trapped against the Indonesian archipelago, the warm pool can rise as much as 15 inches above sea levels farther east. Clearly, this state of affairs cannot last. And every few years, usually when the winds slacken, this raised pool of warm water breaks out and flows back across the surface of the ocean, right along the equator. As the warm water moves east, the wind and weather systems that it creates follow.

Deprived of their storm-generating weather systems, Indonesia and a wide area of the western Pacific, including much of Australia, dry out. There are forest and bush fires, and crops shrivel in the fields. Meanwhile, the displaced wet and stormy rainforest climate drenches normally arid Pacific islands, and often reaches the coastal deserts of the Americas. Ripples from this vast movement of heat and moisture spread around the globe. They move west through the Indian Ocean, disrupting the Indian monsoon and causing rains or drought in Africa, depending on the season. They move east. Beyond the flooding on the Pacific shores of the Americas, El Niño brings drought in the Amazon rainforest. Its hidden hand alters flow down the River Nile, triggers rains in the hills of Palestine, and damps down hurricane formation in the North Atlantic.

Typically, an individual El Niño event lasts twelve to eighteen months. After it has abated, the system often goes into sharp reverse, with exceptionally wet conditions in Indonesia and fierce drought further east. This is called La Niña. Together, El Niño and its sister constitute a vast oscillation of ocean and atmosphere that in recent times has been the most intense fluctuation in the world's climate system.

Scientists first became aware of the oscillation we now call El Niño in the nineteenth century. But they have been uncertain about how far back El Niño goes. Is it a permanent feature of the climate system, or a minor and occasional aberration? Does it have long-term variability tied to global climate changes? Does the Pacific get "stuck" in either a permanent El Niño or a permanent La Niña?

Reliable climate and ocean records cover only a couple of centuries or so. Delving further requires alternative sources of information. To this end, Donald Rodbell, of Union College, in Schenectady, New York, dug up the bed of a lake in southern Ecuador to chart its past flood levels, in the expectation that, as today, floods would be a feature of El Niño episodes. In 1998, he published a remarkable 12,000-year record of the lake's floods. For the first half of the period, they came roughly once every fifteen years, suggesting a near-dormant El Niño. Then they speeded up quite abruptly, to settle at an average return period of about six years—the classic El Niño pattern until recently. This pattern has been confirmed by Lonnie Thompson's ice cores from nearby glaciers.

The change in the flood pattern also seems to coincide with the same precession shift in Earth's tilt that caused the desertification of the Sahara and the advance of tropical glaciers spotted by Thompson. Rodbell's record was a major breakthrough, implicating El Niño as a key driver of the global climate system. El Niño was no longer just a short-term cycle played out over a few months in one ocean: it had global and long-term meaning. Then came Schrag's chunk of coral.

Through isotopic analysis, Schrag extracted an El Niño signal from his piece of jetsam. When water evaporates, molecules containing the lighter isotope of oxygen—oxygen-16—evaporate slightly faster, leaving behind seawater that is rich in the heavier oxygen-18. When it rains, the oxygen-16 is returned. So in the Indonesian islands during El Niños, when rainfall ceases, both the seawater and the coral growth in those years contain more oxygen-18. Schrag measured the ratio of the two oxygen isotopes in the sixty-five annual growth rings in his ancient chunk of coral. He found two things of importance: First, there had indeed been an El Niño cycle back then. That pushed the longevity of the phenomenon back to before the last ice age, further establishing it as a permanent feature of the climate system. And second, the El Niño cycle looked exactly like that of the modern period from the mid-1800s to the mid-1970s, in which El Niño returned, on average, about every six years. This underlined the idea that six years is the natural length of the cycle—and made the post-1976 period, during which El Niño has developed a return period averaging 3.5 years, appear increasingly unusual.

This sense that El Niño may have changed in some fundamental way in the past thirty years has been reinforced by another change. The earliest records of the El Niño phenomenon are from the Pacific shores of South America, where a cold ocean current normally works its way north, bringing waters rich in nutrients that sustain one of the world's largest fisheries, off Peru. But during El Niños, the flood of warm water from the west overrides this cold current for a while, and the fish disappear. That has been the classic pattern. But since 1976, the underlying state has changed. The cold current has been pushed to ever-greater depths, even during normal times. The ocean system appears to have become stuck in a quasi-El Niño state.

What lies behind these recent changes? Some say that El Niño is simply on a short-lived, exuberant joyride. They point out that there have always been decades when it is unusually quiet or busy or just plain weird. But Schrag thinks this is unlikely to explain recent events. Publishing his Sulawesi findings, he said: "In 1982–83 we experience the most severe El Niño of the 20th century. According to previous records you wouldn't expect another that powerful for a hundred years. But 15 years later, in 1997–98, we have one even larger." And since then, in 2002 and 2004, there have been two more significant El Niños—not as large as those before, but turning up with ever-greater frequency.

Kevin Trenberth, the head of climate analysis at NCAR, was one of the first researchers to claim that the Pacific entered an unusual state after 1976. He believes that the recent spate of strong and frequent El Niños could well be due to the hand of man. It looks as if global warming, which gathered real pace only in the 1970s, is generating so much warming in the tropical Pacific that the old flywheel pattern in which occasional El Niños distribute the heat that accumulates around Indonesia is not sufficient to handle the amount of energy in the system.

Modelers have been testing this theory, with interesting results. Mojib Latif, at the Max Planck Institute for Meteorology, in Hamburg, developed the first global climate model that was detailed enough to reproduce El Niño. His model predicts that the average climate in the twenty-first century will be more like the typical El Niño conditions of the twentieth century. Cold La Niña events will still happen occasionally, and may even be more intense. But they will become the breakout events.

It would be wrong to suggest that science has somehow cracked the enigma of El Niño. There are still many mysteries. Certainly the idea that a strong El Niño is necessarily associated with warm times could be a gross simplification. Schrag's coral, along with other evidence, suggests that El Niño kept going right through the last ice age, when, even in the western Pacific, temperatures were several degrees lower than they are today. There is even some suggestion that El Niños were more common in the colder phases of the ice age, whereas La Niña held sway during the warmer periods. Likewise, the warm early Holocene era, before 6,000 years ago, saw El Niño largely in abeyance. It recovered during a cooler period.

Clearly, El Niño is not a simple planetary thermostat. But its operation in the past may have had more to do with changes in solar radiation that were reflected in alterations to the tropical hydrological cycle than with temperature. It is possible to imagine a climate system in which those changes triggered different temperature signals at different times. So efforts to tie past El Niños to temperature trends may not provide a good guide to what happens in a world of pumped-up greenhouse gas concentrations.

But what is becoming clear is that El Niño is a phenomenon that influences basic planetary processes such as the transfer of heat and moisture in huge swaths of the tropics. That it has big swings that operate on timescales varying from months to thousands of years. That it leaves its calling card in different ways right around the planet. And that its variability seems to be keyed into critical external drivers of past climate such as the precession and Bond's 1,500-year solar cycles. You would not bet against its playing an equally important role in moderating or amplifying global warming caused by greenhouse gases. What is not yet clear is which way it will jump.

Perhaps scientists should put aside their models and search for some wisdom on El Niño from Peruvian farmers, who have grown potatoes high in the Andes for thousands of years. Throughout that time, El Niños have become stronger and weaker, more frequent and less frequent, and have influenced potato growing all the while. For many centuries now, farmers have gathered in mid-June (the Southern winter) to gaze up at the night sky in the Andes and observe the eleven-star constellation known as Pleiades, or the Seven Sisters. If the stars are bright, they set to planting quickly, confident that there will be good rains and a healthy harvest.

For years this folklore was dismissed by agriculturalists as mumbo-jumbo—until Mark Cane, one of the world's foremost modelers of El Niño, heard about it from a guide while traveling in the Andes. Intrigued, he checked meteorological records, and discovered that typically about six months before an El Niño, thin, high, and almost invisible clouds form above the Andes. These dim the brightness of the constellation. So a dim constellation means a dry spring, while clear skies and a bright constellation mean good rains.

The farmers had thus perfected many hundreds of years ago what climate modelers like Cane have only fitfully managed in the past twenty years—a way of forecasting El Niño. Cane says the Peruvian potato farmers' forecast is better than his. "It's a brilliant scheme, really quite a feat. I still wonder how they possibly worked it out." Perhaps, he muses, the Peruvian potato farmers have had the key to the world's climate all along.

FEEDING ASIA

What happens if the monsoon falters?

More than 3 billion people today are fed and watered thanks to the Asian monsoon. It is the greatest rainmaking machine on the planet—and possibly one of the most sensitive to climate change. Its mechanism is extremely simple. It is like a giant sea breeze operating over the world's largest continent. In winter, the vast Asian landmass becomes cold—extremely cold on the high ice caps of Tibet, the largest area of ice outside the polar regions. It cools the air above. That air descends, forcing cold, dry winds to blow off the land and out across the Indian and Pacific Oceans. Asia is mostly rainless for nine long months. But come summer, the land warms up much faster than the oceans. Warm air rises, and as it does, the winds reverse and moist winds blow in off the oceans. For about a hundred days, monsoon rains fall across Asia. The rains burst rivers, fill irrigation canals and water fields. Across the continent, rice farmers take their opportunity to grow the food that sustains half the world's population.

A failed monsoon has devastating consequences. They happened repeatedly in the nineteenth century. British colonial administrators in India watched in bemusement as tens of millions died in the famine of 1837–1838, and again in 1860–1861, 1876–1878, and 1896–1902. The Asian monsoon remained an unruly beast through the twentieth century. But despite tenfold increases in the populations of most monsoon countries, the death toll from famine has fallen. There are many reasons for this, one of which is that the rains proved more reliable in the twentieth century than in the nineteenth. That was a good news story. The question is: Can it last? The Asian monsoon has appeared for the past century to be self-contained and invulnerable. But, like other big features in the global climate system, it may have an Achilles heel. If the monsoon proves less reliable in the twenty-first century, there could be real trouble ahead—for about 3 billion people.

The monsoon's vulnerability in past centuries seems to lie in its links to two other parts of the global climate system. One is El Niño. Strong El Niños often seem to switch off the Asian monsoon. British imperial scientists discovered more than a century ago that most of the great Indian famines coincided with marked climatic fluctuations in the Pacific. El Niños seemed to draw heat away from Asia, and so to drain the monsoon's strength. But the argument has become a little academic in the past thirty years, because El Niño has intensified without any widespread weakening of the Asian monsoon. The break in the old link has been both a scientific surprise and a humanitarian godsend. But nobody knows what has caused it and whether it will last. If the Pacific climate system does what many predict, and in the twenty-first century leans heavily toward a permanent El Niño–like state, and if the monsoon resumes its former relationship, then the rains may soon fail over Asia more often than they succeed.

The second link is with the Atlantic. This was dramatically established in 2003, when Indian and U.S. researchers assembled a 10,000-year record of the strength of the Indian monsoon. They did it by counting fossilized plankton found in ancient marine sediments off the Indian coast. The plankton thrive when strong monsoon winds cause an upwelling of the nutrients that provide their food. The study found huge variability in the monsoon's strength over the centuries. And it confirmed that, over time-scales longer than individual El Niño years, "weak summer monsoons coincide with cold spells thousands of miles away in the North Atlantic," according to Anil Gupta, of the Indian Institute of Technology, in Kharagpur, who worked on the project. Strong monsoons go hand in hand with warm waters off Europe and North America.

It had been known for a while that the Indian monsoon turned off during the last ice age but probably flickered on briefly during the warm episodes that punctuated the glaciation. The new study showed that the strength of the monsoon also shadowed the flutters of the Atlantic system during the postglacial era, faltering during the Younger Dryas and the chill of 8,200 years ago, for instance. The changes clearly followed Bond's

1,500-year solar pulse. Thus the last faltering of the monsoon came during Europe's little ice age, which ended in the final decades of the nineteenth century. Soon, as colonial records confirm, the monsoon was regaining its reliability.

But this pattern, impressive though it is, does not explain how the link with the Atlantic works. Does the Atlantic tell the monsoon what to do? Does the monsoon tell the Atlantic what to do? Does Bond's solar pulse independently determine both? Or is there another element not taken into account? Where does El Niño fit in, for instance?

Jonathan Overpeck, of the University of Arizona, one of the authors of the monsoon history, holds that the Atlantic has the whip hand. He says that a warm North Atlantic sends heat east on the winds, warming Asia in spring, and allowing a rapid melt of the Tibetan plateau and an early start to the rain-giving monsoon winds. But when the Atlantic is cold, he says, "more snow on the Tibetan plateau in spring and early summer uses up all the sun's heating, because it has to be melted and evaporated before the land can warm." If he is right, then should the ocean conveyor falter in the coming years, the effects for Asia could be even more grievous than for Europe. "There could be a weakened monsoon and less water for all the people who depend on it," says Overpeck.

The tropical school disagrees with this analysis. It holds that both the cooling of the Atlantic and the weakening of the monsoon are likely to be triggered by changes in the heating of the tropics. According to this theory, a cooling of the tropics will weaken monsoon winds and rains, while at the same time sending less warm water north in the Gulf Stream. The theories of the polar and tropical schools are on this occasion not mutually exclusive. In fact, they are mutually reinforcing.

But right now, neither theory offers much enlightenment about what might happen to the Asian monsoon in the coming decades. Global warming driven by accumulating greenhouse gases without a solar component may have different features and different outcomes from the solar-dominated scenarios of the past. The situation is further complicated because across much of monsoon Asia, warming is itself severely compromised and sometimes extinguished by the aerosols in the Asian brown haze. As we have seen, the haze's biggest impact is on the radiation bal-

ance between the land surface and the air aloft—a vital parameter in de-
termining the strength of the monsoon. The fear is that the haze may break
the seasonal heating cycles between land and ocean, and turn off the mon-
soon. It hasn't yet, but it may. And, valuable though reconstructed histo-
ries of the Asian monsoon may be, it is unlikely that they will ever be able
to provide a firm prognosis for the monsoon.

VII

AT THE MILLENNIUM

32

THE HEAT WAVE

The year Europe felt the heat of global warming

At a zoo near Versailles, outside Paris, keepers kept twenty-seven polar bears cool by feeding them mackerel-flavored ice. In Alsace, the electricity company trained water cannons on the roof of a nuclear power reactor as temperatures outside soared to 118°F. In Rome, tourists queued up to pay the fine for bathing in Trevi Fountain. It seemed like a good deal, they said. Crops died; forests burned; power blacked out as office air conditioners were turned to full power; rivers from the Danube to the Po and the Rhine to the Rhone were at or near record lows.

This was by no standards an ordinary summer heat wave. For one thing, it killed at least 35,000 people: 20,000 in Italy and 15,000 in France. Old people, many of them abandoned in apartments without air conditioning as their families took their August holidays, suffered most. Dehydrated and short of breath, they died by the thousands in temperatures that often exceeded 104°F during the day and stuck close to 86°F at night. It was Europe's hottest summer in at least half a millennium. At the heat wave's peak, on August 13, 2003, the twenty-four-hour death toll in Paris was eight times the norm. In parts of the city, there was a three-week wait for funerals. More than 400 bodies were never claimed by relatives.

It wasn't just the mortuaries that were rewriting their record books. This was the first single weather event that climate scientists felt prepared to say was directly attributable to man-made climate change. In the past, the assumption had always been that any individual weather event could be the product of chance. But the 2003 heat wave was different, says the Oxford University climate scientist and statistician Myles Allen. "The immediate cause, I agree, was a series of anticyclones over Europe. They always raise temperatures in summer, and we can't say those were made any more likely by climate change. But we can say that climate change made the background temperatures within which those anticyclones operated that much higher."

There is no doubt that average temperatures have been rising strongly for years. In much of Europe, the summer average at the start of the new century was 0.9 to 1.8°F warmer than it was in the first half of the twentieth century. In the summer of 2003, temperatures averaged 4.1 degrees warmer. Judging from past averages, the heat wave was probably a once-in-a-thousand-years event. But, says Allen, "small changes in average temperatures make extreme events much more likely."

One of the nicest confirmations of how exceptional the summer of 2003 was came from a study published at the end of 2004. The French mathematician Pascal Yiou, of the Laboratoire des Sciences du Climat et de l'Environnement, had collected more than 600 years' worth of parish records showing when the Pinot Noir grape harvest began in the Burgundy vineyards of eastern France. There is a clear relationship between summer temperatures and the start of the harvest, so he extrapolated backward to produce a temperature graph from the present to 1370. The results showed that temperatures as high as those typical in the 1990s were unusual, but had happened several times before. "However," Yiou said, "the summer of 2003 appears to have been extraordinary, unique." Temperatures in Burgundy that year were almost 11°F above the long-term average. And if Yiou's formula was accurate, the highest previous temperature had been just 7° above the average. That happened in 1523, in a warm interlude during the little ice age.

"The 2003 heat wave was far outside the range of normal climate," says Allen. It was not impossible that it could have happened without global warming, but it was very improbable. "Our best estimates suggest the risk of such a heat wave has increased between four- and sixfold as a result of climate change." Many scientists continue to argue about how we might recognize "dangerous" climate change, he told me. "Well, for the thousands of victims in Europe in the summer of 2003, it is clear we have already passed that threshold."

And the big heat is only just beginning. Allen says that by midcentury, if current warming trends persist, the extreme temperatures experienced in 2003 in Europe could occur on average once every two years. Richard Betts, of Britain's Hadley Centre, says that for people living in cities, the risks are even greater. They are already feeling the worst of climate change, because they also suffer the "urban heat island effect." During heat waves, the concrete, bricks, and asphalt of buildings and roads hold on to heat much better than does the natural landscape in the countryside. In the typically windless, anticyclonic conditions of a European heat wave, the effect is even more marked. The air just stays in the streets and cooks. The effect is especially marked at night, which doctors say is a critical time for the human body to recover from daytime heat.

Betts says global warming will push the urban heat island effect into overdrive. Doubling carbon dioxide levels in the air will triple the effect, he calculates.

33

THE HOCKEY STICK

Why now really is different

It was a seductive image. So seductive that the IPCC put it right at the front of its thousand-page assessment of climate change, published in 2001. The panel hoped that it would become as talked about as the Keeling curve. And scientists gave it a snappy caption: this was the graph they called the "hockey stick." As I don't play hockey, I was initially left wondering why. But if you lay a hockey stick on the ground and look at its shape as a graph, you will see that the long, flat shaft has at the end of it a short but sharply upturned blade, the bit you hit the puck with. And that, according to the IPCC authors, is the shape of the world's temperatures over the past thousand years: about 900 years of little or no change, followed by a century with a short, sharp upturn.

The assembly of the data behind the hockey stick graph has become a political cause célèbre. It began with high hopes: it was to be the first serious attempt to piece together a global picture of climate over the past millennium from a wide variety of different kinds of sources. Rather than carrying on the well-established work of reconstructing past temperatures from analysis of tree rings, it sought to add in other proxy data from ice cores, coral growth rings, and lake sediments. The idea was to lose the built-in bias of tree-ring chronologies, which must rely on trees from Northern Hemisphere regions outside the tropics, because those are the trees with well-defined annual growth rings.

The hockey stick graph was first put together in 1998. The politics soon got going. That year turned out to be the warmest in the instrumental record. So it wasn't much of a stretch to argue that the hockey stick revealed 1998 to be the warmest year in the warmest century of the past millennium. That got headlines. And brought trouble—not least for the voluble, self-confident, and likable collator of the hockey stick data, Mike Mann. Even though the IPCC published other data sets showing much the same, Mann was accused of concocting a spurious case that late-twentieth-century warming was exceptional and therefore, presumably, a result of man-made pollution.

It probably didn't help that at the time, Mann was based at the University of Virginia, home of the biggest voice among the climate skeptics: Pat Michaels. Soon Mann was fraud-of-the-month on the Web sites of the climate skeptics. But the criticism went beyond the normal community of climate skeptics: some serious climate researchers expressed misgivings about Mann's methods.

When I finally met Mann, he had moved from Virginia to Penn State University, where he is now director of the Earth Science Systems Center. But the flak had followed. Some was fair; some was unfair; some was deployed as political hand grenades; some was just a part of the normal adversarial flow of scientific debate; and some was just plain personal —like Wally Broecker's bad-mouthing of Mann, quoted at the start of Chapter 23. Mann was even damned in Washington, where Senator James Inhofe of Oklahoma accused him of playing fast and loose with the data, and Representative Joe Barton of Texas summoned him to provide his committee with voluminous details about working procedures and funding. Some called it a McCarthyite vendetta. But Mann seemed up for it, dismissing Inhofe as "the single largest Senate recipient of oil industry money."

I will now entertain some of the criticisms that have rained on Mann, because they matter. But it is worth saying first that nothing I have heard impugns Mann's scientific integrity, credentials, or motives. He is just braver than some, and more willing to have his debates in public—and to fight back when the brickbats start flying. (You can read him in action on the Web site he started with scientific colleagues at www.realclimate.org.) Some researchers have suffered real personal and psychological damage from attacks by skeptics. I hope that won't happen to Mann. I wish more scientists were like him.

First, does the hockey stick fairly represent the temperature record? Does Mann's take-home conclusion, that the last century warmed faster and further than any other in the past thousand years, stand up to scrutiny? The short answer is yes—but only just.

The world of proxy data trends is a statistical minefield. This is partly because the physical material that shows past climate loses detail with time. Tree rings, for instance, get smaller as the tree gets older, so annual and even decadal detail gets lost. "You lose roughly 40 percent of the amplitude of changes," says the tree ring specialist Gordon Jacoby, of Lamont-Doherty. But it goes far beyond that. To make any sense, analysis of a single data set—for instance, from the tree rings in a forest—involves smoothing out the data from individual trees to reveal a "signal" behind the "noise" of short-term and random change. The kind of analysis pioneered by Mann, in which a series of different data sets are merged, involves further sorting and aggregating these independently derived signals, and smoothing the result. And Mann's work involves a further stage: meshing that proxy synthesis with the current instrumental record.

Some, including Jacoby, complain that by combining smoothed-out proxy data from past centuries with the recent instrumental record, which preserves many more short-term trends, Mann created a false impression of anomalous recent change. "You just can't do that if you are losing so much of the amplitude of change in the rest of the data," Jacoby told me. Mann argues the contrary—that in fact he was one of the first analysts in the field to include error bars on his graph. "The error bars represent how much variance is lost due to the smoothing," he says.

But the accusation that he has somehow fixed the data analysis continues to dog him. The most persistent line of criticism, and the one most widely championed by anti-IPCC lobbyists, came from two Canadians: Stephen McIntyre, a mathematician and oil industry consultant, and Ross McKitrick, an economist at the University of Guelph. They claimed to have found a fundamental flaw in Mann's statistical methodology that biased the temperature reconstruction toward producing the hockey stick shape.

The argument is a technical one that hangs on how Mann used well-established mathematical techniques for classifying data called principal component analysis. McIntyre and McKitrick claimed that Mann's method had the effect of damping down unwanted natural variability, straightening the shaft of the hockey stick and accentuating twentieth-century warming. Mann agrees there was some truth in this charge. He analyzed the data in terms of their divergence from twentieth-century levels, and this had the inevitable effect of giving greater significance to data showing the biggest differences from that period.

But the critical charge was that he had somehow created the hockey stick out of nothing—"mining" the data for hockey-stick-shaped trends, as his critics put it. McIntyre and McKitrick produced their own analysis, showing an apparent rise in temperatures in the fifteenth century, which, they claimed, may have been as warm as the twentieth century. The shaft of the hockey stick had a big kink in it. When it was published, in 2005, this analysis was hailed by some as a refutation of Mann's study.

But while Mann was open to attack, so were McIntyre and McKitrick. Would their "refutation" of Mann stand up to critical attention? During 2005, three different research groups concluded that Mann's findings bear scrutiny much better than do those of his critics. They had bent the statistics more than he had, arbitrarily leaving out certain sets of data to reach their conclusion. Remove all the biases, and the real data looked more like Mann's—a conclusion underlined in early 2006, when Keith Briffa, a respected British tree-ring analyst at the University of East Anglia, published the most complete analysis to date, showing the twentieth century to have been the warmest era for at least the past 1,200 years. Briffa's take was confirmed in June 2006 by the U.S. National Academy of Sciences, which, in a long-awaited review of the hockey-stick debate, endorsed Mann's work. The analysts expressed a "high degree of confidence" that the second half of the twentieth century was warmer than any other period in the previous four centuries. But they said that although many places were clearly warmer now than at any other time since 900, there was simply not enough data to be quite so sure about the period before 1600.

If the key to successful science is producing findings that can be replicated by other groups using different methodologies, then Mann is on a winning streak. Upward of a dozen studies, using both different collections of proxy data and different analytical techniques, have now produced graphs similar to Mann's original hockey stick. Not identical, for sure, but with the same basic features of unremarkable variability for 900 years followed by a sharp upturn in temperatures in the final decades.

The one unexplained factor is that most of these studies show paltry evidence for the medieval warm period and the little ice age. But an answer to that conundrum now seems at hand. There is growing agreement that the most substantial evidence for the existence of both a medieval warm period and a little ice age comes from the northern latitudes. "What we know about the cold in the little-ice-age era is primarily a European and North Atlantic phenomenon," says Keith Briffa. Most interesting, there is growing evidence from a range of new proxy data that other parts of the world were seeing climate trends opposite to those going on in Europe. The tropical Pacific appears to have cooled during the medieval warm period and warmed during the little ice age. One ice core from the Antarctic shows temperatures during the medieval warm period that were 5°F colder than those in the little ice age. Under the circumstances, says Mann, it is not surprising that his more global assessment of temperatures does not spot much difference during these earlier climatic shifts. They undoubtedly had major influences on regional climates, but the cumulative effect on global temperature was small.

It is no part of this book's case that climate didn't change in the past. Parts of the world clearly saw substantial warming and cooling during the medieval warm period and the little ice age. Other parts saw other changes. In the American West, there were huge, century-long droughts during the medieval warm period. Even Broecker, who holds that the little ice age was global, admits that the evidence of a global medieval warm period is "spotty and circumstantial." But there is a good case for saying that over the millennium until the mid-twentieth century, most climate change concerned the redistribution of heat and moisture around the globe rather than big changes in overall heating. Only recently has there been a major additional "forcing," caused by the introduction of hundreds of billions of tons of greenhouse gases into the atmosphere. Recent warming may be the first global warming since the closure of the ice age itself.

The argument over the hockey stick is an interesting sideshow in the debate about climate change. But it remains a sideshow. Right now, it matters little for the planet as a whole whether the medieval warm period was or was not warmer than temperatures today—or, indeed, whether it was a warm period at all. The subtext of the climate skeptics' assault on Mann's hockey stick has always been that if the current warming is shown not to be unique, then somehow the case that man-made global warming is happening evaporates. But this is a spurious argument. Briffa is not alone in arguing precisely the opposite. If it was indeed very warm globally in the medieval warm period, that is truly worrying, he says. "Greater long-term [natural] climatic variability implies a greater sensitivity of climate to forcing, whether from the sun or greenhouse gases. So greater past climate variations imply greater future climate change."

34

HURRICANE SEASON

Raising the storm cones after Katrina

Corky Perret lost everything when Hurricane Katrina hit. His house on the beachfront out on Highway 90 between Gulfport and Biloxi, Mississippi, was reduced to matchwood by 130-mile-an-hour winds, and sucked away by a 30-foot storm surge that washed up the beach and over the highway. "Nothing is left; it was totally destroyed," he told me weeks later. Out in the Gulf of Mexico, barrier islands that once provided protection against storms had also succumbed. Perret didn't know if hurricanes would be worse in the future, but without the islands, the effects would probably be worse anyway.

The houses along the section of Highway 90 where Perret lived, along with the hotels and resorts, had been built mostly between the 1970s and the 1990s, a period of quiet in the Gulf when there were few hurricanes. Hearing reports that no letup is likely anytime soon, some of his neighbors were going for good. They could see only more hurricanes and more havoc. They were off to Jackson or Dallas or Memphis, or anywhere inland. But when we spoke in late 2005, Perret still had his job as director of marine fisheries for the state of Mississippi, and was unsure what to do. He wanted to stay and rebuild, but was that wise?

The year 2005 had been an extraordinary one in the Atlantic. There were so many tropical storms that for the first time meteorologists ran out of names for them. Wilma became the most powerful Atlantic storm ever recorded. Katrina brought an entire U.S. city to its knees. It was the second hurricane year in a row to be described by meteorologists as "exceptional" and "unprecedented," and it came after a decade of rising hurricane activity that stretched the bounds of what had previously been regarded as natural. So what was going on? Are hurricanes becoming more destructive as global warming kicks in? Is there worse to come? The answer matters not just to the people in the firing line around the Gulf of Mexico and the Caribbean, or across the tropics in the Indian Ocean and the Pacific: if there's more severe disruption to oil production in the Gulf, or super-typhoons hit economic powerhouses like Shanghai or Tokyo at full force, we'll all feel the impact.

Until 2005, most of the world's leading hurricane experts were san-guine. The upsurge in the number of hurricanes in the North Atlantic in the previous decade had been just part of a normal cycle. Hurricanes had been strong before, from the 1940s through the 1960s. Climate models suggested that even a doubling of carbon dioxide levels in the atmosphere would increase hurricane intensity by only 10 percent or so. But that year the consensus was shattered. A flurry of papers claimed that hurricanes had grown more intense during the past thirty-year surge in global tempera-tures. Not more frequent, but more intense, with stronger winds, longer durations, more unrelenting rains, and even less predictable tracks. The trend was apparent in all the world's oceans, they said. From New Orleans to Tokyo, nobody was immune.

One of the authors, Kerry Emanuel, of the Massachusetts Institute of Technology, said: "My results suggest that future warming may lead to an upward trend in tropical cyclone destructive potential and—taking into account an increasing coastal population—a substantial increase in hurricane-related losses in the 21st century." Coming just weeks after the destruction of New Orleans, that sounded like a clear message to Corky Perret and the people of the Gulf Coast. No point in rebuilding, because the next superhurricane could be just around the corner. But the claims produced a schism among the high priests of hurricane forecasting. Many, like the veteran forecaster William Gray, of Colorado State University, said that they saw no upward trend and no human fingerprint. They accused the authors of the latest papers of bias and worse. So who was right?

Hurricanes are an established part of the climate system. There have al-ways been hurricanes. They start off as clusters of thunderstorms that form as warm, humid air rises from the surface of the tropical ocean. As the air rises, the water vapor condenses, releasing energy that heats the air and makes it rise even higher. If enough storm clouds gather in close proximity, they can form what Emanuel calls a "pillar" of humid air, extending from the ocean surface for several miles into the troposphere. The low pressure at the base of the pillar sucks in more air, which picks up energy in the form of water vapor as it flows inward, and releases it as it rises. This lowers the pressure still further.

Meanwhile, the rotation of Earth, acting on the inward-flowing air, makes the pillar spin. If conditions are favorable, a tropical storm can rapidly turn into a hurricane as wind speeds pick up. Its power is staggering: Chris Landsea, of the National Oceanic and Atmospheric Administration, in Miami, has calculated that an average hurricane can release in a day as much energy as a million Hiroshima bombs. Luckily for all concerned, only a tiny fraction of this energy is converted into winds.

Worldwide there are about eighty-five tropical cyclones each year, of which about sixty reach hurricane force. That figure has been fairly stable for as long as people have been counting hurricanes. But the distribution of the hurricanes varies a great deal from year to year. In 2005, for example, the Atlantic was battered but the Pacific was relatively peaceful. On the face of it, global warming is likely to make things worse. The initial pillar of humid air forms only when the temperature of the sea surface exceeds 78°F. As the world's oceans warm, ever-larger areas of ocean exceed the threshold. There has been an average ocean warming in the tropics of 0.5 degrees already.

What is more, every degree above the threshold seems to encourage stronger hurricanes. When Katrina went from a category 1 to a category 5 hurricane back in August 2005, the surface of the Gulf of Mexico was around 86°F, which, so far as anyone knows, was a record. Whether or not climate change can be blamed for the record sea temperatures (and most would guess that it can), those temperatures certainly helped Katrina strengthen as it slipped across the Gulf from Florida toward the Louisiana coast.

This simple link between sea surface temperatures and hurricane formation and strength has encouraged the view that a warmer world will inevitably lead to more hurricanes, stronger hurricanes, and the formation of hurricanes in places formerly outside their range. But the world is not that simple, says William Gray. What actually drives the updrafts that create the storm clouds, he says, is not the absolute temperature at the sea's surface but the difference in temperature at the top of the storm. Climate models suggest that global warming will raise air temperatures aloft. So, if he is right, while the current sea surface temperatures necessary to create hurricanes may be 78°F or more, it could in future rise to 82° or more. In the final analysis, Gray argues, the hurricane-generating potential of the tropics may remain largely unchanged.

There are other limitations on hurricane formation. However hot the oceans get, air cannot rise everywhere. It has to fall in some places, too, whatever the ocean temperature. And many incipient hurricanes are defused by horizontal winds that lop off their tops. Climate models suggest that global warming will increase wind speeds at levels where they would disrupt hurricanes. Other disruptions include dust, which often blows across the Atlantic during dry years in the Sahara.

But some trends will make big storms more likely. Most tropical storms fizzle out because they lose contact with their fuel—the heat of warm ocean waters. This happens most obviously when a hurricane passes over land, but it also happens at sea. As the storm grows, its waves stir up the ocean, mixing the warm surface water with the generally cooler water beneath. The surface water cools, and that can be the end. In practice, a hurricane can grow only if the warmth extends for tens of yards or more below the surface. But with every year that passes, warm water is penetrating ever deeper into the world's oceans. That is clearly tied to global warming. And it is setting up ideal conditions for more violent thunderstorms. Katrina is again an object lesson here. It continued to strengthen as it headed toward New Orleans, because it moved over water in the Gulf of Mexico that was very warm, not just at the surface but to a depth of more than 300 feet.

The past decade in the North Atlantic has seen a string of records broken. The period from 1995 to 1998 experienced more Atlantic hurricanes than had ever before occurred in such a short time—a record broken only in 2004 and 2005. The 1998 season was the first in a 100-year record when, on September 25, four hurricanes were on weather charts of the North Atlantic at one time. And not long afterward came Hurricane Mitch, the most destructive storm in the Western Hemisphere for 200 years. Feeding on exceptionally warm waters in the Caribbean, it ripped through Central America in the final days of October 1998, its torrential rains bringing havoc to Honduras and Nicaragua and killing some 10,000 people in landslides and floods.

The Atlantic is also generating hurricanes in places where they have never been seen before. In March 2004, the first known hurricane in the South Atlantic formed, striking southern Brazil. That the hurricane, later named Catarina, even formed was startling enough. What caused the greatest shock was that it developed very close to a zone of ocean pinpointed a few years before by Britain's Hadley Centre modelers as a likely new focus for hurricane formation in a warmer greenhouse world. But they had predicted that the waters there wouldn't be up to the task till 2070. Many saw Catarina as a further sign that global warming was making its presence felt in the hurricane world rather ahead of schedule.

The billion-dollar question (literally so for insurance companies) is whether there is now a discernible climate change component at work in the frequency and intensity of hurricanes. Kerry Emanuel, for one, argues that whatever the natural variability, the "large upswing" in hurricanes in the North Atlantic in the past decade is "unprecedented, and probably reflects the effect of global warming." Jim Hansen weighed in at the end of 2005, insisting that climate change was the cause of a warmer tropical Atlantic and that "the contention that hurricane formation has nothing to do with global warming seems irrational and untenable."

The matter of North Atlantic hurricane trends is likely to be debated for many years yet. The "signal" of climate change will be difficult to disentangle from the "noise" of natural variability. But while it is easy to become obsessed with hurricanes in the North Atlantic, they amount to only around a tenth of the global total—and a rather smaller proportion of those that make landfall in a typical year. The biggest source of hurricanes is, and is likely to remain, in the western Pacific, where they terrorize vulnerable and densely populated nations like the Philippines, Vietnam, and China. So it is the global picture that both matters most and is most likely to resolve the issue of the impact of climate change.

Several research groups have been scouring records of past hurricanes worldwide to see if there is any evidence of a trend as the world has warmed. Emanuel has concluded that, on average, storms are lasting 60 percent longer and generating wind speeds 15 percent higher than they did back in the 1950s. The damage done by a hurricane is proportional not to the wind speed but to the wind speed cubed. And Emanuel's results suggest that the destructive power of a typical hurricane has increased by an alarming 70 percent. "Global tropical cyclone activity is responding in a rather large way to global warming," he says.

Others are coming to agree. Only weeks after Emanuel's paper appeared, in the autumn of 2005, three other leading hurricane researchers published a similarly alarming conclusion. Peter Webster and Judy Curry, of the Georgia Institute of Technology, and Greg Holland, of NCAR, concluded that while there had been no overall increase in the number of hurricanes worldwide, the frequency of the strongest storms—categories 4 and 5—had almost doubled since the early 1970s. They now made up 35 percent of the total, compared with 20 percent just three decades before. The trend, the researchers said, was global, and they agreed with Emanuel that it was clearly connected to the worldwide rise in sea surface temperatures. That made it extremely unlikely that natural cycles, which are relatively short-term and confined to single ocean basins, were causing the trend. "We can say with confidence that the trends in sea surface temperatures and hurricane intensity are connected to climate change," Curry declared.

William Gray and some other traditional hurricane forecasters have contested the findings, claiming that some of the data, particularly old estimates of wind speed from the Pacific in the 1970s, are flawed. In an increasingly vitriolic exchange, Gray argued that the papers simply could not be true. Emanuel and Webster agree that the data are not as good as they might like. But "Gray has not brought to my attention any difficulties with the data [of] which I was not already aware," Emanuel said, with some irritation. Webster says Gray is "grasping at thin air."

So where does that leave us? There is as yet nothing unique about recent individual hurricanes, though Katrina, Wilma, and Mitch clearly stretch the bounds of what can be regarded as normal. The largest and most powerful hurricane ever recorded, Typhoon Tip, with wind speeds of more than 180 miles per hour, grazed Japan a quarter of a century ago, in 1979. The storm that hit Galveston in 1900 killed 10,000 people, many more than Katrina. Both pale compared with a hurricane in 1970 that may have killed half a million people in what is now Bangladesh.

But even if we don't yet see "superhurricanes," evidence is emerging of a human fingerprint in the rising number of stronger, longer-lasting hurricanes. It is not yet proof of a long-term global trend tied to global warming, but the striking finding from both Emanuel and Webster that there is a consistent, global connection between rising sea surface temperature and rising storm strength is strong evidence of such a link. Whatever the theoretical concerns, for now it seems that, as the climatologist Kevin Trenberth, of the National Oceanic and Atmospheric Administration, puts it: "High sea surface temperatures make for more intense storms." In a paper published in June 2006, Trenberth calculated that about half of the extra warmth in the waters of the tropical North Atlantic in 2005 could be attributed to global warming. This warming, he said, "provides a new background level that increases the risks of future enhancements in hurricane activity."

One puzzling question is how scientists have until now failed to spot the sharply increased destructiveness of modern hurricanes. There is no dispute that, taken together, hurricanes have been doing a lot more damage in recent years. In badly organized countries, such as many in Central America, that has often meant a heavy loss of life. Elsewhere, if evacuation systems work, it has simply meant a huge loss of property. Insurance claims for hurricane disasters have been soaring for some years.

The prevailing view has, until recently, been that the problem is one of bad planning, rising populations, and more people putting themselves in harm's way. The beach resorts along Highway 90 and the large squatter colonies spreading along low-lying coastal land in Asia give some support to that view. But the new data suggest that there is more to it than that. A lot more. And that most of the extra damage is being caused by the storms themselves becoming more intense. The trend seems set to continue.

35

OZONE HOLES IN THE GREENHOUSE

Why millions face radiation threat

Joe Farman is a scientist of the old school. String and sealing wax. Smokes a pipe and drinks real ale. He has the faraway look in his eyes that you often see in men who have spent any length of time in Antarctica. He is retired now from the British Antarctic Survey, where he spent virtually his entire working life in a worthy though less than exalted capacity. Or he did until 1985, when he wrote one of the decade's most quoted research papers. He is the man who discovered the ozone hole over Antarctica. And the way it happened—or, rather, almost didn't happen—is revealing.

A quarter of a century ago, Farman was in charge of the BAS's Dobson meter, which for many years had been pointing up into the sky measuring the depth of the ozone layer in the stratosphere from the BAS's base at Halley Bay, on an ice shelf off West Antarctica. For several years his bosses had been trying to halt the observations and bring the old instrument home. After all, they pointed out, nothing interesting had happened for years, and satellites orbiting Earth were by then measuring ozone levels routinely. Ground-based observations were deemed superfluous.

But Farman resisted, and in 1982, he noticed a series of unusual and abrupt fluctuations in the ozone readings, just after the sun reappeared following the long polar night. It happened again the following year.

"I asked the Americans if they had seen anything similar from their satellites," he told me later. "They said they hadn't. So I assumed that my old machine was on the blink." But he was intrigued enough not to leave it at that. He found another Dobson meter back in Cambridge, and took it south in 1984 to check the readings. It recorded the same thing—only more so. Farman's data were by now unambiguous. He was seeing a deep hole opening in the ozone layer over the base. It lasted for several weeks before closing again. "We were sure then that something dramatic was happening," Farman said. In places, more than 90 percent of the ozone was disappearing in what appeared to be runaway reactions taking place in just a few days.

The ozone layer protects Earth's surface from dangerous ultraviolet radiation from the sun. Without this filter, there would be epidemics of skin cancers, cataracts, and many other diseases, as well as damage to vital ecosystems. Life on Earth has evolved to live under its protection, and would find things much harder without it.

For more than a decade, scientists had been concerned about the ozone layer, fearing that man-made chemicals such CFCs in aerosols might cause it to thin. But nobody had thought of a hole forming. Least of all over Antarctica, which was as far from the source of any ozone-destroying chemicals as you could get. And certainly not in a runaway reaction over just a few days. Earth was simply not supposed to work that way.

Farman bit his pipe and got to work. No more checking with NASA. He had his data and was intent on an urgent publication in the scientific press. Perhaps he sensed it was his moment of fame. He was certainly scared by what he had found—scared enough to miss all the office parties in Cambridge in 1984 to finish his paper titled "Large Losses of Total Ozone in Antarctica." He posted it to *Nature* on Christmas Eve.

The editors didn't quite share Farman's sense of urgency. It took them three months to accept his paper, and another two months to publish it. When the paper finally appeared, NASA scientists were confused. They still had no inkling of anything amiss over Antarctica. But they could hardly ignore the findings of two Dobson meters, however ancient. They re-examined the raw data from their satellite instruments and were shocked to find that their satellites had seen the ozone hole forming and growing over Antarctica all along, even before Farman had spotted it. But the computers on the ground that were analyzing the streams of data had been programmed to throw out any wildly abnormal readings. And the data showing the ozone hole had certainly fitted that category. The episode, as Farman was not slow to point out, was a salutary lesson for high-tech science. It was also a triumph for the string-and-sealing-wax school, and for the dogged collection of seemingly boring and useless data about the environment.

Paul Crutzen—who had unraveled much of the complex chemistry of the ozone layer—swiftly tied Farman's findings to specific chemical reactions involving CFCs that took place only in the uniquely cold air over Antarctica each spring. Below about -130°F, unique clouds form in the stratosphere above Antarctica. These are called polar stratospheric clouds. It turned out that the runaway reactions happened only on the surface of the frozen particles in these clouds. The reactions required both the cold to create the clouds and solar energy to fuel them. And there was a window of a few weeks when both were supplied—after the sun had risen, but before the air warmed enough to destroy the clouds. After that, the air warmed and the ozone recovered, though the repair job took some months.

Farman's discovery and Crutzen's analysis finally pushed the world into taking tough action against ozone-eating chemicals. The Montreal Protocol was signed in 1987. Slowly, very slowly, the amount of CFCs and other ozone-eaters in the stratosphere is declining. And the Antarctic ozone layer is equally slowly starting to heal, though it could be a century before it is fully repaired, even if every promise made by government negotiators is met. But it had been a close call.

And things could have been a lot worse. "Looking back, we were extremely lucky that industrialists chose chlorine compounds, rather than the very similar bromine compounds, to put in spray cans and refrigerators early in the last century," says Crutzen. Why so? Bromine compounds make refrigerants that are at least as effective as their chlorine equivalents. But atom for atom, bromine is about a hundred times better than chlorine at destroying ozone. Pure luck determined that Thomas Midgley, the American chemist who developed CFCs, did not opt for their bromine equivalent. "It is a nightmarish thought," says Crutzen, "but if he had chosen bromine, we would have had something far worse than an ozone hole over Antarctica. We would have been faced with a catastrophic ozone hole, everywhere and at all seasons during the 1970s, before we knew a thing about what was going on."

The world has been very lucky. Or has been lucky so far. The same combination of low temperatures and accumulating gases that combined so devastatingly over Antarctica can also occur over the Arctic in some years. The conditions are not quite so favorable for ozone destruction, because the atmosphere is not quite so stable and the extremely cold temperatures occur less frequently. But there have been some near misses.

One occurred in January 2005. Anne Hormes, who runs the German research station at Ny-Alesund, in Svalbard, told me the story when I visited there a few months later. Temperatures in the lower stratosphere above Svalbard had for a few days fallen to -144°F, fully 14 degrees below the threshold necessary for the formation of polar stratospheric clouds, and extremely low even by the standards of Antarctica. "We feared that a real, big ozone hole would form," she said. "And if the temperature had stayed that cold for a few more weeks, till the sun came up to drive the chemical reactions, we would certainly have seen one." It would have been the Arctic's first full-fledged ozone hole, and in all probability a major world environment story.

Her concern is shared. The ozone expert Drew Shindell, of the Goddard Institute for Space Studies, says: "Overall winter temperatures are going down in the Arctic stratosphere—2005 was very cold. But actual ozone loss is very time-critical. So far, we have been lucky." But he doubts that our luck will hold. How so? Why are the risks of an ozone hole still growing, even though the chemicals that cause it are now in decline in the stratosphere?

The problem is this. In the lower atmosphere, greenhouse gases trap heat. But in the stratosphere, they have the opposite effect, causing an increase in the amount of heat that escapes to space from that zone of the atmosphere. This is happening worldwide, but some of the most intense stratospheric cooling is over areas with the greatest warming at the surface. Like the Arctic, where the air increasingly resembles the air high above Antarctica.

There is another risk factor, too. The warmer troposphere, with stronger convection currents taking thunderstorm clouds right up to the boundary with the stratosphere, may be injecting more water vapor into the stratosphere. As far as we know, the stratosphere has always been very dry in the past. So extra water vapor is potentially a big change. And more water vapor will make more likely the formation of the polar stratospheric clouds within which ozone destruction takes place. "If it gets a lot wetter, that will make ozone depletion much worse," says Shindell. There is some evidence that that is happening, though data are scarce. "Water vapor levels in parts of the lower stratosphere have doubled in the past sixty years," he says.

No hole formed in the Arctic ozone layer in 2005, because the sun did not rise when the air was at its coldest. But the spring of 2005 nonetheless saw the largest Arctic ozone loss in forty years of record-keeping. More than a third of the ozone disappeared, and losses reached 70 percent in some places. Air masses with reduced ozone levels spread south across Scandinavia and Britain, and even as far south as Italy for a few days. One year soon, the sun will rise when temperatures are still cold enough for major runaway ozone destruction. And when it does, millions of people may be living beneath. This will be another unexpected consequence of global warming.

VIII

Inevitable surprises

36

THE DANCE

The poles or the tropics? Who leads in the climatic dance?

As we have seen, researchers into the global history of climate, especially in the U.S., divide into two camps. One believes that the key drivers for past, and therefore probably future, climate change lie in the polar regions, especially the far North Atlantic. The other believes that the real action happens in the tropics.

The most outspoken advocate for the polar school is Wally Broecker, of Lamont-Doherty. As described in Chapter 23, he is the man behind the idea of the ocean conveyor, which begins in the far North Atlantic and which, he argues, is the great climatic amplifier. It has, he says, a simple on-off switch. It pushed the world into and out of ice ages; it modulates the effects of Bond's solar pulse, including its most recent manifestations in the medieval warm period and the little ice age; and it could be a big player in directing the consequences of global warming. Around Broecker is a whole school of researchers who have spent their careers investigating the dramatic climate events of the North Atlantic region, as recorded in the ice cores of Greenland.

The rival, tropical school has often looked to two characters. One, just down the corridor from Broecker at Lamont-Doherty, is Mark Cane, a leading modeler of El Niño, the biggest climate fluctuation in the tropics. The other is Lonnie Thompson, the man who decided thirty years ago to stop investigating polar ice cores and switch instead to drilling tropical glaciers. They argue that Broecker's ocean conveyor is at best a sideshow, relevant to the North Atlantic and the countries that border it, but not the great global amplifier it is claimed to be. For them, the important climatic levers must be in the planetary heat and hydrological engines around

Earth's girth. The debate between the two schools has, at various stages, become quite personal. "It all came from one man: Wally Broecker," says Cane. "You were for him or against him. And I found myself against."

The polar people deploy their polar ice core data to show that climate change has been more dramatic and sudden in the far North, so that must be the cockpit of climate change. This is where the Gulf Stream turns turtle and drives the ocean conveyor; this is where ice melting and changes in freshwater flow can freeze the ocean virtually overnight and send temperatures tumbling by tens of degrees; this, above all, is where the great ice sheets of the ice ages formed and died. They have a point. There can be little doubt about the importance of ice formation to the ice ages. Virtually the whole world cooled then, and two thirds of that cooling was caused by the feedback of growing ice sheets and their ability to reflect solar radiation back into space. And nothing except a huge rush of meltwater from the receding ice caps could have plunged the world into the Younger Dryas, 12,800 years ago.

But that doesn't mean that the Arctic tells the whole story. What pulled the world out of the Younger Dryas, for instance—an event that happened even faster than its onset? And while big climate change during and at the close of the ice ages does seem to be associated with polar events, the evidence concerning climate change since is far less secure. Thompson argues that most of the global climatic shudders of the Holocene, such as events 5,500 and 4,200 years ago, must have been tropical in origin: "In climate models, you can only make such things happen in both the Northern and Southern Hemispheres by forcing events from the tropics, and I am convinced that is what is happening."

Hockey-stick author Mike Mann, though not a fully paid-up member of the tropical school, says: "I increasingly think that the tropical Pacific is the key player. When you see La Niña dominating the medieval warm period and El Niño taking hold in the little ice age, it begins to look like the tropics, rather than the North Atlantic, rule." The argument is that heat flows from the tropics are the true intermediaries between Bond's solar pulse and temperature fluctuations in the North Atlantic.

The tropical school also accuses the polar fraternity of being blinkered about what constitutes climate change. Besides overly focusing on events in North America and Europe, it stands accused of being overly concerned with temperature. In the tropics, the hydrological cycle matters more than the temperature. Megadroughts are as damaging as little ice ages, and the rains, rather than extra warmth, bring plenty. Witness the drying of the Sahara 5,500 years ago, and the importance of the vagaries of the Asian monsoon.

The tropical school doesn't stop there. Its adherents argue that many of the big climatic events in the Northern polar regions have their origins in the tropics. The tropics, by delivering warm water into the North Atlantic, are just as capable of flipping the switch of the ocean conveyor as is ice formation in the far North Atlantic. And if there is a tropical equivalent of Broecker's switch in the North Atlantic, they say, it is probably the warm water pool around Indonesia—an area they often call "the firebox." This is the greatest store and distribution point for heat on the surface of the planet, with a known propensity for threshold changes via the El Niño system. It is also the biggest generator of water vapor for the atmosphere, which is both a potent greenhouse gas and a driver of weather systems.

If this region can trigger short-term El Niños that warm the whole planet, and La Niñas that cool it again, then might it not also trigger long-term climate changes? Might not events here have been important in turning a minor orbital wobble into the waxing and waning of the ice ages? The waning, certainly. For cores of ocean sediment recently taken from the tropical Pacific suggest that temperatures started to rise there a thousand or more years before the Northern ice sheets began to shrink.

But after some years of standoff, many protagonists in this debate are now seeking common ground. Not Broecker, of course. But Richard Alley, a polar man but also a fan of Thompson's, now thinks that the location of the climate system driver's seat may change with time. It is easy to imagine the power of ice and meltwater to hijack the world's climate during the glaciations, when a third of the Northern Hemisphere was covered with ice. But with less ice around in the interglacials, he concedes, the argument is less persuasive. And, with characteristic pithiness, he admits to past regional bias. "Suppose the North Atlantic circulation did shut down. Sure, Europe would care. They might have a midseason break in football in Britain. Manchester United wouldn't be playing on Boxing Day. But in the Great Plains of the U.S. and in the Pacific Ocean, would it be so important?"

Meanwhile, on the tropical side, Cane admits: "I am less absolutist than I used to be." He agrees that his great enthusiasms, El Niño and the tropical Pacific, might not be behind everything. He still believes that the role of the ocean conveyor is hopelessly hyped, but he concedes the possible importance of the "sink or freeze" switch for sea ice in the North Atlantic. The divide between the polar and tropical schools is "a slightly false separation," says Peter deMenocal, of Lamont-Doherty. "You cannot at the end of the day change one bit without changing the other. They are all part of the same pattern, whether leading or following." Earth functions as an integrated system, not as a series of discrete levers.

That view seems to be confirmed by Steve Goldstein, of Columbia University, who has used analysis of a rare earth called neodymium, which has different isotopic ratios in different oceans, to reconstruct the order of events at the starts and ends of the ice ages. He argues that orbital changes, as expected, lead events. But the first feedback to respond is the ice-albedo feedback. It caused an initial cooling at the start of the last ice age that was most pronounced in the far North. Prompted by that initial cooling, the chemistry and biology of the oceans started to change, removing carbon dioxide from the atmosphere and accentuating the cooling further. Only then, some thousands of years later, did the ocean conveyor start to shut down. "The conveyor follows; it does not lead," he says. If his analysis is confirmed, it will be a blow to Broecker, but it will also confirm that both the tropics and the polar regions were deeply implicated in the elaborate dance that took the world into and out of the ice ages.

Paul Crutzen has been in the forefront of research in both spheres, helping crack the mysteries of the Antarctic ozone layer while making a strong case for the dynamic properties of the tropical heat engine. "Big planetary changes happen in both the tropics and the very high latitudes," he says. "The tropics are where the high temperatures drive a lot of the chemistry and dynamics of the atmosphere. And the polar regions are the homes of the big natural feedbacks that could accelerate climate change: things like melting ice and permafrost and alterations to ocean currents." That is probably as good a compromise statement as can be found right now. At the end of the day, the system is bigger than the individual parts.

37

NEW HORIZONS

Feedbacks from the stratosphere

Is that the end of the story? I don't think so. Constantly, in writing this book, I have been struck by how little we know about the way Earth's climate and its attendant systems, feedbacks, and oscillations function. This story contains some heroic guesses, some brilliant intuition, and, no doubt, occasionally some dreadful howlers—because that is where the science currently lies. More questions than answers. Beyond the cautious certainties of the IPCC reports, there is a swath of conjectures and scary scenarios. Some criticize the scientists who talk about these possibilities for failing to stick to certainties, and for rocking the IPCC's boat. But I suspect we still need a good deal more of the same, because we may know much less than we think. I think Wally Broecker and his colleagues deserve praise for developing their scenarios about the global conveyor. They have produced a persuasive narrative that has transformed debate. Of course, producing a persuasive story doesn't make it right, but it does generate new research and new ideas that can be tested. It is time someone in the tropical school produced something comparable.

Equally important, there may be other narratives that need developing. Richard Alley must be right that there are more "inevitable surprises" out there—outcomes that nobody has yet thought of, let alone tested. One area where unconsidered triggers for global climate change may lie is in and around Antarctica. While sinking cores into Antarctica as well as Greenland, the polar school has yet to devote much attention to generating theories about events in the South Atlantic. This may be a mistake. Much of the action in Earth-system science in the next few years will happen there, I am sure. Any place capable of producing something as remarkable as the ozone hole in the stratosphere is surely capable of storing up other surprises.

One new idea emerging from the battle between the polar and tropical schools is that the real driver of climate change up to and including the ice ages may actually lie in the far South. During ice ages, the theory goes, the ocean conveyor did not so much shut down as start getting its new deep water from the Antarctic rather than the Arctic. A certain amount of deep water has always formed around Antarctica, though in recent times it has played second fiddle to the North Atlantic. But, as the ice sheets grew across the Arctic and the chimneys in the North Atlantic shut down, the zone of deepwater formation in the Southern Ocean seems to have strengthened and may have taken charge of the conveyor.

Some go further and say that there must be a "bipolar seesaw," in which warming in the Southern Hemisphere is tied to cooling in the North and vice versa. That would certainly make sense of some of the Antarctic ice cores that show warming while the North was cooling. The question then is: Which pole leads? Does the North Atlantic end of the system shut down, closing off the Gulf Stream's northward flow of warm water and leaving more heat in the South Atlantic? Or does some switch in the South trigger the shutdown of the Gulf Stream and leave the Northern Hemisphere out in the cold, with the North Atlantic freezing over?

The idea that the South may lead in this particular dance gained ground late in 2005, when results were published from new ice cores in Antarctica. A European group found that the tightest "coupling" between temperature and carbon dioxide levels in the atmosphere is to be found in Antarctic cores, rather than their Greenland equivalents. "The way I see things is that the tropics and Antarctica are in phase and lead the North Atlantic," says Peter deMenocal, of Lamont-Doherty. "Even though we may see the largest events in the North Atlantic, they are often responding, not leading." By this reading, the onset of the Northern glaciation may have its origins in the Southern Hemisphere.

This apparently obscure debate could matter a great deal in the twenty-first century. Right now, the world has become worried that melting ice in the Arctic could freshen the far North Atlantic and shut down the Gulf Stream. This is a real fear. But maybe, while we are researching that possibility, we are ignoring the risk that large stores of freshwater in the Antarctic might break out and disrupt deepwater formation there. Arguably, the risks are far greater in the South, where, besides the potential breakout of ice from Pine Island Bay, recent radar mapping studies have revealed a large number of lakes of liquid water beneath the ice sheets of Antarctica. They might set off a cascade of freshwater into the Southern Ocean, similar in scale to the emptying of Lake Agassiz. Yet nobody, so far as I am aware, has studied what the effects of such a breakout might be for deepwater formation and the Southern arm of the ocean conveyor.

Or, rather than shutting down deepwater formation in Antarctica, might we be about to trigger a switch in the bipolar seesaw, so that deepwater formation in the South takes over from that in the far North? Could that switch be flipped in the South, rather than in the North? And if so, how? And what might happen? It would certainly lead to the Southern Hemisphere's hanging on to very large amounts of heat that currently head north on the Gulf Stream. The Southern Ocean might warm dramatically while the North Atlantic froze. And if the Southern Ocean were to warm substantially, says Will Steffen, the former head of the International Geosphere-Biosphere Programme, "it could result in the surging, melting, and collapse of the West Antarctic ice sheet." Ouch.

If anybody doubts that plenty of new surprises are waiting to be discovered, then the work by Drew Shindell, of the Goddard Institute for Space Studies (GISS), should offer food for thought. His story starts with an apparent success for climate modelers. Since the days of Arrhenius, most climate models have predicted that global warming will be greatest at high latitudes, where known feedbacks like ice-albedo are most pronounced. So rises in temperatures of up to 5°F over parts of the Arctic and the Antarctic Peninsula in recent decades have often been taken as the first proof of man-made climate change.

But there has been a persistent and troubling counterargument. The warming in the polar regions appears to be linked to two natural climatic fluctuations, one in the North and one in the South. In the North, the fluctuation is known as the Arctic Oscillation, an extension of the better-known North Atlantic Oscillation. It is the second largest climate cycle on Earth, after El Niño. The oscillation itself, as measured by meteorologists, is a change in relative air pressure, but its main impact is to strengthen or weaken the prevailing westerly winds that circle the Arctic. Like El Niño, the Arctic Oscillation flips between two modes. In its positive mode, air pressure differences between the polar and extrapolar regions are strong, and winds strengthen. Especially in winter, the winds take heat from the warm oceans and heat the land. So, during a positive phase of the Arctic Oscillation, northern Europe, Svalbard, Siberia, the Atlantic coast of North America, and Alaska all warm strongly. Likewise, when the oscillation is in its negative phase, the winds drop and the land cools.

The strength of this effect depends on the warmth of the oceans, and in particular on the Gulf Stream and the health of the ocean conveyor. But for most of the past thirty-five years, the Arctic Oscillation has been in a strongly positive mode, helping sustain a long period of warming. Modeling studies suggest that at least half of the warming in parts of the Northern Hemisphere is directly due to its influence, leaving global warming itself apparently a bit player. Except that there is growing evidence that global warming is driving the Arctic Oscillation, too. And it does so from a surprising direction.

Enter Shindell. He likes to occupy the unpopular boundaries between scientific disciplines. His particular interest is the little-studied relationship between the stratosphere, the home of the ozone layer, and the troposphere, where our weather happens. He studies this with the aid of the GISS climate model, one of the few that can fully include the stratosphere in its calculations. Most models show little relationship between global warming and the Arctic Oscillation. The GISS model is the same when the stratosphere is not included. But Shindell discovered that when the stratosphere is hooked up, the result is a huge intensification of the Arctic Oscillation and the westerly winds around the Arctic. In fact, with current levels of greenhouse gases, he has reproduced a pattern very similar to the current unusually strong positive state of the oscillation.

What is going on? One of the problems with climate models is that it is not always easy to pinpoint exactly which of the elements in the model is causing the effects that you see in the printout. But here the role of the stratosphere is clear. And Shindell reckons he has the links in the chain explained, at least. As greenhouse gases cool the stratosphere, this cooling alters energy distribution within so as to strengthen stratospheric winds. In particular, a wind called the stratospheric jet, which swirls around the Arctic each winter, picks up speed. This wind, in turn, drives the westerly winds beneath, in the troposphere. So they go faster, too. In this way, a stratospheric feedback is amplifying global warming in the Arctic region by pushing the Arctic Oscillation into overdrive and strengthening the winds that warm the land. It is a brilliant, startling, and, until recently, entirely unexpected feedback.

Might the same apply to events in Antarctica? The GISS model suggests so. There, the dominant climatic oscillation is the Southern Hemisphere annular mode, or SAM. Like the Arctic Oscillation, the SAM is a measure of the air pressure difference between polar and nonpolar air that drives westerly winds sweeping around Antarctica. The geography is somewhat different from the Arctic's. The winds whistle around the Southern Ocean and hit land only on the Antarctic Peninsula, which juts out from the Antarctic mainland toward South America.

The climatologist John King has studied the SAM for the British Antarctic Survey. He says that, like the Arctic Oscillation, it has been in overdrive since the mid-1960s, driving stronger westerly winds. And, again like the Arctic Oscillation, it is amplifying warming along its path. The Antarctic Peninsula has seen air temperatures rise by 5°F since the 1960s—the only spot in the Southern Hemisphere to show warming on this scale. The effects include the melting of the peninsula's glaciers and the dramatic collapse of its floating ice shelves, such as the Larsen B. Additionally, by bringing more warm air farther south, the SAM winds are warming the waters that wash around the edges of Antarctica and beneath its ice—helping destabilize the West Antarctic ice sheet.

Here again, Shindell's model suggests that the strengthening of the SAM is the product of a cooling stratosphere and a strengthening of stratospheric jets. There is an important additional element here in the thinning ozone layer, which makes an additional contribution to stratospheric cooling.

All this is alarming evidence of a new positive feedback that intensifies warming in two particularly sensitive regions of the planet, where that ex-

tra warming could unleash further dangerous change. Glaciologists say
that the Greenland ice sheet could collapse if warming there reaches 5°F.
The huge stores of methane beneath the Siberian permafrost and the Ba-
rents Sea could be liberated by similar warming. And "the SAM warming
now includes parts of the West Antarctic ice sheet, as well as the Antarc-
tic Peninsula," says Shindell's boss, Jim Hansen. "This is a really urgent
issue."

The discovery of the stratospheric feedback also helps answer another ques-
tion that has long bothered climate scientists: Why do variations in solar
output that are probably no more than half a watt per 10.8 square feet cause
the big climate fluctuations in the North Atlantic identified by Gerard
Bond in his analysis of the 1,500-year solar pulse? Conventional climate
models without a stratospheric dimension suggest that such a solar fluc-
tuation shouldn't produce temperature changes of more than 0.35°F. But,
although the global temperature change may well have been close to that,
in parts of Europe and North America the pulses produce changes ten
times as great.

Researchers have struggled to find amplifying mechanisms that might
have caused that. Sea ice, the ocean conveyor, and tropical flips like El Niño
have all been suggested, but none seems up to the task. Shindell says the
answer is his stratospheric feedback. The heart of the mechanism this time
is ultraviolet radiation. While the total solar radiation reaching Earth's
surface during Bond's pulses varies by only a tenth of a percentage point,
the amount of ultraviolet radiation reaching Earth changes by as much as
10 percent. Most of the ultraviolet radiation is absorbed by the ozone layer
in the stratosphere, so its impact at ground level is small. But the process
of absorption causes important changes in energy flows in the stratosphere.
These eventually change the stratospheric jets, and with them the Arctic
Oscillation in the Northern Hemisphere and the SAM in the South.

Shindell modeled the likely effects of the last reduction of solar radia-
tion at the Maunder Minimum in the depths of Europe's little ice age, 350
years ago. The GISS model without the stratosphere was unmoved by the
tiny change in solar radiation. But with the stratosphere included, it de-
livered a drop in temperatures of 1.8 to 2.6°F in Europe, but only a tenth

as much globally—results remarkably close to likely events in the real world. The declining flows of ultraviolet radiation into the stratosphere triggered a slowdown in the westerly winds at ground level, says Shindell. That, in turn, caused winter cooling, particularly over land, in the higher latitudes of the Northern Hemisphere.

The stratosphere and its influence on polar and midlatitude winds thus seem to be a hidden amplifier that can turn small changes in solar radiation into larger changes in temperature in the polar regions of the planet. This is not the only amplifier in those regions. Ice and snow are important, along with the ocean conveyor and, maybe, methane. But it appears to be the critical ingredient that turns minor solar cycles into big climatic events. It makes sense of Bond's solar pulse and, perhaps, of tiny short-term variability in solar radiation.

Climate skeptics have sometimes argued that sunspot cycles correlate so well with warming in the twentieth century that greenhouse gases could be irrelevant. Mainstream climate scientists dismissed this idea because they could not see the mechanisms that might make this happen. The changes in solar radiation seemed much too small. Shindell's finding of a powerful stratospheric feedback to the solar signal have forced a rethink. But Shindell has not joined the climate skeptics. Far from it.

His conclusion is that for the first half of the century, the correlation between estimated solar output and Earth's temperature is not bad. And the stratospheric feedback might show how the sun could have driven some warming early in the century, followed by a midcentury cooling that made some fear an oncoming ice age. But since then, there has been no change in the solar signal that could be amplified to explain the recent warming. During the final three decades of the twentieth century, average solar output, if anything, declined, while global temperatures—not just at high latitudes but almost everywhere—surged ahead at what was probably a record rate. So, Shindell says, "although solar variability does impact surface climate indirectly, it was almost certainly not responsible for most of the rapid global warming seen over the past three decades."

For that most recent period, he says, it is clear that rising concentrations of greenhouse gases are the primary driver. But besides producing a general global warming, they have generated changes in the stratosphere that have produced a specific positive feedback to warming in the polar regions and the midlatitudes. The positive feedback has manifested itself through the apparently natural Arctic Oscillation and the SAM—cycles that appear to have gone into overdrive.

Only a fool would conclude from this that we don't need to worry so much about man-made climate change. On the contrary, Shindell's dramatic discovery of the stratospheric feedback suggests that the natural processes of temperature amplification are much stronger than those in most existing climate models. His newly discovered feedback seems set to continue, driving up temperatures in Arctic regions beyond the levels previously forecast. That additional warming is likely to unleash other feedbacks that will melt ice, raise sea levels, release greenhouse gases trapped in permafrost and beneath the ocean bed, and perhaps cause trouble for the ocean conveyor.

Relieved? I don't think so.

CONCLUSION: ANOTHER PLANET

Over the past 100,000 years, there have been only two generally stable periods of climate, according to Richard Alley. The first was "when the ice sheets were biggest and the world was coldest," he says. "The second is the period we are living in now." For most of the rest of the time, there has been "a crazily jumping climate." And now, after many generations of experiencing global climatic stability, human society seems in imminent danger of returning to a world of crazy jumps. We really have no idea what it will be like, or how we will cope. There is still a chance that the jumps won't materialize, and that instead the world will warm gradually, even benignly. But the odds are against it. There are numerous feedbacks— waking monsters, in Chris Rapley's words—waiting to provide the crazy jumps. Climatically, we are entering terra incognita.

The current generation of inhabitants of this planet is in all probability the last generation that can rely on anything close to a stable global climate in which to conduct its affairs. Jim Hansen gives us just a decade to change our ways. Beyond that, he says, the last thing we can anticipate is what economists call "business as usual." It will be anything but. "Business as usual will produce basically another planet," says Hansen. "How else can you describe climate change in which the Arctic becomes an open lake in the summer, and most land areas experience average climatic conditions not experienced before in even the most extreme years?"

I am sorry if you have got this far hoping for a definitive prognosis for our planet. Right now, the only such prognosis is uncertainty. The Earth system seems chaotic, with the potential to head off in many different directions. If there is order, we don't yet know where it lies. No scenario has the ring of certainty. No part of the planet has yet been identified as holding an exclusive key to our future. No feedback is predestined to prevail. On past evidence, some areas may continue to matter more than others. But "the story of abrupt climate change will become more complicated before it is finished," as Alley puts it. "We have to go looking for dangerous thresholds, wherever they may be."

For now, we have checklists of concerns. Melting Arctic ice, whether at sea or on land, could have huge impacts, both by raising sea levels and by amplifying global warming. Glaciological "monsters" could be lurking in Pine Island Bay or the Totten glacier. The whole West Antarctic ice sheet could just fall apart one day. El Niño may get stuck on or off, triggering megadroughts or superhurricanes. The Amazon rainforest may be close to disappearing in a rage of drought and fire that would impact weather systems around the world. The oceans may turn into a giant lifeless acid bath. Smog may cripple the hydroxyl cleaning service or shut down the Asian monsoon. And the stratosphere may contain yet more surprises.

Methane is always lurking in the background, ready to repeat the great fart of 55 million years ago, if we allow it out of its various lairs. And the North Atlantic seems to hold a particular fascination. I keep coming back to Alley's disturbingly simple choice for the Gulf Stream as it surges north: sink or freeze? And to Peter Wadhams's lonely chimney, stuck out off Greenland somewhere northeast of Scoresby Sound, endlessly delivering water to the ocean floor. Until it stops. Who knows when? And who knows what will follow?

Quite a lot of this book has been taken up with climatic history. This is deliberate. The past shows more clearly than any computer model how the climate system works. It works not, generally, through gradual change but through periods of stability broken by sudden drunken lurches. And the past operation of the climate system reveals in their fully conscious state the monsters we may be in danger of waking.

But past climate does not provide a blueprint for the future. There are no easy analogues out there. We have already strayed too far from the tracks created by Bond's solar cycles and the other natural oscillations of the Earth system. Greenhouse gas concentrations are already probably at their highest level in millions of years; temperatures will soon join them. But the distinctive nature of our predicament goes a long way beyond that. Give or take the occasional asteroid impact, past changes have almost all been driven by changes in solar radiation, beamed down to us through the stratosphere. Earthly feedbacks such as biological pumps and spreading ice sheets, and threshold changes to marine currents and terrestrial vegetation, followed on the solar signal. This time, we are starting from the ground up, with a bonfire of fossil fuels that has shaken the carbon cycle to its core. Not only that: we are simultaneously filling the atmosphere with aerosols and assaulting key planetary features like the rainforests and the ozone layer. There can be no certainty about how the monsters of the Earth system will respond. We can still learn from the past, but we cannot expect the past to repeat itself.

When I first wrote at length about climate change, back in 1989, in a book called *Turning Up the Heat,* I warned that we passengers on Spaceship Earth could no longer sit back for the ride. We needed to get hold of the controls or risk disaster. But it was at heart an optimistic book. I figured that if *Homo sapiens* had come through the last ice age as a mere novice on the planet, then we could make it this time, too. We had the technology; and the economics of solving the problems wouldn't be crippling. I compared the task to getting rid of the old London pea-soupers of half a century ago. Once the decision was taken to act, the delivery would be relatively easy. We'd soon be wondering why we had dawdled for so long.

Fifteen years on, the urgency of the climate crisis is much clearer, even if the story has grown a little more complicated. But we are showing no signs yet of acting on the scale necessary. The technology is still straightforward, and the economics is only easier, but we can't get the politics right. Even at this late hour, I do believe we have it in our power to set Spaceship Earth back on the right course. But time is short. The ship is already starting to spin out of control. We may soon lose all chance of grabbing the wheel.

Humanity faces a genuinely new situation. It is not an environmental crisis in the accepted sense. It is a crisis for the entire life-support system of our civilization and our species. During the past 10,000 years, since the close of the last ice age, human civilizations have plundered and destroyed their local environments, wrecking the natural fecundity of sizable areas of the planet. Nevertheless, the planet's life-support system as a whole has until now remained stable. As one civilization fell, another rose. But the rules of the game have changed. In the Anthropocene, human influences on planetary systems are global and pervasive.

In the past, if we got things wrong and wrecked our environment, we could pack up and move somewhere else. Migration has always been one of our species' great survival strategies. Now we have nowhere else to go. No new frontier. We have only one atmosphere; only one planet.

APPENDIX: THE TRILLION-TON CHALLENGE

All the world's governments are committed to preventing "dangerous" climate change. They made that pledge at the Earth Summit in Rio de Janeiro in 1992. (The signatories included the U.S. and Australia, which both refused to ratify the subsequent Kyoto Protocol and its national targets for emissions reductions.) But what constitutes dangerous climate change? And how, in practice, can we prevent it?

For some people, dangerous climate change is already a reality. Many victims of recent hurricanes, floods, and droughts blame climate change. Such claims are usually impossible to prove. But that doesn't mean that our weather is not changing, says Myles Allen, of Oxford University. In essence, climate change is loading the dice in favor of weird and dangerous weather. "The danger zone is not something we are going to reach in the middle of this century," Allen says. "We are in it now." The 35,000 Europeans who died in the heat wave of 2003 were victims of an event that would almost certainly not have happened without the insidious increase in background temperatures that turned a warm summer into a killer.

But, despite such local disasters, most would argue that the critical aim in the quest to prevent dangerous climate change is to avoid crossing thresholds in the climate system where irreversible global changes occur—especially changes that themselves trigger further warming. There is no certainty about where such "tipping points" lie. But there is a growing consensus, especially in Europe, that the world should try to prevent global average temperatures from rising by more than 3.6°F above pre-industrial levels, or about 2.5 degrees above current levels.

Unfortunately, there is no certainty either about what limits on greenhouse gases will achieve that temperature target. We don't yet know how sensitive the climate system is. Current estimates suggest that to stack the odds in favor of staying below a 3.6-degree warming, we probably need to keep concentrations of man-made greenhouse gases below the heating equivalent of 450 parts per million of carbon dioxide. In practice, that probably means keeping carbon dioxide levels themselves below about 400 ppm. Let's call this the "safety-first" option.

Forgive me if I now abandon this language of parts per million. I find it an irritating and unnecessary abstraction. It seems to me much more sensible to talk in terms of tons of carbon instead. Then we can establish how much there is in the atmosphere and see more clearly how much we can afford to add before the climate goes pear-shaped.

The simple figures are these. At the depths of the last ice age, there were about 440 billion tons of carbon dioxide in the atmosphere. As the ice age closed, some 220 billion tons switched from the oceans to the atmosphere, raising the level there to about 660 billion tons. That's where things rested at the start of the Industrial Revolution, when humans began the large-scale burning of carbon fuels. Today, after a couple of centuries of rising emissions, we have added another 220 billion tons to the atmospheric burden, making it about 880 billion tons. If we want to keep below the safety-first concentration, we have to keep below 935 billion tons. So we have only about another 55 billion tons to go.

Currently, we pour about 8.2 billion tons of carbon into the atmosphere annually. Of this, a bit over 40 percent is quickly taken up by the oceans and by vegetation on land. The rest stays in the air, where its life expectancy is more than a century. So, for practical purposes, we are adding about 4.4 billion tons of carbon dioxide a year to the atmosphere. Even at current rates of emissions, that means that we will be above our 935-billion-ton safety-first target before 2020; and assuming that emissions continue to rise at the current rate, we will be there in less than a decade. Frankly, barring some global economic meltdown, there is now very little prospect of not exceeding 935 billion tons. If we had acted quickly after 1992, we could have done it. But the world failed.

If we are lucky—if climate sensitivity turns out to be a little lower than the gloomier predictions suggest—the 3.6-degree target may still be achieved while we allow carbon dioxide levels to rise significantly above 935 billion tons. We cannot be sure. There is already about 1 degree of warming "in the pipeline" that we can no longer prevent. But if we are feeling lucky—and with a nod to both round numbers and political reality—we might allow ourselves a ceiling of a trillion tons. Some would call that a "realistic" target, though others would brand it a foolish bet on a climate system we know little about.

The "trillion-ton challenge" is still a tough call. Literally, whatever target we set will require drastic cuts in emissions. Nature will probably continue to remove a certain amount of our emissions. But experts on the carbon cycle say that we must reduce emissions to around a quarter of today's levels before nature can remove what we add each year. Only then will atmospheric levels stabilize; only then will climate start to stabilize. The quicker we can do it, the lower the level at which carbon concentrations in the air will flatten out. Reaching the safety-first target of 935 billion tons of carbon dioxide would require an immediate and dramatic ditching of business as usual in the energy industry worldwide. Global emissions would need to peak within five years or so, to fall by at least 50 percent within the next half century, and to carry on down after that. A trillion-ton target could be achieved with more modest early cuts and greater reductions later.

Another consideration is the danger posed by the sheer speed of warming. Many climate scientists say that rapid warming may be more destabilizing to vulnerable systems like carbon stores and ice caps than slower warming. For this reason, it could be important to take some urgent steps to limit short-term warming while we get carbon dioxide emissions under control. And there is a way to do that—through a concerted assault on emissions of gases other than carbon dioxide that have a big short-term "hit" on climate.

Let me explain. Different greenhouse gases have different lifetimes in the atmosphere, ranging from thousands of years to less than a decade. For convenience, climate scientists usually assess their warming impact as if it operated over a century—carbon dioxide's average lifetime in the atmosphere. But this is rather arbitrary. And it has the effect of "tuning" the calculations to make carbon dioxide seem more important, and other gases less so. Most significant here is methane, which, however you measure it, is the second most important man-made greenhouse gas after carbon dioxide. Measured over a century, the warming caused by a molecule of methane is about twenty times as great as that caused by a molecule of carbon dioxide. But methane does most of its warming in the first decade, its typical lifetime in the atmosphere. It has a quick hit. Measured over the first decade after its release, a molecule of methane causes a hundred times as much warming as a molecule of carbon dioxide.

By following the scientists' conventional time frame, Kyoto Protocol emissions targets have underplayed the potential short-term benefits of tackling methane emissions. It is unlikely that the politicians who signed the protocol were even aware of this.

But underplaying the benefits has had an important effect on policy priorities. To take one example, if the British government decided today to eliminate all methane emissions from landfill sites, it would meet only a fraction of the country's Kyoto targets, because the Kyoto rules measure the impact of foregone emissions over the whole of the coming century. If the initiative were measured instead on its impact over the first decade, the benefits would be five times as great. The methane specialist Euan Nisbet, of London's Royal Holloway College, reckons that the short-term hit would be almost as great as banning all cars on the streets of Britain. And, if the rules had been drawn up differently, it would have been enough to entirely meet Britain's Kyoto target.

If the world is mainly concerned about the effect of greenhouse gases in fifty to a hundred years' time, then we should probably stick with the existing formula. But if we are also concerned about quickly reducing global warming to stave off more immediate disaster, then there is a strong case for coming down hard on methane now—on leaks from landfills, gas pipelines, coal mines, the guts of ruminants, and much else. "Cutting carbon dioxide emissions is essential, but we have neglected methane and the near-term benefits [acting on] it could bring," says Nisbet. He wants the Kyoto Protocol rules narrowed to a twenty-year time horizon. Jim Hansen takes a similar view. "It makes a lot of sense to try to reduce methane, because in some ways it's easier," he says.

Hansen also advocates action on soot, which he calculates to be the third biggest man-made heating force in the atmosphere. Soot, as we saw in Chapter 18, has a local cooling effect but a wider and more considerable warming effect. It sticks around in the atmosphere for only a few days, but while it is there, its effects are large. Action against soot and methane would not stop global warming. But it would give the world time to introduce measures against the chief culprit: carbon dioxide.

Kyoto Politics

The Kyoto Protocol, signed in 1997, was the first, tentative step toward implementing the Rio pledge to prevent dangerous climate change. Some forty industrialized nations promised to make cuts in their emissions of six greenhouse gases, including the "big two": carbon dioxide and methane. Different countries accepted different targets, and the countries of the European Union later internally reallocated theirs. Those cuts averaged about 5 percent, measured between 1990 and the first "compliance period," which runs from 2008 to 2012. The protocol included various "flexibility mechanisms" aimed at making more effective use of cleanup investment funds. They allow countries to offset emissions by investing in cleanup technology abroad and in planting trees to soak up carbon dioxide from the air, and to trade directly in pollution permits.

The protocol did not impose targets on developing countries, because their emissions per resident are mostly much lower than those of the rich industrialized world (some conspicuous exceptions include South Korea, Singapore, and several oil-rich Gulf states). The U.S. and Australia originally signed up to Kyoto targets, but then pulled out. The protocol came into force in 2005, and at the end of that year, its signatories agreed to start negotiations on tougher cuts to come into force after 2012.

So far, so good. But the current Kyoto targets are very small compared with the cuts in emissions that will eventually be needed. And the delay has effectively shut off the option of a safety-first limit on carbon concentrations in the atmosphere. Some European countries have set themselves informal targets of a 60 percent emissions reduction by midcentury, which is closer to what is needed. But even if all the Kyoto nations did likewise, they are responsible for only a minority of emissions today. So more cuts by other nations would still be needed.

Eventually, if the climate regime develops as many hope, every country and every major energy and manufacturing company will need a license to emit greenhouse gases. The system, some say, could even be extended to individuals. If we are to stop dangerous climate change, the number of licenses available will have to be very limited. So the question of how they should be shared out becomes critical. It is political dynamite. The very suggestion sets the industrialized and developing worlds at loggerheads. This is partly because the industrialized countries of Europe and North America have already used up something like half of the atmospheric "space" available for emissions, and partly because developing nations are coming under pressure to reduce their emissions before they have had a chance to industrialize.

Big developing nations like China and India may have high national emissions. But measured in ratio to population, their emissions remain low. While the U.S. and Australia emit around 5.5 tons of carbon a year for every citizen, and European countries average around 3 tons, China is still around 1 ton, and India below half a ton. Developing countries feel they are being asked to forego economic development to help clean up a mess they did not create. On the other hand, they increasingly see that climate change threatens their prospects for economic development. The only solution is to institute a rationing system for pollution entitlements, based on a shared view of fairness.

Perhaps the simplest blueprint is "contraction and convergence." Developed by a small British group called the Global Commons Institute, it is attracting support around the world. The contraction half of the formula would establish a rolling program of annual targets for global emissions. The targets would begin roughly where we are today, and would fall over the coming decades. They would be set so as to ensure that the atmosphere never passed whatever limit on carbon dioxide concentrations the world chose.

The convergence half of the formula would share out those allowable global emissions each year according to population size. So national targets might begin at about 1 ton of carbon per person and then fall to maybe half a ton by 2050 and to that much less again by 2100, depending on the global target chosen. Of course, at the start that would leave rich nations with too few permits and many poor nations with more than they needed.

So they would trade. The costs of buying and selling pollution licenses would be a powerful incentive for a global cleanup.

Fantasy politics? Maybe. But something on this scale will be needed if we are to prevent climatic disaster. And if the rich world wants the poor world to help clean up its mess, and save us all from dangerous climate change, then some such formula will be needed.

TECHNOLOGICAL FIXES

Politics aside, what are the practicalities of stabilizing climate? President George W. Bush may have become a pariah in environmental circles for refusing to sign the Kyoto Protocol, but he is right on one thing: ultimately, it will be technologies, rather than politics, that solve the problem. The only question is what politics will best deliver the technologies that will allow us to "decarbonize" the world energy system. Those technologies fall into four categories: much more efficient use of energy; a switch to low-carbon and carbon-free fuels; capturing and storing or recycling some of the emissions that cannot be prevented; and finding new methods of storing energy, such as hydrogen fuel cells.

The task sounds daunting. But, in truth, much of it goes with the grain of recent economic and industrial development. In the past thirty years, global carbon dioxide emissions have grown only half as fast as the global economy—thanks mostly to improved energy efficiency. And many of the new energy technologies we will need are already in use, offering benefits such as cheaper or more secure energy. The replacement of coal with lower-carbon natural gas, oil with ethanol made from biofuels, the development of wind and solar power, the proposed expansion of nuclear energy, and investment in energy efficiency all fall into this category. What is needed first is faster progress in a direction in which we are already headed.

The top priority should be energy efficiency. More than half of the immediate cheap potential for reducing carbon dioxide emissions lies in improving energy efficiency in buildings, transport, and industry. Much of it could be done at zero or even negative cost, because the cost savings would outweigh the investment. This is also the area where we as individuals can most easily make a difference—by buying energy-efficient light bulbs and appliances, insulating our homes properly, cutting down on car use, and choosing energy-efficient models such as hybrids.

Also in the short term, there is huge potential to equip the world's fossil-fuel-burning power stations with "scrubbers" to remove carbon dioxide and deliver it via pipelines for burial underground. The technology is already developed and only needs scaling up. The potential global storage capacity in old oil and gas wells alone approaches a trillion tons of carbon. The British government's chief scientist, David King, says that by 2020 Britain could be burying a quarter of its power-station carbon dioxide emissions in old oil fields beneath the North Sea.

Other technologies will take more development before they become cost-effective on a large scale. These include solar power, which is available but currently too expensive for widespread use, and turning hydrogen into the fuel of the future for transport. The idea here would be to manufacture hydrogen in vast quantities for use in batteries, known as fuel cells, to power cars. Hydrogen would become the "new oil." Hydrogen is manufactured by splitting water into hydrogen and oxygen, which is a very energy-intensive process. So if the energy for splitting water were generated by burning fossil fuel, there would be little environmental gain; but if the energy came from renewables, such as solar or wind power, that would change everything.

The hydrogen fuel cell is not so much a new source of energy as a new way of storing energy. It could be the only way to make cars truly greenhouse-friendly. And it may turn out to be the best way of utilizing fickle renewable energy sources like wind and the sun. The big problem with these energy sources is that wind cannot be guaranteed to blow (nor the sun to shine) when the energy is needed. But if the energy is converted into hydrogen, it can be kept for future use.

So what, exactly, would it take to deploy all these technologies in order to bring climate change under control? The most ambitious attempt so far to produce a simple global blueprint comes from Robert Socolow, an engineer at Princeton University. He admits that when he checked out the plethora of options for cutting greenhouse gases, he was overwhelmed, and figured that most politicians and industrialists would be, too. So he decided to break the task down into a series of technological changes that would each cut global emissions of carbon dioxide by about 25 billion tons over the coming fifty years. He called them "wedges," because the impact of each would grow gradually, from nothing in the first year to a billion-ton emissions cut in the fiftieth year. They would each cut a "wedge" out of the graph of rising carbon dioxide emissions.

Socolow proposed more than a dozen possible wedges, but said that seven would be necessary to stabilize emissions at current levels. But we need to do more than that: we need to stabilize actual concentrations of greenhouse gases in the atmosphere, and that would require reducing emissions from their current 8.2 billion tons a year to around 2.2 billion tons. So I have adapted Socolow's blueprint to allow for that tougher target. We might choose the following twelve wedges, each of which could cut emissions by about 25 billion tons over the coming half century, and reduce global emissions from the projected 15.4 billion tons a year by 2060 to 2.2 billion tons:

- universally adopt efficient lighting and electrical appliances in homes and offices;
- double the energy efficiency of 2 billion cars;
- build compact urban areas served by efficient public transport, halving future car use;
- effect a fiftyfold worldwide expansion of wind power, equivalent to 2 million 1-megawatt turbines;
- effect a fiftyfold worldwide expansion in the use of biofuels for vehicles;
- embark on a global program of insulating buildings;
- cover an area of land the size of New Jersey (Socolow's home state) with solar panels;
- quadruple current electricity production from natural gas by converting coal-fired power stations;
- capture and store carbon dioxide from 1,600 gigawatts of natural gas power plants;
- halt global deforestation and plant an area of land the size of India with new forests;
- double nuclear power capacity;
- increase tenfold the global use of low-tillage farming methods to increase soil storage of carbon.

ECONOMICS OF THE GREENHOUSE

How much might all this cost? In 2001, a team of environmental econo-
mists assembled by the IPCC reviewed estimates for stabilizing atmos-
pheric concentrations of carbon dioxide by 2100. They ranged from a low
of $200 billion to a high of $17 trillion—almost a hundred times as much.
It seems extraordinary that estimates could range so widely. But, when
these are boiled down to their basics, it appears that much of the difference
depends on whether the modelers assumed that the necessary technical and
social changes would "go with the flow" of future change, or that every-
thing would have to be grafted onto a society and an economy heading fast
in a different direction.

Put simply, the high estimates guessed that, under business as usual,
rising wealth would produce and require almost equally fast rises in emis-
sions from burning cheap carbon fuels. Diverting from that path would
thus require preventing emissions of trillions of tons of carbon using ex-
pensive technologies that would not otherwise have been developed. The
lower estimates assumed that the world was already slowly losing its ad-
diction to carbon fuels, and that all we would need to do is make the switch
faster. They also took a rather different view of technological development,
seeing it as molded by a range of economic incentives. In this version, gov-
ernments could shape technological development by stimulating markets.
Once the process was under way, innovation would go into overdrive, and
prices would fall away.

Some of the people involved in the IPCC study were instinctively hos-
tile to major efforts to cut carbon dioxide emissions. The Yale environ-
mental economist William Nordhaus suggests that "a vague premonition
of potential disaster is insufficient grounds to plunge the world into de-
pression." But let us assume that the real costs will be toward the top end
of the range. Would their adoption really push the world into recession?

The veteran climate scientist Stephen Schneider, of Stanford Univer-
sity, redid the arithmetic in 2002, assuming it would cost $8 trillion to
stabilize carbon dioxide concentrations by 2100. He found that the same
economists who predict doomsday if we try to tackle climate change also
believe that citizens of the world will be, on average, five times richer in a

hundred years than they are today. So he took the economists at their word and asked: How much would the $8 trillion bill for halting climate change delay those riches? The answer was just two years.

"The wild rhetoric about enslaving the poor and bankrupting the economy to do climate policy is fallacious, even if one accepts the conventional economic models," he told me when his analysis was published. Coincidentally, that was the week that Australia's prime minister, John Howard, announced that his country would not ratify the Kyoto Protocol because it would "cost jobs and damage our industry." Poppycock, said Schneider. "To be five times richer in 2100 versus 2102 would hardly be noticed." It was a small price to pay.

A small price to pay for what? What would we be buying with this trillion-dollar investment in a stable climate? That, of course, is impossible to answer, because we don't know the extent of what would be avoided. But we can easily see the scale of things, even today. Evidence of the cost of extreme weather is everywhere. The 1998 El Niño cost Asia at least $20 billion. Insured losses from extreme weather in 2004 hit a record $55 billion, which was promptly exceeded by an estimated $70 billion for 2005. Total economic losses for 2005, including uninsured losses, are expected to be three times higher: cleaning up after Hurricane Katrina alone may eventually cost $100 billion. Incidentally, a simple extrapolation of trends in insurance claims stemming from extreme weather in recent years suggests that they will exceed total global economic activity by 2060. That may be slightly wacky math, but it is sobering nonetheless.

Not surprisingly, economists disagree about the cost of inaction on climate change as much as they do about the cost of action. Some have attempted to assess the "social cost" of every ton of carbon put into the air. One recent review found a range from approaching $1,700 per ton down to zero. The British government, which commissioned the review, settled on a figure of $70 per ton. One reason for the wide range is accounting practices. Economists routinely apply a discount to the cost of anything that has to be paid for in the future. Dealing with climate change that may happen decades or even centuries ahead allows for huge discounts. Some economists say that very long-term impacts—such as the rise of sea levels as ice caps melt—should be discounted to zero.

This discounting of the future may be a convenient device for corporations, or even governments in their day-to-day business. But it is less clear how sensible it is for the management of a planet. If corporate finances or a nation's economy go wrong, shareholders can sell their shares and governments can print money or go cap in hand to the International Monetary Fund. But the planet, our only planet, is rather different.

Moreover, the existing estimates of social cost are based on IPCC studies that so far have not included many of the irreversible positive feedbacks to climate change that this book has concentrated on. So nobody has yet even asked what price should be attached to a century-long drought in the American West, or an enfeebled Asian monsoon, or a permanent El Niño in the Pacific, or a shutdown of the ocean conveyor, or the acidification of the oceans, or a methane belch from the ocean depths, or a collapse of the West Antarctic ice sheet, or sea levels rising by half a yard in a decade. Though, on reflection, these are perhaps questions best not answered by accountants.

GLOSSARY

Aerosols Any of a range of particles in the air, including soot, dust, and sulfates, that can intercept solar energy, sometimes scattering it and sometimes absorbing and reradiating it. Under different circumstances, they can either warm or cool the ground beneath and the air around.

African Humid Period The period after the close of the last ice age and before about 5,500 years ago, characterized by wet conditions in Africa, notably in the Sahara.

Albedo A measure of the reflectivity of a surface.

Anthropocene A new term to describe the past two centuries or so, during which human activities are seen to have dominated some key planetary processes such as the carbon cycle.

Arctic Oscillation A climate oscillation that occurs on timescales from days to decades. Measured by differences in air pressure between polar and nonpolar areas, and manifested in changing wind patterns that alter temperature. Related to (and sometimes synonymous with) the North Atlantic Oscillation.

Biological pump The process by which living organisms in the ocean draw carbon dioxide out of the atmosphere as they grow, and then deposit carbon on the ocean floor following their death. Has the effect of moderating the accumulation of CO_2 in the atmosphere.

Biosphere That part of Earth's surface, atmosphere, and oceans that is inhabited by living things.

Carbon dioxide fertilization effect What happens when higher concentrations of carbon dioxide in the air "fertilize" the faster growth of plants or other organisms.

Carbon cycle The natural exchange of carbon between the atmosphere, oceans, and Earth's surface. Carbon may be dissolved in the oceans, absorbed within living organisms and soils, or float in the air as carbon dioxide.

Carbon sink Anything that absorbs carbon dioxide from the air. Anything that releases carbon dioxide is a carbon source.

Chimneys A term coined by Peter Wadhams for giant whirlpools in the far North Atlantic that take dense water to the seabed. The start of the ocean conveyor.

Climate model A normally computerized simulation of the workings of the atmosphere. Often used to predict the effect of future changes such as an accumulation of greenhouse gases.

El Niño A periodic switch in the ocean currents and winds in the equatorial Pacific Ocean. A major perturbation in the global climate system.

Feedback Any by-product of an event that has a subsequent effect on that event. A positive feedback amplifies the original event, while a negative feedback dampens it. Key climate feedbacks include ice, water vapor, and changes to the carbon cycle. See also ice-albedo feedback.

Fossil fuel A fuel made from fossilized carbon, the remains of ancient vegetation. Includes coal, oil, and natural gas.

Gaia The idea, developed by James Lovelock, that Earth and its living organisms act in consort, like a single organism, to regulate the environment of the planet, including atmospheric chemistry and temperature.

Global warming Synonym for the greenhouse effect and climate change.

Greenhouse gas Any one of several gases, including water vapor, carbon dioxide, and methane, that trap heat in the lower atmosphere.

Gulf Stream The tropical ocean current that keeps Europe warm, especially in winter. Part of the ocean conveyor, and may be turned off at times, such as during ice ages.

Holocene The geological era since the end of the last ice age. Sometimes regarded as recently succeeded by the Anthropocene.

Hydrological cycle The movement of water between the oceans, the atmosphere, and Earth's surface through processes such as evaporation, condensation, rainfall, and river flow.

Ice ages Periods of several tens of thousands of years when ice sheets spread across the Northern Hemisphere and the planet cools. Believed to be triggered by Milankovitch cycles and amplified by positive feedbacks. Recent ice ages have occurred roughly every 100,000 years. The last ended 10,000 years ago.

Ice-albedo feedback A positive feedback on air temperature caused by the presence or absence of highly reflective ice. Thus, during warming, ice melts and is replaced by a darker surface of ocean or land vegetation that absorbs more heat, amplifying the warming. The reverse happens when cooling causes ice to form.

Ice sheets The largest expanses of ice on the planet. There are currently three: Greenland, West Antarctica, and East Antarctica.

Interglacials Warm periods between ice ages.

Intergovernmental Panel on Climate Change (IPCC) A panel of scientists appointed by the UN through national science agencies to report on the causes of, impacts on, and solutions to global warming.

Isotope One of two or more atoms with the same atomic number but containing different numbers of neutrons. For example: oxygen-16 and oxygen-18. The ratio of the isotopes in the air or oceans can vary according to environmental conditions, but will be fixed when the isotopes are taken up by plants, or air bubbles are trapped in ice. Thus isotopic analysis of ocean sediments, ice cores, and other leftovers from the past can be a valuable way of reconstructing past temperatures and other conditions.

Kyoto Protocol The 1987 agreement on climate change, whose provisions include cuts in emissions by most industrialized nations during the first compliance period, from 2008 to 2012. The U.S. and Australia subsequently pulled out.

Little ice age The period from the fourteenth to the nineteenth century when parts of the Northern Hemisphere were cooler than today.

Medieval warm period The period from the ninth to the thirteenth century when parts of the Northern Hemisphere were notably warm.

Methane clathrates Crystalline lattices of ice that trap large volumes of methane. Usually found at low temperatures and high pressures beneath the ocean bed or in permafrost.

Milankovitch wobbles   Various wobbles in the orbit of Earth than can influence climate over timescales of thousands of years. Believed to be the trigger for ice ages. Named after the Serbian mathematician Milutin Milankovitch, but originally investigated by the forgotten Scottish amateur scientist James Croll.

Nuclear winter   The theory that in a nuclear war, there would be so many fires that smoke would blanket the planet, causing massive cooling.

Ocean conveyor   Global ocean circulation in which dense surface water falls to the ocean floor in the Arctic and near Antarctica, travels the oceans, and resurfaces about a thousand years later in the warm Gulf Stream of the Atlantic. Prone to switching on and off, and perhaps a major determinant of global climate.

Ozone hole   An extreme thinning of the ozone layer seen in recent decades. Found each spring over Antarctica, but potentially could occur over the Arctic, too. Caused when man-made "ozone-eating" chemicals accumulate in the ozone layer. The immediate trigger for ozone destruction is low temperatures and sunlight.

Ozone layer   The ozone within the lower stratosphere, which protects Earth from harmful ultraviolet radiation from the sun.

Permafrost   Permanently frozen soil and rock found in the tundra regions of Siberia, Canada, Antarctica, and some mountain regions. Can reach a depth of more than 1.2 miles.

Precession   One of the Milankovitch wobbles that affects the axis of Earth's rotation. Changes the season when Earth is closest to the sun. Implicated in some climate changes during the Holocene.

Rainforest   Forest that depends on frequent rainfall, but also generates rain by recycling water into the atmosphere from its leaves.

Southern Hemisphere annular mode (SAM)   The Antarctic equivalent of the Arctic Oscillation. Responsible for strong warming of the Antarctic Peninsula in recent decades.

Stratosphere   A layer of the atmosphere starting about 6 to 9 miles up. Home of the ozone layer. Greenhouse effect causes it to cool, but it may act to amplify warming in the troposphere beneath.

Thermal expansion   The warming and resulting expansion of water in the oceans. Along with the melting of land ice, it is causing a worldwide rise in sea levels.

Troposphere   The lowest layer of the atmosphere, occupying the 6 to 9 miles beneath the stratosphere. The area within which our weather occurs. Greenhouse effect causes it to warm.

Ultraviolet radiation   Solar radiation with wavelengths shorter than light but longer than X-rays. Harmful to living organisms, which are largely protected from it on Earth by the ozone layer.

ACKNOWLEDGMENTS

Where to start? In my twenty years of reporting on climate change for *New Scientist* magazine and others, innumerable scientists (and not a few editors and fellow journalists) have helped me get things mostly right. To all of them, thanks. I hope this book brings their work together in a form that many of them will find enlightening.

My greatest debt is to the synthesizers within the scientific community—the people who have tried to see the whole picture and to put their work into what seems to me an ever more frightening context. Their names recur throughout this book. But those who have specially helped me in person include Jim Hansen, Paul Crutzen, Jim Lovelock, Wally Broecker, Peter Cox, Peter Wadhams, Mike Mann, Richard Lindzen, Will Steffen, Richard Alley, Lonnie Thompson, Terry Hughes, Jack Rieley, Sergei Kirpotin, Euan Nisbet, Peter Liss, Torben Christensen, Crispin Tickell, Richard Betts, Myles Allen, Meinrat Andreae, Tim Lenton, Chris Rapley, Peter deMenocal, Joe Farman, Gavin Schmidt, Keith Briffa, John Houghton, Dan Schrag, Bert Bolin, Jesse Ausubel, Drew Shindell, Stefan Rahmstorf, Mark Cane, Arie Issar, Hans Joachim Schellnhuber, and the late Charles Keeling and Gerard Bond.

One always gets ideas from fellow writers. So thanks, too, to John Gribbin, Mark Lynas, Bill Burroughs, Doug Macdougall, Mark Bowen, Jeremy Leggett, Gabrielle Walker, and two historians of the climate change debate, Gale Christianson and Spencer Weart, whose books I have referred to in preparing this work. Thanks also to the organizers of the Dahlem conferences for making me welcome at an important event; to Carl Petter Niesen, in Ny-Alesund; and to the many people who have helped turn a germ of an idea into a completed book, including my agent, Jessica Woollard, and the editors Susanna Wadeson and Sarah Emsley.

NOTES ON THE REFERENCES

This is a far from complete list of the sources used in writing this book. But it includes the main written sources as well as others, summarizing information that could be of use to readers.

PREFACE

Wadhams's work on chimneys appears at greatest length in "Convective Chimneys in the Greenland Sea: A Review of Recent Observations" (*Oceanography and Marine Biology: An Annual Review* 2004, vol. 42, p. 29–56) and also in *Geophysical Research Letters* 2002 (vol. 29, no. 10, p. 76). Wadhams also spoke with me at length. For more on William Scoresby, see my article "Hell with a Harpoon" in *New Scientist,* 18 May 2002.

INTRODUCTION

The proceedings of the British government's Dangerous Climate Change conference appear at www.stabilisation2005.com. The resulting book can also be found at www.defra.gov.uk/environment/climatechange/internat/dangerous-cc .htm. Hansen's address to the AGU in late 2005 is at: www.columbia.edu/~jeh1/ keeling_talk_and_slides.pdf. Three overviews on abrupt climate change are: Richard Alley's *Abrupt Climate Change: Inevitable Surprises* (National Academies Press, 2002), especially chapter four; "Abrupt Changes: The Achilles' Heels in the Earth System" by Steffen et al. in *Environment* (vol. 46, p. 9) and Rial et al., "Non-Linearities, Feedbacks and Critical Thresholds with the Earth's Climate System" (*Climate Change,* vol. 65, p. 11).

1. THE PIONEERS

The journal *Ambio* had a special issue on Svante Arrhenius and his legacy in 1997 (vol. 26, no 1). I wrote about him in *New Scientist* in "Land of the Midnight Sums," 25 January 2003. Other sources include Gale E. Christianson's book *Greenhouse: The 200-Year Story of Global Warming* (Constable, 1999), which is also good on Callendar and Keeling. Many useful obituaries of Keeling were posted on news Web sites following his death in June 2005—for instance in the *Daily Telegraph* (www.telegraph.co.uk/news/main.jhtml?xml=/news/2005/06/24/db2402

.xml). And a good personal description of his early work appears at: www.mlo
.noaa.gov/HISTORY/PUBLISH/20th%20anniv/co2.htm.

2. Turning Up the Heat

The British newspaper mentioned in the first paragraph is the *Daily Mail.* The
column, by Melanie Phillips, "Global Warming Fraud," can be read at her Web
site: www.melaniephillips.com/articles/archives/000255.html. Christianson cov-
ers much of the early history of researching greenhouse gases. Brindley's paper
on the planet's radiation balance is in *Nature,* vol. 410, p. 355. See also: www
.imperial.ac.uk/P2641.htm.

The definitive consensus overview of the science of climate change in 2001 is
provided by the *Third Assessment Report of the Intergovernmental Panel on Climate
Change* (www.ipcc.ch), which will be superseded during 2007 by the *Fourth As-
sessment.* However, the *Fourth Assessment* is already out of date. It only accepted ev-
idence published in peer-reviewed literature by the summer of 2005—missing
much new evidence of tipping points in the climate system.

Sherwood's 2005 research appears in *Science* (vol. 309, p. 1556). Parker's work
on the urban heat island appears in *Nature* (vol. 432, p. 290). For references to
Mann's work see the notes for chapter 33. Lassen and Friis-Christensen's origi-
nal 1991 paper was in Science, vol. 254, p. 698. Lindzen is better known as a
polemical and op-ed writer (for instance www.cato.org/pubs/regulation/reg15n2g
.html), but he does have a track record of interesting research, such as "Does the
Earth have an adaptive infrared iris?" *Bulletin of the American Meteorological Society,*
vol. 82, p. 417.

Pat Michaels is another media regular. His exposition of the paradigm prob-
lem appears in his diatribe on climate science *Meltdown: The Predictable Distortion
of Global Warming by Scientists, Politicians, and the Media* (Cato Institute, 2004). For
a vigorous attack on Michael Crichton's book *State of Fear,* read Jeremy Leggett in
New Scientist, 5 March 2005. Oreskes's review of the scientific literature on climate
change appeared in *Science,* vol. 306, p. 1686.

3. The Year

I visited Honduras after Hurricane Mitch for the Red Cross. I wrote up my find-
ings at www.redcross.int/EN/mag/magazine2001_2/heating.html. First reports
on how exceptional 1998 was appeared the following year (see, for instance, www
.sciencedaily.com/releases/1999/03/990304052546.htm). This was underlined in
2001 in the *Third Assessment Report of the IPCC.*

4. The Anthropocene

The proceedings of the Dahlem conference, at which I was introduced to many of the topics discussed here, are published as Earth System Analysis for Sustainability, Schellnhuber et al., eds. (Dahlem University Press, 2004). Crutzen discussed his work at length in his Nobel lecture (http://nobelprize.org/nobel_prizes/chemistry/laureates/1995/crutzen-lecture.html). His discussion of the Anthropocene first appeared in print in 2000 in the newsletter of the International Geosphere-Biosphere Programme (IGBP), no. 41. I interviewed him for *New Scientist*: "High Flyer," 5 July 2003. Alley's report is *Abrupt Climate Change: Inevitable Surprises* (National Academies Press, 2002). Many of the remarks by Alley and Steffen come from my interviews with them in 2003 and 2005.

5. The Watchtower

The reportage follows a visit to Ny-Alesund in September 2005. Kim Holmen discusses its role as "a watchtower for human-induced climate change" in *Polar Science in Tromso* (Polarmiljosenteret, 2004). Kohler's mass balance study appears in *Polar Research* (vol. 22[2], p. 145). Dobson's story can be read at www.atm.ox.ac.uk/user/barnett/ozoneconference/dobson.htm. The Bear Island research appeared in *Environmental Pollution,* vol. 136, p. 419.

6. Ninety Degrees North

McCarthy revealed the ice-free North Pole at http://news.bbc.co.uk/1/hi/world/americas/888235.stm. Scamdos's work is being updated all the time and appears at: http://nsidc.org/. Polyakov's warm water pulse was reported in 2005 in *Geophysical Research Letters,* vol. 32, L17605, DOI: 10.1029/2005GL023740; available at www.agu.org. The statement by glaciologists on the transformed state of the Arctic appeared in *Eos* in August 2005 (vol. 86, p. 309).

7. On the Slippery Slope

Hansen's "slippery slope" essay appears in *Climate Change,* vol. 68, p. 269. His "dangerous anthropogenic interference" remarks appeared in a lecture of that name to the University of Iowa, available, with much else of interest, from his Web site at: www.columbia.edu/~jeh1/. Box's remarks, and those of Bromwich and Alley, are from interviews conducted in 2005. Zwally's research was published in 2002 in *Science* (vol. 297, p. 218). Data on movement of the Jakobshavn glacier appear in *Nature* (vol. 432, p. 608), and the new findings on Kangerdlugssuaq from measurements by Gordon Hamilton of the University of Maine on a Greenpeace cruise in 2005 can be read at: www.greenpeace.org.uk/climate/climate.cfm?UCIDParam=20050721151314.

8. THE SHELF

The demise of Larsen B is described by Hulbe at http://web.pdx.edu/~chulbe/science/Larsen/larsen2002.html. Alley discusses mechanisms at http://igloo.gsfc.nasa.gov/wais/pastmeetings/abstracts04/Alley.htm. I learned more from interviews with scientists at the British Antarctic Survey, and from Rignot and others at a conference on the Antarctic ice held at the Royal Society in London in late 2005 (www.royalsoc.ac.uk/news.asp?year=&id=3831).

9. THE MERCER LEGACY

I heard the story of Mercer from Thompson during interviews at his lab in 2005, and in correspondence with Hughes. Mercer's 1978 paper is in *Nature* (vol. 271, p. 321), and Hughes's 1981 "weak underbelly" paper was in the *Journal of Glaciology*, vol. 27, p. 518. Pine Island Bay was a major talking point at the Royal Society conference mentioned above, along with the state of the Totten and Cook glaciers. Vaughan's initial findings first emerged at http://igloo.gsfc.nasa.gov/wais/pastmeetings/abstracts05/Vaughan.pdf. Davis's paper on the East Antarctic ice sheet appeared in *Science* (vol. 308, p. 1898).

10. RISING TIDES

The plight of the Carterets reached the world via the BBC. See: www.sidsnet.org/archive/climate-newswire/2000/0093.html. Plans to abandon the islands and Tuvalu were reported by Reuters on 24 November 2005. I interviewed Teuatabo for *New Scientist* in 2000 ("Turning Back the Tide," 12 February 2000). Hansen discussed the history of sea level rise in his December 2005 lecture: www.columbia.edu/~jeh1/keeling_talk_and_slides.pdf.

11. IN THE JUNGLE

Nepstad's drought experiment is discussed in *Science*, vol. 308, p. 346, and at http://earthobservatory.nasa.gov/Study/AmazonDrought/. His plans for an experimental burn are discussed at www.eurekalert.org/pub_releases/2005–07/whrc-whr071905.php. The 2005 Amazon drought was widely reported, see http://news.bbc.co.uk/1/hi/world/americas/4344310.stm, for example. The Hadley Centre predictions appear in its report *Stabilising Climate to Avoid Dangerous Climate Change*, published in January 2005. The report by Gedney and Valdes appears in *Geophysical Research Letters*, vol. 27, no. 19, p. 3053.

12. WILD FIRES OF BORNEO

I visited Palangkaraya for *The Guardian* newspaper shortly after the fires of 1997–98 and received firsthand reports from locals. See also reportage in *Nature* in 2004 (vol. 432, p. 144). Rieley's calculations of emissions from the fires appeared in *Nature* (420, p. 61). The U.S. research corroborating his findings appeared in *Science* (vol. 303, p. 73).

13. SINK TO SOURCE

Fan's explosive *Science* paper appeared in vol. 282, p. 442. Ciais's work for CarboEurope appeared in *Nature* (vol. 437, p. 529), while Angert's paper appeared in the *Proceedings of the National Academy of Sciences (PNAS)*, vol. 102 (31), p. 10823, and Zeng's findings were in *Geophysical Research Letters*, vol. 32, L22709, DOI: 10.1029/2005GL024607; available at www.agu.org. Lawrence's work on permafrost is publicized at: www.ucar.edu/news/releases/2005/permafrost.shtml and in *Geophysical Research Letters*, vol. 32, L24401, DOI: 10.1029/2005GL023172; available at www.agu.org. Peter Cox presented his findings at the Dangerous Climate Change conference (see the notes for the Introduction, above) and published them in *Geophysical Research Letters*, vol. 30, no. 19, p. 1479. I found Canadell's work at: www.esm.ucsb.edu/academics/courses/595PP-S/Readings/VulnerabGlobalC.pdf. Kirk's findings on British carbon appeared in *Nature*, vol. 437, p. 245.

14. THE DOOMSDAY DEVICE

My story on melting permafrost appeared in *New Scientist* on 11 August 2005. Kirpotin's findings had yet to find a peer-reviewed publication in English at press time, but a revised version of his translated Russian paper appears at: www.mindfully.org/Air/2005/Palsas-Climate-Changes11aug05.htm. His findings were corroborated by Ted Schuur a year later in *Nature* (vol. 443, p. 71). I learned of Larry Smith's findings in e-mail interviews. The report suggesting that all plants make methane appeared in *Nature*, vol. 439, p. 187. I interviewed Christensen extensively during my visit to Stordalen in late 2005. His publications include *Geophysical Research Letters*, vol. 31, L04501, DOI: 10.1029/2003GL018680; available at www.agu.org.

15. THE ACID BATH

The Royal Society's study, "Ocean Acidification Due to Increasing Atmospheric Carbon Dioxide," appeared in June 2005, and can be found at: www.royalsoc.ac.uk. Turley presented her findings at the Dangerous Climate Change conference. Orr reported in *Nature* (vol. 437, p. 681). Falkowski's paper appeared in *Science* (vol. 290, p. 291).

16. The Winds of Change

Kennett and Stott's 1991 paper appeared in *Nature* vol. 353, p. 225. Dickens has published for instance at *Geotimes,* November 2004, p. 18. Alan Judd's seabed explorations were written up by Joanna Marchant in *New Scientist* on 2 December 2000. Norman Cherkis's paper was presented at the American Geophysical Union Spring Meeting 1997. Mienert discussed the Storegga slide in *Marine and Petroleum Geology* (vol. 22, p. 1) and in *Oceanography* (vol. 17, p. 16). Some other material comes from unpublished research he gave me during interviews. Nisbet discussed methane releases in a paper in the *Philosophical Transactions of the Royal Society,* Maths. Phys. Eng. Sc., vol. 360, no. 1793, p. 581. And David Archer produced an inventory of methane clathrates in *Earth and Planetary Science Letters,* vol. 227, p. 185.

17. What's Watts?

Hansen's work on this is synthesized in his paper "The Earth's Energy Imbalance: Confirmation and Implications," published in *Science* (vol. 308, p. 1431) and available at: www.columbia.edu/~jeh1/hansen_imbalance.pdf. Read about the Global Albedo Project at: www-c4.ucsd.edu/gap/. Chapin's findings on Arctic albedo were published in *Science* (vol. 310, p. 627), while Betts's findings are in *Nature,* vol. 408, p. 187.

18. Clouds from Both Sides

The 2004 Exeter meeting was a closed session of IPCC scientists. I was the only outsider attending. But most of the findings have since been made public. Stainforth's work appeared in *Nature* (vol. 433, p. 403), as did Murphy's (vol. 430, p. 768). Likewise, I was the only journalist attending sessions of the 2003 Dahlem Conference (see chapter 4), where Crutzen and Cox made their first calculations about the parasol effect, later written up by Cox in *Nature* (vol. 435, p. 1187). Wielicki responded in e-mail interviews and outlined some issues in *Science* (vol. 295, p. 841). Schwartz's remarks were made in an interview coinciding with the publication of his paper in the *Journal of the Air and Waste Management Association* (vol. 54, p. 1). Hansen wrote about black soot in the *Journal of Geophysical Research,* vol. 110, D18104.

19. A Billion Fires

The INDOEX Web site is at: www-indoex.ucsd.edu/. Remanathan and Crutzen discussed its findings in 2002 in *Current Science,* vol. 83, p. 947. Dale Kaiser's work on dimming appeared in *Geophysical Research Letters,* vol. 29, no. 21, p. 2042. Hansen's ideas appear in *Science,* vol. 297, p. 2250.

20. HYDROXYL HOLIDAY

Prinn gave his warning in *Science* in 1995 (vol. 269, p. 187) and returned to the issue in the *IGBP Newsletter* No. 43 in 2000, and in *Science* in 2001 (vol. 292, p. 1882). Madronich raised his fears in 1992 in *Geophysical Research Letters,* vol. 19, no. 23, p. 465. And also here, a year later: www.ciesin.org/docs/011–457/011–457.html. I wrote a somewhat fanciful doomsday scenario for hydroxyl in a *New Scientist* supplement in April 2001. It can be found at www.gsenet.org/library/04 chm/hydroxyl.php.

21. GOLDILOCKS AND THE THREE PLANETS

Read all about Snowball Earth in the book of that name by my former *New Scientist* colleague Gabrielle Walker (Bloomsbury, 2003). And more from Kirschvink at: http://pr.caltech.edu/media/Press_Releases/PR12723.html. Lovelock gave his Gaian interpretation of the planet's history in books such as *The Ages of Gaia* (W. W. Norton, 1995). His most recent book is *The Revenge of Gaia* (Allen Lane, 2006). I explored Retallack's ideas about "The Kingdoms of Gaia," in *New Scientist,* 10 June 2001.

22. THE BIG FREEZE

The best read on the ice ages and Agassiz and the intriguing James Croll is in *Frozen Earth* by Doug Macdougall (University of California Press, 2004). Shackleton's groundbreaking paper appeared in 1976 in *Science* (vol. 194, p. 1121). I took Berrien Moore III's analysis of carbon movements from the *Global Change Newsletter* No. 40 (December 1999, p. 1).

23. THE OCEAN CONVEYOR

Broecker's writings on the conveyor are extensive. Some key early papers are in *Nature* in 1994 (vol. 372, p. 421), *Scientific American* in 1995 (vol. 273, p. 62) and *Science* in 1997, (vol. 278, p. 1582). I interviewed him in late 2005. Schlesinger's paper appears on the Web site of the Dangerous Climate Change conference, along with Challenor's. Ruth Curry's paper on the great salinity anomaly was in *Science,* vol. 308, p. 1772. And Bryden's paper appeared in *Nature,* vol. 438, p. 655.

24. AN ARCTIC FLOWER

Alley splendidly describes the science of the Younger Dryas (and many other things) in his book *The Two-Mile Time Machine* (Princeton University Press, 2000). Read about how humans fared in William Burroughs' Climate Change in Prehistory (Cambridge University Press, 2005). The latest thinking on the emptying of Lake Agassiz is in *Eos,* vol. 86, p. 465. Chiang's paper appeared in *Climate Dynamics* (vol. 25, p. 477). Alley explored events 8200 years ago in *Quaternary Science Reviews,* vol. 24, p. 1123.

25. THE PULSE

The best study of the events of the Little Ice Age remains the book of that name by Jean Grove (Routledge, 1988). Bond's pioneering work on "the pulse" and its links to the era appeared in *Science* (vol. 278, p. 1257 and vol. 294, p. 2130). His work is summarized at: www.ldeo.columbia.edu/news/2005/07_11_05.htm. Read too Peter deMenocal's paper with Thomas Marchitto in *Geochemistry Geophysics Geosystems* (DOI: 10.1029/2003GC000598) and his essay "After Tomorrow" in *Orion,* Jan./Feb. 2005; plus Shindell's "Glaciers, Old Masters and Galileo" at: www.giss.nasa.gov/research/briefs/shindell_06/; and Christina Hulbe in *Paleoceanography* (vol. 19, PA1004).

26. THE FALL

Useful analysis of how the Sahara became a desert include Robert Kunzig's "Exit from Eden" in *Discovery,* January 2000, Claussen's paper in *Climate Change* (vol. 57, p. 99), and deMenocal in *Quaternary Science Reviews,* vol. 19, p. 347. Haarsma's theories are articulated in *Geophysical Research Letters,* vol. 32, L17702, DOI: 10.1029/2005GL023232; available at www.agu.org. DeMenocal looks at megadroughts through the late Holocene in *Science* (vol. 292, p. 667); and Richard Seager's study is at www.ldeo.columbia.edu/res/div/ocp/drought.

27. SEESAW ACROSS THE OCEAN

The Bodele dust reservoir is discussed in *Nature* as "the dustiest place on Earth" (vol. 434, p. 816). I learned of Schellenhuber's ideas on links between the Sahara and the Amazon in conversations. They seem intuitively sensible but remain, so far as I know, unquantified.

28. TROPICAL HIGH

I interviewed Thompson at length about his career and ideas in 2005. There is also a highly readable book about him called *Thin Ice* by Mark Bowen (Henry Holt, 2005). Key publications include *Climatic Change,* vol. 59, p. 137, and *Quaternary Science Reviews,* vol. 19, p. 19. His Web site is at: www-bprc.mps.ohio-state.edu/Icecore/GroupP.html#lonniethompson.

29. THE CURSE OF AKKAD

The story of Akkad and other tales of climate and civilization appear in *The Winds of Change* by Eugene Linden (Simon & Schuster, 2006). DeMenocal looks at the collapse of Akkad in *Geology,* vol. 28, p. 379. Weiss's original paper appeared in the *Journal of the American Oriental Society,* vol. 95, p. 534. Issar explores similar collapses in the Middle East at the time with Mattanyah Zohar in *Climate Change: Environment and Civilization in the Middle East* (Springer, 2004).

30. A Chunk of Coral

I wrote about Dan Schrag's find and its implications for El Niño in *New Scientist,* 9 October 1999. He published his findings in *Geophysical Research Letters* (vol. 26, no. 20, p. 2139). El Niño has many chroniclers these days, including Richard Grove and John Chappell's *El Niño: History and Crisis* (White Horse Press, 2000) and El Niño in History by Cesar Caviedes (University Press of Florida, 2001). Rodbell's compelling paper is in *Science* (vol. 283, p. 516). Latif's modeling of El Niño's future appeared in *Nature* (vol. 398, p. 694). Read about the Peruvian potato farmers at www.columbia.edu/cu/pr/00/01/pleiades.html.

31. Feeding Asia

Mike Davis wrote passionately about the effects of El Niño and failed monsoons in the late nineteenth century in *Late Victorian Holocausts* (Verso, 2001). Overpeck's analysis of the monsoon's potentially troubled future appeared in *Nature,* vol. 421, p. 354. Analysis of the different interpretations of the links that sustain the monsoon emerged from conversations with Mark Cane, Broecker, Alley, Thompson, and others.

32. The Heat Wave

The 2003 heat wave was summed up at: www.earth-policy.org/Updates/Update 29.htm. The link to global warming was articulated by Allen in *Nature* (vol. 432, p. 610). The study of Burgundy vineyards appeared in *Nature* (vol. 432, p. 289). Betts warned about the extra threat to cities in *PNAS* (DOI 10.1073/pnas .0400357101).

33. The Hockey Stick

Read the IPCC summary for policymakers at: www.ipcc.ch/pub/spm22–01.pdf. Early versions of the hockey stick were discussed in *Nature* (vol. 392, p. 779) and *Geophysical Research Letters* (vol. 26, no. 6, p. 759). Other write-ups of Mann's work and the controversy it created were included in *Scientific American* (March 2005, p. 34) and *Mother Jones* (18 April 2005). McIntyre and McKitrick set out their case in 2003 in *Energy and Environment,* vol. 14, p. 751. Mann's side of the debate, with commentary from some critics, appears on a Web site run by him and others: www.realclimate.org. Recent scientific analyses of the debate include Osborn and Briffa in *Science* (vol. 311, p. 841).

34. Hurricane Season

I spoke to Corky Perret for a feature in *New Scientist,* "Is Global Warming Making Hurricanes Stronger?" (3 December 2005). Webster's paper appeared in *Science* (vol. 309, p. 1844). Emmanuel first predicted a big increase in hurricane destruction in *Nature* in 1987 (vol. 326, p. 483). He was more sanguine when, with others, he reported in the *Bulletin of the American Meteorological Society* in 1998 (vol. 79, p. 19), but returned to the barricades in *Nature* in 2005 (vol. 436, p. 686). Trenberth made his warnings earlier that year in *Science* (vol. 308, p. 1753). Gray's efforts to refute these claims were not carried in the major journals, but can be seen at his Web site: http://typhoon.atmos.colostate.edu/. The story of "hurricane" Catarina is told at: www.met-office.gov.uk/sec2/sec2cyclone/catarina.html.

35. Ozone Holes in the Greenhouse

Farman's landmark paper on the ozone hole appeared in *Nature* (vol. 315, p. 207). Crutzen discussed how lucky the world had been in his Nobel lecture (see chapter 4). Hormes's and Shindell's thoughts come from personal interviews in Ny-Alesund and New York, respectively. The mechanisms that might cause ozone depletion to produce rapid climate change were discussed by Hartmann et al. in *PNAS,* vol. 97, p. 1412.

36. The Dance

The debate between the polar and tropical schools has never been properly articulated in the journals, so this chapter is pieced together from interviews with the participants, many of them in New York. Goldstein's paper appears in *Science* (vol. 307, p. 1933). Crutzen's comments came from an interview I conducted.

37. New Horizons

Similarly, much of this chapter derives from conversations rather than written papers. The idea of a bipolar seesaw is discussed by David Sugden in *Planet Earth,* journal of the Natural Environment Research Council, in autumn 2005. Read about lakes beneath the Antarctic ice at: www.earth.columbia.edu/news/2006/story01-26-06.html. Recent changes to SAM are reviewed by King in *Geophysical Research Letters,* vol. 32, L19604, DOI: 10.1029/2005GL024042; available at www.agu.org. Shindell's key papers appear in *Science* (vol. 284, p. 305 and vol. 294, p. 2149) with useful summaries at www.giss.nasa.gov/research/news/20041006/ and www.giss.nasa.gov/research/briefs/shindell_04/.

Conclusion

My earlier book, *Turning Up the Heat,* long out of print, was published by The Bodley Head in 1989 and in paperback by Paladin later the same year.

Appendix

Much of what appears here was presented at the Dangerous Climate Change conference, whose proceedings can be found at www.stabilisation2005.com.

INDEX